Michael Banim, John Banim

The bit o' writin' and other tales

Michael Banim, John Banim

The bit o' writin' and other tales

ISBN/EAN: 9783741140082

Manufactured in Europe, USA, Canada, Australia, Japa

Cover: Foto ©Thomas Meinert / pixelio.de

Manufactured and distributed by brebook publishing software
(www.brebook.com)

Michael Banim, John Banim

The bit o' writin' and other tales

THE

BIT O' WRITIN'

CONTAINING

BY THE O'HARA FAMILY.

A New Edition, with Introduction and Notes.

BY MICHAEL BANIM, ESQ.,

THE SURVIVOR OF THE "O'HARA FAMILY"

NEW YORK:
P. J. KENEDY,
EXCELSIOR PUBLISHING HOUSE,
5 BARCLAY STREET.
1896.

CONTENTS.

INTRODUCTION TO "THE BIT O' WRITIN'."

"The Bit o' Writin'" originated with me, and was sent to my brother to Paris with "The Mayor of Wind-gap." It was intended by me to be published along with that story. Subsequent to John Banim's return home, and previous to his death, it was sent before the public, in conjunction with the collection of short tales that follow it.

All of the short tales had appeared, from time to time, in the "Annuals" of the period, which periodicals, it will be remembered, were the favorites of the day. Highly embellished volumes they were, as to illustration, type, paper, and binding—suiting them for the drawing-room table.

These republications from the "Annuals" were all written by my brother, with one exception—"The Hare-hound and the Witch," which is mine.

When transmitting "The Bit o' Writin'" to my copartner, Barnes O'Hara, I copied accurately, in its proper place, the original "Memorandle o' Sarvice," assumed to have been written by Murty Meehan, at the dictation of "the Ould Admiral," with the intention of having it inserted as it came to my hands. The printers were, however, provided with no font of type from which a *fac-simile* could be produced, so that my copy of the original went for nothing.

"The Memorandle o' Sarvice" was given to me, as a curiosity in penmanship, by Garret Byrne, the "public writer," whose person and occupation are slightly sketched in the tale, and with whom I was on terms of intimacy for my own purposes. "The Ould Admiral" was a crony of mine too. In my angling excursions I often met with him, and as often listened to his marvellous adventures with apparent interest and assumed credence. Nearly all his yarns were, however, like the fiction about his nose—out of the range of probability.

As the incidents of the tales forming the present volume do not afford opportunity for annotation to any extent, I will, with the reader's permission, insert here the few words of reference I think it necessary to make.

Garret Byrne is, as I have said, a very slight sketch of an original character, who followed the profession of "public writer" in Kilkenny shortly before "The Bit o' Writin'" was put together. He occupied a miserable room in one of the lanes branching off from the main or "High" street of our city, over the entrance door to which was a sign-board, black letters on a white ground, announcing—

"GARRET BYRNE, PUBLIC WRITER."

When Garret Byrne was the "public writer" of Kilkenny, few and far between were the occasions for his services. It is safe to say, comparing his day with the present, that the writing of letters is now four hundred fold; so that, even elevated above the illiterate as Garret Byrne may have been, his profession produced him only meagre fare, evidenced by his shrivelled body, covered with scanty make-out attire.

Kilkenny is not without its "public writer" at the present day, and our existing scribe is seldom unemployed. Terry Walshe is now the "public writer," and, like the "the wine that needs no bush," he has no necessity to designate his residence by a sign-board. Terry Walshe is of repute in his calling, and his "ready pen" is seldom idle. His appearance at the post-office, with two or more of his employers under his guidance, is of constant recurrence. He professes to know as much about the postal arrangements as does the guiding secretary himself. To the exact second of arrival and dispatch of all mails, whether inland or foreign, he is able to give incontrovertible information to his customers; and when he calls out at the post-office window for "shillingy stamp for America," or "sixpenny stamp for Australia," or "tenpenny stamps for the overland mail," he does so with an air of decision and authority sufficient to convince his wondering and admiring clients that he knows his business, and can not only transfer all they have to say to paper, but send the letters, when written, as directly to the mark as a crow flies, notwithstanding all the chicanery of the post-office folk. Terry Walshe is constantly at work; but I apprehend that the fee in kind, "the glass of sperrits," he receives for the stamping and posting of his productions, and which is distinct from his charge as an amanuensis, by imparting an alcoholic longing to his palate, induces him to liquify the shillings he receives for his penmanship.

A little dell named " Lacken-na-mono," or the Woman's Hill, is at Lavistown, two miles from Kilkenny. The spot was pointed out to me as the scene of the tragedy made use of in " The Bit o' Writin'," where a girl, wiled away from her home by a stranger, was murdered by her seducer, that he might appropri- ate to his exclusive use the money he had induced her to steal from her father's chest.

THE HAREHOUND AND THE WITCH.

THE fact of a witch of the olden time having been hunted, after having assumed the form of a hare, was related to me as a verity. All doubts I might have as to the reality of the event were assumed by the narrator to be removed by the circumstan- tial detail, that a mouthful of flesh had been bitten by the fore- most dog from the haunch of the counterfeit hare—which mouth- ful of flesh was found, as all the world of the time and place could testify, to have been torn from the witch—her person having been examined before she had had time to exercise her healing art on herself.

The witch, I was told, had taken the shape of a hare, with the impish design of precipitating down the cliff above her cavern three of her most troublesome persecutors. And I was further- more informed, that her speed as a hare was not to be wondered at, inasmuch as witches, although shaky and decrepit while in human shape, and obliged to bestride anointed broomsticks for expeditious travelling, become endowed to the utmost perfection with the qualities of the animals they represent while in a state of metamorphose.

THE ROMAN MERCHANT.

THE tale of " The Roman Merchant" has an actual occurrence for its foundation.

A foreigner, a dealer in different outlandish commodities, and supposed to be wealthy, was murdered in Kilkenny many years ago. He resided in a small house in the street leading to the Cathedral, known as Dean-street. It was customary with " the Roman Merchant" to shut up his dwelling, and be absent for weeks together, travelling, it was supposed, either to vend his wares or to replenish his stock. Whether the imputed reason for his frequent disappearance were accurate or not was a matter of surmise only. He lived entirely to himself, holding little or no communication with his neighbors, and altogether there was a mystery about him that was a source of curiosity, and interest, and conjecture to those among whom he had settled.

When his little shop was found closed one morning, and days passed by without his reappearance, the occurrence created only the usual observations, and there was no suspicion of foul play.

That he had been murdered was discovered, however, by accident. A remarkable circumstance, leading to the discovery, was not known to my brother when he wrote the tale, which, had he been acquainted with, he would, no doubt, have used to heighten the interest of the chance revelation.

The churchyard surrounding the old cathedral of Ossory is now very befittingly surrounded by a high wall, and access to the burying-ground can be gained only through secure gates, which are kept locked, except during the hours of church service, or when an interment is to take place, or when visitors apply for admission.

At the time when "The Roman Merchant" dwelt in Dean-street, there was a pathway through the churchyard, across the graves, giving a short passage from one portion of the town to another, and there were stiles for public convenience.

On a certain night, when the moon was at the full, there was a total eclipse of our satellite, and the people of the neighborhood assembled on a high bank or terrace, which may yet be ascended, in the cathedral cemetery, and which looks northeast. This was a favorable spot whence to view the phenomenon of the night.

Few, if any, of the observers were astronomers, and the inky shadow that for a time covered the silver surface of the moon excited superstitious forebodings of various hue and conjecture. Among the more serious and reflective of the lookers-on was a group of urchins, who, when their favorite reappeared in splendor, sung out the rhyme they had often before chaunted—

> " I see the moon, and the moon sees me—
> God bless the moon, and God bless me ;"

and, with shouts of gladness and recognition, they scampered down the terrace and in among the graves, singing another of their boyish refrains—

"Boys and girls, come out to play—
The moon she shines as bright as day ;
Up with the kettle and down with the pan,
Come into the moonshine, boy, girl, and man ;"—

their glee at the restoration of the planet causing them to forget altogether that they gamboled over the dead. One of the shouters stumbled and fell, and his scream of terror brought his companions around him. There, fully in the now unclouded moonlight, the affrighted boy lay prostrate, while a hand and arm protruded upwards from a grave, and, as the child in his terror imagined, about to descend and strike him because he had disturbed the rest of the dead, and who, as his fellows receded from the spot horror-stricken, lay where he had fallen, unable to rise, and expecting the ghostly hand to smite him if he attempted to move.

The hand and arm which the boy regarded with such terror was that of "the Roman Merchant ;" and thus it was ascertained that he was not away on one of his usual excursions, but that he had been murdered. His body had been hastily interred in a very shallow grave, without a coffin, and in his usual attire ; and one of his arms that had been kept down by stones and earth, being freed from the pressure by the boy's fall, suddenly regained the extended position in which the muscles had stiffened while, as it was conjectured, he had endeavored to keep off his assailant.

The people did not fail to connect the shadowing of the moon with "the Roman Merchant's" fate. The murderer was never discovered. At that day, much detective vigilance was not exercised, and the murderer was unpunished.

I had my account of the circumstance here related from an old man, himself the identical boy who had looked up in the moonlight at the threatening hand above him.

Shortly after the publication of "The Roman Merchant," a discovery referring to the story was made in the burying-ground where the body had been accidentally found.

A young medical practitioner, who had a penchant for antiquarian research, went through the churchyard of St. Canice to enjoy his leisure, examining the inscriptions over the occupants of the graves. Close by the porch of the old cathedral he found a very lowly headstone, almost entirely hidden by the long grass and rank weeds that find vigorous nurture from the decay they spring from.

The inscription on this little humble tablet had been rendered am'o'iguous by the obliterating hand of time, and further doubtful by the rust-colored moss that will fill up the cavities of mortuary relics. After much assiduity and laudable perseverance, the ex plor succeeded in deciphering the partly illegible memento. It ran thus:

"Here lyes ye body of Mr. Timothii Carroll Glasi, who departed this life Iune ye 29, 1728.
R.I.P."

The reader was repaid for his labor. Here was the grave of "The Roman Merchant" of Banim's tale. Here the murdered man had received Christian burial, after exhumation from his first hurried concealment.

The discoverer eagerly sought out a fellow-antiquarian—a medical gentleman also. A learned man he was, grave and astute, as it became him to be, and of great expertness and acuteness in legendary lore.

The young and the elderly revealers, as they knelt together for the purpose of bringing themselves on a level with the little slab they studied, felt certain that their knees rested on the grave of—

"Timothii Carroll Glasi,"
"The Roman Merchant."

A certain clergyman, who, I daresay, recollects the denoue-ment, was passing into the cathedral just as the two friends had compared notes and satisfied each other. He hurried over, that he might, with them, enjoy the perusal, letter by letter, of the memorial they had brought to light.

The new comer, however, read the epitaph differently: he made it out most convincingly to be—

"Here lyeth ye body of Mr. Timothy Carroll, Glazier, who departed this life Iune ye 29, 1728.
R.I.P."

So, then, the grave of "The Roman Merchant" turned out to be the last resting-place of Timothy Carroll, the glazier.

The second l in Carroll had been mistaken for an i, and an "er," for which there had not been continuous space on the little slab, had been chiselled above ; and so "glazier" was read "Glazi."

This was a mortifying result for the two learned decipherers.

THE BIT O' WRITIN'.

THE BIT O' WRITIN'.

CHAPTER I

On a fine morning in the month of May, Murty Meehan was occupied "threnching his little pee-aties." By the term "little" applied to them, Murty did not by any means wish to convey the idea that his growing staple-crop was confined to a small space. In truth, the sloping potato-ridges occupied a goodly portion of the hill-side upon which they were planted. Nor did he convey any apprehension that they must prove of diminutive size, owing either to his choice of seed or to an unfavorable season, or to any other cause which the uninitiated can easily imagine. His "little pee-aties" he, however, called them—signifying thereby (and his neighbors so understood the adjective), first, that they were his—his own ; second, that, even in embryo, he bore them a particular affection.

The French people would understand the term, in the double sense mentioned, better than the English. But to a portion of the rather unfigurative community for whose edification we write, it seems incumbent on us to explain why Murty Meehan applied to his fine sprouting plot of potatoes the epithet "little."

By Murty's reasoning, then, they were little—yet almost every thing to him. They were dear to Murty—dearly loved ; therefore little. They had cost him, and were costing him, considerable trouble ; and, until piled up at home, or in a pit in their own soil to protect them against the frost, would cost him a good deal more ; therefore he owed them a paternal regard. Under Providence, they were to prove, for many a month after gaining maturity, the staple dish of his family, himself, and his "slip of a pig ;" ay, for the whole coming year, they were to stand him and his human dependents in lieu of beef, mutton, lamb, veal, venison, and turtle : hence they were his very, very "little pee-

aties." And just as "little," in Murty's eyes, or according to
his vocabulary, were his "little wife" (a strapping, though a
simple dame), his "little daughter" (a full-grown woman), and
his "little cow," and his "little horse," though neither animal
shamed the standard proportions of its species.

Using, therefore, the term in the fond sense infused into it by
Murty Meehan, we repeat, that on a fine morning in May he was
employed "threnching his little pee-aties ;" which consisted in
digging between the potato-ridges, in the interstices which separated them, and throwing the fresh earth among the growing
plants.

His position, as has been intimated, was on a hill-side. This
hill-side sloped down to the banks of a little rivulet, covered with
the freshest green grass, among which grew a profusion of wild
flowers, and Murty's cabin stood within view and sound of the
rippling water. Across the stream the ground again rose high,
and was mostly wooded ; so that our friend resided in a solitary
and peculiarly beautiful little valley, owing to the curvings of
which, on both sides of the stream, and upward and downward
with its arbitrary course, no other dwelling could be observed
from his and our point of view. A pleasing impression of seclu-
sion, without desolation, was therefore conveyed to the mind by
the simple scene. Something of the same kind might have been
its attractions to the unusual numbers of small singing-birds
which frequented it—to the linnet, the chaffinch, the robin, the
thrush, the blackbird ; to all birds, in fact, not omitting even the
chirping, flirting wren, who were made by Providence to pipe or
twitter a single note of joy or of contentment.

So Murty Meehan's "little cabin" is situated amid features of
much natural beauty, aided and heightened by cultivation. In
this case his favorite and generally bestowed epithet came true
in every sense. "Little," indeed, was his mud edifice—so little,
that some surprise might be expressed as to how he managed to
get in or out of its doorway, or even to stand upright under its
straw roof—for Murty was a man of no common stature. Having been his own architect as well as chief workman, one might,
at all events, safely assert that in constructing it he had not
studiously calculated either his natural height or his personal
convenience. But no matter. Such instances of disproportion
between the miserable houses of his countrymen, and even their
own bones and muscles, to say nothing of the . bounty and love-
liness of nature all around them, were and are sufficiently numer-

ous to remove from Murty's architectural practices, according to his means, any thing like a charge of waywardness or singularity.

So Murty "threnched" away, the birds we have spoken of singing loudly to him ; he, as if by mere loudness he would make them admit themselves over-matched in melody, bawling out, in tones to which the sweet little hollow rang again, the song which has the frequent chorus of

> "Cuishla-ma-chree, did you not see
> What, the rogue, he done to me?
> Broke my pitcher, and spilt my wather,
> Kissed my wife, and married my daughter!
> Cuishla-ma-chree !"

To observe Murty Meehan at his task, the looker-on might, with some slight assistance from imagination, gain a tolerably accurate notion of the lusty ease and dexterity with which Hercules must have performed his labors : indeed, were our amateur a statuary, he need not have searched further for a model from which to chisel a god of strength. In Murty's person were combined accurate symmetry of parts, with almost gigantic proportions ; he stood to the full height of six feet four inches. His face, though not a very intellectual one, was comely, honest, and well-meaning ; but, for reasons to be mentioned, we ought, perhaps, to limit to one or two days in the week all opportunity for deciding either on its character or its claims to be considered handsome or ugly. In fact, upon one day alone, out of the seven, he got shaved—this was on Sunday ; the next, his beard began to sprout again, and even so soon some change was thereby induced over his physiognomy. By noon on the Tuesday it—"the afther-grass," as he styled it—gained a goodly growth ; thenceforward, day by day, till shaving-day came round in course, so disguised was his face by the great crop of black bristles surrounding it, that it would be very difficult to decipher its cast, hue, or general effect. Light blue eyes hinting good-nature, indeed, continued visible, with spots of wholesome red just under them—about half a nose, and a forehead above it. And these were the only glimpses of feature distinguishable amid the luxuriant "afther-grass."

Notwithstanding all his natural qualifications, so far as person went, for bullying his way through the world, and notwithstanding, also, the proverbial pugnacity of his countrymen of every stature, Murty Meehan was a quiet, easy man, using his rare strength chiefly for the right lawful purpose of executing, in full ratio with his superior capacity for the task, an extraordinary portion of field labor. But if he otherwise made no display of himself, his neighbors boasted of him. The district in which he resided was called, far and near, Murty Meehan's parish, as if the honor of having given birth to him entitled it to that distinguishing appellation. We must explain.

Although never known to have quarrelled with any human being, and seldom proposing himself a trial of strength with a neighbor in a friendly way, Murty, without his knowledge, was often staked by his admirers against all comers. Then, for the honor of the parish, he would quietly submit to be led forth against his ambitious challengers, and with invariable and immeasurable success, he exhibited his hidden might in tossing a stone, almost a rock, or in flinging a sledge-hammer, or in performing, beyond chance of competition, any other of the various rustic feats, in the doing of which massive force is the only qualification for excellence. And on the occasions of his proceeding to the place of trial, he might be seen surrounded by the young and the old, the boys, the girls, and the aged men and women of his little secluded valley and its vicinity, towering above them all, and—without our meaning a threadbare pun—looking down on his escort with all the simple good-nature of his character, and smiling on their enthusiasm, just as any other assured great man might at that of his humble adherents.

But we are not going to exhibit Murty Meehan in his most distinguished and famous light. Upon a matter widely different from his prowess either in the laboring field or in the arena of manly contention, it is our present duty to record the achievements of this redoubtable personage ; readers may form their own notions of the manner in which he acquitted himself of the business in hand. One thing is, however, certain—namely, that it proved to honest Murty himself a task much more difficult than if he had engaged to toss a metal weight of one hundred pounds over the roof of his own house.

Before entering further into the affair, a few lines must be devoted to a sketch of the individual at whose instance, and for whose advantage, he undertook this serious matter.

The man in question, for reasons yet to be given, generally went by the name of " the Ould Admiral." Standing at Murty Meehan's side, he appeared to no advantage in point of stature ;

yet, pigmy he was not, unless a person of nearly six feet high deserves that epithet. His air, his mode of speech, and carriage were bluff—bluff almost to a challenge to box with you. A cicatrized gash, commencing under his left eye, traversing his nose, and terminating at the right corner of his mouth, diagonally severed his face into two tolerably equal portions, of which one-half of the nose belonged, or seem to belong, to the upper, and the other half to the lower portion of his physiognomy This division of property, of identity, indeed, rested, according to his own account, on grounds other than that suggested merely by the line of demarcation.

It occurred, he asserted, on "boord the ould Saint Vincint," during the American war; and his story of the transaction, among all the stories he told of his battles, victories, and dreadful escapes from death, which were topics of standing wonder to his friend, Murty Meehan, as well as the whole neighborhood—was not the least surprising. The crew of the Saint Vincent were in the act of boarding an enemy's ship. Terence O'Brien—our hero's name—figured away, of course, in the thick of the *melee*—a slash from an opponent's hanger—"a curse-o'-Cromwul, French loober, he was,"—conferred the whole gash in question, into the channel of which "he could run his five fingers," and at the same time "whipped away, clane an' clever, more than the biggest half of his ruddher." Well, what of that? it was not till the action ceased, and the Frenchman had been made a prize of, and Terence about to put in a rightful claim for some half-and-half grog, that he ascertained his loss; and "a thrifle grieved" he felt, to be sure, when he first brought to mind, at the moment, what an appearance he must make in future, when—

"Terry O'Brien, a-hoy! would you know this, I say?" sang out to him his shipmate and fellow-countryman, Tom Ryan, holding up to view what seemed to Terence indubitably the lopped portion of his nose. He was in a great hurry, doubtless, at the time, and did not take particular notice, but Tom Ryan assured him it was a slice of his own features he beheld; and so, to the cock-pit they made their way together with it, and the surgeon stitched it on, as well as he could—and—

"May my ould hulk of a sowl never float aloft," continued Terence, "if I do not tell the blessed thruth. It wasn't the rest o' my natural nose he fixed on, at all—and that cat-head pet, Tom Ryan, knew the same from the beginnin' (my heavy curse on his tack, wherever he is!)—but a bit of a d—d to-the-divvle

French loober's snout that Tom picked off deck from among
other odds and ends, afther the scrimmage, an' that never belonged to myself." And that was the reason why, to the present
day, the whole nose on his face, such as it was, never seemed of a
piece. "And no blame to the surgeon, by any manes—for may I
sink five fathoms deep, but he was as clever a hand as ever spliced
a timber ; didn't I see him, wid my own eyes, saw off the right
arm from my hulk, while I could shout out ' grog,' and no more
about it, only throw it for a tit-bit to the sharks ? An'—my ould
bones to ould Davy—only he *did* get through the nose job so
well, but I'd haul down the *parly's* bit o' had flesh agin, an' throw
it into the say, to pison the hungriest fish that ever swum."
   There were some obvious collateral proofs of the truth of
Terence O'Brien's biography of his nose to which he did not fail
to allude. "He spoke through his nose," as the saying goes ;
" and didn't all the parbleus do the same, like so many pigs o' the
divvle." Again—it was well known that from his cradle up to
the day of the accident, he had boasted a long hook-backed
nose—but what was it like now ? the upper half of it, which had
always been on his face, might do well enough, to be sure, and,
indeed, gave promise of the beginning of such a conformation as
that mentioned ; but only look at the lower half—the Frenchman's half of it ! "cocked up towards his forehead, like the
chaplain's eye that had a squint in it, towards the sky-rakers,
when he sang out prayers of a Sunday."
   During his term of sea-service, Terence O'Brien had unconsciously contracted some characteristics which rendered him a
puzzle to his present neighbors, and indeed a contradiction to
himself—or, at least, to Terence O'Brien that then was, and
Terence O'Brien that used to be, once upon a time. For instance :
In his more youthful days, he had engaged in some one of those
many rustic combinations for which the Irish peasantry are celebrated, and which can best be accounted for by considering that
their wants make them discontented, and the injuries that often
produce those wants, reckless of all consequences, when their object is vengeance on the nearest palpable aggressor. Terence
and his associates violated the law of the land ; rewards for their
apprehension were offered ; some of them were discovered, tried,
and hanged ; and he himself, to avoid the fate that seemed to
await him, absconded from his native place, "and never cried
stop, nor let the grass grow under his feet," till he arrived in
" Cork's own town," distant about one hundred miles (Irish)

from his starting-post. There, scarce yet pausing to take breath, he entered on board a man-of-war, as his most secure hiding-place ; and thus the wild Irishman, who but a few hours before had been denounced as almost a traitor to the State, became one of its sworn defenders. Ay, and in a very short time, if not at that very moment, one of its most loyal and sincere defenders. This character grew upon him, and in it fully confirmed, he returned home after a long absence, in peaceful and oblivious times, much to the non-edification of his stationary neighbors, as has been intimated.

Further. As a White-boy, before going on his travels, Terence had mortally hated England, England's king, and the very name of every thing English ; in the same ratio, had loved England's foes, of all denominations—the French, her "natural enemies," as they have been somewhat strangely called, above all others. But none of these youthful prejudices did Terence bring home with him. " Long life and a long reign to King George !" was now his shout, while the hairs on his head bristled in enmity against "parly-woos ;" and good reason why, for both senti-ments—sensations rather. During half his amphibious existence, Terence's grog had been sweetened by pouring it down his throat among his ship-comrades, with a grateful mention of the name of his Britannic majesty, and Terence's only thoughts and efforts constantly directed towards the discomfiture of the ill-wishers of that august personage. The loss of his arm and of half his nose, with the disgraceful substitution of that half by the half of a Frenchman's "snub," gave him personal cause to detest the Gallic race. So that he might be said to loathe the French to the marrow of his bones—yea, even of those portions of his bones which had been severed from his body and cast to the sharks.

Some other exotic peculiarities Terence also transplanted to his native valley. His language seemed, among his old play-fellows, absolutely a new dialect—and so indeed it was. Grafted on his ancient brogue, which had never quite slipped off his tongue, sea-terms and sea-phrases, and, above all, sea-oaths and impre-cations, luxuriantly sprouted out : the former would make his auditors laugh themselves into fits, while the latter astounded or shocked them. We must, in truth, admit that, in the use of those unnatural profanations of speech, Terence was indeed too lavish. With some one—if not two—of them he always began a sentence, and they served him, rhetorically, as conjunctions, copulative and disjunctive, and sometimes to point his periods.

His parish priest, a man of some humor as well as of sincere zeal in his vocation—and every parish priest of an Irish congregation, at least of a rustic one, ought to have a spice of humor in him—was fond of listening to Terence O'Brien's accounts of his battles, and other adventures. He it was who had laughingly dubbed Terence "the Ould Admiral;" though the title was un hesitatingly and gravely accepted and retained, as well by the veteran as by most of his present friends and associates. But the good priest felt it his duty to take Terence to task on the head of his outlandish cursing, swearing, and imprecating. The sinner acknowledged his offences, and promised to give them up; yet, at the very next encounter between him and his spiritual director, did he salute the chaplain with a good merman oath, at the beginning, in the middle, and at the end of the well-meant greeting.

His clergyman, still in pursuance of his sense of duty, then prevailed on Terence, after much salutary stratagem, to attend the confessional. Again the penitent was so far amenable, and did "attend with the rest of the crew;" principally because he understood the "*station* of confession" to be a kind of muster of all hands on deck." But the zealous priest soon began to feel hopeless of a real reformation in the nominal convert. Even while at his clergyman's knee, Terence would confess his very transgressions against piety of language with new and awful oaths in confirmation of the truth of his self-accusations. And while acknowledging other sins of a different and perhaps still more heinous character, he would, as his energy arose with his vivid recollections, still swear, through thick and thin, to his own great condemnation, so that the priest was obliged to make a drawn battle of the matter. The good man's conscience did not warrant him in permitting the irreclaimed and irreclaimable Terence to approach the Sacrament ; and his feelings of comfort were much augmented by the declaration, on Terence's part, that "—— to his ould soul, if he would boord him any longer !"

He had been kept so long coming and going, he averred, "now on this tack, now on that, an' still no say-room made, but all an' the same 'station,'—one time with the wind, the next moment breeze right ahead—so that the ablest sayman in the service could make no port, and have sich a steerage. His hulk to ould Davy ! but he would hoist sail, an', for the rest o' the voyage, steer in the ould thrack. Ay (another tremendous oath), if he didn't, might ould ship never weather another gale!" So hoist sail he did, and "scudded afore the wind, steering his ould hulk by the ould compass, au' laving the rest o' the looberly crew to the looberly chaplain." That is, he continued to curse and swear away right and left; although, in other respects, Terence could not be called a very wicked sinner.

CHAPTER II.

SUCH was the man who now accosted Murty Meehan on the potato-covered hill-side of their native glen.

So intent upon his work, as well as upon his marvellous song of "*Cuishla-ma-chree*," had Murty been, that the deafening sound of Terence's voice, very near to him, was the first intimation he received of the presence of his esteemed neighbor.

"Ould ship a-hoy!" shouted the admiral, bellowing through his truncated fist, by way of speaking-trumpet, almost into the tympanum, as we have intimated, of Murty Meehan's ear. So sudden, so proximate, and withal so tempestuous, that a man of less tension of nerve than that possessed by our honest friend might, without much censure to his presence of mind, have lawfully started and quaked at it. Murty only turned quietly round, however, pushed his old hat up from his eyes, and smiled good-humoredly, as he answered the hail.

"Hah! then, musha, God save you, Admiral!"

"What cheer, lad, what cheer?"

"What cheer, a bouchal, is it? English that to me, if there's no offence."

"What cheer, I say, what cheer?"

"Well, I must thry to English it myself, I suppose. It's all as one, I'm thinkin', as if a country *spalpeen*, like myself, 'ud say—'How is your four bones, Murty?'"

"All the same lingo, shipmate."

"Why, thin, I'm brave and harty, Admiral, as is asy to be seen by lookin' at me. I give thanks to you for axin."

"A fair breeze in your sheets every day you turn up, my hearty."

" An' success purshu *you*, is what *I* say, ould Admiral, aroon."

" I've steered ahead to your station, shipmate, to ax your service on a conthrary little mather, d'ye see me."

" Och, then, Admiral, isn't it yourself knows well I'd go a sthart or two any day from my road to do a turn for you. An' not mooch noise I'd make about that same."

" An' for that rason, and becase I knows it well, d'ye see me, I'm now alongside o' you, my hearty. In the days when I was nothin' but a bit of a loblolly boy—"

" A loblolly boy! an' what quare sort of a boy is that, Admiral ?"

" A gorsoon, a gorsoon, as they used to call me here in Muckalee."

" Ay ; now I'm on your manin', I think. A gorsoon is a gorsoon, in the counthry : but whin he goes to say, it's a loblolly boy they call him, Admiral ?"

" Ay, ay. Well, shipmate, whin I was a gorsoon at home here, d'ye know, the schoolmaster could'nt by no manes cut the larnin' into my lanthron, though it's often an' often, he thried it, at the cat-head, the old Muckalee loober !"

" At the cat's head ? Why, thin, that was a curious thing for him to do. I never heered of a schoolmasther havin' that fashion afore, Admiral, honey. Stop ; wait ; och, but maybe I have you now; maybe it's wid the cat's-tail he thried you ? You know the breed o' cats that does the scratchin' at the loblolly boys at school, Admiral ?"

" All much the same, jolly lad ; all much the same. Cat, head or tail. Ay, many's the day he lent me the rope's end, as if 'twas the mainmast he was layin' it on—to ould Davy wid his hulk, to scuttle it well, for the same !" (We have, during our report of this conversation, sunk some of Terence's oaths and imprecations, and it is our intention to do so in future.) " Little doubt, shipmate, but he *is* undher hatches long ago ; an' if ever I happen to steer on that tack," continued Terence, getting animated, and flourishing his one arm, as if it were giving a preparatory shake to the rope's end, " if I ever steer on that tack, and when I see him lashed up, getting his own round dozens—as surely will be the case—if I don't sing out, ' Lay on, ould Davy ! lay on, my jolly lad !'—if I don't, Murty, may——shiver my timbers to a parfact wreck, Murty ! Ay, or maybe I'd take on to the work myself, shipmate, an' pay him back on his —— looberly stern-quarters some o' the ould score wid my own hand !"

" Bee the gonnies! an' only right," grinned Murty through his

" afther-grass," highly amused with the time, place, and circumstances of the Admiral's threatened vengeance.

" A broadside to my sowl in glory, if I don't then ! But,
Murty, my hearty, as I was a sayin', I never could pick up as
much o' the larnin' as 'ud help me to box the littlest bit iv a
compass that ever swum ; an' for that same rason I was only fit
to do the work of an able-bodied sayman, all the blessed days of
my say life, aboord the ould ship, d'you see me. Howsomever
Murty, when the decks were cleared for action, an' the guns roar-
in', and the saywather was bilin' hot, you'd think, round about
'em, I could stand by my own gun, or jump aboord a—jabberin'
French inimy, wid my pike or my hanger in my hand, well
enough. Ay, shipmate, I'd do that for the honor an' glory of
ould King George, an' ould Ireland, an' Saint Patrick into the
bargain, as well as ever a Johnny-raw Englishman that ever
reefed a sail, Murty ! Them Englishers is bould enough, to be
sure, but they're not fit to stand by the side of an Irish sayman, for all that. The fightin', Murty, comes more naatril to
us : by land or by wather, it's all the same—the one as welcome
as the other."

" Why, we're handy at it, somehow, I believe, beyond all
doubt, Admiral."

" Why, again, Murty. As I tould you twice over, I never
could come at the larnin', my jolly boy. But no matther now ;
it's all one, when the ould ship's a hulk. Only this, Murty Meehan, I'm informed as how there's a power o' prize money sarvin'
out to the ould crew o' the ould Saint Vincint, or to as many o'
them as is over saywather, anyhow, wherever they be's to be
found. An' I come to you on the head of it, 'cause I hear, for
sart'n sure, you're a good scholard."

" Musha, I'm thankful to the neighbors for their good word,
Admiral," said Murty, blushing, if the occurrence could only
have been seen through his crop of black beard and whiskers at
this acknowledgment of his literary superiority. " But surely
you could get as good a hand as ever I was among your own
people, avich. There's the born brether o' you, to say nothing
of his son, your own namesake—"

" Avast now, shipmate !" interrupted Terence, gruffly and
stentoriously. " Hah ! the ould reg'lar sayman isn't goin' to
hoist signal for smugglers and pirates to come aboord. The
born brether o' me ! No, no, nor that bit of a cockboat he has
in tow, his son, either What ! when I cum back only to give

him a hail, afther my last cruise, didn't the —— landloober tell
me to sheer off, an' say I had no call to a berth in my own ould
ship, now that the ould commodore, the father of us, had slipped
cable ?   An', aint I ever since here, in Muckalee Station, scuddin' from port to port, not able to ride at anchor among the
whole squadhron o' ye ?   An' now, whin the shinars is to be pu
into the locker, am I to sing out to him to help me to keep the
kay, or ax him for any help at all that might let him into the
acret, or give him a right to jaw for share?   No, no, I say
again.   —— to my ould timbers! if ever he sees a yallow boy
o' mine.   You're the man, Murty, an' you only, that must turn
out for this musther ; an' what I have to ax o' you is to write
down wid your pen what we used to call a memorandle o' service."

"Why, thin," replied Murty, " that's not so mooch to talk
about, that we'd say no to you, for a one, Ould Admiral.   An'
so we'll do it for you ;" and Murty "elevated his figure to its
full height," again silently triumphing in the testimony borne to
his scholarship, and at the distinguished light in which it placed
him.

"Here, then,—yee-o-ho ! heave away, my hearty ! yee-ho !"
piped the Admiral, passing his single arm through one of Murty's, and lugging him down the hill-side.   And Murty, sticking
his shovel in the soil, allowed Terence O'Brien to hurry him still
downward toward his cabin ; his features wearing a serious cast,
and, indeed, his whole mind bent upon the important task of
clerkship which he had undertaken.

———————

CHAPTER III.

AFTER nearly doubling himself in order to enter the door-way
of his dwelling, and when he had stood (almost) erect again, in
the middle of its clay floor, Murty addressed his wife.

"Chevaun, aroon, where's the poor gorsoon's bit of an inkhorn, I wondher ?"

"What cheer, vanithee, what cheer ?" demanded the Old Ad
miral, in the same breath, as he kindly, though rather smartly,
slapped the good woman between the shoulders.

"Why, thin, brave an' hearty, Admiral honey," answered the
housewife Chevaun. "Here's the inkhorn, Murty acuishla;
musha, my heavy hatred on it, for one inkhorn!"

"Au' why so, Chevaun!" asked Murty.

"Why! I'm as sart'n sure as that I spake the word, that
Paudeen put more o' the ink of it on the Sunday *shanavast**
than he did on the copy-book, Murty."

"Bee gonnies! an' likely enough sich a thing 'ud happen,"
ssented her husband. "I remember the first time I was put
upon my larnin' the pen-writin' myself, Admiral. Sure it's
nothin' nd sarve my turn, in thim days, but I must go an' scoop
out amost all the ink in the horn, an' put it all over my clothes,
on every spot where it could be obsarved; ay, an' my two fists
'nd have the color of a blackamoor's paws. An', bee this pin my
hand! I done it for no rason in the world only to let the neighbors see, whin they'd meet me comin' home from the school of
an evenin' or a mornin', that I was makin' use o' the pen, wid
the masther himself. 'Twas by way o' braggin' o' myself, afther
a manner, Admiral."

"Aha!" replied the Admiral, "well for you that you hadn't
my ould commodore, Fitzgibbon, to pipe you on deck, shipmate,
on the head o' that same; the ould loober, with his ould three-
decker of a flax wig, that commanded over our crew whin I was
at the schoolin'! Split my mainsail to tatthers! if he would
not have you up to the cat-head for wastin' the ship's tar. Sink
my hulk to Ould Davy, if he wouldn't!"

"Arrah, then, Admiral, aroon," inquired Mrs. Meehan, "who's
that same Ould Davy you're always sinkin' your hulk to, afther
sich an unnaatural fashion? I'm tould it's your own self you
call bee the name of a hulk. Sure it's a quare name for a
Christhen to be puttin' on his body, that has a sowl to be saved
tied to it. But who is this one Ould Davy, I'd be thankful to
know?"

"Who is he? blow us all up sky-high, if I very well know
myself, misthress." He paused to examine, with a knotted brow
and a gruff, puzzled face, a question which be had never before
taken into consideration.

"It's like enough, mistress, he's some kind of a *duoul*,"† he
resumed, after a pause. "Ay, ay; he must be a duoul, I'm
thinkin'. I hard 'em aboard jawing about his cloven foot, an'

* Waistcoat. † Devil.

duouls have sich timbers. Yes, an' he hauls away at the parley-woos whin they foundher in action. When we used to be givin' 'em a broadside, we had a fashion o' sayin', send the d—d loobers to Ould Davy ! Ay, ay"—he paused again to recapitulate in his mind those weighty reasons for investing with a certain character the personage in question,—the Jupiter or Pluto, as it might be, of his marine mythology. Then Terence continued, " Ay, misthress, I b'lieve he's all as one at say, as what you call your *duoul* here on land; though this isn't quite clear to me, neither ; because, d'ye see me, Ould Davy has *his* locker at the bottom o' the say, that's sert'n sure ; and your *duoul* is undher hatches—down here, undher ground. But they're close related. Ay, ay, the one is born-brother to the other chap, no doubt of it. An' he bears a hand wid sailors, as your *duoul* does wid your landsman—wid this differ, that he takes all foundered sowls as belong to him in the jolly-boat, or in a barge, or in a pinnace, according to the rank aboord. Yes, misthress, he's our say-div-vle, nothin' less—my hulk to Ould Davy, but he is !"

" The Lord purtect us from him, and from all his sort, bee say an' land, now an' forever, amin !" ejaculated the attentive Chevaun Meehan, crossing her forehead.

" ' Bee the gonnies !' as Chevaun says," remarked her husband ; " Goodness save us from his two paws ! But if a body got his pick an' choose o' the both, I believe it would be betther, as the man said to his wife—I mane neither myself nor you, Chevaun—it would be betther to keep the *duoul* we know than the *duoul* we don't know, Admiral, honey. Though wid good help we won't be throublesome to ather the one or the other o' them, plaise God.

" Musha, an' gracious forbid, Murty agra," piously assented Chevaun.

" That's not my way o' thinkin' teetotally, shipmate," dissented the admiral, gruffly. " For whinever I'm bound for the other world, if 'tis a thing I must steer for any sich d—d port of it, d'ye see me—"

" Ye may call the port bee that name, sure enough, Admiral, an' no sin on you for cursin', this time, anyhow," interrupted Murty.

" D—d or no d—d, shipmate," now bellowed Terence, becom-ing vehement ; " Ould Davy's jolly-boat for me, far beyant any way o' goin' by land, undher your land *duoul's* colors. Your laudamen are all sharks, as I heered from my cradle up. And

your land *duouls* goes by the same fashion of course. So none
o' the d—d horned loobers for my money, but Ould Davy forever—hurrah!"

"Well, all the harum I wish you, poor Ould Admiral, is, that
you may keep clear o' the ugly place—you know yourself where
I mane—by land or water ; to go in a boat might be the most
cooramuch* way, no doubt. Only, for our three selves, an'
them we wish well to into the bargain, we'd rather not to be on
the voyage, at all, at all."

"It's a bad sarvice, afther all, shipmate," half agreed Terence,
beginning to be cooled by his friend's moral reflections ; "but
hurra! an ould able-bodied sayman that does his duty is never
clapped undher hatches, foundher as he may, or whenever or
wherever he may. No, he goes aloft, my hearty—'tis as
naat'ral for him as to ship his grog. An', barrin' Ould Davy's
press-gang claps me aboord, an' thin scuds off wid me, all canvas crowded, never will I take on wid him or his crew. For,
d'ye see me, Murty, when once a man is nabbed by the press-
gang, an' lugged 'boord ship, he must stick to his gun, bee course,
or be tried for mutiny in the sarvice. So, if Ould Davy 'lists me
that way, I must stand before the mast, and make the cruise ;
but if I ever boord him by my own free-will, may I be d—d for
it, ueighbor."

"You needn't pray the prayer at all, Admiral," smiled the
facetious Murty. "But I wondher what sort of a pen for the
writin' is this," putting on a face of much business, approaching
the doorway, holding the pen between him and the light, and
with much knowing scrutiny examining it. Then he tried its nib
on his nail.

"Looks if it had seen sarvice," remarked Terence ; "but all
the betther for that, may be, shipmate. A sayman is never the
worse, getting into fresh action, for havin' been in two or three
scrimmages afore."

"Sarvice or no sarvice, as regards the pen," pursued Murty,
"it's so long since my own self thried my hand at the writin'
business, that I don't well know how it will turn out in the long
run, neighbor."

These words of modest doubt were accompanied, however, by
a smile of self-sufficient confidence.

"But here goes, in God's name, anyhow, to venture our look,

* Comfortable.

the best way we can." And while he leisurely pulled the cross-legged table to the door, Murty continued to speak in assured good-humor.

"When I was in the habit o' goin' to the school, Admiral, the masther usen't to be over-an-above ashamed o' the scholar—though it's mysef says the same, that oughtn't to say it, Admiral."

"No doubt of it, no doubt. Aboord o' the ould Saint Vincint, it's purser's mate they'd make o' you, long ago, to a sart'nty," flattered the Admiral, willing to keep Murty in good-humor, that he might get his own business the better done. Not, indeed, that he in the least doubted the scholarly qualifications of his chosen private secretary.

"Maybe it's jest as well wid me as it is, Admiral. Who's wise enough to say but that if we were a sailor all this time, from the schoolin' up, but we'd have a bit of a Frenchman's snout upon our poor face, instid of our own naath'ral nose, this blessed day?"

"Ay, like enough—every mother's sowl's hulk o' them to Ould Davy!" assented the Admiral, reddening with anger. Thereupon he gave his own nose—or what served him as his own, or, at least, as half of his own—such a pull, that had not the surgeon of the Saint Vincent done his office well, Terence must have torn it from its usurped position.

"But we had betther go to our work at onst," resumed Murty—and he fell to scraping, with more strength than skill, at the inside of his little son's inkhorn.

"Musha, I wondher what *meeaw* is on it, this turn, for ink?"

The ink which the amanuensis essayed to get into his pen had been produced by the squeezing together of elderberries. To prevent it spilling out of the horn, which hung by a leathre strap from a button of Paudeen's jacket, as he trudged to school, the primitive little vessel had been half filled with old linen, scraped into lint; into this pulpy substance the liquid became absorbed; and it required a certain schoolboy knack, acquired by long practice and many failures thence to press and scoop it into the funnel of the quill.

After sundry awkward attempts, Murty Meehan succeeded in charging his pen, brimful, and began to stir his fingers, wrist, and even arm, when he suddenly exclaimed, "Och! tundher—tundher an' ages! an' sure we forget oursefs, intirely—where is the paper, Admiral? Here was mysef goin' to set about writin' widout the paper—an' that's a thing the schoolmaather, his own four bones, couldn't do, I believe."

"May my hulk go floatin' to Ould Davy!" began Terence O'Brien.

"Musha, Admiral, 'tis a schandle for you, an' a great sin, to be goin' on that-a-way, wid your Ould Davy and your strange curses," remonstrated Chevaun. "Loock or grace can niver come of it to the writin'."

"I desarve your word, misthress—I desarve it, but won't agin this long time." Terence felt selfishly penitent. "Here's the paper, shipmate ; I had it in the locker all tho while."

"An' see how it wouldn't spake out for idsef," remarked Murty, with a condescending smile, such as any man of parts might vouchsafe to those who admit his possession of them, and whom he was about to amaze with a proof of their excellence. And, while thus smiling on the undisguisedly ignorant Admiral, Murty proceeded to smoothen down, as he honestly believed, the paper, which had become much crumpled in the Admiral's locker, i. e. under his jacket, and therefore seemed to require some such adjustment. But Murty's hard, raspish hands only produced a rough, fuzzy surface on the sheet which was intended to bear the impress of his scholarship. It was at length properly set before him, and he again succeeded in filling the tube of his pen to the utmost it could hold.

"Now, Admiral, what's the writin' to be about?" he demanded, approaching the pen to that point of the paper whence he intended to set forth upon his voyage of venture through the dimly apprehended ocean of letters—when, lo! the overcharged instrument immediately voided its contents on the paper, and they flowed over it a little sable current.

"Spilt milk, bee the soukins," said Chevaun, with wife-lik sorrow and sympathy.

"The divil welcome id, I say," lamented the penman. "Couldn' it stay quietly where it came from? But wait a bit," winking on the sailor, and resumed his self-assured smiles. "We had a way in the school, long ago, to get over a misfort'n like that. I'll bet you any thing but you'll see I don't forget my larning to this blessed day." And (shudder, civilized reader!) Murty protruded his long tongue, and with it began to sponge out of the rivulet of elderberry ink.

With much relish for the experiment, the Admiral sedately looked on. "That's what we call swabbin' decks, shipmate," he observed; "an' the very thing to do afther shippin' a say, sure enough, barr:n' it's a heavy say intirely, an' thin the words 'bale out', afore swabbin,' d'ye see me?" He paused, still evidently pleased with the dexterity of the operation, which Murty continued with his winks and smiles of promised success.

But Murty was not quite triumphant over this obstacle to his penmanship. His first efforts only spread the ink in rather a lighter shade over a much larger surface than it had previously occupied. A necessity thus arose for extending and persevering in the process of extraction. And when, at length, the paper was, in his estimation, and in that of his friend and his wife, pretty free from positive stain, its whole superficies had become thoroughly damp. But this latter circumstance did not occur to Murty nor to his observers.

"Now, at any rate, for the writin'," he said, again scooping out his "tent o' ink." Lest it should serve him the trick it had before done, he cautiosly held the pen level till he had stolen it round his back, and then, with a calculating jerk, Murty tried to get rid of the superfluous quantity of ink it held.

"Oh!" screamed his wife, Chevaun, suddenly slapping her left eye with her right hand; "oh, oh! Murty, it's now you done the *dhunnus** intirely!"

The elderberry juice had lodged full in the handsome, though too inquisitive, eye of Chevaun. The good dame was in that state of health in which, according to a quotation that has often served writers—

" Ladies wish to be who love their lords ;"

and her words of alarm expressed a fear, and so Murty well knew, though their meaning was not fully expressed, that "the young Christhin," who, by this time, was far on his road into the world, would make his appearance among us with, upon his cheek, such a black tear as now welled down that of his mother.

Murty was at her side in a moment, anxious to reassure her, though almost as much alarmed as herself. "No, no, *ma-chree*," he cried, in his tenderest accents ; "no harum can come of it. There now."

We are almost ashamed, this time, to crave pardon of, or otherwise to conciliate, the refined patron of our humble studies

* Mischief.

from nature. But we must indicate the shocking fact, that the anxious and loving husband did use to his wife's cheek the very same horrid sponge which he had, with so much felicity, just before applied to the stained paper. And when he conceived that, as in the former initiating case, success had crowned his efforts, Murty kissed the sufferer.

"Cleared out for action at last, or my hulk to Ould Davy!" said the patient, never-doubting Admiral, who had observantly regarded this second piece of cleverness on Murty's part with the same profound interest bestowed on the first.

"Ay, by *gonnies!* Now or never, as the ould sayin' goes, Admiral, *a hager.*"

Once more the amanuensis sat, right in the door-way, to his cross-legged table, and once more with increased sedateness, disposed himself to his task. Murty was now a wiser, because a more experienced man. Previous failure and mishap had taught him extreme caution. After a third time imparting ink to his pen, he carefully examined it, in order to ascertain whether or no it contained the necessary measure of liquid, and no more. In properly fixing it between his two fingers and thumb he spent a reasonable portion of time, and, in the eyes of his neighbor and spouse, evinced much ingenuity—the operation being effected by seizing the top or feathery part of the quill with the fingers of his left hand, and by their aid drawing it upwards and downwards, and twisting and turning it, till it was poised to his satisfaction. Still, by the joint agency of both hands, Murty guided it to the paper.

"Choice steerage, my hearty," said the ever-watchful Admiral, with glee.

"Nately done, of a sart'nty," agreed Chevaun.

All seemed, indeed, most happily ready. The pen took dead aim at the place on the sheet which it was first to hit; the scribe's mouth screwed itself up, his eyes intently fixed on the paper, and his head twisted round towards his left shoulder, where stood the Admiral, ready to "pipe" when the signal was made for action. A double-loaded musket, at full cock, levelled at a target, and only wanting a touch on its trigger to discharge it, would convey an idea of Murty at this big moment. Having waited a second or two—"Now, Admiral, say out, and don't be afeared, what we're to put down," he said, solemnly.

"We had a fashion o' callin' this sort o' writin' a memorandle o' sarvice. Put down that, first," said his employer. But sud-

denly interrupting himself, he sang out shrilly, "No, no; avast
there—no, not yet, shipmate. Afore any other thing, d'ye see
me, put down the time o' the watch."

"The time o' the watch, avich? Musha, never a one in the
poor house; nor a clock neither, as you know well yourself.
But couldn't we guess the hour o' the day it is by the sun, as
we're used to do, an' seldom go wrong, somehow?"

"Jaw, jabber! Ax pardon, shipmate; didn't by no manner
o' manes intend an offence. But what I want you to put down
isn't the time o' the hour, d'ye see me, but the date o' the month
we have, wid the day of the year."

"Och, ay! The day o' the month and the figures o' the year
is to go down first, Admiral; that's what you mean, we b'lieve,"
corrected Murty. "An' you're right. Yes, the year an' the
day goes down, at the first offer, by course." The penman
went on, still very cautiously bringing his instrument to bear on
the long-severed point of attack. "Well; this is the year
aighteen hundred an' one, isn't it?" There was silence, and he
paused a moment in deep study. "Yes; aighteen hundred an'
one." From a confused recollection of the dashing manner in
which "the masther in the school" used to commence similar tasks,
he gave two or three flourishes of his pen, at a civil distance,
however, from the paper, as many a boastful man will make a
show of fighting without soon coming to blows.

"Aighteen hundred an' one," continued Murty, and he
repeated the words five times at the least; and then, giving up
his affected mastery over the pen, he once more very cautiously
moved it thrice, resolved on a beginning.

The Admiral watched him with the keenest attention. Chevaun,
sharing his feelings in her own way, pulled her stool close to her
husband, and poked her head almost over the table.

The pen at length touched the oft-threatened mark. But
Murty's difficulties were not thereby lessened. It will be recollected that, since the sponging process, the paper had remained
damp, and that previously Murty's hand had rasped it into a
fuzzy surface; so that, in this state of preparation, as soon as
Murty now described upon it the first figure which he meant to
stand at the beginning of the year's date, the lines of that figure
chose gradually to swim and mingle together under his astounded
eyes, and so went on till they ended in one unintelligible blot. He
paused: his lower jaw dropped, and he stared at the self-defacing
lines as if he had witnessed witchcraft.

"Ill loock agin—an' more an' more of it!" at last groancd Murty; "an' what *bolgh* is on it now, I wondher ?"

"Haze ahead," cried the Admiral, slapping Murty, in what he meant to be an encouraging manner, between the shoulders, for he had noticed the undisguised drooping of the man of letters, and sought to prop him up. "Haze ahead, and that's all. Cheer up, my jolly boy. Hard tackin', sometimes, getting out o' port. But when you once make say-room enough to spread canvass, nine knots an hour won't catch you—sink me to Ould Davy, if they will!"

"Musha, maybe it's wet is on the paper," surmised Chevaun.

"Faix, and I believe it is," agreed her husband, somewhat relieved.

He arose and held it to the fire, kneeling to his task; and in this position turned round his head to address his hearers.

"Well, well; the praises for all. There's no tellin', now-a-days, when a poor boy sits down to do any one thing, what crosses an' what conthrary things may come to pass afore he— och! tundher an' agis!" Thus did Murty interrupt his own moralizing, as the paper suddenly caught fire, blazed up, and scorched his fingers, causing him instinctively to let it go. "Ulla—loo—oo!" he went on; "never sich a misfort'nit writin' met me in my born days afore—sure there was some curse on you!"

With a countenance of extreme mortification he watched, still kneeling, the expiring ashes of the paper. The breeze came in sharply at the open door, and hastening to get out of the house again as fast as possible, whisked up the wide chimney, and soon carried with it even those relics of old raggery.

"There!" resumed Murty. "Ould Nick has you now, an' let *him* write on you, if he can."

"Ould ship blown up," announced the Admiral, beginning him self to feel at last discomfited in his hopes of "a memorandle o' sarvice."

"An' haven't you ne'er another scrap o' paper about you, Admiral?" asked his secretary.

"Scuttle and sink me to ould Davy—no! Locker cleaned out this voyage, shipmate."

"Maybe I'd find a bit," said Chevaun; and her husband and his friend fixed their eyes on her movements. When—

"Fresh squall comin' on—heavy cloud right ahead!" piped the Admiral.

"Never a welcome to whoever it is," grumbled Murty.

CHAPTER IV.

A FIGURE suddenly darkened the door-way. It was that of a female wearing the deep-blue peasant mantle of the district. She stood still and silent, with her back to the inside of the house, and, of course, to our friends. The ample cloak, falling close to her shoulders and down her sides, in two straight lines, while its gathered hood was drawn over her head, baffled observation as to who or what she was, neighbor or stranger.

"Never a welcome to whoever it is," grumbled Murty.

"Amin, say I, till the writin' is over," echoed Chevaun.

"Ship ahoy—ii !" hailed the Admiral, angrily, through his speaking trumpet.

The person slowly turned sideways on the spot where she stood, and even in her movement there was sadness. Her left hand and arm now appeared through the folds of her cloak, and a pair of new light-blue worsted stockings hung from the latter. She spoke a few words in a low tone, and they fell on the ear like the melancholy, though musical, trickling drops of water in a little basin, half covered with sedge, in a lonely place. They were spoken tears.

"I don't think you know who it is that's keepin' the May sun from your dour-stone, Chevaun," she said ; and still her face was quite hidden by the cloak-hood which almost closed in front of it.

"Ochown ! bud sure I know your own poor voice now !" cried Chevaun, in great interest, as she endeavored to push her way to the visitor by the side of the cross-legged table, " Mary, alanna ! how are you, the mornin' ?"

"In good health, I give thanks, Chevaun, an' I'm only come wid the first o' my knitten' for Murty."

She held out the stockings on her arm. The mistress of the house had now gained her side, and greeted her kindly.

"Och then, Mary ! an' is it you ! An' how is every inch i' you, asthore ?" exclaimed Murty, his inhospitable tone also changed for the better, as, in his turn, he seized the visitor's hands, and shook them violently.

"Ship on her beam-ends !" proclaimed the Admiral, somewhat reprehensively, as he sprang to set up again the table which, in his amiable haste, Murty had overturned.

" Come in, acuishla, come in," resumed Chevaun. " Sure this
this is no place for you to be standin' !"

" Yes, rowl in the four bones o' you!" said Murty, throwing
an arm around her waist ; and Mary passively suffered herself
to be led, or rather hurled, into the house.

The two women proceeded towards the fireplace. Chevann
at on the hob, almost facing the door, so that her face remained fully visible ; the other on a " boss,"* confronting Mrs.
feehan, the hood of her cloak still unmoved, and her features, as
well as her person, still a mystery to the " Ould Admiral."
Murty deposited himself on a second boss, on one side of the
women, with the air and manner of a person who, without much
intrusion, had a right to loiter within ear-shot of whatever they
were about to say. Terence O'Brien remained where he had
been, after adjusting the table, his legs apart, his one arm hanging straight by his side, his one fist clenched, and his eyes and
whole face angrily, one would think, regarding the group.

" An' the poor ould mother—how is she, *alanna-ma-chree ?*"
resumed Chevaun, stooping her head close to that of the person
she addressed.

Mary answered in a still lower and more saddened voice that
she had used at the door, accompanying the mournful sounds with
a slow rocking motion of the body. A conversation went cu
between her and Chevaun, of which the Admiral caught not a
sentence, though it might be supposed, from the expression of his
visage, as well as from his set attitude, that he listened attentively
—which, however, was not the case. Whatever art might or
might not have done to make him a gentleman, the Ould Admiral
was by nature one in heart, and he would have spurned the idea
of turning eavesdropper upon the confidential discourse of any
persons, gentle or simple. But he could not help observing that
Mary's auditors seemed deeply affected with what she told them.
Indeed, Murty's huge, good blue eyes grew moist as they fixed
on hers, and the tears ran outright down his wife's vermilion
cheeks ; while many a sympathizing " och!" and " heart sorry to
hear it!" with other ejaculations of sorrow and compassion, broke
in loud accents from their lips. And so sweetly touching still
were the cadences of Mary's plaintive, though unheard words
whatever they imported, that, as a child would do, Terence almos'
began to follow Chevaun's example ou the occasion, "for com

---

* A low round seat, made solidly with coils of twisted straw.

pany ;" when one other query, now put by that good woman, so as to be heard by him, gave his feelings a new direction.

"An' poor Terry O'Brien, Mary, *achorra?*"

"Ahoy! Here!" answered Terence, making a step forward, and again standing stockstill on his extended legs, as if answering to a "musther on deck."

But Chevaun and Murty only motioned to him to be quiet and mute, while their visitor, after a bound on her seat at the boisterous interruption he had given, drew her cloak tighter round her nead and face, and became, after a long-drawn sigh, quite silent.

All followed her example, and there was a sad pause for some time, which Murty at length broke by softly drawing from Mary's arm the stockings she had already hinted were for his use, and praising them to the skies. Then Chevaun suddenly started up, withdrew into an inner room—if so we may call that portion of the cabin separated from the place where they sat only by a wicker partition, not reaching to the roof, nor even from wall to wall, across the clay-floor—and returned with a little basket, containing some unseen articles, which, with many entreaties, she forced Mary to accept. Terence thought he began to surmise the cause of Mary's grief, and formed his resolutions accordingly.

"Well, I must be stirring now," said the object of his interest. She arose, and, features and person still hidden from him, was passing to the door after a farewell shake-hands on the part of honest Murty, and a kiss, through tears, on that of his spouse. Terence, with another hail and another step, gained her side, and dropped something into her basket. Mary, again starting, picked out of it "a raal balloon guinea," instantly deposited the coin on the table, and saying, "No, no—not from you—no, no!" walked smartly away from the house.

"But you might, though," bawled Terence after her. "It's a thrue yellow-boy, every splice of id, an' honestly got, 'boord ould ship—my bulk to Ould Davy, but it is! But she won't answer hail. Well, well, I see what's in the wind—thinks the ould sayman can't afford it, or else thinks he had it by piracy."

Such were Terence's sagacious guesses at Mary's notions, which, however, he was to live to understand a little better. Chevaun and Murty looked expressively at each other.

"Ay, ay," resumed Terence; "but all's one for that. Since she will sheer off, up goes the shiner into the ould locker again. An' so, shipmate, the ould hulk to shove off, too, on a new tack, without any memorandle aboard—eh, shipmate?"

" Och, no, thin, an' blessings on the kind heart in your body !"
answered Murty, his mind more full than ever of anxiety to do
the Admiral a service, notwithstanding the many interruptions his
previous efforts had undergone. In fact, his own honest nature
was grateful for Terence's proof of sympathy towards poor Mary.

" No, no, don't stir a step yet, for the life o' you !" seconded
Chevaun, in something of the same spirit.

Again she moved, and again the eyes of her husband and
Terence followed her. Chevaun made her way to the cupboard,
and was about to open it, when she paused, turned towards her
friends, and solemnly addressed them.

" I'll tell yez what was a loocky thing, afther all."

Murty anxiously demanded, " What ?"

" That when the paper tuk fire there was none o' the writin'
on it."

" Bee gonnies ! an' so it was," cheerfully assented her husband,
rejoicing in any set-off against his undeniable ill-luck.

" Ay, ay, right, misthress," also agreed the Admiral. " Good
chance iv a sart'uty, that none o' the crew were aboord when ould
ship blew up; for up along with it they'd ha' gone, and not a
sowl saved, d'ye see me ?"

" See that now," resumed Mrs. Meehan, congratulating herself
upon her ingenious remark ; " there's nothin' so bad in this world
but it might be worse. An' so, Murty agra, don't be down-
hearted any longer." She laid her hand on that of her husband,
and looked commiseratingly into his face. " Let bygones be bygones ; what's past can't be helped, if a body were to lay down
a life for it."

" Thrue for you, Chevaun ; but will you be able to make out
another scrap o' the paper ?"

" There's the gorsoon's copy-book in the cupboard—can't we
just tear a lafe out o' that, Murty, *acuishla-ma-chree ?*"

" Beo gonnies, an' so we can ! you war always an' iver a kind
sowl, Chevaun," smiled Murty, greatly relieved. " The heavens
prosper you."

It may be surmised that, previous to his wife's happy thought
of the gorsoon's copy-book, Murty Meehan had, from his repeated failures. become somewhat cooled in his first estimate of his
own capability to master the task before him, and, notwithstanding his seeming anxiety to persevere, might perhaps have half
wished to elude it—up the chimney, if he could—with the burned
paper. Now, however, Chevaun's presence of mind left him no

excuse for drawing back. Either he prepared to renew his efforts in a kind of hopeless determination to do his best, or else the sight of the fresh leaf of paper really renewed his courage, and endowed him with the spirit, and, joined to his experience, with the tact which—we are proud to say it—insured his ultimate success.

"Yes, plaise the pigs, we'll mind oursef this time, at any rate --and a watched season is never scarce," was the philosophical dage with which he now set down to recommence the "Bit o' Writin'."

"Sink my ould hulk to—" began the Admiral.

"Whist, Terry O'Brien," suddenly interrupted Chevaun ; "we'll have none o' the saltwater cursin' now, if we want to escape more o' the *dhunnus.*"

The Admiral fidgeted, but stood convinced, reproved, and silent.

"The date o' the year," said Murty.

"Ay, ay, the date o' the year, first of all, shipmate."

"Aighteen hundhred an' one, then," Murty repeated, slowly muttering ; and as in deep thought he strove to call to mind the shapes of the figures which should designate the era, his pen described above the paper two or three cautious flourishes almost as before.

A figure of 8, lying on its back—thus, ∞—was described. He snatched up the pen, and looked earnestly at the real commencement of his task. All was right. Neither pen, ink, nor paper played him false "this turn." He moved the sheet from side to side, accompanying it by wagging his head from shoulder to shoulder. He resumed, still repeating "aighteen hundhred an' one."

Two additional figures were produced, and the embryo document became antedated by about one thousand years. The whole of the figures stood thus, "∞ 01."

"There's the date o' the year, plain to be seen, we b'lieve, Admiral," he said, glancing at his neighbor with ill-disguised pride.

"I like the cut o' their jibs well, my hearty ; they're o' the right sort of a sart'inty. Ay, ay, able-bodied saymen, every kind o' them."

"Musha, the Goodness be praised," said Chevaun, with a happy sigh ; "an' see what it is to get the larnin' arly. Not brought up to the handlin' the paper like a cow or a horse."

"An' isn't the day o' the month to be your tack now, jolly boy ?"

"That's to be put in, by all manes, Admiral."

There were a few more passing flourishes, and then ensued the actual operation. The pen went up and down, heavily grating against the rough paper.

"Yee-ho! yee-ho! ho-yee!" sung Terence O'Brien, keeping time to the pen's movement and shrill harsh noise; "undher way at last, my hearty. I like the sound o' your tackle; it's like the ould ship in a stiff breeze—yee-ho!"

Murty smiled with the conscious glee of certain success, thus added to by the Admiral's approbation, while, at his other side, his wife further encouraged him.

"Didn't I know, Murty, *acuishla*—didn't I know the second offer 'ud thrive—that, and barrin' the cursin'?"

And so Murty went on producing, by degrees, a full crew of "able-bodied saymen;" not an unapt term, by the way, when applied to his striding, straggling, burly characters.

For two good hours was the amanuensis's hand at work. He would stop in the middle of a word; spell over the letter of it which he had just written; oblige the admiral to repeat it for him; endeavor to ascertain how much of its sound he had succeeded in typifying; get the remainder into his mind in a jumble, and then proceed very ambiguously to express what had been very ambiguously apprehended. His "saymen," therefore, stood quite independent of each other, or, at least, but seldom linked together.

And while placing a point over an i, Murty would steal down the pen, and not always exactly fix it over the proper character, and then turn it round and round, until the point became swollen to a goodly size; or in crossing a t, his first essay was very gradually made, and the whole process amusing. He would, as the Admiral called it, steer his instrument with his left hand, and then quietly and slowly scrape it across the upright letter. But, indeed, on this one matter practice gave him courage as he got on; for at length he would make a bold dash with his pen, and deviating from a horizontal course, divide into two parts, not invariably equal portions, whatever letters happen to come in his way. And pretty nearly thus, till his task was quite completed, did Murty reduce to paper the stentorian dictation of the Ould Admiral.

But his task was indeed finished. He slowly arose to dry the paper at the fire; but in full recollection of a former adventure, as well as in obedience to Terence's warning of—"Fire-ship

ahead—ahoy !" and of Chevaun's—"Have a care now, Murty,
agra !" he kept it well clear of the turf-blaze.

Dried the document became, without hap or injury. Murty,
suspending it by a corner, strode the few strides which he could
take on his cabin floor, and slowly held it up to the full view of
his admiring spouse, who well understood his glance and smile to
mean—

"See, Chevaun, what it is to have a scholar for your hus
band."

Nor was he slow in apprehending that the answering drawing
up of the muscles about Chevaun's mouth, the poking forward
of her head to the invited scrutiny, and the wide-open expression
of her eyes as they afterwards met his, plainly said—

"Yes, Murty, a wondher o' the world you are, an' good rason
I have to be proud o' you."

"Here it is now for you, Admiral," said Murty, presenting
the document to its owner. "An' it's loock we wish you wid
it, Admiral, avich !" His tones, air, and manner, were graciously patronizing.

CHAPTER V

AFTER due reflection and consultation on the matter, Terence
O'Brien, or the Ould Admiral, arrived at several pretty accurate
conclusions touching the further disposal and progress of the
"memorandle o' sarvice."

He had heard—beyond doubt he was sure—of such a place as
the Admiralty Office, "in the port of London," and judged that
thither he ought to forward it. As a first step towards this, he
soon became aware that the document should be "put aboord
the post-office," in the neighboring town, and thence that it was
to continue its voyage "aboord the mail-coach." Right well
was he aware that he at present lived on an island, separated
from another island in which was the "port o' Lunnon," by a
sea. That his "memorandle" was to be received and forwarded
on and from the coast of that first island, as one of "ould ship's
papers," without at the same time shipping the mail-coach or its

other contents, Terence rather suspected, but, indeed, could not be quite certain of the fact. Nor did he find Murty Meehan, who had never yet caught a glimpse of the sea, nor received or forwarded a letter of any kind in his life, able to enlighten him on the subject. It might be so, or it might not be so ; thus they decided between them ; and eventually the Admiral, suddenly struck with the conviction that the question, turn out as it might, was no concern of his, made up his mind to leave it undecided. "The captain o' the post-office" was the man whom it concerned, and not him, Terence O'Brien. Every commander of a vessel knew how every thing ought to be done aboard his own ship, from the splicing of a cable to the firing of a broadside ; and agreeably to this notion of the postmaster's competency in his duties, Terence argued that his paper, once delivered into the hands of that person, just as it had come out of Murty Meehan's hands—by-the-way, unfolded and undirected—ought to arrive safe at the end of its voyage ; a mere announcement of its destination being obviously sufficient to enable the captain to supply and superintend all the detail of its progress upon the way.

"What else was the ould loober upon that station for ?" and so Terence set forward for the post-town nearest to his residence.

The postmaster was in the act of delivering the morning letters, and a crowd of people gathered round the window of his office. Had we leisure we might attempt to produce some pathetic and some ludicrous surmises as to the different feelings in which different individuals of the throng stretched forward their hands and exerted their voices, claiming their expected dispatches. But we must not pause to indulge our speculations or show our skill at the expense of the reader's patience. With one person alone, of all present, we dally for a moment.

He stood on the outskirts of the crowd, quietly waiting his turn to go to the window, saying nothing, pushing or hurrying nobody, and resting both his hands upon his stick. He seemed a very personification of patience and humility. Either he had never, even in youth, possessed any dash in his character, or the pinching poverty now visible in his sharp features and peculiar attire had long ago frozen it out of him. His head-gear was very ancient, and yet made the most of ; he would seem fully to have studied and approved the celebrated adage, that "the life of an old hat consists in cocking it." His person was draped in a kind of frockcoat of coarse gray kersey, reaching below his knees, so fashioned as to save him from the sarcasm of going too heavily clad in summer, or of having an appearance of almost nakedness in very cold weather : for the garment could not be called an outside coat at the one season, nor a thin coat at the other. Originally his leg had been well shaped, and at such a period of its existence had first taken possession of that part of the pantaloon which at present covered it ; but abstemious living for many years since then had shrunk its calf, so that it now allowed its vesture to ruffle in wrinkles to the wind. And it was not difficult to conjecture from his general appearance, and the hints supplied by his face and deportment, that his blay stocking had been "darned" by his own careful hands ; while his shoes were water-proof in sole, upper, and quarter, because, from year to year, they had been diligently watched, and the moment time made a rent or a crack in them, no matter how small, immediately and intently patched in the frail place, with a view to prevent each breach from widening.

We have not much to do with this man, so we crave pardon for volunteering this sketch of him.

"Ahoy, my hearty !" bellowed Terence O'Brien at his ear, in a tone that would have made him start, or at least look offended had he not long abandoned all hastiness of movement or of feeling, or he might have deemed that, as the term "hearty" could certainly not apply to him, he was not the person addressed. At all events, he only turned, slowly and quietly, his sharp little face to the speaker.

"Post-office thransport ahead—eh, my jolly lad ?" still questioned the tar, pointing to the window.

"If it's the post-office you want, yes, there it is ; though it's no thransport, as I know of, my honest man," answered little Patience.

"Scuttle my hulk to Ould Davy ! you don't mean to call it a frigate, do you ?"

"You have my lave to call it a man-o'-war, if that same gives you the laste pleasure."

"No—shiver my timbers to splinters if I do ! Hah ! do you want to come over the ould sayman that way, you loober ? I'd spy out a man-o'-war seven leagues to windward, you landshark."

"Well, well, just as you like."

"Capt'n gives ordhers at the gunnel—eh ?"

"I don't well undherstand your meaning."

Muttering something like contempt for the ignorance of all "land-loobers," Terence steered direct for the post-office window "Scud, scud—avast, my heartics? I say," he bellowed forth, forcing his way through all opposition ; and he presented his unique visage at the open wooden-pane through which letters were distributed.

"Ship's paper—ould ships—will your honor take it aboord ?" and he held out his "memorandle o' sarvice."

"What do you want? what do you call this ?" questioned tho postmaster.

"Sink my hulk! what do I call it? Why, are your lights out, capt'n, or can't you take an observation ?"

The captain peered and peered. He took off his spectacles and wiped them in the ample, though rather soiled, muslin frill of his shirt. He peered again, and his lips moved, as if in an honest effort to spell his way through the manuscript. He raised up his head and looked attentively from it to the disfigured face of the "sayman;" then to the paper again ; and then to that index visage again.

"What is it at all, man? and what do you wish me to do about it ?"

"Why, don't you see it's a memorandle o' sarvice? What else would it be ?"

"And pray, inform me how am I to dispose of such a dirty piece of nonsense ?"

"Avast there, capt'n, you loober! Fair weather between us ; 'tis as thrue as the log, every word of it."

Once more the good-natured postmaster bent his eyes studiously upon Murty Meehan's penmanship, and began to mutter—" 'Terry O—O'Brien'—I suppose ; um—um—' a la burbe'—um—um—' shot close to his body'—here, my man"—interrupting himself, and handing back the document, as many impatient voices called aloud for their letters—" I can make no hand of your paper or yourself ; take it away, and leave the window clear."

"Take it away, capt'n," echoed poor Terence, rather crestfallen ; "it wasn't to take it away I towed it in here from Muckalee ; you'll just ship it for the Admiralty Boord—eh, capt'n !

"Get away with it ; take it out of my hand, I tell you ; there—go—get it properly written ; stand back, and let sensible people come for their letters."

Beginning to entertain some slight doubt of the clerkship of his Muckalee friend, the Ould Admiral was obliged to retire with his "memorandle ;" not, indeed, until he had fought hard to have it received "aboord." Having cleared the crowd, he stopped in the middle of the street to ponder what next was to be done.

The little man he had before accosted followed him closely though quietly, at a cat's pace, when she steals, step by step within springing distance of a fat mouse. He had overheard the dialogue between Terence and the postmaster, and it was not quite thrown away upon him. In his imagination—we use an inapt word—in his sober, unromantic, practical calculations, we should rather say—the document had already set the kettle singing and the pot boiling for a better breakfast and a more substantial dinner than he had for some time been intimate with.

When he arrived close to Terence, that worthy fragment of a Jack was holding the paper close to his eyes—and, to help him still more, turned upside down—endeavoring to discover in what respect it was deficient for a voyage " 'boord the post-office thransport."

" Looking as wise as a pig at a sun-dial," commenced his future friend to himself; then he continued aloud—

" Honest man, was that wrote wid a spade or a shovel—which o' the two ?"

" What jaw, now I what jaw ?" demanded Terence, angrily and ominously.

" I say it's either the spade or the shovel wrote that paper."

Terence nearly lost all command of temper at this double slight of his own importance, and of the zealous, and hitherto but slightly questioned, services of an esteemed neighbor. " It's a lie, you loober I it's a lie !" he thundered forth, raising the document to slap it across the face of the commentator.

Notwithstanding the incivility of the commencement of their dialogue, these dissimilar men were, however, in a short time, better acquainted. However ignorant at first of the right road to an object, self-interest is generally a ready scholar in finding it out.

Very gradually the uselessness of the document became explained to Terence, and was comprehended by him ; and the little half-starved man and he eventually struck a bargain on the business, and were seen to walk down the street together.

The Admiral was led up a narrow, dirty lane, and he and his

convoy entered a dilapidated house, over the door of which was a sign-board, announcing it as the abode of

"GARRET BYRNE,
PUBLICK WRITTER."

The personage so described, Garret Byrne, fixed a wicker-backed chair as his desk, sat to it upon a three-legged stool, and, without a tithe of poor Murty Meehan's preparations, with none of his failures or misfortunes, and devoting to his task an incredibly short portion of time, in the opinion of Terence O'Brien, produced something like a proper letter to the Admiralty Board. It was even folded, directed, and wafered, and then Garret Byrne asked and received a reward, dishonest in him to propose, and very improvident in his employer to bestow. Finally, Terence saw him "put it aboord" at the post-office ; after which, the public writer and his dupe adjourned into a dram-shop, to pour down, at the expense of but one of the party, libations to its prosperous voyage.

CHAPTER VI.

AFTER the sailing of his dispatches, the Admiral kept a sharp lookout for an answer. But he was not impatient in point of time. He made due allowances for the weather-gauge, and reckoning a certain number of knots to an hour for the out-bound and the in-bound voyage, did not begin to hail "the post-office thransport" again till his nautical experience told him he was warranted in doing so. Nor was Terence much out of his calculations, when a letter directed to him—absolutely to him—appeared at the post-office in due course.

It did not, however, contain money, nor an order for money ; it only called on him to prepare and forward various certificates and affidavits. No matter. The certificates and affidavits were soon ready, under the superintendence of his now established agent, Garret Byrne, and a check for a good round sum came at last.

At the bank of the town, being conducted still by Garret Byrne, the Ould Admiral sunk " all thim bits o' notes to Ould

Davy," and would accept nothing but gold—"the yallow boys,"
an' nothin' else for him;" and so gold he got. We wish the
reader were present on the occasion to notice the expression of
the eyes and even of the pointed nose of the "publick writer,"·
as the guineas jingled on the counter. But it is enough to say
that out of them he managed to extract a second enormous fee
for his services since the dispatch of the first letter. A second
jorum of grog, too, was shared between him and the sailor, to
the heart's content of Terence and to Garret's slight and momen
tary vivification.

The evening began to fall, and it was time to go homewards
Assisted by his companion, Terence tied up his gold in the use
less sleeve of his jacket, using two strings, one below and another
above the bulk made by his hoard ; he further secured it by
crossing the sleeve upon his breast, and stuffing it into his
bosom ; and then he clutched his cudgel in his left and only
hand, and scudded homeward, every inch of canvas to the
breeze.

"Praise be to the heavens! never, since the day I was born,
did mysef set my two eyes on sich a hape o' the goold," said
Murty Meehan, as he, Chevaun, and the Admiral contemplated
it on their table, where it had been tossed out by its owner among
the pile of potatoes served up for their evening supper.

"It's wondherful to look at it," agreed Chevaun.

"Many a rough gale the old hulk weathered for it, misthress ;
au' many ard n any a broadside went to win it."

"No doubt o' that," continued Murty. "Bud, bee gonnies !
you can't say but you're well paid for all your throubles an'
losses, Ould Admiral, aroon ; it isn't the half o' my nose, but
the whole o' my nose I'd give for sich a fort'n ; ay, even supposin' they stuck a turkey-cock's baik to my face instid—not to
talk of a Frinchman's. Ay, or I'd go widout e'er an arun at all,
or I'd hop on only one leg into the bargain all the blessed days
o' my life, for the honest gainin' o' so much threasure."

"God forgive you, Murty Meehan," said Chevaun ; "take
care o' what you're sayin'. The heavens forbid you'd be spoiled
in sich a manner for the double iv id over again."

"But what, in the name o' wondher, will you do wid it, at all,
Admiral ?"

"Why, d'ye see me, that's just what I'm a jawin' to myself
about, my hearty. But ahoy, my jolly lad! we'll work it in
company—oceans o' grog for say-store, and every sail up while it

lasts!—eh, shipmate? A cruise together—an ould ship scuddin', no matther what point the wind blows from, eh?"

"Och, no, Admiral. That 'ud be a cryin' sin for the both of us."

"'Twould be aflying in the face of the giver, in return for the gift," assented Chevaun.

"A sin?—avast there, avast ; can't cram that down the wizen of an ould sayman. No, no ; mutinee aboord is a sin ; sleepin' or gettin' dhrunk on a watch is a sin ; not standin' up be your gun in action is a sin—an' sich like. The ould jolly boy knows well what they call a sin—ay, as well as e'er a hand aboord. Bud the chaplain himself never said that shippin' grog on pay-out days, whin you're let to sheer off ashore, is a sin. Shiver his hulk ! he couldn't say it, the loober !"

"Why, Admiral, for the mere matther o' that, I would not pelt a stone at a full bottle myself," resumed Murty ; "for I like a dhrop well enough, betimes, maybe. Only wid this differ, that I'd give my vote for the *oneen* widout christenin' it.* That grog o' yours is a wakely sort o' dhrinkin' to my mind, Admiral. Bud all I want to say is, that it would be a robbin' shame au' a schandle to waste so mooch money as this on the table upon dhrink of any kind."

"Then stow it into your own locker for me, my hearty. If it stops 'boord ould ship 'tis gone of a sartinty, d'ye see me ?" and he pushed the gold towards Murty.

"Och ! no, no ; that wou't do, either, my poor Ould Admiral."

"Stow it up for yourself then, I say, shipmate ; and for the misthress-mate there, an' for the brig Peggy, out on her cruise o' sarvice, an' for loblolly Paudeen, d'ye see me one or all. Ye may want it, or know what to do wid it, which I don't, d'ye mind me, barrin' I sarve it out for the grog—my hulk to Ould Davy if I do !"

"No, no, over again, Admiral. We're as heartily thaokful, all as one, as if we made our own of it. But no other man's money will ever burden my conscience ; no, or rear up my child-her, more-betoken. Sure, it's for somethin' o' the like reason I have the *weenochs* on the same place wid me, at all at all ; for whin a very wise body axed me why I was goin' to be married, an' I only a lump of a soft boy, at the same time, Admiral—a

* That is, he would vote for pure whiskey, without watering it.

3

kind o' one of your loblolly boys, you know, only a taste bigger
an' handier at the spade maybe—'why, sir,' says I, 'the reason
is this, sir, savin' your presence, sir,' says I, 'I'm able to work a
start, sir, an' I don't like to be workin' for any man's childher
but my own, sir,' says I."

"Well, well, that's all as it may be. But what *am* I to do wid
the yellow-boys, if you sing out no to the grog, shipmate !"

"Sure, as I said afore, on the head o' the bit o' writin', that all
this goold cum by—" (Terence had been too generous to pain
Murty with intelligence of the failure of his document, or of the
intervention of Garret Byrne thereupon.) "Sure, as I said afore,
there's your brother, Admiral."

"Avast, avast, man ! as *I* tould *you* afore, shiver and scuttle
my hulk to Ould Davy, if he ever touches a stiver of it ! That
same brother is no brother to me, but a d—d laudshark—shuv-
vin' me out to say agin, when I thought to moor my ould hulk
here, in the ould soundin's— 'case why? he said I couldn't work
ship wid him—the greedy unnathral loober ! Ay, ay, adhrift he
turned me, mainmast, riggin', and rhudder gone, an' not a day's
provision aboord ! So jaw no more about him, d'ye you see
me ?"

"'Twas bad usage enough ; we won't gainsay you, my poor
Ould Admiral. But his poor slob of a boy, the son—*he* done
nothin' to you."

"Done nothin' to me ! isn't he one of the crew ? sailing undher
his father's colors and ordhers? an' wouldn't he do by me whatever he's commanded to do, by coorse, or else go to the yard-
arum ? What else could he do ?"

"Well, Admiral, my poor fellow, I'll tell you what kind of a
thought comes to me, then."

"Out wid it, my hearty."

"You're reasonable ould—we can't gainsay that either, you
know."

"Ay, ay, shipmate ; an ould sheer bulk on the wather, goin'
to pieces every say ; but English—I mane Irish—heart of oak,
every plank o' me, howsomever."

"All bud what you call the *ruddher*, Admiral, an' a quare
name it is to give a nose."

"Ay, ay, sink an' d—d it ! I forgot that, shipmate. But let it
go to Ould Davy, an' say your say out."

"Well, aroon ; what I'm thinkin' of is soon said. I'm thinkin'
now, that wid the help of all this goold, an' since you're goin' to

pieces, as you say yoursef, it wouldn't be a bad notion if you had one to look afther you, an' keep you together."

"Hollo! where are you bound for now, my jolly lad?"

"Faix, an' all I mane is, supposin' you was to take on wid a wife, Admiral?"

"A wife!" shouted Terence O'Brien, in utter amazement; "a wife alongside? No, no, shipmate; no one will ever see me join company with that kind o' craft. No, no; grapple to the locker is the word aboord with all sich—grapple to the locker; an' when no more say-store is left, then shove off, d'ye see me? No; never a painted schooner of 'em shall take the ould hulk in tow."

Terence was calling to mind some kind of wapping adventure.

"An' sorry we'd be, Ould Admiral, to see the best among them use her toe to you, or her five fingers either. But little's the danger o' that here, in Muckalee. Them sort you spake of lives by the sayshore; but our honest counthry girrels isn't given to any sich kind o' doin's."

"Avast, lad, avast; all she-pirates and sharks, one wid another. When first I steered home here to Muckalee, 'case I didn't carry bags o' goold for ballast, didn't your whole squadron of that craft cock up their noses at me, as your land-sayin' goes?"

"Bud, sure, you ped 'em back in their own coin, and widout any throuble," smiled Murty, again venturing the sore allusion.

"Ay, ay: but sink that, I say. Didn't one of 'em call me as ugly an ould fish as ever swum! and another say I was a *farh brecghoch*,* an' ax me to let her stick me in her father's whatefield? An' that young fire-ship, Nance Dulhanty, didn't she— the craft wid the red lauthron at her poop, I mane—didn't she set my pigtail a-blaze at her ould granny's wake? An' Kitty Doyle! I was a cruizin' on the top o' the hill, d'ye see me, an' she an' a fleet o' doxies wid her, at the bottom; an' she hails me to join company, an' I tacks to bear down on 'em; an' she an' they ties the long land-grass right across the channel, an' I strikes on id, and comes on my bame-inds—ay, over an' over, till the ould hulk righted again—an' the whole crew o' them singing an' pipin' out to me, all the time, in make-game like? Avast, I tell you, shipmate; they're all the same, by sayhore or by land-shore —all the same."

"Why, thin, we're much behouldin' to your good word, misther Admiral," remarked Mrs. Meehan.

* Scarecrow

"Didn't mane you, jolly misthress; didn't never mane you. You're not one of the sort. I mane the young light deck ers, as scuds on every tack, in all weathers, flyin' in every breeze."

"Sure, then, we'll get one for you as old as the hills, if you like," said Murty.

"And that won't go down neither, my hearty; luff, luff; two sheer hulks, bobbin' shivered planks together every swell—never do; singin' out, too, ' avast, avast,' in every cap-full of wind—ay, or if there was ever gun left aboord, exchangin' shots, I warrant you."

"Faith, an' you're a'most in the right, now, we b'lieve, though you did live so long on the wather, Admiral," grinned Murty.

"Musha, an' I'm afeard he is, Lord purtect us," added Mrs. Meehan, more seriously.

"But," resumed her honest man, "sure you don't see much o' the robbin', or vastin', or toein', or scuddin', or singin', or shootin' betwixt Chevaun here, au' my own sef, Admiral?"

"No, no; all fair sailin' in company there, an' breeze right ahead."

"Well, an' wouldn't you like Chevaun's likes for a voyage, as you call it?"

"Hallo, shipmate! goin' to change tack? Only say the word, an' I'm for the cruise in your stead, d'ye see me—ay, wid all my heart and lights, my hearty!" He took the flattered Chevaun by the hand, and shook it upwards and downwards, in approval of what he understood to be Murty Mechan's proposal for a transfer of his wife; and Terence spoke—we stake our veracious character on the fact—in perfect, simple seriousness.

"Ho, ho, ho! we couldn't manage that matter so asily—none of us, Admiral."

"What jaw, then; what jaw?"

"Why, God forgive you, man, sure isn't poor Chevaun an' mysef to be in company, as yoursef has it, till death does us part?"

"Foundher to Ould Davy, then, an' lave the misthress-mate au' I say-room."

"We don't want to have a call to that fellow, I tould you afore, Admiral."

"Go aloft, then, you loober."

"An' I cau't pleasure you that way, neither—at laste till we have the little pee-aties out o' the ground, asthore."

"Well, an' what port are you steerin' for, then?"

" No port at all ; I'll stay in the port where I am ; an' Chevaun an' I will be pleasant company wid one another, these hundred years to come, plaise God. Bud, Admiral, there's one little
Moya Moore, an' she's the born sisther o' Chevaun—nearer to
her she couldn't be ; an' she's very like Chevaun, only a younger
girrel, an' she's a'most as purty as Chevaun, and she's a'most as
good as Chevaun—an' that's a great word."

" Ay, ay ; I spoke wid Moya Moore, shipmate, the night o'
my cruise to Nance Dulhanty's granny's wake—an' 'twas she put
out the fire 'boord ould hulk when Nance set the rishlight to my
pigtail ; ay, spoke wid her then an' often afore an' since. Ay,
ay. Now that I call to mind, that little craft Moya is the only
one o' your jade squadron that never says nothin' to jibe the ould
sayman—never does an' never did. Ay, ay."

" She'd make a nate, an' a clane, an' a laucky* wife for the
Ould Admiral," observed her prudent sister. " Yes, an' you
spoke to her later than you think, Admiral ; she was here the
day o' the writin'."

" Whin you gave me sich a hail by my name, misthress, an'
she an' you ajoinin' together? an' I never knew her from the
new cut of her canvass. But why wouldn't she share a little
say-store wid me ! why sheer off in a rumpus at only the sight o'
the shiner ?"

" Shy she was, maybe, Admiral, to take any help from a body
that wouldn't be a blood relation to her ; don't blame the poor
erature for that."

" Help ! distress aboord, then, though no signal hoisted ?
But why did you sing out, ' the Terry O'Brien ahoy !' misthress,
if I was to bear no hand, d'ye see me ?"

Chevaun and her husband interchanged a look similar to that
which had passed between them upon the very occasion alluded
to. Evidently they thought Terence in some misconception.

" Never mind about the hoy, Admiral, for the prasent. But,
yes, asthore—disthress, sure enough, is come on poor Moya ; the
ould mother has a nice bit o' land, to be sure, only there's a'
ould arrear over it ever since her husband died. An' she an
Moya will be turned out on the world-wide this May, barrin'
somethin' takes it off for 'em."

" Sent adhrift ? sink my hulk, but they sha'n't, though ! Show
me the loober that daare think of it, an' if I don't blow him clane

---

* Tidy and gracious.

off the wather at the first broadside, scuttle me for Ould Davy."

"That wouldn't be the way, Admiral," said Murty; "the thing to be done is to blow the arrears off o' the land. And now listen well to me; your houest goold could do that, if you an' Moya Moore was once man an' wife. Ay, an' more than that; stock the farum, too, afther clearin' it; an' then all would go well to the world's ind."

"Ay, ay; but this little galley, the Moya, would she be puttin' the ould hulk undher any new ordhers—short allowance o' grog, or sich like—d'ye see me, eh, shipmate?"

"Niver fear that, Admiral; she wouldn't say one conthrary word to you from year's end to year's end, an' I know her well."

"No squalls, at a hand's-turn, to get ould ship on her bames' inds?"

"The dickens a squall she'd give the crature! barrin' you gave her rason, Admiral," answered Murty; "an' you're not the man to do sich a dirty turn. No; Moya is as quiet as the lamb. No; but she'd mend for you, an' she'd make for you, an' she'd sing a purty little song for you at her wheel; an' you'd have a house o' your own, Admiral, an' no one to cross or conthrary you; an' the stock an' the crops 'ud be thrivin' on the land; an' in a rasonable time there 'ud be little weeny Admirals runnin' about your legs, an' they'd be tumblin' over head an' heels on the flure to divart you, an' you'd be a 'sponsible man."

"Hurrah!" cheered Terence, as the picture glowed before his ardent imagination.

"And then let me see the one that 'ud call you an ugly ould fish, or tumble you down the hill, or put the fire to you're pig's-tail, or as much as snap an eye at you, my poor Ould Admiral."

"Hurrah! hurrah! hurrah!" again shouted the Admiral, three times distinctly, as we have noted it down—now taking off his hat, and waving it round his head, while the deafening pitch of his voice startled the echoes in the little glen outside the house.

It was finally settled that Terence should indeed go a-wooing—by proxy, however, in the first instance. He was loth to venture, as he intimated, out of "say-room," such as he was used to, into a strange, unknown harbor, without taking soundings; for there might be rocks, or sands, or breakers ahead enough to make the best ship afloat go to pieces, and to baffle the steering skill of the ablest hand that ever grappled a helm or boxed a compass. In fact, Murty Meehan was deputed, and gladly accepted the commission, to break the business to Moya and her mother; while Terence O'Brien should await his return in the next public house, administering to the thirsty wants of some of his neighbors, in return for their decent attention to his stories of wondrous adventure on the ocean; containing many charms for them, doubtless, though deficient in that of novelty, and deficient we venture to say, in another sense, veracity,—something in the same style as the substitution of the nose, almost all of them.

CHAPTER VII.

SITTING down to this story, we made up our minds that it should not, if possible, be solemn, from the beginning to the end of it. Now, even when it is plain that, with close regard to truth, it must take some such turn in spite of us, we would fain avoid the contingency, if, we repeat, circumstances permitted our choice; so anxious are we to have it to say, that we possess the talent of selecting, for once in our lives at least, as the subject of a tale occurrences and persons always of a sunshiny character.

But the course of human affairs is, we fear, against us. The clear blue sky and the cloud of life, the sun and the shower, work alternately with each other in whatever succession of true events our experience can bring before us. And it is to be even so with our little history, henceforward. We promise, however, to stay out in the sun as often and as long as we can, and not to chill you under the cloud-shadow, or wet you with the shower, except when there is no running in-doors from the approach of either.

Moya Moore deserved the character jointly given of her by her sister Chevaun and by her good brother-in-law, Murty Meehan. She was, indeed, an excellent-hearted girl; very pretty, too, with as tender and loving a blue eye as ever lighted up a rosy cheek. We have often paused, with others, to admire her modest beauty, and her soft, retiring manner, as she stood by one of the pillars of our market-house, with some half-dozen pairs of woollen-hose hanging over her arm, all of her own knitting—nay, the materials of all carded and spun by herself. And we have as often thought, while engaged in our innocent studies of Moya, that the cooing, pipy murmur of voice in which she used to recommend the quality of her merchandise must have convinced many bidders of their excellence.

But Moya Moore had been more blooming some years before our approaching introduction to her than she is at present. Care and sorrow, and her efforts, from morning to night, to supply, with untiring industry, to her old broken-spirited parent the comforts her age required, had lately made sad work among the roses on her cheeks. After all, little could she effect to soothe her mother's lot. The profits of her little household manufacture were inadequate to pay men to till the old farm, to stock it, and above all, to clear it of the heavy arrears of rent with which it was burdened.

Murty has already hinted to his friend, the Old Admiral, something of the present position of Moya and her mother. We must be a little more particular.

Mrs. Moore had once been a bustling, consequential personage. Perhaps she used to pride herself on the station she enjoyed in the world. She had been an heiress—after the fashion following. Her father held a small, compact tract of land, but having no male issue—no child but herself, in fact—caused her husband, when she married, to come and reside with his wife in the house in which she was born, and help them to cultivate and take care of the land, and be in every respect a son unto him—which, indeed, Daniel Moore was, until the old man died, leaving him, in right of his spouse, the envied possessor of a comfortable independence.

And still every thing went on prosperously. Mrs. Moore became the mother of two sons, who in time proved industrious lads, and, directed by their father, increased the profits of the farm ; and so, year after year, the heiress, all along covered by her natal roof, saw herself and her family gain much repute in the neighborhood. But a sorrowful reverse was doomed to her. A malignant fever broke out in her district, and, within a few weeks of each other, hurried her husband and her sons to the grave. And now, her broken-heartedness and her consternation assisting the ultimate result, the widow gradually became first embarrassed, and then involved beyond hope of redemption.

At the time of her first misfortunes, her daughter Chevaun had during some years been married to Murty Meehan, and her second daughter Moya, was a child of nine or ten. At present that child is nineteen, so that for a long period poor Mrs. Moore has been vainly struggling. almost alone, still to live, and if pos

sible die, under the roof which sheltered her father, herself since
her birth, her husband since he became such, to the day of his
death, and her fine young sons to the day of their untimely de-
mise also. And at last she has but one melancholy prospect
before her—that of seeing herself and her innocent Moya turned
out upon the world, poorer than beggars, because in debt—and
the one helpless from age, and the other on account of her youth
and tender character.

As Murty Meehan crossed the farm to Mrs. Moore's house,
bent upon his matrimonial diplomacy, bitterly did he lament over
the face of dilapidation worn by every thing around him. The
fences were all broken down ; the land overrun with stones,
weeds, thistles, and bramble. Over that part of it which had once
afforded pasture to a goodly herd of cattle and a fine flock of
sheep, a single half-fed cow—a present from himself by the way
—now ranged, untended and mournfully.

Nor did the once comfortable farm-house and its adjuncts present a better appearance than the land. The disjointed gate of
the front yard lay in the mire. No sturdy swine grunted and
lorded it over the back yard ; no grand chorus of cackling geese,
gobbling turkey-cocks, and quack-quack quacking ducks greeted
his ears from its recesses ; two or three old-maid hens alone, who,
by sharing Moya's scanty meal of potatoes, just contrived to live,
uttered some fretful sounds in one of the corners. One end of the
barn had fallen in. The house itself was fast bending to decay
and ruin. Here and there the thatch had slid off its roof, or been
blown away by the winds, and was all over that greenish hue
which indicates, in such material, a speedy approach to decompo-
sition, while rank grass, moss, and weeds flourished through it.
The once decent though small windows of the humble mansion
were shattered, and their framework shaken. Before the door,
on both sides, lay a broken plough, a broken harrow, and the wreck
of a farming cart ; all had gone to pieces in the weather, as well
as from the want of an eye and a hand to keep them in repair.

We have said that Murty Meehan scanned with a feeling heart
all these symptoms of distress. One thought, however, brought
him comfort. The Old Admiral's gold would put every thing to
rights. In the scattered heap of it which he had just seen on his
supper-table, there was surely enough for the purpose. And deriving spirits from this reflection, Murty crossed the threshold of
the house.

8*

Moya was seated to her knitting, inside the door, when he suddenly appeared before her with the usual "God save all here." Murty never paid a visit to the widow's abode without bringing some little present, or else volunteering and performing some little piece of service. His placid, good-natured face was ever welcome. His sister-in-law sprang up, threw her arms round his neck, and kissed him cordially.

"Achorra-machree, Moya, how is every little inch o' you ?"

"Thank God ! Murty, I'm as well as my heart could desire ;" such was now her habitual answer, while her cheek, her eye, her very voice contradicted her.

"An' the poor ould mother, achorra, how does she hould up ?"

"Och, Murty, only poorly, poorly. She's making my heart to bleed for her—in good truth she is ;" and while Moya pressed the tears from her eyes with one hand, she pointed towards the widow with the other.

The old woman was seated in a far corner, brooding, as usual, over her troubles. They presented to her mind the one monotonous subject of bitter study and chagrin. She had been comfortable—she was a pauper ; happy, and she was miserable ; the respected mistress of a plentiful home, and she did not now know how soon she must leave it forever, to die under a strange roof, or, perhaps, on the road-side. A plentiful home !—and now there was no butter in her dairy, no sides of bacon in her chimney, no brown loaf in her cupboard ; the small vessel full of inferior potatoes, which simmered on a low fire, and a scanty allowance of milk from the ill-nourished "sthripper," presented to her by Murty Meehan, were her only food.

Seated on a very low stool, the tail of her tattered gown was turned over her head, and pinned partially round her face, as if to shut her up with her own melancholy ; her knees were crippled up to her mouth—a favorite position, as we have noticed among our humbler people, of hopeless poverty. As if such a cringing and doubling of the person were meant to express the sense of self-humiliation weighing upon the heart. Her fingers were dove-tailed across her knees ; and with an exaggeration of the rocking movement before noticed in her daughter Moya during her visit to Mary Meehan, she swayed her body to and fro—the low wailing which occasionally timed the motion imparting to it a character at once wild and despairing.

"How do you come on, my poor sowl ?" asked Murty Meehan,

bending his gigantic figure till his head came on a level with hers in her lowly position, and his tones expressed deep and extreme commiseration.

Startled from her wretched abstraction, she suddenly turned round, and fixed her sombre eyes on his. But it was some time before she could perfectly recognize and bring to mind the features of her son-in-law.

"Murty Meehan, is that you?" she at length said. "I didn't know you at onst. The sighth o' my eyes is goin' from me—the very blessed sighth o' my eyes; yes, the way every thing else is goin' from me. Husband and sons—they're gone—gone, this many a year; paice an' comfort, house an' land—they're gone, too, or else goin', fast, ay, fast, fast; an' maybe 'tis well that the ould eyes will be fadin' too; the good Christhins may be more open-handed when they see that the widow that begs a cowld pee-aty from them is blind as well as poor."

᾿ "She's frettin' herself into the grave from me this away," said Moya, still weeping. There's no use in my tellin' her that God is good, and that he never shuts one door on us but he opens another. Mother, I'm sthrong, an' young, an' able to do for you."

"That child puts the vexation on me, Murty Meehan," resumed the peevish, and therefore selfish, old woman. "Just listen to the words of her mouth; she goes on talkin' o' doin' for me!—does she call givin' me half a mayle o' pee-aties doin' for me? Is she able to put her hand agin the rascal of a sheriff an' his bailiffs, an' shuv 'em from the dour? Will she stock the land, and till the land? Will she pay the black-hearted landlord his rent? Will she keep me in the house where I was born, as I used to be kept in it? I'm not to be under this roof another week."

"Mother, mother! don't be so cast down in yourself," comforted Murty, as Moya turned away, hopeless and pained, though not feeling offended, and weeping more than ever. "Betther times is comin'."

"Betther times! well, ay; I know that. The day I'm sent adrift over that threshold, the heart will burst in my body; an' then there will be betther times—in the grave. Betther times, becase I can't call to mind there the times that are gone. Ay, ay; I know it well; an' I'm thankful to you for your comfort, Murty."

"She's sore afflicted," whispered Moya, coming back, and wishing by her remark to soften to Murty's ear her mother's bitter and hurtful words.

" Mother, you'll want none o' the grave's comforts yet a start, plaise God. You'll be livin' undber the roof that covers you an' that you was born undher, this many a day to come ; an' you'll be liviu' undher it prosperous an' happy."

" Did you stalk over here on your long legs, Murty Meehan, thinkin' you had a witless woman, as well as a broken-nearted woman, to make your mock at ? You have a house to cover you ; don't jibe them that'll soon be houseless, an' that onst had a home o' plenty. Go to your own place, Murty Meehan, an' laive me to myself. Go to your own place, an' take your gorsoon on your knee, an' promise him a coach an' four horses, if he stops cryin'. But don't bring sich stories to the ould widow in her misfortunes."

" Och, mother, mother !" gently remonstrated Moya ; "Murty 'ud never come to your hearth-stone to mock you."

" Mother, the colleen says the truth," cried Murty. "I was never given to say or to do what 'ud give pain to the heart of a sthrauger, not to talk o' you. An' I tell you again, an' I know what I'm sayin', that you'll live in the ould house to the ind o your days, I say, au' comfortable an' happy, if you like."

Moya had begun to listen to Murty with a beating heart ; now she looked at him in breathless interest. The widow relaxed her clasped fingers from her knees, put back, with one hand, the neglected gray hairs from her face, and rested the palm of the other on her low stool. that so she might enable herself to turn round and gaze her full wonder into the speaker's face. Her fluent words ceased.

" First an' foremost," Murty went on, " you don't owe a *laffina* o' rint in the world wide, this blessed moment! There's the landlord's resate in full, to the prasant day." He laid it on her knees. " An' will you b'lieve me now, mother dear ?"

Moya, uttering a low scream of joy, suddenly knelt, clasping her hands, looking upwards, and moving her lips in prayer. The aged woman snatched up the paper, started on her feet, flung back the gown which had been hooded round her head, tottered to the rushlight in the middle of the floor, read the writing, and saw there was no mockery.

" May the ould widow's blessin's," she began, also kneeling, " fall in a plentiful shower on the head that—that—" she could not go on ; a passion of tears interrupted her speech. Mary fervently finished for her the intended blessing, adding, " An' mine with it, our Father in heaven! mine—the blessin' o' the poor

widow's orphan child on whoever it is that takes my mother out
of her sore throuble, this holy and blessed night!"

" 'Tis more nor two years," resumed Mrs. Moore, wiping with
her apron the plentiful moisture from her eyes and her wrinkles,
" more nor two years since a tear fell from me. My heart was
crusted over wid bitterness, like the wather when the frost is
upon it. An' I'm cryin' now becase the thaw is come to me.
Don't be afeard, Moya; don't let it throuble you; nor you,
Murty, asthore; it's the joy makes me cry, an' it will do me
good."

For some time the certain tidings that she was not to be
turned out of her house—the home of her fathers, of her youth,
of her womanhood, and of her matronly consequence—were sufficient tidings for the Widow Moore; and as she professed to receive relief from her tears, Murty allowed her to indulge them
without interruption.

Moya also experienced a temporary abstraction of joy, though
not of a nature so selfish as that indulged in by her mother; in
fact, her heart thrilled with pleasure because her mother's had
been comforted. Both, however, awakened, at length, to the interest of the new question—how had Murty obtained the money
to pay their rent?

" Sit where you are, mother, quiet an' asy, an' I'll soon tell
you the whole story. The body that gave me the money to free
you o' the landlord won't stop his hand there. He'll stock the
farum for you; an' he'll make the ould land and the ould place
to look the same it onst looked for you; an' he'll come an' live
undher the same roof wid you; an' he'll be a son in your ould
days to you. An' I'll let you call me a born gandher, if he
doesn't turn out to be a good son, into the bargain."

" Yes, Murty; yes, avich," gasped Moya, changing color, in
an ill-boding, and fidgeting with her fingers.

" An', to ind all, in one word, he'll just marry wid my little
Moya, here. An' if he doesn't make mooch of her, why I'm
asthray intirely."

Moya slid down quietly in a sitting position, her face now very
pale, and her eyes staring at Murty

" Who is he, Murty dear?" she asked in a whisper scarcely
audible.

" Yes, Murty, aroon; what name is on the gorsoon?" echoed
her mother.

" Gorsoon?" questioned Murty, with an innocent smile—that

is, with a smile meant to be received as quite innocent, though it really did not, so much as his usual ones, partake of that honorable character. "Gorsoon! why, then, barrin' he's a gorsoon bee raison of his bein' a bachelor boy, I'm thinkin' it's time for him to be a man at the prasant day. Sure, ye both know Terry O'Brien, the—the—" Murty hesitated.

Moya started into an expression which it would be difficult to define, as with the slightest possible approach to impatience, she resumed, "Terry—Terry O'Brien, the—the what?"

"The—the—Admiral," answered Murty, at last, in a hurry. He could not, on the present occasion, bring himself to honor Terence with his usual title in full.

Moya's figure suddenly sank lower as she sat, and with clasped hands, and a face of utter misery, she looked towards her mother. Neither that good woman nor Murty Meehan, however, noticed or understood the present meaning of her manner and features.

"Terry O'Brien, the *Ould* Admiral?" queried Mrs. Moore, very slowly, supplying Murty's delicate omission ; and it half seemed that even her selfishness could not at once reconcile her to poor Terence as a husband for her daughter.

Murty went on—"Call him bee whatever other names ye plaise, Terry O'Brien is the man ; a power o' the goold cum to him, from his ould ship, for prize-money, bee manes iv a bit o' writin' that one poor Murty Meehan, a neighbor, dhrew up for him ; an' we all know he had a thrifle o' the guineas aforehand along wid it ; an' every *laffina* of it all that's left afther payin' the landlord he'll pelt into little Moya's lap, to do what she likes wid it. There's no denyin' that Moya might get a younger boy, an' maybe a one more likely an' comely to look at ; bud would he bring her or you, mother, out o' the throuble that's on ye? would he rise up all our heads again, an' bring back the ould times? An' salvation to my sowl, if there's a more *laucky* crature than my poor Terry walkin' Ireland's ground. He'll be like a little dog about the house ; he'll do every thing ye bid him do. Moya 'ill be his Queen o' the May. An' if 'tis a thing that he's taste ould, why, he's hearty, an' not bad to look at whin you come to be used to him."

Moya still continued silent, her looks fixed on her mother, as a culprit at the bar of justice, on trial for his life, watches the face of the foreman of the jury returning into court with his brethren, after having agreed upon a verdict. She soon knew her doom.

"Moya won't say the ' No,' " decided the old woman ; "Moya

always cared for her mother, an' she won't be the cause of her ayin' broken-hearted at last. Moya wouldn't put the mother's blessin' from her.

The young girl drew in her breath, making a slight hissing sound.

" I tell you again, Murty Meehan, if it came to pass that I was thrust over that dour-stone, I'd lay down my head on its threshold an' die. And Moya wouldn't send her father's widow an' her own mother out o' the world that way."

A visible shudder ran through Moya's frame, but again her agitation was unnoticed.

The garrulous Mrs. Moore went on in great glee—" No, no, Moya would not. An' so all will be as it used to be agin, plaise God ! The flitches will be in the chimbly agin ; the cows will come to the baun, lowin' to be milked, agin ; we'll have the sheep-shearin' agin ; an' the churn-dash will be goin' by the fire. We'll have our little parlor nate an' purty agin. Whin the lark is sing-in' above our heads, in the mornin', we'll ramble through the green fields to to look at the lambs sportin', and to hear the ewes blaitin' to 'em. There will be nothin', widin an' widout, but pace, an' plenty, an' happiness, an' heart's rest. Oh ! the praises be given above ! Och ! 'tis a blessin' that Moya is bringin' on her-self an' me ! She was always good—the widow's comfort in all her sore throubles an' misfort's ; an' now she'll be the manes o' lettin' me die undher the roof where I first saw the light. Och, the blessin's on my Moya ! Come an' give the ould mother one kiss, my Moya-bawn ! Come, acuishla !"

Mechanically, and with some difficulty in her motions, Moya arose from her crouching seat on the floor, and went to obey her mother's commands. The lips she touched to those of the old woman where white and cold.

"The mother's blessin' be upon your head, my own chorra-ma-chree," added the good dame, laying her hands on Moya's head, after embracing her ; "but is it shiverin' wid the cowld you are ?"

Murty Meehan also noticed, at last, the girl's wretched appear-ance and manner, but accounted for them on the grounds of maid-enly surprise and bashfulness. He was not quite so much in Moya's confidence as was his worthy spouse. And after some further conversation between him and Mrs. Moore, honest Murty took his leave, convincing himself—though in the teeth of a lurk-ing little suspicion to the contrary—that he had acted as a dutiful son-in-law and an affectionate brother-in-law ought to have done. All along, doubtless, he had admitted to himself—as, indeed, we have heard him acknowledge to the girl's face—that Moya might very naturally prefer a younger and a sprucer bridegroom. Yet was it Murty's serious conviction that, by the proposed match, he consulted her personal happiness as well as her worldly advantage—so very high was his opinion of the Old Admiral.

As to the Widow Moore, her sudden change wrought by the joyous prospect thus suddenly opened to her, from moping despair to brisk good spirits, was truly surprising. She seemed to have regained the vigor of her early days. So soon as Murty had departed, she became wordy and bustling to excess, to the almost unconscious eyes and ears of her still silent child. She took Moya with her through the house, and, late as it was, through the yards and out-buildings, to point out the repairs and improvements which were to be immediately undertaken by means of the fortune so providentially supplied to them. Seated within doors again, she ran over the arrangements for the wedding-feast; numbered the dishes to be placed on the tables; selected the guests; and even prescribed the fashion, colors, and quality of the bride's wedding garments. Moya only felt that a word of dissent or discouragement, on her part, to all this selfish and vain anticipation would break her mother's heart, and deprive her of her mother's dying blessing, and she was still and silent.

At length the widow retired to bed. Even after she had lain down, Moya sat enduring her loquacious and, to the poor girl, terrible visions of happiness and importance in the world. Sleep fell on her; Moya watched till she was sure her mother slumbered soundly, and then she stole on tiptoe to the door of the house, raised its latch quietly, stepped out, closed the door again, ran down the slope of a hill, gained the edge of the little stream that whimpered at its foot, and cast herself down there. Now, as she wrung her hands in agony, the sobs and the tears which had been so long kept in swelled through the echoing nooks of the lonesome spot around her, and pattered into the shallow water over which she bent.

"Oh!" she cried, "may the Lord of heaven have pity on me this black night! The heart's rest my mother spoke of—the heart's rest! Oh, I was only poor before—poor, and fatherless, and brotherless—but now! now! now!"—she rung her hands with increased energy and bitterness—"the fortune! och, yes!

the fortune to be sure! But isn't there *another* would do the same for my mother an' me, only he's poor, poor, poor like ourselves? Mother, it will cost me dear to keep your last blessin' on my head, an' to laive you undher the roof-three of your father's house! Mother, mother, it would break your heart to be turned out o' that house, an' it will break mine to keep you in it! Oh! the Lord look down ou me! Oh! I am the most miserable crature on the face of the earth this moment! Oh! what, what is to become of me?"

Thus did Moya make her moan, but the running stream that received and bore away her tears failed to carry with it her young sorrows too. The gray morning began to break before she became alive to a necessity for calming herself. Then, however, amid continued sobs which almost rent her bosom, she tried to cool and wash away the tears from her burning eyes. At length she walked up the hill to the house, slowly and heavily, that she might be in time for her mother's wakening hour, and take her place to listen to renewed descriptions of the happiness in store for her.

CHAPTER VIII.

AFTER spending, as a matter of etiquette—indeed, almost of necessity after prize-money—two or three days and nights at the alehouse, drinking King George's health, and confusion to all his enemies, but particularly to his French ones, Terence O'Brien steered up to the Widow Moore's abode, to promote in person his matrimonial suit.

To this step he had been induced principally by Murty Meehan's frequent representations of its being indispensable in the eyes of all "dacent neighbors of people, livin' on firrum land." For Terence's own part, he saw no use in jawing over the business; "it wasn't sayman-like." When "boord ould ship," they always cleared for action without any such palaver. So soon as Mother Moore chose to give the word, he was ready to come to close quarters, and what else could be required of him? In boarding an enemy who ever thought of speaking her fair? What was a broadside for but to bring her to her senses, without wasting a word?

With his usual kind consideration, Murty Meehan labored to convince the Admiral that there was no parallel between the present proposed encounter and that of an action at sea. That, in fact an' truth, Moya Moore was no enemy of his, nor he an enemy to her; but that, ou the contrary, they were both good friends already, and that the object in view was to make them the best and closest friends in the world,

"We cruise ahead together, then, my hearty—the Murty and the Terry alongside—eh?"

"By all manes, Admiral;" and, accordingly, they proceeded to Mrs. Moore's together.

Upon this occasion the Admiral looked as well as his personal accidents could permit. From top to toe, he wore a new suit, perfectly in sailor trim. Blue jackets, blue trousers, scarlet waist-coat, white stockings, and single-soled pumps. His gray hairs were smoothed backwards from either side of his forehead, his new furry hat hung towards one ear, his pig-tail was freshly bound and ribboned, and around his throat he had coiled a flaming silk hand-kerchief, which

"Waved like a meteor in the troubled air."

Before the inmates of the house could see him, his stormy "Ould ship ahoy!" sounded in their ears from the middle of the accent to their threshold. At the hail, Moya, who had been moping about, sank on a seat in a dark corner. The widow, on the contrary, bounded from her stool, adjusted her attire, hastened to the open door-way, and there stood with a preparatory face and air, expressive of much welcome and cordiality. And there did the Admiral first address her.

"Aha, ould frigate! all right and tight aboord—eh?"

"He's axin' you, mother," said Murty Meehan, in an "aside," as Mrs. Moore's features began to wear a very puzzled expression, "he's axin' you, in his say-gibberish, how is all in the house."

"Why, then, we're brave and hearty, thank God, an' to your-self, sir, for the axin'," answered the dame, addressing Terence; an' glad in the heart to see you undher our poor roof."

"Splice timbers, here, my ould frigate."

The Widow Moore was again at a loss to comprehend the Admiral's phrase, but the action accompanying his words proved sufficiently intelligible to her. Terence jerked forward his one hand: she advanced one of her's to meet it; and then he set to work at her arm, along with that hand, as if he had been at the pump aboard, five feet of water in the hold. The old woman's joints were nearly dislocated in their sockets; and the struggle of her heart to restrain screams expressive of her torture, and of her countenance to keep up a show of good-humor, became pitiable. Her son-in-law elect went on :

"I'll tell you a piece of my mind, now, misthress. I hate jawin'. A sayman isn't never used to it. He laives it to your land loobers an' the parley-wows. But never mind for all that; he'll do his duty without it as long as a plank of him sticks together. And now, agin, here's a bit o' log, d'ye see me. Murty Meehan, my jolly shipmate here, he cruised a start round your port t'other night to take soundin's; an' he spoke wid you, an' so you know our present tack. See here—I'll put the rhino aboord—I'll work ould ship for you here, as well as one timber can do it, hearty and sayman-like—I'll tug when you cry, 'Ye-ho!' —I'll keep the tackle thrue, and the canvas fair to the breeze. Maybe I'd thry my loock at the helm, off an' on; but I'm no great hand at that part o' ship's work, an' I'll tell you so, plump, afore we weigh anchor. An' that's all I've got to palaver about. If it's a bargain for the voyage, I'm aboord; if not, only say the word, an' I'm off on the ould course—eh, my ould frigate?"

Again, Mrs. Moore wot not what to say, for again she wot not what had been said to her. She believed, however, that notwithstanding the pumping she had undergone, she was still called on to manifest great content and satisfaction. So, as the best thing to be thought of, she bobbed many curtesies. But again Murty Meehan considerately acted as interpreter between her and what he was pleased to call, in his own pride of knowledge of the English language, the "say-gibberish" of his friend.

"It's what he's demandin' of you now, mother, is—would you be plaised wid him, goold an' all, for a husband for the colleen?"

"An' troth, an' why not? An' sure we'll do our endayvor to make the place an' the house agreeable an' comfortable to him, an' to any friend of his," she replied. "Paice an' plenty widin an' widout, *laucky* times, an' happiness *galore.*"

"But mind, misthress—mind one thing. Sayman's allowance of grog, an' no stintin'."

Murty promised there would be no stint : he was supported, upon explanation, by Mrs. Moore; and matters being so far understood, Terence again "spliced timbers" with the ould frigate, and a second time wrought so hard that, in order to conceal her real feelings, she forced herself into an affected burst of laughter, while the sourness of her aspect plainly denoted that a hearty fit of crying would have more honestly expressed her sensations, and the state of her temper.

"Sink my hulk to Ould Davy!" then bellowed the Admiral, "where's the little craft I'm to join company with? Ahoy, there!" as he discovered Moya in her dark corner; "alongsid here! alongside, my little schooner!" and he seized her hand, and tugged her into in the middle of the apartment. "What cheer, now, what cheer—eh? Scuttle me but her canvas shivers in the breeze. But cheer up, cheer up; 'twill right soon—eh? Shiver my timbers, but you *are* a thrim little vessel—prize for an Admiral. And if the ould jolly boy doesn't fight, broadside to broadside, for you, against any seventy-four that ever swum, may he be sent uudher hatches for a skulker! A buss, my little hearty, an' all's settled." And before the terrified Moya could recede from his advance, he snatched the favor he had proposed. "My hulk to splinters, shipmate!" addressing Murty Meehan, "but she's a well-built little vessel—aint she? Lookee; painted, pin-nace-like, d'ye see me, and right well wrigged from stem to stern. Don't you shiver so, my hearty; cheer up, I say. I never knew a land-jack that wasn't afraid o' salt wather, at the settin' out; but you'll not be long before the wind till you bear a hand bravely I know it—so cheer up." The Old Admiral again saluted his bride! and Moya, then pulling herself somewhat free of his gripe, retreated to her corner.

Her mother next boarded the seaman, engaging him in a discussion of all her plans of improvement and management in the house and on the farm. For a short time he listened to her with some little seeming attention; but, fatigued with her "jaw," suddenly bounced off his seat, told her that he left the whole business of the outfit to his shipmate and herself, snatched a parting *bonbouche* from his little pinnace, and scudded away, full before the wind.

Terence felt perfectly satisfied with the state of affairs. All was now settled, and so no more talk about it. Mrs. Moore could not be smoother nor kinder. Moya seemed shy, to be sure; but, as he had intimated to her, so were, according to his recollections and experience, all fresh-water jacks at the first sight of the sea. She had not repulsed him—she had not said, "No." And seeing that she was gifted with a tongue in her head, such must have been the case did she really dislike the proposed "cruise in company." On board the old Saint Vincent, all his life long, his shipmates and he always spoke their mind honestly to each-other, and he had no other rule of judging people's opinions, and he would have none. No meant no, and yes meant yes ; or, what was even better, for it saved jaw, if you asked a "shipmit" will you? and he said neither yes nor no, but just held his tongue, and at the same time did not knock you down, or give any similar indication of dissent, why you had an answer much plainer than all the languages in the world could convey it, to the effect of, "To be sure I will." So that our honest Admiral left the Widow Moore's "ould ship," experiencing pretty nearly the same sensations he used to feel when about to make a fresh cruise, after riding some time at anchor—careless and hearty, and his spirits up, from an undefined hope of something novel about to happen to him.

How often, with the best intentions in the world, do the best people in the world go near to break the hearts of the unhappy in an endeavor to do them good !

And why ?

Because they don't, or won't, or can't understand.

And ah ! that little word "won't" contains matter for chapters upon the curious and contemptible compound of our nature, take it, upon the average, at it's best.

But—"to the deuce with your sentiment."

With all our heart. Don't be afraid, "gentle reader."

CHAPTER IX.

THE news of the intended nuptials soon spread abroad, and among the guests selected by Mrs. Moore on the occasion great preparations ensued to grace the widow's roof upon the appointed day. Under that roof itself a still greater bustle went on to do honor to her invitations. Before the arrival of the priest, there is something to be noticed.

The high-road leading to the principal country town ran at the distance of about a mile at right angles with the front of the Widow Moore's dwelling. From it a *borheen*, or narrow way, diverged, and took a circuitous route towards the humble abode, and by a branch track communicated directly with its threshold. Along this route horses and carts, or—as the primitive machines which then substituted carts were called—cars, could journey to and from market. But pedestrians chose a shorter cut to the main road, as well from her house as from other solitary dwellings near her.

Upon the night when she first became informed of Terence O'Brien's proposal of marriage, Moya Moore, as we are aware, ran down from her mother's door to the side of a little stream, there to vent her feeling in solitude. This stream, having its source among high hills in the recesses of the country, had, before Moya arrived at its banks on that spot, passed close by Murty Meehan's cabin, about half a mile up from her, and continued to flow on from her feet to the high-road already spoken of, which it crossed ; thence pursuing its course to the river, with which it soon became confounded. While sketching, at the opening of our story, Murty Meehan's residence and its surrounding features, we believe we hinted that the tiny rivulet ran a very zigzag race near to his threshold. We have now to say that it did the same thing all the way it had to run, its aberrations being caused by the nature of the ground through which, like a dog on a scent, it seemed to nose its way. At every twist it was almost shut up among puzzling inequalities, in one little solitude or another, from all sight of whence it had come, or whither it was to go. Now the little active stream found itself safely rippling over smooth sand or pebbles ; then among sinkings or swellings of cultivated fields ; now stealing amid rushes, dock-leaves, and sedge, through lumpish land, neglected or naturally barren ; and anon it chafed, and beaded, and sometimes grew important enough to foam through a jumbled group of rocks and stones, great and small, doing its best to escape from the fastness. Yet, crooked as was the line along its edges to the high-road, foot-passengers, thither bound for Mrs. Moore's abode, or from the residences of her neighbors, chose it in preference to the cart-way already described, for no other reason that we could ever discover except that they deemed it the pleasanter.

At the point where a dislocated row of stepping-stones afforded a crossing from the footpath at one side of the brook to the opposite one, Moya Moore sat down on the night we have mentioned ; and on the next night, and the next ; her hot tears still making bubbles, like blisters, upon the surface of the clouded water. Girls of all degrees are, we are told, timid ; and those

of Moya's class in life superstitiously so. It is therefore remark
able that in so often frequenting this lonely place at such late
hours, she did not feel uneasy under the influence of its character,
nor yet on account of a time-out-of-mind story of which it was
the scene.

A story! Yes; an old and terrible story! We cannot
help it, but had better recount it in as few words as possible.

The rising ground to Moya's back, as she sat, was called
" Lacken-na-Monh," or "the Woman's Hill." Opposite to her,
at the other side of the stream, just where the pedestrian from
the high-road should begin to cross it on his near approach to
her mother's house, arose a huge rock of granite, streaked in a
kind of deep dim color, with a figure something like a cross.
From a murdered maiden had the hill been named : at the foot
of the rock she had been found dead and stiff ; and the cross
had been made four generations ago (though no weather could
since erase it) with her blood. The unhappy girl had loved, in
secret, a stranger. He prevailed on her to leave her father's
home with him—she engaged to rifle, beforehand, for his advantage, her father's coffers ; she kept both her promises but too
well. He watched for her at night, by appointment. On her
progress to him, after her elopement from her hitherto innocent
dwelling, he saw her steal down the Lacken-na-Monh to the
stepping-stones. He received her with extended arms. After
crossing the stones, he led her under the ominous shadow of the
pile of granite ; ascertained that she came freighted with the
expected booty ; struck her down ; followed up the blows till he
killed her, and then escaped with his prize ;—for all along the
villain had not in the slightest degree responded to her guilty
love. At her father's gold alone he had aimed ; now, that gold
in his clutch, he did not want her to encumber him, or to help
him to spend it.

Such was the well-accredited story connected with Moya
Moore's chosen nook of solitary sorrow. Yet, as we have
noticed, it had not the effect of keeping her away, under her
mother's roof, or even of sending her to spend her hours elsewhere out of doors. Though respectable authorities added to
the horrors of the tale we have glanced at, by asserting that very
often, under the clouds of the night, the spirit of the murdered
girl might be heard shrieking terrifically over and around the
place, and sometimes seen, too, exaggerated to an unearthly size,
and draped in white upon the top or at the base of the desecra-

ted rock. Still all this seemed to make no disagreeable impression on Moya; or if, during her repeated visits to the haunted and unholy ground, natural fear did come over her recollections, either she was too much engrossed with her own grief to care about any thing further that might happen to her, or she had some particular reason for braving the terrors of the spot. We believe both feelings combined to shape her conduct.

At all events, upon the third night preceding that appointed for her marriage with the Old Admiral, Moya Moore was again sitting at her own edge of the stream, opposite to the "stone of the bloody cross." A smart breeze whistled along the brook, and eddied at her back against the "*Lacken-na-Monh.*" The stars were now hidden by stormy clouds, and now shone free of the obstruction. But on this occasion Moya need not have given way, as much as upon former nights, to supernatural terrors, for she did not sit alone at the stepping-stones.

Her companion was a very young man, athletic and comely: but whatever might be the character of his brow, as stamped naturally by his disposition, it was now dark and wrinkled. When he spoke, his accents were sometimes vehement ; sometimes they sank into a cadence of despairing entreaty. Moya's voice, in reply to him, was invariably heart-broken and wailing, and often interrupted by sobs. In his right hand he grasped her right hand, his left arm encircled her waist tightly. Often, in moments of excessive grief, the girl allowed her head to fall on his shoulder.

"No, no, I cannot pass the sthrame with you," she said, "nor stay out from my mother, even where we are, any longer 'Twas a wrong thing for me to come to meet you at all ; for 'tis sorer to part than I thought it would be."

"Don't forsake me, Moya," groaned the young man. "Don't, for the Saviour's sake."

"Never lay the blame to me, gorsoon. Oh! would I, would I forsake you, if I could help it ?"

"Moya, if you loved me,—I am ill, some way, I don't know how, an' I can spake but a few words to you at a time,—if you loved me—if ever you loved me—you would surely help it, Moya."

"An' never say that to me, my poor gorsoon, of all words out of your mouth. Love you!—och, you have no rason to say 't. God, who hears my prayers and sees the heart, knows you

huve not. Feel Moya's heart this moment, ma *bouchaleen**—
'tis heavy, heavy ; heavy, like a lump o' lead ; broke, I believe—
broke, I hope—I hope! An' the sleep never falls on my eyes the
night long: whenever I am in the bed, I sit up in it, cryin'."

"Moya, ma-cuishla, we won't part—we won't go from one
another."

"Och, the sorrow is on my heart to know that the time for
partin' has come !"

"No, no, Moya! no—it would be a desthruction to both of us."

"I know it will be the desthruction of one of us, at any
rate. Listen to me well, my own bouchal ; I'm thryin' to get
ready to laive the world. There's somethin' tells me that I
won't live out the night that takes me from you ; that the next
mornin's breakin' will look down on the corpse o' Moya Moore !"

"An' you tell me to quit your side, Moya, in the same breath
that tells me that ! You love me as well as that, an' you bid
me laive you! Cuishla, I'd give up house an' home, kith an'
kin, land an' goold, if land an' goold were mine, for *you*."

"An' I'd do the same for you, my poor gorsoon, if so doin'
only concerned myself in this world, an' laid up no evil for me
in the next. But I wouldn't break the ould mother's heart, and
airn her dyin' curse."

"Och, my own colleen! what is to become of us, then?
Moya, Moya, the love is on my heart for you ever since we were
little childer, goin' to the school together! an' now I see that
you're in want o' the pity as mooch as mysef!"

"I remember the time you spake of well. There was a day
that I climbed up an' spilt the master's ink, an' you took the
blame on yoursef, widout my knowin' it, an' you never cried
when they punished you, but suffered like a stout little man for
my sake. An' I call to mind when we used to come home
together of an evening, an' when the rain would be fallin', you'd
take off your coat to cover me, an' walk in the peltin' shower
widout a tack to shelter you from it. An' I remember the
singin' birds you'd bring me, and the nosegays you'd pull for
me. Avoch! I remember every thing—up to the very May-
mornin' when you tould me I was your own cuishla-gal-machree.
An' if I was the misthress of a coach-an'-six to-night, not the
weeniest word or deed that ever passed between us could Moya
forget, my poor bouchal bawn."

* Little boy.

4

" An', afther all, Moya, you talk of goin' from me ?" One
only idea was at present in the lad's mind, that one expressed,
with but little variation of words, every time he spoke.

" I'm goin' from you into the grave ; but then I'll die free of
my mother's death an' of my mother's curse, and maybe God
will give me a comfort in the life to come.   What grieves me
most of all at present, is the knowledge that I must laive *you*
broken-hearted too for your poor Moya."

" Moya," he said, trembling, while she wept and sobbed in
his arms, " if things are to turn out that way, God's heavy
curse on my heart, if it does *not* break !"   His tears now flowed
fast with hers.   She started, sat erect, and looked across the
stepping-stones.

" What is it ?" he asked.

" Did you see nothing over the sthrame ?"   He answered,
" No."   " Not hear any noise ?   But there's no one to be seen
now, an' nothin' to be heard but the whistlin' wind an' the runnin' wather—an' sure I was only puttin' foolish things into my
own mind."   Again her head rested on his shoulder, as, amid
tears and sobs, scarcely lessened or interrupted by her momentary fright, she uttered in a very low voice the young man's
name ; and when he replied, she went on—

" You know the berrin'-place of my unfortunate people, my
poor gorsoon?   Yes, you do—only you'll know it betther when
you follow another coffin there.   I remember well, you walked
afther my father's, and afther my two brothers' coffins, to it.
So you'll come there of a Sunday ; an' you'll kneel down, bareheaded, on a new-made grave, an'—"

" Cuishla ! cuishla ! stop them words—I won't listen to them !
An' I won't part you, neither ! I can't part you ! never will I
part you ! My father is poor, and has nothing to give me ; but
I'm an able boy ; I can go through a day's work with any other
that ever held a plough.   I'll take a bit o' ground ; I'll dig on
it ; we'll build a little cabin on it.   I'll labor in our little garden
afther the day's work for the farmers, and afore the day's work
—afore the sun rises, an' long afther the sun goes down.   An'
I'll work so well for others, as well as for you, that the rich
farmers will come to seek me out, and to hire me.   I'll keep up
your mother an' yourself.   An' if there's a fort'n to be made on
Ireland's ground, or a penny, I'll earn it for my colleen.   We'll
be happy together ; happy, though not very rich.   But to part
from you ! Sittin' here wid you :to-night, an' my arms about

you— to talk of partin' from you! Moya, I say again, we'l: never part.

"Avoch! many's the time my own thoughts an' my own heart brought before me the bit o' land, an' the little cabin, an' the little garden, an' every thing you spake of—ay, an' more ; I seen my own self helpin' you in the garden, or makin' or mendin' for you at the cabin dour; or busy about the floor, inside, to be ready for your comin' home in the evening. But it was all a dhrame—an empty dhrame—though a very happy one ! As empty as the wind that whistles on the hill behind us, an' as unthrue as the stars are dancin' in that wather, though *that* seems thrue enough too. No, bouchaleen. The mother's curse an' the mother's grave rises between us, and opens between us ! We *are* parted forever in this world—an' may God help us both !"

"I say no, still, Moya! no, no! do *you* listen to me now. We are promised to one another in the holy Name, an' nobody on earth has the right to stand between us!"

"Is it the anger is comin' upon you, bouchal-bawn ?" she asked.

His looks and accents, as well as his words, told that a change began to work within him.

"An' why shouldn't the anger come on me, if it did come? Why should your mother desthroy us both for the sake of a wasteful dinner or a new gownd, or a courteshy an' a 'God save you, ma'am ?' Us—two young people in the mornin' of our days—long life an' many hopes before us. Cover my Moya undher the sod o' the grave, and send me—if I didn't soon lie by her side—send me, a mad creature, over the face o' the earth, killin', I believe, any live thing that would stand up afore me. By the night that's above our heads, I'll not go from you, Moya! There's no one, I say, has the right over you but myself, an' I hould you close—an' I will hould you close !"

"Och, bouchal ma-chree ! don't say them cross words to me, an' don't press me so hard. Would you hurt me, as well as frighten me, now? Take away your hands, an' let me be goin' home to my mother, in the name o' God."

"Home you'll not go, Moya—never !"

Still holding her in his arms, he suddenly started up with the terrified girl, bore her rapidly across the stepping-stones, laid her at the base of the granite rock, and cast himself by her side.

"What did you bring me here for, ma-bouchal ?" she whispered, standing up; as well as she was able; after a shrinking glance around which informed her where she was. He did not answer; but she saw him turn upon his breast, and cover his face with his hands, while his limbs shook, and sounds of great passion escaped him. Ay, the master-fit was upon him. "Now, my poor boy, you frighten me more and more—the good-night to you, for I must—"

He again interrupted her, starting up to her side, and clasping her wildly. "No, Moya, no ; not the good-night!—no, no !" and amid showering tears and choking sobs, he impressed upon her lips and cheeks kiss after kiss, in rapid succession. Moya was unable to struggle against his strength and blind impetuosity.

"Free me !" she could only say, in a low voice, "free me ! an' tell me, I ask you again, why have you brought me to this evil spot ?"

His paroxysm grew less ; now, in his turn, his head fell on her shoulder ; and though he still held her, his grasp relaxed, as he at length answered, "I don't know why, Moya ; I can't tell you why ; it has gone out of my mind, I believe, if ever it was in it. Or I brought you here only to bring you somewhere—no matter where—with me, maybe—yes, that's the truth."

"Let us quit it, then. 'Twas here Norah Grace lost her life. An' they say that when two thrue lovers stand together near this stone, in the night-time, bad fortune is in the path of one o' them, or both o' them. Come."

"Yes, so they say. An' we are two thrue lovers—an' we are standin' near the stone—an' the sayin' will turn out to be a right sayin', if you don't hindher it, Moya."

Silence ensued, while, in the imperfect light, she endeavored to read the meaning of the young man's features. "Moya," he resumed, in a broken, hoarse tone.

"What is it ?" she asked, ill at ease, and speaking with difficulty.

"Will you come your ways with me, and be my own Moya ?"

"Where with you, bouchaleen? where could we go together?"

"Anywhere that gives our heads a shelter—there can be love anywhere."

"Oh, bouchal, bouchal! you will let me home to the poor ould mother, an' Heaven will have a blessin' in store for you."

"I give you the warnin', Moya. Don't say the no to me, this night."

"An' well you know I wouldn't cuishla, if the mother's death an' the mother's curse were not in our road afore us !"

" Moya, you must or—"

" Or what ? Why do you stop? Is it hurt or narm you'd put on your own poor Moya ?"

" No !" he roared out, stamping on the sward. " No ! There ! —I free you ! I take my arms from around you! Go your ways, now, to your mother if you like ! Only listen to me first— listen well to me. By the cross o' blood on this stone—" He was stepping closer to the rock, his hand raised.

Moya interrupted his words, crying loudly, " Don't lay your hand on it to swear by it ! Don't touch it !"

" By the cross o' blood on this stone," he repeated, slapping his palm against it so smartly that the little solitude rang to the sound he produced by the action.

Moya flew after him, tore away his hand, flung herself on his neck, and, after glancing round her, much terrified, and in great apprehension, whispered, " An oath was sworn, afore now, on that cross, an' the man that swore it was forced to keep it ! It became his fate to keep it, though he grew sorry for takin' it, and wanted not to do what it bound him to do ! So don't do it; bouchal-bawn ; don't swear the oath, but come out of this unlucky place, at this unlucky hour. Come, we'll talk more goin' back the way towards the house. Come, a-grawgal machree !

She saluted his cheek entreatingly. But her moody lover was not to be shaken—in his present purpose, at least. He swore the oath. A certain terror-moving ballad had been, if we remember aright, written about the time of which we speak, but was certainly unknown to the rustic lad ; and yet his oath contained a threat very similar to that used by " a warrior so bold" to " a virgin so bright." " By that cross," said he, " I swear that if you marry any man but me, Moya Moore, I will take my own life on the sod where we stand ; and if ever a departed soul came back to this world, I swear that my ghost will be seen at your wedding-supper. That's my oath ; and half of it I'll keep, as sure as the stars are twinklin' above us, and the other half too, if I can."

" The Lord preserve us !" said Moya. " Oh, bouchal, you know that a bad spirit has power in this place, an' now hears your oath."

" Then let the bad spirit be a witness for me."

The young man yelled aloud this raving speech, and as fearful a yell as his own replied to him ; while, to one side of the granite rock appeared, elevated from the ground, a whitish form vaguely

resembling the human shape, but, to Moya's terrified glance, wav·
ering, as if it were disjoined—nay, as she afterwards averred, head-
less, and

"Was so thin and transparent to view,
You might have seen the moon shine through."

Moya instantly disengaged herself from her lover, and with a
shriek, which produced a second yell all around her and above her,
darted across the stepping-stones of the stream, ran up the Lacken-na-Monh, gained her mother's door, burst it open, and, one step
beyond its threshold, fainted and sank down "a weary weight."
It was not of her lover she was then afraid—nay, in her wild
race, she did not even think of him. And he, daring as had hitherto been his words towards the "bad spirits," and all-engrossed
as he had seemed with the idea of losing his mistress, became,
even sooner than Moya, a victim to his unspeakable fears, falling
the instant she left his side senseless and motionless at the base
of the "Rock of the Bloody Cross."

And now we have placed ourselves in a dilemma which produces
some fear, though not of the ghost, for ourselves.   Be lenient to
us, O gentlest of readers! while, in the next chapter, we afford
ourselves breathing time, to deprecate thy offended dignity.

----◆----

CHAPTER X.

DEAREST reader, there was—But how can we bring ourselves
to say the words—to shape them so as that the avowal they must
contain shall meet thy severe eye in the form best calculated to
win thy forgiveness.

Hast thou ever, when a schoolboy, been called in from the play-
ground to account, before thy master's face, for some abominable
act of riotousness, observed by him while haply taking his breakfast at a—by thee—forgotten window?   In similar feelings to
those thou mayest have experienced on such an occasion, do we
now hang down our head before thee.   And yet, dearest reader,
why should we hang down our head?   Thou mayest complain,

doubtless, when the murder is out—as out it must surely come—
that we have been guilty of an unwarrantable imposition upon thy
good sense, or have descended into clap-trap to produce, for an
instant, "a thrilling interest," or brought so closely together the
extremes of the pathos and the bathos, or of the picturesque and
the burlesque, or of the plausible and the ridiculous, that the contact is insufferable—is—in one damning word, is "in bad taste."
Some of this, or all of this, thou mayest say ; but could we have
avoided the plain truth for the mere purpose of writing on, according to the best approved rules of poetical propriety ? That
is our first point of defence. Our next is a solemn declaration
that we never intended to impose on your sense, good, bad, or
indifferent, as it may be, but merely to give you a faithful account, just as we got it ourselves, of how poor little Moya Mooro
and her athletic lover were imposed upon, in a state of feeling
which left *them*, at least, few claims, for the time, to sense or
rationality of any kind. Thirdly, we plead an inherent, hearty,
healthy, abhorrence of clap-trap. Fourthly, we beg to ask thee,
do not such extremes as thou wouldst object to sometimes, nay
often, meet in the quick succession and incongruous linking together of the most real events of this strange life. Hast thou
never known pathos whine itself down into a provocation to its
own laughter? or the absurd, in some curious, whimsical, ara-
besque way, dovetail itself in any instance with the awful ?

For our own part, we know of an elopement which, had it
taken place, must have left to the world's pity—that is, scorn—
a father and his six legal sons and daughters—hindered, and forever hushed up, by a noise heard by the lady in her dressing-
room, as she was putting on her bonnet, in the dark, to steal
down the back stairs, because she believed it to be a supernatural
noise—a warning, sent to waken her conscience (or else her husband) ; and it proved, after all, to be caused only by a mouse
gnawing at her rouge-box. We know of another proposed elopement,—a less improper one—one, in fact, between two devoted
lovers,—also frustrated by the sudden appearance in their path of
a very harmless poor fellow, Billy Taylor by name, who could
never have dreamed of intercepting them or pursuing them ; but
who was so generally voted a pest in conversation, that appear
wherever or whenever he did, merely in the hope of addressing a
word to his fellow-creatures, the established usage was for all
who saw him approach to turn their backs, and crying out, "But
here's Billy Taylor !" run away from him. And so it happened

in the case of the lovers we speak of; they, too, fled from Billy,
retracing a good portion of the road they had come from the
house of the lady's father to their carriage, until they ran plump
against that very latter-named gentleman, so that the lady was
taken home again and locked up. Nay—we have heard of a
downright murderer frightened away from his victim's throat by
the entrance on the midnight scene of a witness in the shape only
of a little black terrier. But why, dearest reader, overpower thee
with pleas of extenuation of the admission we are about to make?
To the following instance of a running-in upon one another, and
blurring together of the very distinct lines of solemn and absurd,
we were witnesses.

Late upon a winter's evening, a maiden lady was alluding, in
her niece's presence as well as ours, to an early attachment,
gloomed forever by the death of her lover. After his death, his
spirit appeared to her, and she went on bringing before us with
much effect the appalling circumstance, when suddenly her nervous niece, strangely—and for ourselves laughably, though for
herself painfully excited—suddenly sprang from her chair, just at
the spirit's appearance, and with a sharp and, we thought, spite-
ful tap of her extended palm, broke the spectacles on her aunt's
respected nose into shivers.

And so, dearest reader, hoping to have now prepared thee,
somehow or other—though we are not sure exactly how—mercifully to hear us, we at length venture to say out in full—

There was no apparition of a murdered maiden at the granite
rock.

True, we have asserted that the impertinent thing

> "Was so thin and transparent to view,
> You might have seen the moon shine through."

And so you might—that is, had the moon been in the sky—and
no wonder, when, after Moya had fled, and her cowardly companion had dropped senseless at the sight, old Terence O'Brien
moved two or three paces from the rock's side, and stood over
the latter, still yelling and waving on the top of his stick a new
white muslin dress which he had gone to the market-town to purchase for Moya, and which he meant her to wear on her marriage-
day. And—"Ahoy!" still bellowed Terence, stirring with his
foot his prostrate rival—"Ahoy, you loober! take a white say-
mew in the offing for a seventy-four? but you're only fit to be a
parley-woo, an' not a heart-o'-oak British sayman! An', shiver

my hulk, but 'tis to Ould Davy he's gone, sure enough, I believe!"

He again stirred the lad, and soon saw him jump up, however; and then ensued some stormy discourse between them.

CHAPTER XI.

THE wedding evening came, with all its guests, and all its bustle of preparation to receive them. There were flesh-pots boiling, and spits turning, and servants and helpers, hired and volunteers, toiling before the great fires, at the pots and at the spits. Every thing and everybody under the superintendence of the Widow Moore, now fully reinstated in her former responsibility and importance of character. In the little parlor, alone, two pipers blew away in rivalry, until the perspiration teemed from their foreheads; while, at some distance, in the barn or banquet-hall, three other professors of the same musical instrument surpassed them, if possible, in zeal and melody. And parlor and barn were crowded with youthful visitors, footing it heartily to their strains, while the elderly and the old looked on. It seemed as if the national sport, pursued to its utmost, were to give a keener appetite for the viands in preparation for supper.

It is etiquette at bridals such as the present one in Ireland, that if the bridegroom does not happen to be by nature a very shame-faced, modest person, he should do all in his power to enact that character—to

"Assume a virtue, if he have it not."

In fact, he ought not, and in all proper respectable cases he does not, make his appearance before the overwhelming crowd of company, until the wedding-feast is dispatched, the bridecake cut up, and the very ceremony, which cannot well dispense with him, waiting his presence.

All this had Marty Meehan earnestly and often represented to his friend, Terence O'Brien, but with little effect. The Ould Admiral, with one of his usual oaths, swore that he was "commodore aboard," and his deck he would walk, fore and aft, to see that all was trim and tight, and ready for action, upon the eve of

4*

so momentous an engagement. So here and there and everywhere he pushed and strided among his guests, or, as he called them, "his crew," commanding and ordering—few of his orders understood, by the way—as if he had indeed received an admiralty-commission to bandy them about. And Terence was met upon all hands with large and good-natured allowances for his departure from the more "Christhen-like" usage of bridegrooms—his ocean-life and habits being generally taken into consideration ; while among every group, and in every corner, his outlandish phraseology occasioned infinite mirth. He, in turn, took the laughter of his crew in good part, excusing his want of discipline and of respect to a commander because of the "jovialthry" of the occasion ; and it was only with a pleasant bluffness that he threatened to "mast-head," or to put them all into bilboes.

Terence was, above every thing, delighted with the great ranges of tables in the barn, when they became properly freighted with the great, the enormous, heaps of food, which they were just able, and no more, to support. When all was ready, the Ould Admiral placed one of his pipers on a barrel at the head of the feast, dubbed him boatswain, and commanded him to pipe all hands on deck, instructing him to use no variety of notes on the occasion, but keep up one unbroken monotonous scream until the guests had taken their places.

If, as we have noticed is customary, the bridegroom at an Irish country wedding is expected to demean himself modestly, much more, with the exception of absence from the banquet, is anticipated of the bride. Retiring, silent, passive, abstracted, and, in consideration of her approaching separation from her parents or other friends, somewhat sorrowful she must be. And, at these nuptials, retiring, silent, passive, abstracted, and sorrowful was Moya Moore ; and sometimes more besides. Her abstraction seemed a wandering of her mind in mazes of terror ; her sorrow, a stupified despair. From the continued expostulations of her bridesmaids, and even of her mother, she vaguely conceived that it was expected she should now and then smile ; but when she made an effort to do so, her smile was dreary and chilling, and inspired no answering one on the countenances of those who beheld it. Unquestioned, Moya scarce spoke at all ; and her replies to repeated interrogatories were abrupt, unmeaning, and from the point.

It became necessary that she should take her place beside the priest at the festive board ; her bridesmaid was obliged to lead

her out of a corner where she seemed to have become torpid.
And though she sat, without resistance, at the clergyman's right
hand, it might be seen that she sat without consciousness also.

The supper went on. Moya looked around her, and, for the
first time since she had entered the barn, became fully aware
that it was a wedding-feast she saw, and that the guests were
come. She turned suddenly to her left, fixed her eyes on the
clergyman, and gazed at him for some time wildly, and in terror.
But a slight relief seemed to steal over her when she was able
properly to call to mind the person whom she regarded. Then,
in renewed apprehensions, she turned to the individual at her
right ; and again recognizing in that of her bridesmaid a face
different from the one she feared to behold, partial composure
calmed her brow.

Still, however, as if in the most unallayed apprehension of discovering a dreadful object, her glance roved from one to another
of the guests ranged at the different tables, while her breath came
short and loud, her bosom panted, and her features worked. To
every question now addressed to her she answered hastily, "Yes,
yes." And when, imputing to her maidenly feelings alone all this
absence of manner, the loud laugh arose at her expense, she would
sometimes echo it in a manner so hysterical that the mirthful became chided and silent.

Her plate remained untouched before her ; she was pressed to
eat : whispering, "Thankee, thankee," she snatched up a knife
and fork, and put a morsel to her mouth—but it fell untasted
from her lips, as she again scrutinized the features of those around
her and near her.

Her allotted husband, while seemingly all engrossed in his attentions to his crew, had kept his eye on Moya. Now he came
behind her unperceived, and laid his hand heavily on her shoulder
Without turning to regard him, Moya suddenly put her palms
over her eyes, and shrieked so piercingly, that the roof-tree of the
barn rung to the sound ; then she hid her face in her bridesmaid's
bosom, and clung to her in a paroxysm of terror. The guests,
after vainly glancing here and there to discover some cause for
agitation, exchanged looks and whispers with one another ; and,
for a moment, it was the opinion that Moya Moore was to become a wife against the wish of her heart.

"Shiver my hulk to splinthers !" cried the Admiral, in explanation ; "the little pinnace is afraid o' the sarvice. But no matther
for that ; once launched, d'ye see me, she'll scud, sthramers mast high.

And the former general surmise now seemed banished by tne seaman's words, or else was soon forgotten in the resumed gratification of palate and stomach.

The wedding-feast was over—the grace was said—the bridecake was cut up by the priest ; he then put on his stole, opened his book, and stood up ; all arising with him to yield grave attention to the marriage ceremony.

Her bridesmaid led the pallid, shivering bride closer to the clergyman. The poor girl went pausing at every step, and feeling the ground with her feet, as if she were blind. Yet her eyes were distended beyond their usual compass. In fact, just as she suffered herself to be conducted from the table, her former unexplained terrors seemed to have become tenfold confirmed upon her, and now possessed her to extremity. At every unconscious move towards the clergyman, she glared—her head turned over her shoulder—towards the remote and half-lighted end of the barn ; and although her young companion held her arm, one of Moya's fingers pointed in the direction of her look. The priest spoke to her. Without turning her eyes to him, she waved her arm as if she would silence the sound of his voice, or direct his attention to whatever it was which so strangely absorbed her own.

"The name, sir—the name ?" she said, when the priest demanded her own name, "Terence—Terence O'Brien !" in a voice of excessive fright and alarm.

"Not yet, my good young friend," half-smiled the good-humored priest, "not yet, for a little while."

There was a general titter at poor Moya, on account of—as was supposed—only her fidgety mistake. She unbent her set glare, for a moment, as if to ascertain the cause of this mirth, which she felt to jar unnaturally on her present feelings ; and when her eyes resumed their former bent, it became evident, from their expression, that the object which had so long fascinated them was not now to be seen where they had observed it. Then they wandered, as had before been the case at the supper-table, from face to face, all around her.

"What is *your* name ?" asked the clergyman of his old penitent, the Admiral.

"Terry O'Brien, chaplain—an able-bodied sayman o' the crew, i' th' ould Saint Vincent, seventy-four."

"Take off your hat, Terence O'Brien ; it is necessary you should be uncovered for this ceremony.

"My hulk to Ould Davy, chaplain ! I command the ship this

cruise, and no capt'n never hauls down his sky-rattlin' for no loober of a chaplain, barrin' whin there's prayers on deck."

"Well, sir," again smiled the clergyman, "and we *are* going to have prayers on deck."

"Ay, ay, sir; that changes tack, d'ye see me; ay, ay, sir;" and the Admiral stood uncovered.

The marriage-service commenced. The icy hand of the bride was placed in that of the Old Admiral, Moya not sensible of the circumstance; for again, through an opening in the crowded cir cle of guests near her, she seemed to have rediscovered, at a dis tance, the cause of her previous consternation, and again a finger of her disengaged hand pointed vaguely. The clergyman con tinued:

"Terence O'Brien, will you take Moya for your wedded wife, to—"

"Will he! to be sure he will; scuttle and sink me if he don't!" interrupted Terence.

The priest sternly commanded the Admiral to abstain from all profane language, and further commanded him to answer the question properly, in the first person singular.

"That is, chaplain, I'm to make answer to your hail, yes or no, if *I* will take Moya Moore to be my wedded wife?"

"Yes, sir, or why are you here—why are we all here? Listen, man, I shall repeat the question."

"No use, chaplain, no use; jaw an' jabber for nothing, d'ye see me; I got your hail plain enough, and here's my answer— No; I will not!" shouted in a tremendous voice, at which all started; while the guests stared, as well as the priest, at the disfigured, bluff, and gruff countenance of the tar, not knowing whether to join in the grave surprise of the one, or laugh out right at what they deemed to be the sea-eccentricity of the other.

"What do you say, man?" inquired the clergyman.

"An' you didn't hear me, chaplain? Here's at you again, then, chaplain. "May Ould· Davy send a rattlin' broadside into my hulk, if the little craft ever sails under my colors!" And before any one could recover from the grand amazement he occa· sioned, the Ould Admiral, now bellowing through his fist, wen on: "Ahoy there! namesake, ahoy! Scud up, my hearty scud up here! aft here, the Terry O'Brien! aft here, you loob er! where are you, you skulker?" And from the quarter in which Moya had been glaring, his young nephew made his way through the crowd—she shrinking down, almost double, from his near approach.

"Think 'tis the ghost of him, my little pinnace, and that he will bite, aboordin' o' you, like the—parley-woos in action? Never fear, howsomever ; 'tis no ghost ; though he promised to turn himself into one, among the crew here to-night, for your divarshin. I say, chaplain, splice this young couple, an' be d—d to you ! Here, my little galley ; I resign command to the land-jack ; for he's the capt'n you'd rather make the voyage with, if I hard right, alongside the ould hulk-rock, t'other night. Come, chaplain, splice 'em—splice 'em."

A word aside, and indeed something else, on the part of young Terence O'Brien, went a good way, conjointly with the Admiral's assurance, in beguiling Moya of her apprehensions that she had to do only with a disembodied spirit in the present instance ; and a few additional sentences made her understand the noble, the maguanimous part which the poor old sailor had adopted towards her and her lover, as soon as, from their sad conversation at the stepping-stones, and at the granite rock, mostly overheard by him, as well as from his subsequent cross-raking of his nephew, after Moya's flight from the muslin ghost, the Admiral got a clear notion of how matters really stood.

In the first reflux of the tide of happiness round her despairing heart, Moya drew back a step from the uncle and the nephew, glanced quickly twice or thrice from one to the other, in a hesitating way ; but soon taking her resolution, extended her arms, and threw herself on the tar's neck, crying and sobbing, and kissing his unsightly cheeks, forehead—nay, lips—and hugging him tight to her relieved bosom. Her lover, instead of looking jealous, smiled, and even shed some grateful, as wel as happy tears along with her ; and the true state of the cas soon becoming known through the barn, many an eye among the generous-hearted male portion of the guests, to say nothing of all the eyes of all the woman-kind present, followed young Terence's example.

"Avast, avast there, you little she-pirate !" whimpered the Admiral himself—tears ("as big as beans," Murty Meehan said) rolling through the ugly channel across his face, and making it beautiful, as doth the fresh mountain-stream the rocky cleft in the mountain's side—"avast there, I say ! off wid your grapplin' irons, or sink my bulk to Ould Davy ! I'll change the sailin' ordhers, and take you in tow for the cruise myself, afther all that's jawed about, d'ye see me ! The young Terry, ahoy ! chaplain, ahoy ! Here, you loobers, free me of this craft ; I've got enough of her."

Striding to the head of the supper-table, Terence the elder counted down one hundred guineas as his nephew's fortune, and then scarcely allowing any one, including the priest, time enough to recover from their many surprises, or to know what they were doing, had him married to Moya Moore. And when all resumed their places at the nuptial board, it was not upon his own generous feelings and conduct that the Old Admiral grew egotistical, but upon what he thought a great deal more of—namely, his own unsurpassable cleverness in hoaxing the young pair with an appearance of the ghost which he had overheard them "jawin' about ;" and afterwards in keeping Moya in the dark—a punishment for her having hung out false colors when he "spoke her," her mother in company, on the head of their proposed cruise—as to the real Terry O'Brien she was eventually to sail under.

"An' so," quoth our Old Admiral, "seein' as how I never was much a-gog mysef,—not half so much as my shipmate, Murty Meehan—for a new voyage off o' all the ould tacks, an' that all I wanted, an' all I want, is safe moorage for ould hulk until it foundhers (and be d—d to it) ; an' seein' how, furthermore, the young Terry alongside never done me no spite, though his commandher, the born brother o' me, did—why, afther all this, d'ye see me, it's no great shakes if I gives up full command for the rest o' the voyage, an'—with fair sayman's allowance o' grog, Misthress Moore, d'ye mind me—take on wid first-lieutenant's berth aboord the ship."

"Here's your health, an' long life, an' may your ould hulk niver foundher at all, my poor Ould Admiral, darlin' !" cried Murty Meehan, his eyes still running over with admiration and love of his protegé. "An' here's another toast to go along wid that one—here's what brought the showers o' goold an' good loock to the whole of us—here's 'The Bit o' Writin'.'"

It would be doing injustice to the Widow Moore not to say that, to the hour when, notwithstanding Murty Meehan's bacchanalian prayer, his old hulk did founder at last, she never infringed on the Old Admiral's "sayman's allowance," nor, indeed, in any way upon his comforts under the family roof. Of Moya's attentions, or of her husband's, to their eccentric bene-

factor, nothing need be said. So that our excellent friend and
hero lived happily many a long year ; long enough, indeed, to
instruct a very, very little Terry O'Brien in all his sea terms—
thus insuring them fame in his third generation—and to build
and launch for him, on a pond formed by damming in a corner
of the brook at the celebrated stepping-stones, two seventy-four-
gun ships. It is recorded, however, that upon afterwards bring
ing those vessels into action, as separately English and French,
himself commanding the one, his grand-nephew the other—" the
lubberly French flag" adorning the latter, the gay and gallan*
Union Jack flying over the decks of the former—it is recorded,
we say, that the Old Admiral, forgetting in the heat of the engagement its mimic character, and giving way, for an instant, to
all his habitual hatred and contempt of the Gallic enemies of
Great Britain, made real war on the Lilliputian ship-of-the-line,
and, with one kick and one dread oath, consigned and sent it
" to Ould Davy."

THE IRISH LORD-LIEUTENANT
AND HIS DOUBLE.

THE IRISH LORD-LIEUTENANT
AND HIS DOUBLE.

IT is really quite true that some time ago, and not long ago either, there was a London gentleman who took a strange fit of ambition into his head. His partial friends, or himself alone of his own accord, or he in concert with them, believed that he bore, in face, air, and even in the upper part of his figure, a striking resemblance to a certain nobleman who had become highly distinguished by brilliant qualities of various kinds. In truth there was a likeness, but a general one only, between him and the celebrated Duke or Marquis (at present we cannot declare which ought to be the proper title), and, highly flattered by this personal compliment of nature, he did all in his power to seem "the very image." He studied his original as closely as the nobleman's appearance in public—in the streets, in the parks, or in "the house"—gave him opportunities for doing; and, in consequence of his observations, he changed his elongated hat for one of a round fashion, and his light hair for a sandy-colored or haply (for we hate being as demonstrative as he himself was) a raven-black wig; he instructed his tailor how to cut his coat; he spent hours before his glass, practising the very tie of his neckcloth—to say nothing of the hours occupied, by its aid, in trying to imitate a bow, a smile, a turn of the lip, or a droop or a toss of the head. But, although much was gained by all these adaptations and labors, something yet remained to be done in order to procure a public and general misconception of who he was; for the Double's great longing consisted of a wish to have people gaze after him in the streets, in proof of how well he enacted his mute lie; and here—as regarded self-exhibition in the streets—lay his difficulty. At home, indeed, or in the houses of his particular friends, while he *sat* quietly at table, he succeeded amazingly well, because, in fact, in a sitting posture you could not so easily detect that his figure was considerably shorter than the noble one of his supposed counterpart. But one cannot well sit down out of doors in a thronged metropolis ; unless, indeed, one sits in a saddle. And even if one could do the former-mentioned feat, it were of no avail in this particular case, inasmuch as the man to be cheated out of the admiration due exclusively to his own person, never did it ; and as to sit ting in a saddle, our gentleman had no saddle, not to talk of a horse's back to put it on. Truth must out. Although "a real gentleman," the high prices at which human existence, with a reasonable share of enjoyment superadded, must be purchased in London, had deterred his hitherto economical mind from attempting the keep of a steed worthy of being seen in and about the great city.

But what will not high ambition endeavor on the road to its object ? The Double, after pondering the matter some time, started off after breakfast, one morning, to scrutinize the studs of sundry livery-stables of respectable character though reasonable charges ; and, with a vivid recollection in his mind of the often contemplated horse most usually ridden about town by his own original, he selected, before dinner, an excellent likeness of the animal, and hired it, for two days in each week, at a not very extravagant price. And now, if ever a man were on his hobby-horse, surely he was on his. Twice every week, for months afterwards, we have seen him, at fashionable hours, walking or trotting, nay, even galloping, his new acquisition up and down Piccadilly, and by Hyde Park Corner into Grosvenor Place, and where not ; and veritable attention did they both draw from individuals of the passing crowds, who, having never seen the true man and horse anywhere but in the open air, were promptly imposed upon. Nor was that all. Once or twice, in the Ring in Hyde Park, we, and others along with us (for at the time we speak of he was beginning to be blown among us, knowing ones, as Master Shallow might say), have seen him bowed, or smiled, or kissed finger-tips to, out of carriages which he rapidly passed in the direction opposite to their motion ; and oh, intoxicating spirit of fame ! what a happy glow did not those palpable hits impart to the countenance of the successful aspirant !

Indeed, it cannot be guessed by what process of reasoning, to say little of feeling, he thus deemed himself honored in his own mind, on account of only being mistaken for a celebrated person. What, then, were the grounds upon which the poor Double so anxiously would have disowned his identity?—so anxiously, indeed, that we do believe he was ready and willing to sell himself to the devil, as Dr. Faustus did, could the bargain have insured to him as perfect a change into the likeness he thirsted after, as was the change from age to youth insured to the doctor by *his* bargain. But 'tis useless multiplying questions or conjectures on the subject. We only know that, in a vein of perfect consistency, he was nearly as proud of the deception practised by his hired horse as of that toiled after by himself ; that he often wished the poor brute were conscious of the laurels he had gained ; and that (wiping his brows with a handkerchief in a way he had once seen his better self do), he has been heard to say, after returning from a day's exhibition about town—"I do own myself grateful and proud for having been cast in the same mould with that great man !"

So, for months, as has been said, he passed a very happy life; when suddenly there arose a prospect of great interruption to the gathering of the triumphs of his deceptive existence. It is clear that if the nobleman were known to have left London, he could scarce hope to make people go on believing that he was still in London, unless, indeed, he wished to frighten passengers in the streets out of their senses, by being taken for the *wraith* or *fetch* of the absent public character. In fact, to continue in the glory of the occasional doubt that he was somebody else, the Double was necessitously chained to the place, though not to the spot of the place, inhabited by that somebody. Considerable, therefore, were his anxieties, and regrets, and sense of humiliation, when he read in the papers that the noble and gallant —— of —— was to go over immediately to Ireland, as its Viceroy, or Lord-lieutenant.

True, the high appointment flattered his vanity, in a kind of personal way. He felt it as an additional homage very nearly paid to himself ; and strongly was he tempted to spend the summer, at least, in the Irish metropolis, in the hope of coming in for his just share of•the usual public—that is, street—worship to be paid to the representative of the representative of royalty. But then, first of all, he feared, if he did not dislike, the Irish; and they were, at that time, more to be feared than ever—many of the counties of their country being in open insurrection, famine, and typhus-fever. Next, what was he to do for his well-esteemed horse in Dublin? He could not think of purchasing him—the price was too much even for ambition to pay, taking purse into account; yet by no other arrangement could he prevail on the the owner of the livery-stables to allow the distinguished animal to float within view of Ireland's eye (the little island so called in the bay of Dublin). In a word (and alas !) the newly-appointed vice-king sailed for his Irish capital, while his disconsolate Double remained, still torn by indecision, in London.

Scarce a month had elapsed, however, after the Lord-lieutenant's arrival in the land of (sometimes) potatoes, when the good folks of Dublin began to be puzzled, as their brethren of London had been, by the vision of his copyist riding about the main streets, or along the beautiful quays, or in the Phœnix Park ; the horse too, whether the London one or not, being a very good similitude. One fortunate circumstance was in favor of our adventurer. The Lord-lieutenant (though he stuck no great bunch of shamrock in his hat or on his breast, and pointed at or pressed his hand upon it, as some people had done before him) was beginning to be very popular, in consequence of a mode of conduct as manly, and as suitable to his nature, as it was good in policy. In truth, from almost the day of his arrival, he had thrown himself upon the confidence of the people, asking the higher classes of them to share his hospitality, or good-humoredly sharing theirs ; and showing himself in public, with the least ostentation possible, to the other classes. To come to our point ; he began soon to ride through the streets, very often quite alone ; and here, it will be perceived, was the circumstance in favor of his untired and untiring mimic of which we have already spoken. Here was the vice-sovereign in a situation susceptible of perfect imitation by one man and horse. And it is quite true that the lonely impostor sometimes succeeded to his heart's content in consequence; hats and caps were taken off to him by men and boys at either side of the streets, as he rode along, bowing and smiling with a degree of similarity only conferable by long practice. And having heard that the object of his mixed adoration and self-esteem had alighted one day at the door of a pastry-cook's shop, and chatted amiably with the pretty girl behind the counter, he also did dismount at the door of another shop of the same kind, and did also overwhelm with a sense of being inexpressibly honored, and lifted out of herself, the not as pretty handmaiden of the rival establishment. After all which, he would steal away, horse and self, to deposit the former in his livery-stable, and then win, by circuitous and unfrequented ways, his own humble lodgings, and sit down, a delighted man, to his chop or his steak, not playing the Lord-lieutenant of Ireland to his orderly landlady or her smoke-dried daughter—though indeed, it added to his notions of self-consequence in the house to hear them begin to say, even while he strove to disrobe himself of the character, how "very like h was."

But his happiness was again doomed to be sadly interrupted. It was announced that the Lord-lieutenant would speedily set out upon a tour through some of the counties in Ireland, and some of the disturbed ones too! For all the reasons—and more with them—given for his troubles, when he heard of the intended voyage from London to Dublin, he felt agitated anew. Doubtless the Irish he had met with in Dublin itself were not so much to be dreaded as he had laid the thing down in his own mind. But the barbarians of the insurrectionary and remote quarters of the country; the savages, whooping among the hills and bogs, with scythes and pikes in their hands!—his soul, although nothing of its darling's thirst for renown had abated, shrank from such a prospect of peril. Besides, would there be much glory, worthy of the name, to be gained by the mistakes of his person, committed by the populace of small towns or villages, or by peasants on the road-side, even supposing he should escape danger? Yes, and a new and brilliant ray of future fame flashed on his soul. Yes! by some happy combination of circumstances, in his character of Lord-lieutenant, he also—and he, really—might allay an Irish rebellion, or staunch the wounds of civil discord. But fears, deadly fears, came on him again—his horse, too, as in a former case. In truth, we must a second time part from him undecided, and a prey to conflicting wishes and doubts, longings and terrors; and in the mean time, after some other things, let us occupy ourselves a little with his reality.

This was not a year of rank insurrection in any of the usually disturbed (that is, starving) districts of Ireland. Great outrages were not committed by the neglected, uneducated, and despairing peasantry. The chief feature of their refractory spirit, for the season, was evinced in combinations and determinations not to cut down the corn of any of their land owners, no matter of what creed, who, during the speechifying of a recent election, we believe, had thought proper to give them rather hard words.

"An' so we're not as much as to lay a finger on the poor capt'n's whate, aither, Con?" asked one of a body of legislators among them, who were assembled, by stealth, at a late hour of the night, in an old barn, for the purpose of organizing the rebellious proceedings of the next day. It will be understood that the querist spoke in a tone of mock compassion for "the poor capt'n," while his features expressed a bitter sneer.

"The divil a grain of it 'll ever lie in shafe, wid help from ou. holy Roman reaping-hooks, Micky, ma-bouchal," answered Con, who might be termed chairman of their committee of public safety, though, indeed, he was only squatted on a thin layer of straw, accidentally found in the empty barn.

"Och, an' it's like, if we don't cut it for him, that he'll be forced to send a little way to the North for the nate Orange hands," remarked a third. "Becase, ye see, boys, we're all only a set o' baste brutes o' Romans that's to be found about him in these parts, and that he said, out afore all the gintlemen, tho other day ; we wasn't fit to be touched wid a pair o' tongs, so we wasn't. The Lord look down on us !"

"Amin," assented Mick ; "an' since he can stop his nose at us afore the whate is ripe, he can do widout us, when it's ready to shell idself about the fields."

"That's a thruth," said another. "An' sure, when the people that God plaised to put in a counthry aren't fit to cut the harvest that God put in it too, why, thin, the capt'n must only thry for the Orangemen, the few hundred miles away, as my gossip here tould ye afore me, or else see me how many rale, honest boys, like 'em, he'll be able to get in the barony.

"An' they're asily counted," resumed Con, the chairman ; "four of 'em, all in a lump. Ould Spear, wid de head shakin' on his shouldhers, like the last lafe on the top of a poplar—h that cries 'amin' to his reverence, the ministher, in the church, every Sunday—Ould Spear, I say, is one ; then there's the twc Hucks, brothers, the wavers—the only bodies that hears Ould Spear in the church, or does be there to hear him, barrin' the ministher's own wife and childher, and the capt'n himself—long life to him ! an' to his whate, too ! The Hucks is—stop—Ould Spear is one—yes ; the two Hucks is three—craturs so worn away with the shuttle, an' goin' in winther to a cowld church, that—but, look up there, boys !" cried the speaker, suddenly interrupting himself, as he stared towards the roof of the barn. The eyes of all the other rebels followed his, and fixed upon the face of a man which was visible through a rent in the thatch, and which earnestly regarded them.

"It's Connors, the informer!" shouted Micky; "out wid us, boys, an' let us give him what some of us owes him, at last!"

"I'm no Connors, and I'm no informer," said the man overhead; "stop where you are, boys, and look at my fatures again."

"By the mortial man!" cried one of the conspirators, a young taciturn, sad-browed fellow, who previously had not uttered a word, though he now spoke with remarkable liveliness of voice and manner, as he sprang from his primitive seat on his heels by the rough wall of the building; "by the mortial man, an' he says thrue!—it's poor Ned Cahill is iu it, if he's a livin' man this night!"

"You're not far off from the mark, Peery O'Dea," replied the intruder; "and now that you're sure o' me, won't you and the other boys let me drop down among ye, to discoorse one word?"

He prepared to descend throught the aperture, as he spoke; his face disappeared from it; his legs, his body, took the place of the former; then he swung an instant by the hands from the rude joists of the roof, and saying, "'Tisn't the same way some people 'ud like to see me hangin', boys," he alighted firmly on his outspread feet, in the middle of the earthen floor of the barn.

There were ease, agility, and boldness in all his motions, while accomplishing this not unperilous descent; and now the rushlight, which illumined the council of the disaffected Irish, showed the person of a slight-limbed man of thirty or thereabouts, with broad chest and shoulders, and a well-favored face, of which the only disagreeable expression was the suspicious curl of the brow, and the sidelong, quick glance of the eye.

"Musha, my poor fellow! my poor Ned!" resumed Peery O'Dea, hastening to him, and there were tears in Peery's eyes, and a tremor in his limbs, while they interchanged the usual salute—kissing each other's cheeks as they held each other's hands. The other peasants looked on, with various expressions of countenance. Some showed sympathy; some anxiety, perhaps for themselves; and one or two regarded the new-comer as if forming a selfish resolution towards him.

"And how is Nelly, ma-bouchal?"

"The only sister o' you is brave an hearty!" answered Peery O'Dea, "if it wasn't for thinkin' a great dail about you, Ned, an' cryin' morning, noon, and night, on the head of it all."

"An' her wcenoch?" continued Cahill.

5

"As fine a lump of a boy as ever you—" began the vain father. His brother-in-law interrupted him.

"Oh, well—sure I know, Peery; Nelly's gorsoon 'ill want no praises you can give him. But that's not the business, now. I come here a good stretch o' road to spake o' something else to you and the boys foreuent me; only I'm hungry, not to say drouthy, an' 'ud ax a bit an' a sup afore I make my narration. So you'll *tust* step out, *avich*, and beg a mouthful for me from Nelly, and tell her I'll see her maybe the night, afore I take to my thravels again."

"I'll run out," volunteered one of the two men whom we have mentioned as glancing at Cahill in a questionable way, "I'll run out, Peery, an' you can be stoppin' wid your brother-in-law."

"No," said Cahill, fixing upon him an expressive look; "no, neighbor; we're all neighbors afther a manner, though I won't take it on me to say I ever saw much of *you* afore. But no; neither Peery nor you need go now. Con, my boy," turning hastily to the ex-chief of the assembly, "you and I are ould friends, an' you'll think it no great throuble to run and ax a morsel to ate for a hungry and a tired man."

"You're afther just sayin' it, Ned *avich*," responded Con; and he arose and strode towards the badly secured and crazy door of the barn. "I'll let you out my own self," continued Cahill. "There!" holding the door only a little way apart, while he again glanced keenly around him. He shut the door, and secured it as he had found it. "An' you and I, Perry, can just step, the closest of any to the dour; for who knows who might be on the scent of one of us abroad. There's great temptation, boys"—turning to the legislators, as he drew a pistol from his breast—"great temptation, even among neighbors sometimes, in the reward offered for the head of a poor outlaw."

Short answers, yet such as sympathized with Cahill's well known position, or seemed to do so, came from the greater number of his hearers after he had spoken. But Peery O'Dea was greately moved, his friends heard him groan, as he turned away his face.

"It's a long time since you come this road afore, Ned," remarked the Micky before named; "though we hard tell of you showing yourself, here and there, in other places."

"Ay, Micky, the life I'm forced to lead isn't the pleasantest. Here an' there, as you say, good weather an' bad; sleepin' little, and never two nights together on the same road, an' never undher a Christian roof, but out on the fields at the snug side of a stack, or in a wood, or in a plantation, or near the fox's hole, or down by the river near the otter's bed ; and all for fear of what I said a moment ago. The neighbors are very good to me—I'll never deny it ; and, as yet, I've no rason to be in dread or doubt of any one, but the reward in the proclamation is a heavy one,—that's all I have to say."

He started slightly, Peery sharing his emotion, as a woman's voice came to the door at the outside, high in anxiety, if not lamentation. Cahill, after listening a moment, hastily undid a second time the fastening of the door, using, however, some caution still, and, after saying in a whisper to Peery, "Look about you," opened his arms to embrace his only sister, whom he had not for a long time seen, and who was his nearest surviving relation.

Their meeting evinced deep and true affection on both sides. The young woman had an interesting, if not handsome face ; and it and her person just began to indicate the matronly change which her duties of wife and mother were bringing about. She wept abundantly, while her arms surrounded his neck, and her face lay hidden on his bosom ; but for some minutes her attempts to speak could not get beyond, " O Ned ! O poor Ned !" Nor was the rough man she clung to unmoved.

At length they began to talk a little more freely, and, calling to mind the claim which her brother had forwarded by Con upon her hospitality, Mary O'Dea caused the outlaw to sit down near the door, with his back to the wall, upon her ample cloak, folded into a temporary cushion ; and, confronting him, sitting also " on her hunkers," she gave him to eat of the plain fare she was able to snatch up at home, and to drink, too, out of a bottle of " potheen," diluted with water. During her attentions, the provisions rapidly disappeared. Mary looked every other instant at her brother's features, or scanned his person, and perhaps the state of his attire, while tears still flowed down her cheeks, and plaintive mutterings escaped her. Poor Mary, poor as she was, deserves to be called a good specimen of the only really beautiful existence under Heaven's sun—a true-hearted and gentle-hearted woman ; she possessed, too, as may appear, what (thank Providence !) often mixes up with female excellence in the softest shape - -a strong, prompt mind, and a sacred sense of right and wrong.

" An' won't you stop wid us the night, Ned *agra* ?" she asked, towards the conclusion of his hasty meal.

" You oughtn't to say to me, *won't* you, but *can* you, Ned ?"

he answered, turning his head to the door to note if Perry continued to do duty at it, with the pistol he had slipped into his hand ; "that's what you ought to say to me, Mary, machree. But little's the use in thinkin' of the thing the heart 'ud like best to do, when the body isn't able to do it."

" *I'*ll do something to get *you* lave to do *that*, Ned, my dear, afore I'm many days oulder," resumed Mary, glancing at her husband, and, with a nod of her head, looking expressively at her brother, while she spoke in a low, cautious voice.

" Mary ! Mary, *asthore ?*" he said, in the lowest whisper, although its cadence betokened sudden and deep emotion, "what are you for saying, girl ! Get up, and come this way wid me."

He took her by the arm, and led her into a corner of the barn, where they were far removed from the peasants.

" What's this, at all ?" he continued ; "tell me in one word, Mary !"

" I know all about it at last, Ned ; and I'll do my best to free you from the outlawry," she replied.

" *Duoul !*" he cried, impatiently ; "the woman has taken lave of her seven senses ! all about what ? And what would you dhrame o' doing ? and who tould you, Mary, if you *do* know all ?"

" Himself, Ned."·

" Peery, his own self ?" he demanded.

" No other cratur ; who could ? Poor fellow, he couldn't long keep it from me ; the heart in his body is too straight, and it loves and likes us both too well to let him lie down quietly, and you—"

" Whisht, Mary, for your life ! whisht !" He cast his habitually suspicious eyes all round him. " *Musha*, but he's a born fool of his mother to open his lips to you a word about it ! Tell me, Mary, what *are* you goin' to do ? What *can* you thry tha wouldn't be against your own husband—the father of your *weenoch !*" he continued, passionately ; "and daare you, Mary ` —daare you attempt, any thing so unnaatural as that ? Mary, my curse upon your head—and I will pray to our father and our mother to curse you out of their graves—if you let only the thought of it come into your mind !"

She several times strove to speak, he seemed resolved to afford her no opportunity.

"Give over thinking of it, I warn you !" he went on, "and now good-by, and God bless you, if you deserve His blessing ; good-by, Mary, I'll see you again as soon as I can !"

He hastily turned from her, and, standing with his back to the door, continued speaking to the peasants, without an instant's pause.

"I'm goin' my road, boys ; and as my time is short, I must say what I have to say to ye at a hop-and-a-jump ; so here it is The Lord-lieutenant will be down among ye the morrow morning. He's to stop wid a good friend of yours, I hear, and that's like as if he wasn't far off from being a good friend himself. I don't want to advise ye to be good boys forenent his eyes ; sure you'll thrate him well of your own accord, because ye all know he manes well to us (the first of his kind that ever said so, at laste), and morebetoken because he goes about the poor counthry like a man that has thrust in the people ; ridin' his horse sometimes a'most alone, along by roads and *borheens*, as simple, ay, and a great dail simpler, than some o' the little squireens nigh hand to us. Well, if it's a thing that Captain Lighton axes the Lord-lieutenant to ax you to cut his harvest, it would only be a good turn, afther all, not to refuse ; and it may sarve yoursclves, and maybe it might sarve me too, in an endeavor I'm goin' to make to get lave to come home from my rambles, and take to arning an honest mouthful again. And so, there's what I'm come abegging to ye for ; and now, the good-night to ye, boys, or the top o' the morning ; for that matter, the day's breakin' already. God speed ye !"

"Peery O'Dea," he added, whispering his brother-in-law, "help me to open this ould door, quick, quick! and out wid you now like a hurler afore me! and let us run over a field or two together. I want to spake to you, and keep you free of harm. Come, man, hurry !"

He seized Peery's arm, and almost forced him through the door-way ; and when Mary and some of the peasants went out to look after them, the brothers-in-law were nowhere to be seen. Mary pondered a moment, shook her head, and then bent her steps homeward, little changed in the resolution she had taken to try and restore her brother to society.

"What fool's talk has passed between you and Mary, Peery O'Dea ?" asked Cahill, when they had gained their place of concealment—the ruins of an old castle which overhung the main road to their village.

"Ned," answered Peery, "you know I've tould her all ; don't fly in a passion wid me ; I saw ye discoorsin' together in the barn, and it asy to guess what Mary was sayin' to you."

" An' that's the way you keep your promise wid me ?" questioned Ned.

"I couldn't help it, Ned Cahill, *asthore*. It was lyin' like a heavy stone on my heart. Sure enough, we both thought it would be for the best ; I to hould my tongue, and thry to work for her and the *weenoch*, while you were only forced to hide yourself for a start. But I'll tell you what it is, Ned ; the mornin' I hard o' them takin' you, I set off for the jail dour, to give myself up to them in your stead, as it well became me to do ; an' nothin' but the news I larned on the road o' your breakin' jail, and givin' them leg-bail—the thing that put the outlawry on you, afther all, poor boy—nothin' but that sent me home agin. Ay, an' I have more to say to you, Ned Cahill ; the first moment I hear o' your falling into their clutches a second time, I'll be on the road to the jail dour a second time, too ; for I can't ate by day, nor sleep by night, thinkin' o' you. An' afther all we can say about Mary and the child, my heart tells me I'm not doin' a thing that a man ought to do."

" Bother and botheration, Peery ! Do you mane to tell me, even if it did happen that I was locked up agin, that it *would* be the part of a man to start himself off, of his own accord, from wife an' *weenoch*—to say nothin' o' the poor ould father o' you, sittin' at home by the fire—an' let them send you for life across the wide says, if they didn't take the life from you aforehand ? I tell you, man, you have your duties laid out for you on this earth. As for me, no one is dependin' on me, and no one 'ud miss me, barrin' yourself and Mary ; an' even ye only for the sorrow, an' nothin' at all for the loss. An' I'm not a boy given to marryin' ; I don't think the notion of it'll come into my head agin ; for, in troth, Peery, from the day I helped to carry poor Cauth Farrel to the berrin-ground, afthe the long sickness that made her a light load to carry any where afore it ended her days"—Cahill's voice changed, and his eyes fell—"from that day to this, Peery, though I was a younger boy then, I never saw the *colleen* I'd care to be thinkin' of ; no, nor wanted to see her, neither. But we're talkin a power o' *raumaush* here in this ould place. Tell me, Peery, an' don't tell me any thing but the thruth, how much o' the raal business did you blab out to Mary ?"

" I didn't hide a single bit o' the raal business, Ned. I tould her that it was me myself (an' you not wid us, nor in the sacret) that went up to Lighton's house that night for the arms along wid the other boys. An' I tould her you only follied us to get me home out o' danger, when, by bad luck, you found out what I was goin' to do ; and that when the peelers pursbued us, afther we got the guns and pistols, and were hard and close on my thrack, you ran up to me, Ned, and forced my gun from me, an' made me turn off home by a cross-cut. Och ! Ned ! if it could come into my mind that night what you were goin' to do—"

" Phu, Peery, I never meant they should ketch either of us, when I took your gun, an' if you were bid by me to use your .egs sooner, they never would have to tell that they came up wid me : 'twas our argufying the thing that spoiled all. Well, no matther now. Just listen to me over agin. What's Mary goin' to do, to thry an' get me free o' the outlawry ? Can you tell me that, Peery ?"

Peery solemnly protested he could not. He had never heard his wife mention the subject.

Cahill looked grave, and, after a pause, kindling into a rage, said—

" By the sky over us ! if *my* sisther, my father's and my mother's daughter, ever attempts the like of it, I could kill her with my own hand !"

Peery asked what he meant ; and it was obvious, from his perfectly unconscious manner, that he did not share with his brother-in-law a single doubt of Mary.

Cahill evaded answering him.

" You must stop the day by my side, Peery—that's all ; or as much of the day, at laste, as 'ill be wantin' to do what I mane to do in. An', first of all, let us hide here till the Lord-lieutenant passes by to Mr. Lowe's big house. I'd like to see him, that I may know him again ; an' he'll soon come now, for Mr. Lowe expects him to the great break'ast."

Accordingly, both remained in the old ruin for some hours peering out upon the road, through narrow window slits in its walls. And Ned Cahill seemed to have gained true information as to the movements of vice-royalty. After some time, distant shouts reached them ; they watched the top line of the hilly road ; the uproar came nearer ; clouds of dust arose in view ; and, dimly seen through it, down streamed and trundled the crowds of peasantry, who were drawing his excellency with silken ropes in his open carriage, and the huge crowds who, jumping and capering, were before them, beside them, and behind them ; and Mr. Lowe, and other gentlemen

of the place, on horseback, in front; "an' not a soger nor a
peeler to be seen !"—as the extatic mob declared, and truly declared—the extatic mob, who, not two years before, had been
enjoying the Insurrection Act, and who have not remained quite
extatic ever since that blessed morning.

"I'm tould I'll know him in the carriage by his takin' off
his hat, an' makin' all manner of bows and fine manners to the
people ;" soliloquized Cahill, looking close, as the frantic rout
whirled onward the truly and meritedly popular Lord-lieutenant, often tumbling over each other, in the zeal of each and all
to "have one pull at the ropes."

"Well, an' there I see him, sure enough," resumed Cahill,
"an it 'ill be quare if I don't know him again, after he ates his
break'ast. Much good may it do him, every bit an' sup of id."

At Mr. Lowe's hall-door, the people permitted his excellency
to stop. Their parish priest there read him a litle address, to
which he replied kindly, in impromptu. Again we have to notice the correctness of Ned Cahill's private sources of information. Captain Lighton, who, with other gentlemen, had ridden
out that morning to meet that great man, handed a note into
the carriage. The Lord-lieutenant, interrupting a few words of
conversation with the parish priest, immediately glanced once at
it, and then saying something in a low voice, gave it to his late
reverend panegyrist, who, having perused it in his turn, thus
addressed the assembled thousands :

"My good people ! Down to this present morning, ye have
refused, even against my request, to cut Captain Lighton's corn.
Here is his excellency, the Lord-lieutenant and Governor of
Ireland, and your friend, if you will let him, by deserving his
friendship ; and through my mouth, his excellency is pleased to
ask ye, will ye, or will ye not, save the blessed harvest that
Divine Providence—"

"We will, plase his majisty and your reverence," interrupted
a voice very like that of "Con." "We will, out o' glory to
him for axin' us ; an' for another little rason, becase poor Ned
Cahill, that we're all sorry for, an' love, an' like, is afther bid-
din' us do the same thing aforehand."

"Ned Cahill ! the poor outlaw !" resumed the good priest,
forgetting a little chagrin he had felt on the head of being cheated out of a very pretty peroration by Con's interruption. He
and the Lord-lieutenant began to discourse anew in seeming
earnestness. ..

Ned Cahill and Peery O'Dea soon had proof, from a changed hiding-place, that the people respected Con's pledge as their spokesman. Shouting and capering, and brandishing their sickles, hundreds of them rushed into the captain's fields, and simultaneously attacked all the ripe corn they could find.

And still the outlaw showed a knowledge of how more important people were to act upon that, to him, memorable day Having again spirited Peery along with him to a convenient place of ambush, he watched earnestly the expected approach of the Lord-lieutenant along a by-road leading zigzag from Mr. Lowe's house. Peery knew his purpose by this time, and awaited its issue with his own mental reservations of what he would do, should evil come of Ned's bold thought.

" Whisht, Peery !" cried Cahill, catching his arm, as he glanced over the hedge of the road, with a sparkling eye, and suddenly flaring cheeks. " Here he is, sooner than I or others had a notion of !—an' ridin' quite alone, too, by the powers ! —not an *edge-a-gong*, nor Misther Lowe himself wid him ! well, an' that's quare ! Bud I s'pose they're behind the turn o' the road. At any rate, it's all the betther for me—so here goes, in the name o' God and good luck !"—and springing upon the road, and falling instantly upon his knees, straight before the object of his soul's solicitude and reverence, he continued—

" Oh ! your excellency ! oh, my Lord-lieutenant !—oh, plaise your majisty, hear one word from a poor, heart-sore man !"

" Wha—a—t, what, what, friend ?" stuttered the person he addressed, endeavoring to rein in and quiet his horse, who had been amazingly startled at the sudden vision of Cahill ; and, indeed the horse's master did not speak or look like a man of perfect presence of mind.

" My life ! my life !" resumed Cahill. " Wait, your honor, my Lord-lieutenant, an' I'll hould him for you ;" and he jumped up and grasped the horse's reins. " An' now—"

" Let go, fellow ! let go !" screamed the rider in increased terror ; for, from Cahill's brogue and impassioned pronounciation, he had mistaken the possessive pronoun which the supplicant had placed before the word "life."

" Och, an' won't I, your majisty, won't I, when you only hear me spake one word ! Sure I'm no one else in the world bud poor Cahill the outlaw, that your majisty—"

" Outlaw !" repeated the other. " Savage villain ! do you mean to murder me ?"

6*

"Murder you, my Lord-lieutenant?" repeated poor Cahill, in his turn, letting go the reins, and starting back aghast, with clasped hands. "By the blessed stars in the sky! I love an' like you so well that I wouldn't harm a hair o' your horse's mane, let alone one o' your own head, for the round world stuffed full of goold!"

"And why do you carry that pistol, then?" still stammered the poor Double, now a little soothed by the honeyed flattery of Cahill, and the repetition of the splendid titles addressed to him.

"This—the bit of a pistol, my Lord?" Cahill drew it from his breast, where its butt had not been well hidden. "Och, an' is it me you fear, on the head o' this? Lookee here, plaise your majisty!"

He discharged the weapon in the air, close by the horse's ears. The animal pranced and reared in a frenzy of terror, and his rider, still sharing his feeling, could scarce keep his saddle.

"An' see here agin," continued Cahill, hurling the pistol from him—an action lost to the confounded and dancing eyes of the Double. "And now, at laste, your majisty 'ill plase to hear me!" He renewed his grasp on the horse's bridle, really only meaning well. "You put the outlawry on an innocent poor man, my Lord-lieutenant!—one that never riz a hand for bad in the counthry! Oh, take it off o' me, take it off o' me! Let me go home from the hills and woods, again, to sleep under a Christhen roof, an' to meet my fellow-creatures widout bein' afeared o' them, an' to put my hand to the spade or the plough again, that I may arn the honest bit, and the honest sup, an' that I may go to the house o' God an' kneel down, an' put up my prayers for you an' yours, to the last day I draw the breath o' life! Ochown, take it off o' me, an' may you reign long in glory, an' die happy! It's an innocent boy that axes you, my Lord the Lieutenant—it's an innocent poor boy! Say the word out o' your mouth—say the word, an' do a good action—say the word an'—"

"Well, well, well, man," interrupted the Double, his fears now only divided between the uncertainty whether he had to do with a wild Irish assassin or a wild Irish madman—"d—don't you pull me about so, and we shall see. Let go the bridle, and I *will* say the word. There! stand aside now, and you may regard yourself as a free man."

"Hurrah!" screamed Cahill, jumping up a good height from

the ground, as he smote his breast in ntter joy. "Peery O'Dea, inside the fence there? Peery O'Dea, do you hear that?"

"Hurrah! an' it's I that do!" answered Peery, with another shout, discovering himself.

"It's off o' me! it's off o' me!" continued Cahill, hugging his brother-in-law. "Isn't it, your honor-in-glory—isn't it?"

"It is, it is ; to be sure it is. Have I not said so? I revoke every thing. Only won't you and the other man move away from my horse's head? So—good day to you both—all's right—good day."

Seeing the road at last clear before him, the speaker gave spur and rein to his horse, and was out of sight in a moment, ay, and out of Ireland in some hours after, from the nearest seaport, cured in a degree of performing his absurd and miserable impostures in it.

"There you go! an' may honor an' glory be in your road afore you!" Cahill continued to shout.

"There you go! an' may you never know what it is to have a heart as heavy as the hearts you're afther makin' happy this day!" added Peery.

"Stand!" cried voices at their backs. "One of you is Cahill, the outlaw." They turned, and saw half a dozen police, who, with presented carbines, immediately surrounded them.

"Bother, boys, wid your 'stand!'" answered Ned. "I'm Cahill, sure enough, but no outlaw, this blessed day, thank God! an' his honor the Lord-lieutenant! Hurrah!"

He jumped again.

"Come, come—your arms," said the sergeant of the party.

"Arms! sorrow a one I have, barrin' the two God gave me. A little while ago, to tell thruth, I had a sort of an ould pistol wid me—but I sint the bullet of it up into the air, an' itself after the bullet, to the divvle, entirely ; an' it's my word I give you, masther peelers, my poor fellows, that from this day out—"

"Search him," interrupted the sergeant.

"Here, then—sarch—sarch—sarch—oh, wid all my heart! I tell you, boys, it's only givin' yourselves throuble for nothin'."

"Fall in with the men, then, and march for jail," resumed the sergeant, when the useless search was made.

"Jail? me march for jail? ye're mad to speak of it. It's more than your lives are worth to use the words. Take great care what ye're for doin'."

"Come, fall in! Where are the handcuffs?"

"Handcuffs!" he exclaimed, as he heard them jingling. "Have a care o' your behavior to me, I tell you once again!" continued Cahill, while he vainly resisted the strength used to manacle his hands. "His own self took the ban o' me, masther peelers—his own self, my Lord the Lieutenant, only a minute agone, an' on this very blessed spot! Ay, ye may laugh at me, but I say he did! An' here's Peery O'Dea that's ready to say the same thing, for he hard an' seen him! Didn't you, Peery, didn't you?"

Peery proved, indeed, a ready witness; but still the police sneered, until, after glancing down the road, in the direction of Mr. Lowe's house, the sergeant said, "Well, Cahill, now's the time to get grace from us, if your words are true." The man's tone was still deriding. "Here comes his excellency."

"Which way?" demanded Cahill, glancing up and down the road, in great astonishment. "Eh? the gentleman ridin' up to us wid Mr. Lowe an' the officers? Stop—wait—stop. Eh! By the powers o' man an' it is, sure enough, however the divvle, or by the Lord's will, he got there!" for the Double had retreated in the direction contrary to Mr. Lowe's house. "Peery, Peery, avich!"

"Shove aside, and clear the road," said the sergeant.

The police and their prisoners accordingly stood at the fence, the men presenting arms. The Lord-lieutenant stopped before them, and was about to ask what was the matter, when Cahill broke forward, and failing almost prostrate, prayed his excellency to look on him, and remember him well, and say whether or no he had not, a few moments before, pardoned him his offences; and at the same time he again shouted out for Peery O'Dea to support his assertion.

"The man must be mad," said the Lord-lieutenant to Mr. Lowe. "Both of them must be so; I have never seen either of them in my life before; and yet how apparently sincere is their earnestness. One of them weeps."

At the sound of his excellency's voice Cahill started up, staring in misgiving and dismay on the face of the speaker; and again he called, in a whisper, to Peery, "Peery, avich!" as if for council.

"No, Ned, asthore," replied Peery, after making his own observation; "'tisn't himself is afore us—or it is himself, I mane, or else there's two o' them—or it was the ould divvle that came

the road, first of all, to make you go through wid the foolish
thought o' your mind, and get you taken agin!"

While the Lord-lieutenant was speaking in an under tone with
Mr. Lowe, the sergeant of the police advanced to recapture
Cahill. Peery O'Dea now sprang forward and continued, in a
loud, wailing voice, "But since they have you the second turn,
Ned, it's time for me to do what I said. Plaise your lordship,
Ned Cahill, my wife's brother, though he broke jail, is as inno-
ent as my own *weenoch* o' what sent him there! I am the
man—I, Peery O'Dea, that headed the boys up to the house for
the arms that night—an' Ned wasn't wid us at all, only met me
on the road after we got what we went for—an' forced my gun
from me, an' stood to be seized by the peelers! an' this is the
holy thruth, an' I'll get your honor plenty o' witnesses to say so.
An' now, sure your majisty 'ill tell them to let him go, an' take
me in his place, an'—"

"Don't put thrust in a word the fool of a boy is sayin', glory
to your lordship," interrupted Cahill; "the head of him is
cracked, becase I'm poor Mary's brother, an' he's often not in his
right mind. 'Twas in my hands the gun was found—an' 'twas I
that broke jail—and, by course, it's I that ought to go to jail,
over agin. An' so, misther sergeant, now—the Lord save us!
an' what's this?"

Mary O'Dea held him in her arms, sobbing and weeping alond.
"To jail you'll never go, brother Ned, *machree!*" she cried,
"never, never, praises to the good God, an' our good Lord-lieutenant!"

"*Avich!* you poor cratur! an' did that desaitful divvle come
across you, too, and make you all manner o' promises?" asked
Cahill, returning her embraces.

"Your honor, my lord!" continued Mary, "spake the word
ou promised me!"

Addressing Mr. Lowe, his excellency, touched and affected,
turned his horse's head, "Pray, sir, explain to the poor people."

"Cahill," said Mr. Lowe, "your sister has saved you; at least,
confirmed the Lord-lieutenant's merciful disposition towards you,
previously formed by reason of other circumstances. She contrived to meet his excellency before my house this morning, and,
on condition that a considerable depot of concealed arms, dis
covered by her—she has not said how—(Cahill glanced from
Mary to Peery)—should be delivered up, obtained your pardon.
The tranquillity of the country for the last year, a word in your

favor from your priest and others, and, indeed, from myself, and a wish to show the deluded people that they will be treated mercifully whenever they themselves afford the opportunity—all this helped your sister's prayers. Thank his excellency. You are a free man."

That Cahill did as he was bid it would be idle to enforce. Neither is it necessary to describe the joy of the reunited family. But, indeed, kind English readers—contradictory as the thing may sound—men made of mortal materials similar to those which we believe you like in the brothers-in-law, Ned and Peery, often plunder arms in some Irish counties, nay (and alas for the admission!), use them fearfully, too. Let us hope and pray, however, that such an Irish Lord-lieutenant as we here have sketched for you, acting under the wise instructions which shape his own excellent feelings and inclinations, may soon gain possession of all the hidden depots of destruction accumulated by the wretched people.

As for his Double—

"Peery, *avich!*" said Cahill, after they and Mary had been left alone on the road, "let us run hard, straight ahead, an' thry an' lay hould o' that brute baste of a pretendher!"

END OF THE IRISH LORD-LIEUTENANT AND HIS DOUBLE.

THE

FAMILY OF THE COLD FEET.

THE FAMILY OF THE COLD FEET.

So were called a highly respectable Irish family ; and the appellation is continued to their descendants of the present day, in consequence of the concluding circumstances of the following true narration. Incredulous some readers may be, after having perused it to the end, notwithstanding our intimation that it deals with facts. Should such be the case, we cannot help it ; and shall only add, that while the occurrence, for which we apprehend most question, has authenticated parallels in many countries over the world, its truth, in the particular instance before us, has been vouched to the writer by a member of *The Family of the Cold Feet.* Ay, and cold were his own feet while he told the chilling story ; so inveterately, so inheritedly cold, that the blaze of the jovial fire, at which we sat during his narrative, could not impart to them the least warmth ; and cold, cold were his children's feet—all except one, who obviously took after her mother, as well in constitution as in face and personal conformation ; and cold, cold had been his father's feet—as cold while he lived as when he had been dead three days, and decidedly cold all over ; and his grandfather's, and his grandfather's mother's—which lady brought the inconvenience into the family. And now we begin to tell in what manner.

Antony Skelton, at four-and-twenty, was a tall, well-limbed, fair-haired, ruddy-cheeked, blue-eyed, and half-educated Irishman ; a younger brother, too, though on that account scarce a whit less dangerous to many a blooming girl around him. He lived with his brother, the baronet, in the old cut-stone mansion, called Upper Court, having nothing to do but hunt, fish, shoot, cock-fight, dog-fight, badger-bait, ferrit-chase the rabbits in the warren, and, above all, dear women, to admire you. Profession he would none of ; taking fees, either as attorney, barrister, surgeon, or physician, was very much beneath his family consequence. He might have put his fine, broad shoulders into a red jacket, indeed (or rather long and broad-skirted red coat, as was then good military exquisitism), had there been spirited wars going on over Europe; but it was a time of profound peace ; and he candidly admitted that he did not like the trouble of drilling, and parading, and mounting guard, when very little could be expected to come of it. And he had much rather stay at home, amusing himself as country gentleman, on his brother's grounds.

This sounded in many ears as quite an independent resolution ; but that it really was so may be questioned. There was little doubt that, at an early age, he had, among the pleasures of the Irish metropolis, with great facility disposed of the few thousands which fell to his share, as a younger brother, according to his father's will. So that when he spoke, with a toss of his head, of "staying at home, amusing himself as a country gentleman on his brother's grounds," he must have meant, though perhaps it never struck him, at his brother's expense into the bargain. Sir Roger was fond of him, however, and one of a class of men of that peculiar good-nature besides, who can countenance the expenses of those they are fond of, or, as he would himself have said, "used to," at the risk of their own personal independence. So Tony did very well ; nearly as well as if he had been elder son born, and wrote himself Sir Tony.

Well, gallantry, it has been declared, was, above all others, his amusement on his brother's grounds, and in the neighborhood. For it he would, in truth, give up fox, hare, the river's side, the rabbit-warren, a cock-fight, a badger-bait, any other thing. Of this he boasted, as he ought to have done, to more fair faces than two or three, and was estimated accordingly, for a season at least, by each of those to whom, in turn, he made the avowal in strict confidence. Nor was " Master Tony"—or more expressively, with reference to his virtual reign at Upper Court, " the young master," as the tenants called him—particularly select in the exercise of his talent. His grand passion, or universal passion, asserted and proved itself in a very efficient kind of way, from the "cottiers" comely daughter up through the family of the small farmer, of the "strong farmer," of the gentleman farmer, and of the still more genteel farmer, till it achieved its utmost flight, proportioned to his opportunities, at the fireside of the next 'squire, or locally " square," baronet, bishop, or, haply, real lord. For Tony, certainly had the blessed talent of making himself agreeable, and therefore welcome from the mud cabin to the family seat. We have called him half-educated—that is, he pretended to Virgil and hinted at Euclid ; still he had been a member of T. C. D., and he *could* smatter on, amusingly, among the very best society of his county. While in rhyming—which he devoted exclusively to songs in praise of angling, hunting, fishing, wine, and ladies—Tony was considered a master.

Now any sagacious reader will perceive that so much has not been said about Mr. Tony's characteristics, unless that they must have a good deal to do with the origin and perpetuation of "cold feet" in his family. Such, indeed, is the fact, as we hasten to make evident.

The house of a neighboring gentleman had long been untenanted, save by the trusty servants in whose care he had left it. Mr. Neville lost a well-beloved wife, in her first confinement, and immediately after quitted his home and country to seek forgetfulness of sorrow in foreign lands. The innocent cause of her mother's death, his infant daughter, he deposited in safe and respectable hands, to be nursed through the first years of childhood ; and when Esther Neville gained her sixth year, he sent for her from England, to which country he had just returned from the continent, and thenceforward assumed his natural right as her protector. For some time she was educated in England, afterwards in France and Italy, and ultimately in England again ; and in her nineteenth year her father came back with her to his native country, to instal her as her mother's successor, in his paternal mansion ; announcing his determination never to remarry, and proclaiming her heiress to his considerable estate and funded property.

Antony Skelton, for some long weeks before her arrival within ten minutes' ride of Upper Court, had been rather at a loss for a new object of adoration. He soon got Sir Roger to accompany him to Mr. Neville's on a welcoming visit ; fell in love with Esther ten seconds after he had seen her ; and having contrived to stay for dinner, while his brother returned home, told her as much before he left the house that evening.

Let no one be astonished at this dispatch. It was his way ; he couldn't help it. No, no more than a connoisseur can help expressing raptures at the first sight of an old picture, although he may have seen hundreds quite as old before it. In very truth, Tony could not recollect the time since his sixteenth year, that he had once been able to curb the avowal of his perfect love for any and every woman or girl in the least interesting, by whose side he found himself the necessary number of hours. And we pray, in his behalf, that no ill-natured person will suppose it was because Esther Neville happened to be an heiress, and he a younger brother, that he so soon declared himself, in the present instant. No such thing. Heiresses were by no means new to him. He had been at the knees of one or two before, and given them up in a few months, weeks, or days, as it might be, for th untiring pleasure of once more manifesting his mighty love for the sex in general, in the case, perhaps, of a penniless fifth or seventh daughter. No, indeed ; the least mercenary lover on the earth was Tony. And in some degree to account for this, considering his own pauper state, and a rapid growth of nephews at Upper Court, perhaps it is as well to surmise that, in thus offering fervid adorations, like a lusty sun, to every flower in the female garden, he had not as yet ever thought of becoming entitled, by marriage, to the goods and chattels of one individual woman. But *why* he should not have done so we are utterly unable to explain.

And how sped his, as yet, newest of all wooings? How did Esther Neville take his sufficiently abrupt attack ? Not as she ought to have done had she much experience of the world, or of the various sorts of fools in it. Out of select English boarding-schools, or of continental convents, she had lived but little ; and romance substituted in her mind a wholesome and most necessary knowledge of mankind and womankind. Of such a man as we have sketched Tony Skelton, at four-and-twenty, she had dreamed, as well as of her own powers of striking to the death at first sight ; not forgetting his really fervid and seemingly unchangeable manner in giving her so quick a proof of her good opinion of herself. In truth, although, as the most romantic woman is bound to do, Esther made no response to his first startling speech, Tony had not repeated it, with pretty additions, more than four times, when she did ; and vows of deathless fidelity were forthwith interchanged ; and, in the stolen walks they enjoyed among the wild and solitary scenery adjacent to Mr. Neville's house, plans of future happiness—of happiness that never could, would, should, or ought to tire—towered up, like that same wild scenery, before and round them, till it faded into rich and beautiful vagueness in the distance. And this was as true of Tony Skelton as of Esther Neville. He felt as enthusiastic and as sincere as she did. Yes ; not a doubt of it. He felt, in fact, as he had often felt before, just like a man in love for the very first time; and he could have sworn to the world, as well as to his own heart, that it was utterly impossible he should ever look with the slightest interest on another woman.

In fact, the ardent, quick-tempered Esther was in her paradise —fool's paradise. Once or twice only she thought it odd that, in all their schemes for perennial blisses, her lover never happened to allude to the married state. But, on reflection, this could mean nothing at all; or, if any thing, it illustrated his delicacy, and so helped to raise him in her estimation, if that were possible. It struck her, however, that she might as well tempt him a little on the point; so, one evening, when, as usual, she had stolen out to meet him by the river's side, Esther, after expressing her tremors at the idea of being missed, and asked after by her father, added, "But our little uneasiness on that head, dear Tony, will soon be removed—I mean when you propose for me at home."

"Propose for you at home, dearest Esther!" he repeated, staring at her with great simplicity, and a disinterested observer might have added, something like quandary or stupidity. In truth, it was the first time the idea had presented itself to his mind. And here we again express ourselves unable to make out the peculiar mental economy of our hero. Such as we have found him, however, we give him to the world.

A quick flash from Esther's dark eyes met his strange stare; and she demanded, "Why do you repeat my words?"

"Repeat your words, Esther? Oh, ay; yes, to be sure— what a blockhead I am—! ha! ha! don't be angry with me, gra-machree"—here he slightly interrupted his speech by a little act—" but, as I over and over told you, my darling, looking straight into your beautiful face, always makes me forget what I am saying—ay, or doing either."

Esther constrainedly echoed his laugh; and, though nothing more distinct was said on the subject, all seemed well. On their way homewards, however, she thought Tony a shade graver, or more reflective than usual; and she lay down that night with the germ of something disagreeable in her mind.

The next evening Tony sent her a message, as usual, and they were again alone, in a suitable lover-suiting place. Esther came out, determined to watch him; and having made this resolution, she, doubtless, would have found in his words, looks, and manner, something she suspected him of, had he been as innocent as a babe. Truth must be told, however. Tony really was a changed, or at least a changing man? Why? He no more knew, at present, than he had known, on similar occasions, many a time before. Once only, during the evening, did he appear much-interested ; but the occasion for his alteration of demeanor was no comfort to Esther's heart.

"When my Cousin Mary comes to see me, dear Tony, we must, at once, make her a confidant," said Esther.

"Certainly, Esther. Does she come soon ?"

"To-morrow—some time of the day."

"Indeed ! and that *is* soon." His handsome eyes beamed brightly ; though, alas ! for poor Esther, they turned away, with a kind of a happy, speculative expression. I'm so glad— for your sake, I mean. Your cousin will be such company to you !"

"Thank you, Tony." Esther was quite put out ; she could make nothing of him, no more than ourselves.

"Is she older or younger than you, Esther ?" demanded Tony, still in a calculating way.

"About my own age."

"And like you? Any family resemblance ?"

"Not the least. I am not *very* tall—she *is* tall ; I am a brown girl ; she is a fair one—"

"With blue eyes, light hair, and a good complexion ?" interrupted Tony, vivaciously.

"Yes, as is usual with very fair women."

"*Very* fair, you say ?" again interrupted her waning, waning lover, bewitched with the novelty of the contrast between his present mistress and his future one.

"Yes, Tony Skelton, *very* fair ; as fair as heart can wish," answered Esther, now just beginning to apprehend.

"And only about nineteen, like yourself," cried Tony, not noticing Esther's expressive manner, in the anticipating joy of his simple heart ; "and a bounding, bouncing, charming girl, I'll warrant ; all smiles and laughter, and pleasant conversation ! Yes, I remember you hinted as much to me before, didn't you, Esther ?"

There is no use in continuing the scene between the lovers on this occasion. Tony arrived at home, to rave as much about Esther's cousin as he had done about Esther's self before her arrival at Upper Court. Esther locked herself up in her chamber to hate the merry-hearted Mary, whom she had loved, during their first acquaintance in Dublin, on her way from England to her father's house, and ever since, till this evening ; and, even towards her *beau-ideal* of a lover, and of a constant lover, Tony

Skelton, her heart began to change, and change badly. Un-amiable ingredients had naturally mixed themselves up with the whole of Esther's character ; and the course of her education and experience had not since worked them out of it. As a child, she was self-willed, almost daring in the attainment of whatever she had set her heart on, and resentful if thwarted in gaining her object. Nay, worse, she could brood over her disappointment, and unrelentingly nurse a spirit of retaliation towards its author. Judicious direction of her mind and feelings might, doubtless, have done much towards subduing, if not eradicating, these in-firmities during her growth from child into girl ; or the really good portions of her mind and heart, their generosity, and even romance, might have been cultivated and enlarged, so as to weigh down their dangerous tendencies. Such, we repeat, had not, however, been the case ; and now, at nineteen, she was, there-fore, a passive victim to the unamiable temptations of her nature ; at the impulse, too, of the greatest disappointment any woman can feel, and which Esther Neville felt to an intensity of which few women are capable. In fact, before the summer morning's sun danced dazzlingly through the window on her sleepless eyes, Esther had vowed a vengeance upon the uncon-scious Tony Skelton, for his buoyant spirits the previous even-ing ; nay, she had planned it, and only waited to receive full proof of his delinquency, with a fit opportunity, in order to carry it into execution.

And Tony did not keep her long waiting. He was in Mr. Neville's house when Mary O'Neil entered it, and scarce stirred from her side the whole evening. Esther had to suffer the scene of a laughing, witty, hilarious flirtation between her cousin and her quondam lover, while she sat neglected, looking out through the old bow-window of the sombre drawing-room. She did suffer it, however, silently, and, to all appearance, content-edly ; and, at length, she left them alone—to reconnoitre, how-ever, from an adjacent room ; at the door of which she had not stood a long while till her ears heard the words of perfidy from Tony's importunate lips, and then something else from them, with the aid of those of the laughing, almost scoffing Mary O'Neil, which sounded to Esther like a poisonous reptile's hiss.

And now she took her measures—her first ones, at least. She wrote to Mary's brother, a brave and cool, though fierce old campaigner, quartered with his regiment in a town near at hand. She sought her father, in his library, and conversed with him some time. Then she had to adapt her manner and looks to her purposes, before re-entering the drawing-room, where the new lovers still sat in the twilight.

" Does she laugh at him still ?" thought Esther, again eavesdropping at the door. " No, *now* her voice is gentle enough, and if she *does* continue to reject his quickly conceived, and as quickly told love, it is in maiden murmurs only. Good ! very good ! Mary O'Neil, he shall be mine yet—mine, though it were but to show him how I loathe him, when he *is* so !" And, so meditating, Esther tripped into the room, in seemingly high spirits, rallying the happy pair, and congratulating herself on having been the means of making them known to each other.

Mary laughed, and protested, and remonstrated, and asked, " How could such nonsense enter into her dear Esther's head ?" And Master Tony, what did he say or do ? Was there no appearance of disconcertion in his manner ? no consciousness of being, at the very least, a gay deceiver ? no awkwardness in the presence of the woman to whom, a few hours before, he had been swearing, in good round oaths (as became his rank and bearing in those good old times), adoration and fidelity ? Not a trace of any thing like all this ; and for a very sufficient reason —namely, because he did not feel it. His heart accused him of nothing at all. He stood quite self-acquitted to his own conscience, or rather he had never been at its bar for an instant. He was but following his nature, his vocation. In a word, the matter did not, could not, trouble his mind ; had never done so, and was very unlikely ever to do so. And hence, upon Esther's reappearance, he only joined in Mary O'Neil's laugh, and chuckled, and rubbed the palms of his hands together, and really and truly thought it all exceedingly pleasant and natural, and just as it ought to be.

About three evenings after, Tony and Mary O'Neil were seated in a very nice little place, out of doors. It was a miniature, a fairy valley, abruptly entered, at one point, very near to that where they had chosen to repose themselves after their walk, by a zigzag path down one of its sides—the side, too, opposite to where they sat. A little wailing brook—so little, that it fretted itself in wailing against the mere pebbles which obstructed the would-be perfectly even course of its insignificant existence —was at their feet ; their couch was one of the inland sweeps of its mossy, and daisied, and butter-cupped bank ; and the skylark was bravuring his last evening song for his wife, over their heads. Could there be a better boudoir for two lovers? *They* thought not.

" But can I believe you?" murmured Mary, as Tony's doomed head rested on her shoulder, "this time, your first time?"

"I vow and swear it, dearest, dearest darling, by the round world, and the blue sky over it!—by your two eyes!—and by ₐhis—and this--"

"Stop, stop!" whispered Mary, "there's some one looking at you."

Tony followed her glance with his own. On the top line of the sweeping ground opposite to them stood three figures. Esther Neville, leaning her right arm on her father's, and her left on that of a dragoon officer of about forty. "My brother Peter!" half shrieked Mary, starting up.

The new comers stood a moment observantly, during which Esther, turning her face alternately from one to another of her supporters, pointed expressively towards the lovers.

"What do they want here?" asked Tony, rising.

Esther, her father, and Captain O'Neil, descended the zigzag path to the brook, crossed the tiny stream by stepping-stones, and were soon with their friends.

"Hope you're well, Miss Mary O'Neil, since I saw you last," said the *militaire*. Mary could only run to him, and embrace him.

"Good-evening, Mr. Tony Skelton," began Esther.

"A kind good-evening, Esther," answered Tony; "though I thought we wished each other that before."

"I want to make you acquainted with Miss O'Neil's brother, Captain O'Neil," continued Esther.

"Thank you kindly," responded Tony.

"My service to you, sir," said the captain, bowing low, while the broad skirts of his braided coat stuck out at either side.

"And mine to you, captain," answered Tony, quite cheerfully.

"I may as well make you a little better known to one another, gentlemen," resumed Esther, haughtily taking her father's arm, while her bridled passion made her brown cheeks pallid, and her slight lips ashy colored. "This, Mr. Antony Skelton, is a brave and distinguished officer, who, as yet, cannot count a stain on the honor of one member of his family, male or female, and who is determined he never shall. And this, Captain O'Neil, is the young gentleman who has been trifling with the affections of two of your relations in the short space of a few weeks. The pro-

sumptuous beggar, who began by swearing himself *my admirer*,
and prevailed on me to conceal the dishonor from you, dearest
father ; and who, the very hour Mary O'Neil came to see me, repeated the same oaths to her (Mary shrieked out at these words);
and repeated them again and again, until at last she allowed him
the degree of intimacy we have witnessed from the top of that
height yonder."

" A peculiar kind of business, Mr. Antony Skelton," remarked
the grave and gruff captain.

" I protest—I declare, captain, I don't know, I can't see what
all this means," said Tony.

" Then we must only try and clear your eyesight, sir. *You*
wish to have nothing to say further in the matter, Cousin
Esther ?"

" Me !" repeated Esther, scoffingly, " I scorn the poor adventurer as I do the dust of the road I have come to find him for you."

" Very well," rejoined the captain, " you need be in no passion,
my dear ; I only asked you to declare your mind to his face, just
to give him a hint that, although my own sister is second in the
case, I should have seen you righted before her, if such was your
will, taking into account that *you* were first in the case. Very
well. And so, Mr. Antony, 'tis with Miss O'Neil's help you are
carrying on the war at present ?"

" Sir? what do you say, captain ?" asked Tony.

" That is, in plain words, you are very much devoted to my
sister."

" Devoted ! I adore her on the knees of my heart ! and have
told her as much a thousand times !" assented Tony, joyously.

" Very well, sir. You do my sister and me a great honor."

" Delighted to hear you say so !" cried Tony, pouncing on his
hand and shaking it.

" Very well, Mr. Antony. All very well, so far ; and, of
course, you agree that, particularly after your meeting here this
evening, which any one might have witnessed before your friends
came up, the sooner such matters are brought to an end, the better for all parties concerned."

" I—I must really say," stammered Tony, " that I should be
very, very sorry to bring things to an end so soon between me and
my darling Mary"—his heart nearly failed him at the thought
of *giving her up* so exceedingly soon—" but if you afford me a
little more time, and let me look about me a little, perhaps I may
soon be able to oblige you."

"I can spare very little time, sir," replied the captain, misconceiving him, yet, even on his own understanding, looking dangerous. "My leave of absence extends but to three days."

"Well, captain, well, even in three days a good many things may happen."

"But the business ought to be completed, sir, before I go back to my regiment."

"Well, and perhaps it may—who knows?" assented Tony cheerfully, and with self-reliance.

"Come, come, sir—I don't understand you at all, nor your foolish manner either. In one word, Mr. Antony Skelton, are you prepared to marry Miss O'Neil this evening, under Mr. Neville's roof."

"Marry!" ejaculated Tony, in mortal surprise. But he was soon made more familiar with the new-formed idea, on having the captain's alternative suggested to him. Not, indeed, that he was as much a coward as he was a half-witted country gentleman. Had he disliked Mary, it is probable he would have stood and fired his four or five shots for a chance of escaping her; but, on the contrary, his passion for her still remained as strong as any he had ever felt for any other woman, chiefly, perhaps, because as yet she had not quite fully avowed her adoration of himself, and he wanted that habitual gratification, at any risk. In short, with the nature or extent of his new engagement only very vaguely established in his mind, and while poor Mary, notwithstanding a growing preference, objected on the score of Tony's perfidy to her cousin, as well as on account of the rapidity of the proceeding, married they were that evening, in Mr. Neville's house—her brother emphatically bullying her into compliance by threats of a foreign convent. It should before now have been said that Mary O'Neil was an orphan, her father and mother both dead, and therefore that she stood greatly in awe of a brother so much her elder.

"I wish you joy, Mary Skelton," whispered Esther, directly the marriage ceremony had been performed. Mary half started at the emphasis with which her cousin spoke; it seemed to hide a dangerous meaning. Then she began to wonder at Esther's zeal in so precipitately providing her with a husband, in the person of the very man whom, but a few days before, she had permitted to pay attentions to herself. And the reader's surprise may also be aroused on this point, recollecting Esther's mental resolve, while meanly eavesdropping at the drawing-room door

Marrying Tony to another woman seemed, indeed, a strange step towards making him her own property. But we shall hear her explain the crooked and unique workings of her imperfected mind and unrefined heart.

How Tony was to support a wife, now that he had got one, together with some other little human beings who might follow the event, to say nothing of himself, dogs, horses, cocks, ferrets, and two or three servants, at least, to look after his whole menage; this was a question which occupied his brother-in-law the captain, his host, Mr. Neville, and (in a very slight degree) himself, to a late hour the night of his marriage.

"As for me," said Tony, laughing gayly, "everybody knows that since my last Dublin trip, I have been living on Divine Providence, like my friends the archbishops."

"Your brother may assist you," observed Mr. Neville.

Roger has not a sod that isn't mortgaged twice over," answered Tony; "and I believe I helped him the first time, my own self," he added, again laughing—not a false, forced laugh, but a sincere, hearty one.

"I live on my pay alone," said Captain O'Neil, "having been a little improvident, like yourself, brother Tony, in my younger days, with the wreck of the paternal property which my dear father's tastes, as a country gentleman, properly supporting the family consequence, left me to take care of. Your wife's little fortune remains untouched, however; and with it, suppose we purchase and stock a snug farm for you? Care and prudence might soon make you and Mary rich, and cut out something for the little ones; and 'tis no disgrace to a gentleman to farm his own lands."

"Done!" cried Tony, striking the table with his knuckles. "Disgrace! not a bit; 'tis the most honorable occupation—and that's the worst can be said of it. And as to care and prudence between my darling Mary and me, now that we are to be turned out on our own accounts; never fear, captain; never fear, Mr. Neville. So good-night—and here's our own noble healths. Good-night—hurra!" And, bounding like a stag over the backs of chairs which stood in his way, Tony sallied forth.

Two days after, the new married couple, accompanied by the captain, left Mr. Neville's house to take possession of their own. Esther Neville did not appear to wish them good-by; her father said she was indisposed. Nor had she appeared to them since the moment after their marriage, when she wished Mary joy in rather a remarkable manner. And her father all along gave the same account of her absence ; but it was not the true one. Esther did not stay in the house ten minutes after leaving the drawing-room that evening. Ordering her carriage, she departed in it for the abode of a lady, a relation, in the neighborhood ; and home she did not return till Tony Skelton and his wife had quitted her father's house.

Let us skip over about a year and a half, and visit Farmer Tony in his own house, just to see what "care and prudence" had done for him in the mean time. He and Mary are sitting to a good turf fire, facing each other; and that's one feature of comfort, certainly. Tony has a huge jug of strong beer before him—and that's another. But he is ill dressed, and so is poor Mary; and he looks five years older than when we last saw him, and not so handsome, to say nothing of respectable ; and she looks delicate, and worn, and drooping ; in fact, she is but recovering from her confinement. Glance around the room. Fowling-pieces, fishing-rods, nets, and other weapons and implements of field-sport, irregularly placed over the chimney, hint that Tony is yet able, or recently has been, to follow some of his old pastimes ; nay, a fox-hound rolled up before the fire, and a fresh brush stuck into the muzzle of a fowling-piece, proclaim that, if his hunter is not yet in the stable, he very lately might have been found there. But what shall we say of the torn, and worn, and crumpled carpet on the floor ? and of the rickety, almost shivered deal table before him ; and of the one mean, thin, gawky tallow candle which flickers on it ? and of the broken chairs, and the damp white mould which, in many places, covers the paper on the walls of Tony's parlor ?

A few words of the conversation between him and his wife may assist us to answer—"Never mind, Mary duck ; keep never minding, and all will go right in the long run. If you would just stop talking to me, in that way, about this woman and that woman, and this girl and that girl, you would leave me more heart to look about me, and keep things together."

"Very well, dear Tony, very well ; only I'm told you had a gay time of it while I was up stairs, the last three weeks. But no matter. What we are now to do for common food, or even to keep the old leaky house over our heads—that's the question."

"Well, and so it is, darling," assented Tony.

"You take it very quietly, Tony dear."

"And to be sure I do, Mary pet."

"But what do you mean to do ? There is not a shilling left

of the thirteen hundred spared out of my little fortune, after purchasing the farm, to help us on—is there ?"

" Not a stiver, my love."

" And our stock is driven almost to the last cow, for debts incurred in the mean time ?"

" You speak the blessed truth, duck."

" And we owe more than what they have sold for."

" Indeed and we do, sure enough."

" And no one will give us a loaf on credit any longer."

" So they say, darling."

"Then, where are we to get the loaf ?"

" Buy it—out of that, my dear :" and, to Mary's astonishment,
Tony emptied a goodly sized leathern bag of guineas on the
table.

" In the name of goodness, Tony, how have you come by
that ?"

" Esther Neville's attorney, gave it to me."

" Esther Neville's attorney," repeated Mary, in consternation.

" Yes, love. You know, since the old man's death, she has all
his great riches at her own disposal."

" Yes. Well, she lends it to you ?"

" No such thing ; but, as I was talking of mortgaging our
little purchase, she heard of it, and so sent the attorney to me,
and the business was soon settled."

" Soon, indeed," replied Mary. Then she added to herself :
" Well might you wish me joy, Esther ;" and dismal, though vague,
forebodings pressed on Mary's mind.

" How soon must you repay Esther Neville, Tony ?" she resumed, after a pause, during which her tranquil husband was
whistling a hunting air, and playing with the heap of gold on the
table.

" Esther offered me my own time, darling ; so, to make sure, I
named this day twelve months ; and that's what the little attorney
called a special deed of agreement between us, that the land and
house are Esther's, if we are not quite punctual. But little fear
of that : ' care and prudence' will enable us to meet the debt in
six months, not to talk of twelve."

A comely serving wench here bustled into the parlor, much
agitated. " Misther Antony," she cried, " there's Kitty Larissy,
the smith's daughter, from the other side o' the river, is afther
sendin' in a little brat of a *gorsoon*, to ax you to step out to spake
to her. I wondher what makes her ashamed or afeard to come up

to our door her own self, instid o' snakin' about the house in that way."

"Divvle's in the little fool, what can she want of me?" demanded Tony, bundling out of the room with a very bad grace.

"You're the best judge o' that, yourself, sir," answered the serving wench, stamping after him in evident dudgeon—and dudgeon of that peculiar kind which might have had its source in outraged though tender feelings.

"Twelve months are soon passed over." Again we approach Tony's house upon the day appointed for the repayment of Esther's loan to him.

Something unusual has occurred within. The road, as we come near, is covered with country people ; groups of them also recline on shelving ground over it ; all are grave, and converse in whispers. Looking to the house, we see its window-shutters closed. Entering its little courtyard, Sir Roger Skelton's old lumbering carriage appears at the door ; behind it, those of some of the neighboring gentry : Sir Roger's servants wear long white hatbands and scarfs. At either side of the door stand two mutes in black cloaks, holding long black poles in their hands, surmounted by folds of white linen. Death is in the house. The country people have flocked in to attend the funeral—a duty considered almost sacred among them—and to vie with each other in bearing the coffin on their shoulders to the churchyard. Now they know they have not long to wait ; for the two chairs have just been placed before the door to receive the coffin for a few moments, while the clergyman prays over it before it is lifted up and borne to its destination.

The pause, though short, is very solemn. The country people crowd up to the house, scarce uttering a breath. Hush ! that wild low wailing of women within the house announces the closing of the coffin-lid. The corpse is brought out. Two clergymen, an old and a young man, issue through the door bareheaded, and murmuring prayers ; white scarfs across their shoulders, and white flowing bands on their hats. Then, carried upon men's arms comes the coffin—poor Tony Skelton and his brother following it as chief mourners, their eyes reddened and cast down, their lower features hidden in the collars of their black cloaks. Other mourners, friends and neighbors, also appear in black

cloaks, and the procession is ended by women in close white
mantles, with hoods gathered round their faces, whose wild
lament now swells higher and higher on the ear, and is answered,
suddenly, by the ejaculations and cries of the hitherto hushed
crowd before the house. The coffin rests awhile upon the chairs ;
every head is uncovered, and every knee bent, while the clergymen pray over it. Then four strong men place it on their shoul
ders ; the clergymen still precede it ; the widower and his brothe.
still follow it ; Sir Roger's carriage and servants come after
then the friends and their carriages ; then the women in white,—
and all pass through the country people, abroad, who form ir
regularly in their train, to the amount of perhaps a thousand
souls, men, women, and children. And in this order the procession moves on, by the bank of a shining placid river and through
the windings and inequalities of a road running between sweeping hills at either hand ; the continued wail of the women echoing from height to height, and along the surface of the water.

It was late on a December day when the funeral left the house.
But the churchyard could soon be gained ; it was not a quarter
of a mile distant. Before arriving at it, however, the weather
suddenly changed, as if to try the sincerity of the multitude of
voluntary mourners. Hail, rain, sleet, and wind burst and blus-
tered around them ;—no creature of the assembly turned back.
The coffin was carried to Sir Roger's family vault, the mouth of
which, in the middle of the uninclosed churchyard, was, save
when a fresh tenant approached it, always covered over by a
little oblong building of brick and mortar, surmounted by a
marble slab ; then the slab was removed, and one side of the
oblong broken, to afford free passage for the descent of the
corpse, down a few narrow stone steps. These circumstances it
is advisable to mention. The deluges of rain and sleet, and the
roaring of the wind, increased rather than diminished at the
moment, when, in the somewhat premature gloom of the hour,
the coffin was being conveyed down the steps into the tomb.
There was bustle, confusion, anxiety, and uncertainty. The
steps were slippery from the sleet ; the bearers of the sad burden
missed their footing ; they and it were precipitated into the
depths of the vault, and the result of the accident soon appeared
to be some dislocation of their own limbs, and giving away o.
the screws of the coffin-lid. For the men, help was at hand, for
the other mishap, persons were to be sought after ; the evening
grew darker and blacker : the storm augmented its rage. By

the advice of all friends present, Tony Skelton decided to return home, and wait till morning to have the coffin screwed down again, and the mouth of the vault rebuilt.

We now rapidly approach the close of our history. Sir Roger and the elder of the clergymen accompanied Tony to his house, to remain for the night, and console him in his bereft situation. They found the doors closed ; and this the servants, who had all gone with the funeral, pronounced strange, inasmuch as they had been left open, and, indeed, the house left empty, after the departure of the body for the the churchyard. Tony knocked ; the door was open by Esther Neville's attorney. The widower started and stared. The attorney drew him aside. "Miss Neville, herself, sir," he said, "is in the parlor, and wishes to speak to you alone—quite alone. I'm not sure if— What she exactly means to do I cannot guess. But she insists on seeing you without a witness."

Tony looked still more confounded for a moment ; but a happy thought seemed to relieve him a little. He whispered to his brother and the clergyman what was going on, and stepped into the parlor.

Esther Neville was seated at the fire in the riding dress of the day. A solitary candle scarce gave light to the apartment. To Tony's great comfort she smiled when he appeared, and held out her hand to him—saying—I am glad to see you *in my house*, Tony Skelton."

"In *your* house, Esther ?"

"Don't you remember what day of the month this is ?"

"Yes," muttered Tony ; "and now I guess what you mean, Esther Neville."

"Perhaps you do not. Can you redeem your land and house ?"

"No, not if one gold guinea could redeem them for me."

"Then they *are* mine, you know ; and, as the weather is bad, . intend sleeping here to-night, with some servants, and my attorney. They will contrive a bed for *you*, at Upper Court, I suppose ; or perhaps your friend the clergyman may oblige you."

"Thank you, Esther. I shall go and see."

"Stop a moment, dear Tony." He started and turned round ; she was again smiling at him. "Sit down, and let us have a little chat, something like old times." He did as he was bid ; she drew her chair closer to him.

"Ah, those old times, Tony! when you vowed and swore you loved me dearly !"

"And I did, Esther!" gasped Tony, his happy suspicion before entering the parlor now almost growing into a reality. "I did! as truly as ever man loved woman!"

"'Twas for a short time, however. You soon gave me up for another."

"Ah, dear Esther, a foolish frolic. I did not mean to give you up; and you were to blame, yourself, for separating us, really."

"And perhaps I was, dear Tony. But that can't be helped now, you know. Let us go on, instead of looking back. Whatever attracted you to me a few years ago, is still in me. I am still a very young woman, not yet two-and-twenty."

"To be sure you are, my dear Esther! and improved, if possible, every way. More worthy of true love than ever!"

Did Tony mean and feel what he said? He did. Esther again was a contrast to all other women he had adored since their angry parting. With the tomb unclosed over Mary O'Neil—with her coffin unscrewed—he *did* mean and feel what he said.

They continued their conversation together for more than an hour. Esther's revenge over the paltry mind and heart of Tony Skelton lay within her grasp. She sent him to call in his brother, the clergyman, and the attorney. She invited them to be seated, and spoke as follows—"Mr. Attorney—whatever I say, do not interrupt me. You have assured me there are no means of staying your proceeding against Mr. Tony Skelton, and that his house and lands must pass out of his possession, and he once more become a pauper. But I have found means. I do not scruple to say, gentlemen all, that he and I were once sincerely attached to each other, and that an old love is now renewed, as truly as ever. That being the case, there can be nothing very extraordinary in our becoming man and wife, and, for his sake, as soon as possible. Should we delay a single day—a single evening and night, I mean—*I* must become the possessor of his only earthly property; and, sudden—and, perhaps, something else—as the resolution may appear, I have consented to marry him, this instant, to save him from the humiliation of offering himself to me as a mere beggar."

Tony winced at the tone of her address. It was a little unlike (though he could not exactly say how or where) her honeyed words to him a few moments before. And so was the expression of her face, though he could not define that either.

Esther paused a moment, being interrupted by loud shouts and cries, seemingly of deadly terror, which passed by the house. They subsided, and she continued :

"Yes, gentlemen, there he stands, Tony Skelton, my old lover; Tony Skelton, who partly out of a return of pure, disinterested affection for me, partly from a very natural desire of keeping a roof over his head, presses me"—there, again, thought Tony, why, 'twas *she* pressed *me* !—" to marry him this instant—in this house—the house of death—death's taint and almost smell in it—and while the late wife of his bosom is scarce yet cold in the grave ! But these facts should only increase my love und gratitude, since they show how great is the ardor of his passion. Here I stand, then, dear Tony. When I *am* your wife, you and your friends shall hear a few more of my opinions about you."

They stood hand in hand before the clergyman ; every one but Esther, even Tony, looking stunned and confused. She afterwards declared her plan of revenge : to have married him, in order to prove to the world the base folly and littleness of his nature, which, under the circumstances she had herself enumerated, could permit him to accept any woman's hand, either for whim, or self-interest, or both ; then she would have spurned him to her feet, drawn his own picture to his face, and cast him off forever. But the sweet cup of revenge was snatched from her lips, even while they touched it.

All were suddenly startled by a low, hoarse moaning at one of the windows, of which the shutters fastened inside. They listened. Feeble fingers seemed scratching at the glass ; then the weak, inarticulate voice passed round to the back of the house, accompanied by a trailing noise. A moment after, shrieks and howls of utter terror arose in the kitchen, and Tim Ryan, Tony's man-of-all-work, clasped round the waist by a stout serving wench before mentioned, broke into the parlor, as mad for the time as any two poor creatures in Bedlam.

" *Thonomonduoul !*" began Tim, and *he* was only able to speak, or rather stutter, " God forgive us for cursin' !—bud— here it's afther us, hot-fut !"

His master and friends rapidly questioned him ; he took little notice.

" And the duoul's in me, for a born fool, to run and open the back-door, to let it in ! only that *you* heard it, Winny, and was afeard, and made me go out to see. Murther ! don't ye all hear it !" The trailing noise remarked outside the house was

now more distinct, coming along the passage from the kitchen
"Murther! and do you mane to stay here! Let me go, Winny ; and help a hand to pull open this windee!" He began to
unfasten the shutters. "Oh, your reverence, won't you thry an'
lay it, sir! Let me go, Winny, I tell you!"

But Winny did not let him go ; and they emerged together
through the now fully open window.

Almost at the same moment, Mary Skelton, clad in her grave-
clothes, rent and soiled, and with her hands and feet bleeding,
dragged herself on her knees to the threshold of the parlor door ;
and there, after half-raising herself to give one corpse-like look
at the group within, fainted, and fell across it.

Our story is told. Esther Neville had only half her revenge ;
and in some time, when recovered from the terrors of that
night, she tried to make amends for having ever wished to wreak
any. She shared her fortune with Mary and Tony, who lived
together a tolerably happy couple, during more than twenty
years after—thanks to a false step and bad screws—the father
and mother of sons and daughters—all as much alive all over
their little bodies, as if their mamma had never been waked and
buried beforehand—all over their little bodies, except in their
lower extremities—a deficiency transmitted to them by Mary
Skelton, who, in that respect, never was able wholly to rewarm
herself out of the chill of the tomb, and who thus became the
founder of " THE FAMILY OF THE COLD FEET."

THE
HAREHOUND AND THE WITCH.

HAREHOUND AND THE WITCH.

Your genuine witches, who

——" Seemed not creatures of the earth,
And still were on it ;"

withered old women, who united in their persons the decrepitude
of age with the most marvellous powers of locomotion ; half
spirits, half mortals ; who seemed to live solely for the purpose of
paying back to the whole human race the hatred lavished by men,
women, and children on themselves : who could blight the farmer's
hope of plenty ; cheat his cows of their milk, and his wife of her
butter ; cause the clouds to gather, and the tempest to scourge
the earth ; and yet, creatures of contrarities ! Who, possessed
of all this awful power, could not, or would not, redeem themselves from rags, hunger, and misery ; they, your genuine witches,
as we have already called them, exist not, alas ! at present, in our
green island. Extinct, though not forgotten, is their race, like
that of our noble moose-deer, our formidable wolf, and our as formidable wolf-dog. Degenerate emulators of them, indeed, we
still boast—individual's who dip into futurity by the aid of card-
cutting or cup-tossing, or who find out stolen property, or vent
charms against the peevish malice of the little sprites of the
moonbeam. But compared with their renowned predecessors,
these timid assertors of supernatural endowments may be said to
disgrace their calling. And even they are sinking in repute, as
well as diminishing in numbers.

But we would attempt to preserve in the following pages some
fit idea of the importance of a true Irish witch of the good olden
time. We are aware that the chief event which must wind up
our story, the sudden appearance, namely, of a lost heir (we

have the courage to speak it out so soon), is a threadbare one. It cannot be helped, however : it, at least, is fact, to our own knowledge, although we are not quite as fully accountable for the respectable traditions that surround it with such pleasing wonders as we are about to relate, and which form the real interest of our narration.

On the western coast of Ireland is a certain dangerous bay into it the broad Atlantic rolls his vast waters. Two leagues in land from it mouth, high black cliffs frown over it at both sides, of which the bases are hollowed into caverns. And when the winds blow angrily—and any wind can effectually visit the open and exposed estuary—tremendous and terrific is the roar, the dash, and the foam, which deafen the ears, and distract the eyes of a spectator. That hapless vessel which, in a storm, cannot avoid an entrance into this merciless turmoil of mad waters had sealed its doom.

Formerly, a great number of ships, from different countries, used to be dashed to splinters against the iron-bound coast. A few people conjecture that the diminution of such terrible accidents. in the present day, is partially owing to some improvement in seamanship, or else to the timely warning now given to distant mariners by lights erected at the mouth of the bay. But other persons, and by far the greater number, in the neighborhood, think that the comparative paucity of wrecks may more naturally, and satisfactorily, be accounted for in another way. In fact, there does not now reside, as formerly there did, in an almost unapproachable cavern, high up on the face of one of the black cliffs, " a real witch, of the right sort."

Not that her witchship always dwelt in her cave ; no, her visits to it were but occasional. Nor did it ever become necessary for her to proclaim her presence on the coast by exhibiting her person—the results of her close neighborhood sufficiently " prated of her whereabouts." Farmers' wives toiled in vain at their churns. When no butter would come, self-evident it was that the witch was at that moment in her cavern, seated on her heels before a vessel of water, from which, by drawing a dead man's hand through it, she appropriated the produce of other people's honest labor Cows suddenly went back in their milk ; then it was known that by passing a wheaten straw between her finger and thumb, the witch amply filled her can, while the owner of the animal uselessly wrought at its udder. Cattle swelled and died ; once again every one knew who was in the cave under the cliff. And if none of those events, or similar ones, proved her disagreeable proximity, the direful storms and the frightful wrecks in the bay abundantly warranted it. Often, amid the bellowing of the tempest she had raised, swelled her shrieking voice. And, while the despairing creatures in the doomed vessel topped each short, high, foamed billow, which nearer and nearer dashed them on to their fate, the watchers on the cliff's brow have heard her devilish laugh, until at last it broke into frenzied loudness, as the ship burst, like a glass bubble, against the sharp rocks under her dwelling-hole.

No one could tell from whence she came, or, for a time no longer visible on the coast, whither she went. Occasionally she was observed in conference with certain notorious smugglers ; and the men appeared, it was well known, to petition and bribe her for a fair wind with which to enter the bay, and for a foul one to keep their pursuers out of it ; as was fully proved by the fact that invariably their light lugger got in and was safely moored in some little creek against danger of coming storm, while, the moment the revenue-cutter appeared in the offing, out burst the wildest winds from the witch's cavern, up swelled the sea and the bay in mountain billows, and his majesty's vessel was sure to be wrecked during the night.

Like all of her sisterhood of that famous period, she could change herself at pleasure into various shapes. We give a serious proof of her talent in this respect.

A few miles from the coast which she so despotically ruled, resided a considerable landed proprietor. A great hunter of hares and foxes was he. His wife had just blessed him with an heir to his estate, and the boy was their only child. Of this event the good squire was not a little proud ; for, in case of his not leaving a male issue, his property was to pass away to a distant, obscure, and neglected relation, whom its immediate possessor neither loved nor liked ; for the heir-presumptive was mean in his habits and associations, uneducated, and graceless ; and it would be a sad thing to know that the fine old family acres were to go into such hands.

Shortly after his wife's confinement, and while she and her baby were "doing well," the squire, to dissipate the recent anxiety he had suffered, sallied forth for a hunting. His pack of harriers were his attendants on this occasion, for the hare was the object of the day's sport.

And, surely, never had such a hare been followed by dogs, or "sohoed" by mortal lips, as the hare he and his friends and pack started and hunted upon that memorable day. From breakfast to dinner-time a sweeping and erratic chase did she lead them all; the dogs at full stretch, and the horses at top speed. Various accidents happened to the sportsmen; one maimed his steed, another fractured his collar-bone, some swam| ed in bogs, and none, except our good squire and his huntsmat escaped without injury or disaster. But, from starting to pull ing up, they gallantly kept at the dog's tails.

After an "unprecedented run," the hare suddenly scudded towards the cliffs of the bay, immediately over the witch's cavern. The good harriers pursued, and the eager squire did not stay behind them, his huntsman closely following. The hare gained the verge of the cliff. Sheela, the prime bitch of the pack, just had time to close her, make a chop at her, and take a mouthful of flesh from her haunch before she leaped down the face of almost a precipice. Dogs and horsemen were at fault; none dared follow her.

In some time nearly all the other discomfited members of the hunt came up, soiled, wounded, jaded. They heard of the termination of the chase, and all wondered at the extraordinary freaks of the little animal, which had so distressed and baffled the best harriers and the best hunters in the county, taking men and horses together.

"By ——!" suddenly exclaimed the huntsman, a young fellow of known hardihood of character, swearing a great oath; "I'll tell yez how it is! ye are afther huntin' the witch o' the cave sthraight undher us! It isn't the first time that creatures like her have made a laugh, in this way, of nearly as good men as we are."

Most of his auditors ridiculed the speaker; one or two, however, looked grave, perhaps in patronage to his assertions, perhaps because the pains and aches resulting from their many falls during the day lengthened their faces, darkened their brows, and puckered their lips. The huntsman offered, if any one would accompany him on the dangerous enterprise, to scale down the cliff, penetrate the witch's cavern, and prove his saying. One did volunteer to be his companion—a humble friend of his own —one among the crowd of gaping peasants assembled round the gentlemen hunters.

The adventurers succeeded in reaching and entering the awful cave. Upon their return over the edge of the cliff they reported that they had found the witch at home, stretched panting and exhausted upon some straw in a dark corner of the cave ; that they had dragged her, much against her will (indeed her screams certainly had reached the squire and his friends above), to the light at its opening ; had, with main force, examined her person, and, sure enough, had found a deficiency of flesh in her haunch, with plainly the marks of Sheela's teeth in and about the wound, rom which the blood freely streamed. To be sure, the better nformed hearers of this story, or at least a majority of them, till laughed at it. But whatever they might think, those to whom the talents and capabilities of witches were better known, firmly believed that the squire and his companions had hunted all that day a hare which was no hare after all, and that the courageous little Sheela had tasted flesh of a forbidden kind.

Happy had it been for the squire and his pet bitch, had they proved less eager after their sport. For Sheela died in great agonies upon the very night of that day, and her master was doomed to a speedy punishment for his own audacity.

Nothing daunted at the idea of whom he had been hunting, he took the field again a few days after ; and now, no question could be raised as to the nature of the game he, a second time, started and pursued. Puss did not, indeed, immediately make for the sea ; but this was only a ruse to affect her own malignant purposes. She wanted to get her enemy alone at the edge of the cliff. For this purpose, her speed and her manners quite outdid those of a former day ; so much so, that, in a few hours, even the dare-neck and dare-devil huntsman was thrown out, and returned with a lamed horse and sprained ankle to the gentleman who had suffered before him, leaving the squire alone, close upon the dogs.

For a considerable time, he and his master's friends awaited the reappearance of the persevering Nimrod. Finally they repaired to the cliff, which the huntsman had left him speedily approaching. There they found his horse without a rider ; himself they never again beheld. The unbelievers in witchcraft immediately surmised that his high-blooded hunter had borne him, against his will, to the edge of the cliff ; had there sudden- y started back ; and that, by the quick and violent action, the unhappy gentleman had been thrown forward out of his saddle, and precipitated from rock to rock, hundreds of feet downwards

A few who were able for the effort, cautiously descended towards the sea. On their way, they discovered their friend's hunting-cap on the sharp pinnacle of a rock ; its iron head-piece was stove in ; and it became evident that, after having been loosed from its wearer, by the force of the concussion which fractured it, the squire's body had tumbled still further downwards. They reached the sea's level. His remains were not visible ; they must have fallen into the sea, and been floated away by its tide. The witch of the cavern disappeared with her victim,—her victims, we should say ; for her vengeance on the squire was not limited to his own destruction. At the story of his shocking death, hastily and injudiciously communicated, his wife—yet enfeebled by her recent confinement—sickened, and in a few days died. Nay, nearly within the hour of her departure from this world, her only child, the heir to her husband's estate, disappeared, no one could tell whither, or by what means. Strange enough to say, however, part of the baby's dress was found on the identical pinnacle of rock where his father's hunting cap had been met with ; and, in the minds of the educated and wealthy of the neighborhood, this circumstance started doubts of fair dealing towards father and child. Suspicion, however, could fasten itself upon no object ; inquiry and investigation did not lead to any solution of the mystery. It need not be added that, by far the greater number of the population of the district smiled at the useless efforts to establish a case of human—that is, ordinarily human—agency ; or that they went on tranquilly believing that the squire and his family, not forgetting his harrier, had been punished for the mouthful snatched by poor Sheela from the haunch of a certain person.

———

Twenty years after the time of the tragedy we have detailed ; our story is resumed. The once indigent and despised relation, of whom mention has before been made, sits at his breakfast-table, in the old family house. He is in his forty-fifth year. Like other gentlemen of his day, he carries in his hair the contents oi a large pomatum pot ; four tiers of curls rise over his ears; on the top of his head is a huge *toupée*, and a great *queue* lolls, like an ox's tongue, between his broad shoulders. On his loose, wide-slieved, long-skirted, frock-like coat, is a profusion of gold embroidery; a lace cravat coils round his throat; ruffles flaunt over his knuckles; his gaudy waistcoat reaches only to his knees; satin are his breeches, silken his hose; and ponderous square silver buckles are in his shoes. So much for the outside of the jocular Squire Hogan. As to his interior pretensions, and indeed some of his external ones, too, the least said the soonest mended. He had never been able to raise himself above the homeliness of his youth; but though we cannot present the reader, in his person, the model of the true Irish gentlemen of his day, we do introduce him in the character of—to repeat what every one said of him—"as worthy a soul as ever broke the world's bread."

Squire Hogan, upon the morning when we meet him, paid earnest attention to his breakfast. Cold roast beef often filled his plate, and as often rapidly disappeared. Something seemed to gratify his mental palate as well as his corporeal one. A gleeish, self-contented smile played over his round, ruddy face; his small blue eyes glittered, and, to the accompaniment of a short liquorish laugh, his lips occasionally were drawn up at the corners, as he glanced at his daughter—a good-natured, good-tempered, sensible, and beautiful girl of nineteen—who sat opposite to him, sipping her coffee and picking her muffins. And, whenever their eyes met, well did Catherine know that the chuck·ling of her father had reference to some little triumph which, as he believed, he had cleverly and cunningly achieved over herself. At length the good squire relaxed in his meal; emptied the silver tankard of October which lay at his hand; leaned back in his chair, and laughingly said, "By Jove, Kate, my girl, I nicked you there!"

"Indeed, papa, you played me a roguish turn," assented Kate, convinced, from experience, that it was pleasant to her parent to have the talent of his practical jokes fully admitted.

"Where did I tell you we were driving to, out of Dublin town, eh?"

"You told me, sir, with as serious a face as you could make, that we were only going to visit a friend, a few miles out of Dublin."

"Ho, ho! Good, by Cork! Choice! a capital hoax, as I'm a living sinner! and I told you this confounded lie, with such a serious face, you say?"

"With such a mock-serious face, I meant to say, papa."

"Right, Kate! you are right beyond yea and nay: a mock-

serious face. Yes, and there lay the best of it. If I had not
been able to keep myself from laughing, you might have suspected
something. But I *was* able, as you yourself saw, and as you
now don't deny. Though, by Jove, Kate, it was enough to make
a dead man shout out, seeing you sitting opposite to me, and
believing every word I told you !"

"You kept up the farce cleverly, I must, and do admit it
sir."

"Didn't I, Kate, didn't I ?" And here we are, this morning,
eighty miles from Dublin, in our own house, and taxing no man's
hospitality. But, devil's in it ! there's no fun in playing a good
trick on you, Kate."

"Why so, dear papa ? am I not as easily blinded as your
heart could wish ?"

"To be sure you are ! What else could you be? I never
met man, woman, nor child, that I could not puzzle. That's not
the thing at all. No ; but succeed as I may with you, 'tis impossible to make you a little cross. Why, if I had a lass of
spirit to deal with, there would be no end to her tears, and her
pouts, and her petitions, the moment she found that I was
whisking her away from her balls, and her drums, and her beaux,
and all the other dear delights of Dublin."

"I hope that my merry papa does not really wish to have me
peevish and short-tempered, even for a greater provocation ?"

"Kiss me, Kate ; I believe not. And yet I don't know,
either, by Cork ! There would be fun in tormenting you a bit,
in a harmless way. But, Kate, can you give a guess why I ran
away with you in such a devil of a hurry ?"

"Let me see, papa. I remember you telling me of some original matches you had on hands, here, before you set out for Dublin. Perhaps you have engaged the two cripples to run a race
on their crutches ?"

"No ; that's put off—ho, ho !"

"Or the two old women to hop against time, carrying weight
for age ?"

"Ho, ho ! wrong again !"

"Probably you have succeeded in making the two school-
masters promise to fight out their battle of the squares and
angles with their respective birches ; their scholars standing by
to see fair play ?"

"Ho, ho, ho ! no ; though that's a matter not to be let slip
out of reach neither."

"Then all my guesses are out, papa."

"I'll help you, then. Tell me, you little baggage, what is it on earth you most wish for ?'"

"Indeed, my dear papa, I have no particular wish to gratify at the present moment."

"Get out! get out, for a young hypocrite! Kate, wouldn' something like a husband be agreeable to you ?'"

The girl blushed the color of a certain young gentleman' coat, and drooped her head. Of that certain young gentleman, however, her worthy father knew nothing ; at least, in connection with the present topic.

"Oh, ho! I thought I saw how the land lay."

"Indeed, my dear papa—"

"Say nothing more about it. Leave it all to me, lass. I'll get him for you. None of your half-dead-and-alive fellows, that you could knock down with a tap of your fan. No, he shall be an able, rattling, rollicking chap, able to take your part by land or sea. Did your mother ever tell you how I came by her, my girl ?'"

Kate answered in the negative.

"I'll tell you, then, as true as if she were alive to hear me. Though as poor as a church mouse at that time, I was a hearty young shaver ;* ay, as hearty, though not so matured, as I am this day, now that I am squire of the town-land, and justice of the peace, to boot. By the way, I wish they'd make the parish clerk a justice of the peace in my stead—I hate to be trying to look as grave as a mustard-pot, and as solemn as a wig-block! Well, I was at a Christmas raffle, Kate, and your mother's father was there too ; as comical an old boy as you'd wish to know! I had a great regard for him, by Cork! and so, away he and I raffled, and he lost to me every throw, until at last I didn't leave him a stiver. 'All I've won from you, and my watch to boot, against your daughter Nelly ?' cries I, of a sudden. 'Done!' cries he ; and we threw again ; and he lost, and I won again. And that's the way I got your mother, Kate. Now, do you guess any thing else I'm going to say about yourself, Kate ?'"

"O, papa, I hope—"

"I know you do hope. Yes, Kate, I *am* going to provide for you in something like the same way—"

* One who begins to use a razor.

"Now, good heavens, papa—"

"Don't speak a word more till you hear me out. At the last club-dinner in Dublin, Ned O'Brien calls me aside with a face as long as my own when I'm on the bench ; and after a long-winded beginning, he prays my interest with you, Kate. 'To be sure, man,' says I, 'you must have it.' Then, up sneaks George Dempsey, and his business was the same. 'By Cork, I'll court her in style for you, my boy,' was my word to George. Then Mick Driscoll takes a turn at me, and begs of me, for the Lord's sake, to listen to him ; and I was obliged to listen to him all about his title-deeds and his pedigree ; and he too craved my countenance, with the prettiest girl, and (what he *didn't* call you) the richest heiress in the province. 'By Jove I I'll do my best for you, Mick,' says I ; and Mick nearly pulled the arm out o' my body, shaking my hand. But I'm not done yet. Harry Walshe made his way to me ; and the boy to my fancy is Harry Walshe, Kate. 'I'm up to the saddle-skirts in love with your beautiful Kate,' says Harry. 'Pull away, my hearty fellows,' answers I. Never fear, but I'll give a plumper at your election.'"

"My dear papa—"

"Let me make an end, as I told you, Kate. Well, after dinner, and the bottle going merrily round, and every one of us right jovial, I rehearsed, for the benefit of the whole company, all the promises I had made, and a high joke it was. 'Here's what I'll do among you all, my good boys,' says I ; 'let every one of Kate's wooers be on the turf the first morning of the next hunting season, each mounted in his best style ; let. there be no pull-in from the cover to the death ; no baulking or shying, but smooth smack over every thing that offers ; and the lad that mounts the brush may come a-courting to my daughter Kate.' Well, my girl, you'd think they had all lost their wits at this proposal—such joy among them, such shouting. Many a bottle the rivals emptied, each to his own success. In ten days from this blessed morning the match comes off, my girl ; and whoever wins, Kate will have a wooer worth throwing her cap at."

Kate remained silent ; tears of mortification and annoyance unseen by her father, streaming from her eyes.

"But the cream of the jest I have not told you, Kate. Rattler is in training, privately, the last two months—no one the wiser ; and, harkee, Kate! by Cork's own town, I intend to start for you myself I The brush I'll wear in my own cap ; and then, if I haven't my laugh right out, why, in that case, 'tis the divvle that made little apples !"

And before the sensitive and delicate-minded girl could reply, away went her father to superintend Rattler, greatly chuckling over his scheme ; while poor Catherine sat alone to blush and weep over the mortification of being made, by her own father, the object of a vulgar and foolish contention.

Other sad thoughts mingled with her reveries. The unestated military hero, to whom, while in Dublin, she had all but plighted her troth, had promised, in answer to a letter she dispatched to him from the first post where she halted with her father, on their flight from town, to make his appearance in the country, and try his fortune with the squire. But days had now rolled over, and he came not ; neither did he send a line to account for his absence. This was a sad mortification to the pure ardency of a first love, in the breast of such a girl as Catherine ; particularly when she recollected the disagreeable predicament in which her father had placed her.

The morning of the hunt drew near, and still her lover was absent and silent. The match had become the talk of the whole country. With great difficulty and perseverance, Catherine succeeded in bringing her father's mind to contemplate her position in something of a vein of seriousness. He could not, indeed, "for the life of him," surmise why she seemed so earnest and annoyed. But he did see and comprehend that she was really unhappy ; and the best that he could think of to cheer her, he said and swore. He would break his neck with pleasure, and to a dead certainty, rather than not bring home the brush and fling it into her lap. And when Kate's fears, at this solemn declaration, took, naturally, another turn, the honest squire was again at a loss to account for her tears, her clinging, though gentle embraces, and "her tantrums." He bawled right out in utter mystification at her et-treaties that, come what might, he would not join the hunt. In fact, upon the appointed morning, away he rode towards the fox-cover, mounted on his crack hunter, Morgan Rattler, as full of buoyancy, and vigor, and solicitude as the youngest of the competitors he expected to meet.

Great shouts rent the skies as, one by one, the candidates for the gentle Catherine arrived at the appointed ground. Their horses, as well as themselves, were examined by curious and critical eyes ; and heavy bets were laid upon the issue of the day's chase. The squire, without communicating to any of his rivals his

7

intention to hunt for his daughter himself, had contrived that his own fox-hounds should be in requisition, because he well knew that Morgan Rattler would do surpassing wonders at their tails.

The ruler of the hounds was the same who had held that situation under the former owner of Squire Hogan's estate. In his youth, wenty years previously, we have noticed him as a daring fellow ; we should have added, that he used to be as remarkable for his joisterous good spirits as for his reckless intrepidity. Now, how ver, at five-and-forty, mirth, and even outward dash of every kind, nad disappeared from his character. His face was forbidding ; his words were few ; he never laughed, he never smiled ; and, al together, people regarded him as a dogged and disagreeable man. But enough of our huntsman for the present.

The day promised to be most favorable for the remarkable chase it was to witness.

> " A southerly wind and a cloudy sky
> Proclaimed a hunting morning."

The ground was in prime order, the horses were full of vigor and spirit after their long training, and, except the huntsman's (and he comes in again sooner than we foresaw), every face beamed with joyous animation. In fact, upon this day he was making himself particularly offensive—quarrelling unnecessarily with his hounds, sulkily refusing to take any advice or opinions (commands were out of the question) concerning his treatment of them, giving short answers, and looking " as black as thunder."

" What is the matter with you, Daniel ?" questioned the squire.

" I have no fancy for the work to-day," answered the huntsman.

" Why so, man ? what is all this about ?"

" It was this day twenty years that my ould masther followed the witch down the rocks into the say ; and I was dreaming last night that he and I were hunting here again together, and that he dhruv me down, head foremost, from the brow of the cliff afore him."

" Hutt, hutt, you fool ! there is no witch to hunt now, you know."

" I know no such thing. You haven't heard that she is in her cave again ?"

" Pho, no ! 'Tis impossible !"

" It is not impossible ! 'tis thrue. Let little Tony take my place to-day ; for I tell you, twice over, I don't like the work."

"Bother, Daniel! This day, of all days, I can't and won't spare you. Draw on the dogs. Come, stir; see to your business!"

With mutterings and growlings, Daniel proceeded to obey. He cast the dogs into the cover. For some time they drew through it in silence. Presently some yelpings were heard; then the leader of the pack sent forth his most melodious note; dogs and men took it up; the fox broke cover; away after him stretched the eager hounds, and, close upon them, the no less eager huntsmen.

The squire stood still a moment, willing to let the foremost and most headlong candidates for his daughter's favor blow their horses a little before he would himself push forward. While thus manœuvring, "Whom have we here?" he asked of the person nearest to him. His inquiry was aroused by a strange huntsman who had just then appeared on the ground, no one could tell whence.

"By the good day!" exclaimed the person addressed, "that's Jack Hogan, who fell over the cliff this day twenty years."

"Nonsense, nonsense!" said the squire. The stranger turned round his head, as if he could have heard these words, though he was at a good distance.

"'Tis he, man! just as he looked the last day he hunted! his very dress! See how different from ours! and his black horse! I'd know horse and rider among a million! By all that's good, it is himself!"

The horses of the squire and of his neighbor, a man of fifty, who thus spoke, would brook no further delay. Their riders were compelled to loosen their reins, and allow them to spring onward.

Daniel, the black-browed huntsman, was at this moment immediately next the hounds. Two or three of the rivals for fair Catherine's love rode within a little distance of him. The new comer loitered behind the last of the candidates: of course, the squire and his friend now pressed him hard. Suddenly his coal-black horse, seemingly without an effort, and certainly independently of one from his master, cleared the ground between him and Daniel. The huntsman turned in his saddle, fixed an appalled look on his follower, uttered a wild cry, and desperately dashed his spurs into the sides of his steed. The stranger, still seemingly unexcited, as also appeared his horse, stuck so close to Daniel's crupper, that he could have put his hand upon it.

All were of a mind that the fox outstripped the wind in swiftness. The hounds did their very best, and more than they had

ever done before, to keep near to him. Each huntsman, including
even our honest squire, spared not whip and spur to rival them.
But the huntsman first, and the stranger at his horse's tail, were
the only persons who succeeded in the achievement.

Vain was the endeavor to come up with those two. Every
now and then black Daniel would glare behind him into the face
of his pursuer, and with a new shout of horror reurge his hunter
to greater speed; still and still, although the stranger sat tranquilly in his saddle, Daniel could not gain a stirrup's length ahead
of him. Over hill and valley, over ditch and hedge, over bog and
stream, they swept, or plunged, or leaped, or scrambled, or swam
close upon the dogs, as if life were no value; or as if they were
carried, eddied forward, with supernatural speed, and in superhuman daring. Onward, onward they swept, scarce seeming to
touch the earth, until at length only three other horsemen were
able to keep them even in distant view. Soon after, these three
became two; again, but one followed remotely in their track.
And this one was our excellent friend Squire Hogan.

The sea-cliffs came in view, and straight towards them did the
mad chase turn. In amazement, if not in terror, the squire
pulled up his horse on a rising ground, and stood still to note its
further progress. He saw the panting fox make for the dangerous place over the cliff's brow. For an instant he saw him on its
very line; the next, he disappeared towards the sea. At his
brush came the hounds: down they plunged also. The rival
horsemen followed: they, too, were, in a second, lost to view.
A woman suddenly started up over the perilous pass, gazed below, and then sprang, as if into the air.

The mysterious fate of his predecessor fully occurred to our
squire; and he sensibly vowed to himself that "By Cork! the
faggot of a witch should never tempt him to leave the world by
the same road." He also brought to mind his huntsman's words
that morning; and a struggle arose between his reason and his
superstitious propensities, as to whether or no the man's dream
had been verified.

While thus mentally engaged, one of the baffled aspirants for
Catherine's hand came up, himself and his horse soiled and jaded.
Another and another followed, until almost all the members of
the day's hunt surrounded Squire Hogan. He recited to them
what he had witnessed. Greatly excited, some of them dismounted, and, under the care of an experienced guide, descended
the cliff.

They found that the bewitched hounds and their bewitched followers need not, as the squire had supposed, have jumped direct from the land into the sea ; inasmuch as they might have turned obliquely into a narrow, rocky ravine. Down this pass, however, it seemed impossible that horses of mortal mould could have found a footing. The explorers themselves were obliged to follow their guide very cautiously, as well to avoid tumbling downwards, as to save their heads from the loose stones and fragments of rocks, which almost every step displaced and set in motion.

After having proceeded a little way, they caught, far below them, a glimpse of the dogs, whose cry came up to them, mingled with the roar and chafe of the waters of the sea. Shortly after, they saw the huntsman, still closely pressed by the stranger. The next moment dogs, horses, and riders were lost to view, behind the curve of the tortuous and stony course of the ravine, all hurrying onward and downwards, with whirlwind speed, as if to bury themselves in the waves of the ocean.

Our adventurers, persevering in their descent, suddenly turned a projecting rock, and came in view of a strip of strand, running, promontory-like, into the sea ; this they soon gained. Daniel, the huntsman, lay on his back upon it ; his horse not to be seen. His dogs were squatted around him, each holding a fragment of bone between his teeth. The stranger sat still in his saddle, as if intensely observing the prostrate man. The woman who had appeared to Squire Hogan on the cliff's brow stood on a rock amid the shallow breakers which rippled over the edges of the neck of strand.

As the explorers approached this group the unknown horseman glanced towards them, took off his cap, waved it, and said, " Let no man claim Catherine Hogan's hand till I come to woo it. I have hunted for her ; won her ; and she is mine."

Those of Catherine's lovers who heard this speech were not chicken-hearted fellows. They resolved to ascertain who was the dictatorial speaker. Their friend, Squire Hogan, appeared in view, having nearly completed, at his cautious leisure, the descent to the sea's level, after them ; and they first approached him, momentarily turning their backs on the object of their interest, for the purpose of consulting him, and enlisting him in a common plan of operations. After some discourse with the good squire, and when he and they would have confronted the unknown horseman, no human form but that of sulky Daniel was visible on the patch of strand. There he lay, stretched at his length, and still apparently insensible.

To him their attention became directed. They found him covered with blood, and seemingly a corpse. His dogs continued to crouch around him, holding bones between their grinning teeth ; and they snarled fiercely when the new comers approached them.

"By the blessed light !" exclaimed the squire, "this is part of man's skull that Ranger has his teeth through."

"It is," answered Harry Walshe ; "and not one of the dogs but holds a human bone between his jaws !"

The prostrate huntsman opened his eyes, and glared fearfully around him.

"What has happened to you, Daniel ?" questioned the squire.

Daniel's head turned in the direction of the voice, and he seemed to recognize the speaker.

"Is he gone ?" he asked, faintly.

"Is who gone ? for whom do you inquire ?"

"The masther's sperit—the sperit of the murthered man. The man that *I* murthered, and buried in this sand, twenty years ago !"

Amid exclamations of surprise and horror from all who heard him, the huntsman gained, for a moment, more perfect power of observation. He looked from one to another of the group around him ; then at the dogs ; and then, closing his eyes and shuddering, continued to speak in snatches.

"Ay, and it was a cruel murther. I have never slept a night's sleep since I did it. And every dog of the pack brought me one of his bones to-day. I will hide it no longer. I will own it to the world, and suffer for it. His sperit drove me before him to the spot where I had buried his broken body, after I tumbled him over the cliff—yes, buried it as deep as I could dig. Twenty years passed away, and he came to chase me to his unblessed grave ; and at the sight of it my horse tossed me out of my saddle, and my own accursed bones are broken this day ; and so I have half my punishment Did I see the witch near me, here, a while ago ? I did. The wathers of the say gave her up, alive, to be a witness against me. For, when I was burying him, this day twenty years, I spied her watching me ; and I ran afther her, and saized her, and pitched her far into the waves. But now she is come to hang me. Let her. I will tell· all—all of my own accord. I will ; and·let them hang me for the deed."

He was conveyed to the squire's house ; and in his presence, and that of other magistrates, made a more ample confession.

He had been tempted to commit the murder under the following circumstances :

The mother of his old master had received under her protection a friendless and penniless orphan girl of low birth. The young huntsman loved her to distraction ; and his ardors were seemingly returned, until the squire, then a minor, became his successful rival, seducing, under a promise of marriage at his mother's death, his fickle mistress. Rage, hatred, loathing, took possession of Daniel's heart ; he could have beaten out the brains of his young master with the loaded end of his hunting-whip ; and his amiable feelings were not added to, when, upon a day that he was expostulating, alone, with the estranged object of his affections, the squire suddenly rushed upon him, snatched that identical whip from his hands, and energetically laid it across his own shoulders.

The squire's mother died. The squire cast off his mistress, and married a wealthy wife. It was now the turn of the depraved, bad-hearted, and forsaken girl, to look for her revenge. Upon certain conditions, she offered herself, "soul and body," and without the trouble of a marriage, to her old lover. Daniel's eager passion for her, and his deep detestation of her undoer, had scarce abated. He felt sorely tempted, but hesitated. The girl threw herself in his way from time to time. In almost a year subsequent to the first attempt to make him a murderer he *was* one—nay, a double one ; for, a few days after he had dragged his master off his horse, and hurled him down the cliff, he placed in his tempter's arms, on the understanding that she was to destroy it, the only child of his victim. But, even in the disappointment of his feverish dream of passion, he had a foretaste of the punishment due to his crime. From the moment he committed to her the helpless infant she so much detested he had never seen the authoress of his ruin ; and his belief was, that, after having murdered "the child of days," she had put an end to her own existence.

A few hours after this confession, the huntsman died.

Whether or not the gentle Catherine shared the popular belief that she had been hunted for, and won by, and was doomed to become a spectre's bride, is not clearly ascertainable. True it is, that her cheek faded, that her eye grew dull, and that the smile of contented pleasure forsook her lip, now no longer red nor moist. But these changes may as well be accounted for on less supernatural grounds. Her military adorer still continued absent and silent—he who had so often vowed himself away into worthless sighs, in the big effort to define how much he loved her, and whose only hesitation to declare himself to her father had always assumed the shape of a fear of being regarded as a speculating fortune-hunter ; when, at a glance, it could be ascertained that he was almost an unfriended adventurer, courting the hand of a wealthy heiress.

As for good Squire Hogan, he contrived, or, perhaps, rather tried, to laugh at the whole thing ; vaguely calling it a very good hoax—"a choice one, by Jove !" just to save himself the trouble of trying to unravel it, or else to hide his half-felt ignorance on the subject. Meantime, he got some cause to laugh a little less than usual. Ejectments were served upon his estate, in the name of the lost son of the man whom he had succeeded in it. Squire Hogan only strove to laugh the more, and to affect that he considered the claim as an uncommonly good attempt at " a capital hoax !" practised upon him by some unknown persons, whom, on some past occcasion he must have outwitted " gloriously." But it was a poor attempt at mirth ; and he saw that Catherine, as well as himself, felt it was so.

In fact, he spent many hours alone, mourning for his beloved child, and taxing his brains to shield her from probable and verging misfortune. And a brilliant thought came into his head.

Would it not be a happy, as well as an exceedingly clever, thing to dispose of Catherine before the trial at law, grounded upon the ejectments, should commence, and while the matter was little suspected, to one or other of her ardent admirers at the club-dinner in Dublin—to, in fact, Ned O'Brien, or George Dempsey, or Mick Driscoll, or, above all, to Harry Walshe ? The wise father made the attempt, duly, four times in succession ; and learned thereby that the serving of the ejectments was more generally known than he had imagined.

Still he tried to laugh, however, until one morning, when his boisterousness ended in sudden tears, as he cast his head on Catherine's shoulder, and said : " Oh, Kate, Kate ! what is to become of you ? I think I can bear poverty—but you ?"

" My dear father, do not be cast down," answered Catharine ; "I can earn money in many ways, for us both, if good people will give me employment."

" And you are going a-working to support your father, Kate ?"
He left the room sobbing. His tears affected Catherine to the

quick. Other sad and bitter recollections swelled her sorrow into a flood. She could now account for the persevering neglect of her lover—her tenderly beloved, upon no other grounds than those of her approaching poverty. Ah, that was a heart-cutting thought!

The day upon which the poor squire must necessarily start from the country to attend the trial in Dublin, arrived. He commenced his journey with another magnificent conception in his head; to eke out which, he carried in his pocket, without her knowledge, a miniature of his daughter Catherine. And with this miniature, and a note, expressive of his willingness to compromise the matter by a marriage, he called on the new claimant for his squireship, the evening of his arrival in the metropolis. But, having retired to his own town-house long before he could have thought it possible that his note had received a leisurely reading, he received back the miniature with a technical epistle from his rival's attorney, stating that no compromise could be entered into; that the heir-at-law was determined to accept nothing which the law should not decide to be his right; and, adding, that any attempts to see the young gentleman must prove unavailing, while they would be felt to be intrusive, inasmuch as, in cautious provision against a failure in his attempt to establish his claim, he had invariably concealed his person, even from his legal advisers.

This was the most serious blow our squire had received. Hitherto he had courageously depended on his own innate cleverness to outwit the coming storm. Now, within a few hours of the trial which was to determine his fate, he acknowledged himself without a resource or an expedient, beyond patience, to attend to the grave proceeding, sit it out, and endeavor to comprehend it.

To beguile the remainder of his sad evening, after receiving the attorney's communication, he repaired to his club-room. He found himself coolly received there. Issuing in no pleasant mood into the streets, he encountered, by lamplight, an individual in a red coat, whom he had hitherto considered rather as a deferential hanger-on than as an acquaintance to boast of. Now, at least, by unbending himself he need not fear a repulse; so, he warmly stretched out both his hands, received a very distant bow of recognition, and was left alone under a lamppost.

"By Cork!" said the squire, with a bitter laugh, "the puppy officer thinks I am turned upside down in the world already!"

7*

The case came on. Our good friend's eyes were riveted on every person who uttered a word, upon one side or the other. The usual jollity of his countenance changed into the most painful expression of anxiety ; when any thing witty was said by one of his majesty's counsel learned in the law, at which others laughed, his effort to second them was miserable to behold. Although it was a bitter cold day, the squire constantly wiped the perspiration from his forehead and face ; gnawing, between whiles, a scrap of a quill which he had almost unconsciously picked off his seat. The depositions, on his deathbed, of Daniel the huntsman, were tendered against him. They established the fact of the wretched self-accuser having kidnapped the heir of his then master, and handed the infant to his partner in crime. And the first living witness who appeared on the table, was that witch, supposed to have been long dead, even by Daniel himself. She swore that she intended to destroy the babe ; that, however, having got it into her arms, she relented of her purpose, and gave it, with a bribe, to a strange woman, in a distant district, to expose for her on the high-road. Next came the woman alluded to. She proved that she had followed the direction's of her employer, and after-wards watched, unseen, until an elderly lady of her neighborhood, passing by with a servant, had picked up the little unfortunate. Lastly, the aforesaid elderly lady, who, by the way, had endured some little scandal, at the time, for her act of Christian charity, corroborated this person's testimony ; and further deposed that she had carefully brought up, on limited means, until the day she procured him a commission in his majesty's service, the plaintiff in the case at issue. Not a tittle of evidence, in contradiction to that stated, was offered by the defendant ; and the only link of the chain of proof submitted by the heir-at-law, which the squire's counsel energetically thought to cut through, was that created by the first witness. On her cross examination, it was ingeniously attempted to be impressed on the minds of the jury, that no reliance could be placed upon the oath of a depraved creature like her; that she had really made away with the infant, according to her original intention ; and that the one she had offered for exposure, must have been her own, the result of her acquaintance, with the son of her benevolent and ill-requited protectress. But, without pausing upon details, we shall only say, that during the trial, sound conformatory evidence of the truth of the miserable woman's assertion was supplied ; and that, in fact, without hesitation, the jury found for the plaintiff.

Squire Hogan's look of consternation, when he heard the verdict, was pitiable. For a moment he bent down his head and wiped his forehead with his moist handkerchief. Then, with a wretched leer distorting his haggard countenance, he started up, and muttering indistinctly, bowed low to the judge, the jury, the bar, the public, all, as if he would humbly acknowledge the superiority of every human being. After this, forgetting his hat, he was hurrying away ; some one placed it in his hand ; he bowed lowly, and smiled again. Finally, forgetting the necessity to remain uncovered, he pressed it hard over his eyes and left the court ; carrying with him the sincere, and, in some instances, the tearful sympathy of the spectators.

As fast as horses could gallop with him, he left Dublin, a few moments following.

"By Cork, Kate," he began, laughing, as his daughter, upon his arrival at the house which used to be his home, hurried to meet him. But he could not carry on the farce. His throat was full and choking ; and suddenly throwing himself upon his child's neck, he sobbed aloud.

She understood him, but said nothing ; she only kissed his cheeks and pressed his hands, keeping down all show of her own grief and alarm. Woman ! in such a situation, *you* can do this : man cannot ; it is above the paltry selfishness of his nature.

He rallied, and tried to take up his absurd jeering tone, but soon tripped in it a second time.

"Ay, Kate, by the good old Jove, I'm a poorer man than the day I raffled for your mother ; and you *must* work, sure enough, to try and keep a little bread with us. If there's any thing you think *I* can turn my hand to, only say the word, and you'll see I'll not be idle, my poor girl."

He entered into the details of his misfortunes and mortifications. Among other things, he mentioned the slight of "the puppy officer ;" and neither his wonder nor his curiosity was excited when, now for the first time, Catherine burst into tears.

It shows much good sense to take my Lady Law at her word. Fortune is fickle, but law is fickleness—the principle itself. And so seemed to argue the successful young aspirant to the squire's estate. While yet only expatiating on his past misfortunes, our worthy friend received a note which informed him that, in a quarter of an hour, an authorized agent would arrive to take possession of the house and lands ; and father and daughter had not recovered from the shock this gave them, when the agent was an

nounced, and entered the room where they sat. Catherine turned
away her face ; she could not look at him.

"Possession of every thing in the house, too?" asked the trembling squire ; "every thing, you say ?"

"Every thing," answered the agent, who was no man's agent
but his own, after all. Catherine started at his voice—"Yes,
every thing ; even of the angel that makes this house a heaven."
He advanced to her side. She turned to him—shrieked—laughed
—and lay insensible in his arms. It was the squire's "puppy officer," in the first place ; Catherine's faithful adorer, in the second
place ; the plaintiff in the late action, in the third place ; and the
triumphant hunter for his mistress's hand, in the fourth place.
Surely, dear, fair readers, he had a claim on her. "Yes, if he
account for his neglect, since he left Dublin." Very good. That's
easily done. He had vainly applied for leave of absence ; and
his letter, informing her of the fact, as also of his intention to
take the field for her, dressed in the costume of a picture which,
in the squire's town-house, Catherine had often pronounced very
like him, had miscarried.

"So your daughter is mine, good sir, on your own terms," added
the fourfold hero.

"Capital, by Jove !—capital ! a glorious hoax, by Cork ! capital !" laughed the ex-squire.

"I am delighted you think so. And I assure you, my dear sir,
that I dressed myself up like the picture, merely at the time, to
endeavor to recommend myself to your good opinion, by the od-
dity of the conceit. For I knew you liked a hoax in your very
heart."

"Give me your hand, my dear boy ! Like a hoax ! Ah, don't
I ?—and it is such a prime one ! choice ! capital ! capital, by the
beard of the great old Jove !" And wringing his own hands,
and transported by his feeling, the worthy man left the room, to
describe and praise to his very servants what so much gladdened
his soul.

"You were ignorant of your parentage upon the day of the
hunt?" asked Catherine, after they had been some time together.

"I was. Upon the spot where the huntsman fell, I encounterd
the woman, returned from half a life of wandering, who exposed
me in my infancy : she had been seeking me in Dublin, to unburden her conscience, and do me a tardy justice. I was on the road
for the hunt ; thither she followed me rapidly, and outstripped me
some days ; assuming the garb of the former witch of the cave,

to conceal her identity. I need scarce say, that from her I then received the information which enabled me to prosecute my claim. My beloved Catherine's sense of delicacy will readily suggest to her, why I kept out of her view, from that day, until I could prove the truth or falsehood of her story. And now here I sit, able, thank Heaven ! to show to the woman of my heart, that she lid not quite misplace her generous love, when she gave it to a ʋoor and friendless ensign, and with it the prospect of wealth, and ʌf rank in the world."

It is recorded that, from this hour, Squire Hogan never wore, except, perhaps, when asleep, a serious face. Having resigned, " with a hearty good-will," his commission of justice of the peace there remained nothing on earth to compel him to " seem wise," as Bacon says. He had full leisure to pursue, uninterruptedly, his practical hoaxes ; which he himself, if nobody else did it for him, called " Capital ! choice, by Cork's own town."

THE SOLDIER'S BILLET.

THE SOLDIER'S BILLET.

Some years ago, a regiment marched through the French town in which I resided, on its way to the camp of Charles X. at St. Omer. Two of the soldiers were billeted on me. I had been struck with the face of one of the two as they entered the town—indeed, by his conduct and manner as well as his features. After passing the gate, the regiment, at word of command, I believe, broke their lines and went scampering and jumping, and shouting like possessed creatures down the precipitous main street to the place where they were to get their billets served to them—a most indecorious exhibition to eyes accustomed to the gravity of English soldiers after a march—indeed, upon all occasions. I suppose their pranks were meant to express joy at having gained a resting point for the day and night, with the the near prospect of bread and onions and *bonne soupe*. But I digress. One man among them all cut no such capers as I have mentioned, contenting himself with tramping sedately down the street, his musket held by the middle in the left hand ; nor did he shout or utter any boyish nonsense like his comrades, nor contract his features, as only Frenchmen can do. In fact, though young—about seven-and-twenty—and handsome, too, thought, if not sorrow sat on his open, manly brow, and compressed the corners of his mouth—so far as I could observe his mouth, it so appeared to me ; for not only did he wear mostaches of a prolific growth, but his black beard had been suffered to grow at pleasure—another peculiarity about him— no second man of his regiment having spared his chin from the razor.

After seeing the soldiers come in, I did not immediately return home, and when I got to my door the individual I have been describing was standing at it with his comrade, a lad scarce one-

and-twenty. He handed me his billet, with a grave but courteous bow, asking if he had come to the right number. I told him all was right so far, but that I was exempt from a billet, inasmuch as my house was a furnished one, and that my landlord was to provide him with accommodation for the night. He replied that he knew no mere lodgers in a furnished house could be called on to receive him, and asked how far off was my landlord's residence. I said half a league in the country. He shook his head, and continued to say, still with the utmost civility, if not blandness, that he and his young friend were too tired to take to the road again after a long march, and in such bad weather (the poor fellows were, indeed, soaked with rain, and the mud clung about their feet and legs almost up to their knees); but they would wait till I could send a messenger to my landlord for instructions ; and, if I could allow them to sit down at my kitchen fire in the mean time, they would very much thank me. While he spoke, he leaned his back against the wall of the house, and having reversed his musket, put its muzzle on his shoe, and rested his hands on its butt, and his cheek on them. His manner, his voice, his expression—above all, I believe, his large, mild blue eyes—made a conquest of my precision, and of my praiseworthy attachment to a few francs. I rang at the door after a moment's pause, and telling him he should wait for nothing at my kitchen fire but his dinner, I ushered in him and his comrade to Mademoiselle Phrosyne, who received her guests in a great fluster, but still with the due number of courtesies in answer to their bows. Then she put a chair for each at opposite corners of the fire, and so behold me the host of, as we are told, two of the "natural enemies" of England. I lingered in the kitchen some time. My grave soldier sat down at once, crossing his arms on his knees, and poking his body and head towards the fire. His youthful comrade saved him the trouble of putting his piece in a corner and his cap on a table, and had a kind "Thank you, Pierre," for his good nature. The lad then pulled off his own gaiters in a twinkling, and, tucking up his muddy trousers, ran to the kitchen pump as naturally as if he had been in the house all his life, and set about washing over the sink the first-named articles of dress. Phrosyne offered him her black paste soap, but he declined it laughingly ; and, while proceeding in his work, said he dared her to wash his gaters as well with soap as he should without it, at which mademoiselle laughed too while busy over her saucepans. It was not the first pleasantry they had interchanged, and Phrosyne was a youthful *cuisinière*, and did not shame her name for comeliness. In fact, I saw she was in for a pleasant evening, with one of her guests at least, but the other continued silent and melancholy. He did not hesitate, indeed, to answer my questions promptly and politely, but he never spoke of his own accord. Before I left the kitchen, he had begun to take off his gaiters, in imitation of Pierre, but the lad insisted on having them to wash after his own, adding, "And for this evening, at least, Louis, I will work for two at the muskets, trousers, shoes, and all."

"Are you and Pierre relations?" I asked.

"No, sir," he answered; "but," smiling for the first time, as he pulled Pierre's ear, who was kneeling to get off the gaiters, "we have been friends nearly a year, ever since the day he joined the regiment."

All this interested me, and I went up stairs to interest my wife by telling it over to her. We agreed to do something to make the two men comfortable. A good fire was ordered in their bedroom, at which they might sit to dine, after having cleaned their arms, accoutrements, and clothes. Hours of the evening wore away, and we did not hear their voices or steps in the house: they only sent up their thanks for monsieur's kind attentions. I inquired from time to time how they were occupied; and when I thought they might be at leisure, went down to their sleeping-room to try and get the elder of them into conversation. He was alone, sitting over the fire, which he had suffered to decay, in the same bent position he had adopted in the kitchen. I believe he slumbered, for my entrance did not make him raise his head; so, not wishing to disturb him, after his weary march, I turned into the kitchen to his more lively comrade, whose laugh, mingled with that of Phrosyne and her fellow-servant, attracted me thither.

I spoke to Pierre about his friend, and pointedly noticed his melancholy. In a few minutes I learned the cause of it. Before drawing his *mauvais numéro* as a conscript, seven years before Louis had loved, "not wisely," Rosalie, the only daughter of the richest man of his village—the miller, no less. Rosalie loved him in return, but her father was obdurate. They met in secret. Rosalie became an unwedded mother. But before that event, and while her condition was known to the whole village, Louis again, and repeatedly, solicited the miller to allow her to become his wife, and again and again he was refused. He heard he was a father ; he asked permission to see his child ; it was denied him. The morning the infant was baptized in the church he suddenly appeared amid the family group who surrounded it, kissed it, and claimed it, and insisted that it should bear his name, of which its stern grandfather wished to deprive it. The clergyman was compelled to yield him his right. A few days after he was a conscript ; "and," continued Pierre, "they tell me that, since the first day he came to the regiment, now seven years ago, he has been always, and to every one, what monsieur has seen he is to-day—civil, kind, but very sad. But this does not interfere with his duties. He is one of the best soldiers, if not the very best soldier among us. *I* uphold him to be *the* very best. A good, and true, and most useful friend he has been to me since I joined the Twenty-seventh, and I love him like a brother. Everybody loves him—ay, and respects him too—men and officers, all the same ; and it is pleasure to me, when he will let me do a hand's turn for him, to save him trouble. I wonder will his Rosalie be true to him for another year—after which he may return home to see her and his child ? I hope she will."

"I hope so too," sighed Phrosyne.

"And I," echoed Sophie.

"And I, Pierre," said I, "with all my heart."

"Thank you a thousand times, monsieur," replied Pierre, his face glowing.

Now, were I writing what really did not happen, word for word, and I did not dislike disturbing the honest facts in my own mind, I could very easily go on to say that I had been travelling by chance through Rosalie's village, about a year after, and just in the nick of time to witness the nuptials of her and Louis. But I cannot bear to lie, even poetically, on this subject. The truth is, I know nothing more about it ! and to the truth I limit myself. That I continue to hope what we all hoped that evening round the kitchen fire need scarce be doubted. Nor have I ever seen Louis since ; he had gone to bed before I left the kitchen. I heard from him, however, in the shape of the following note, handed to me by Sophie, after the departure of him and Pierre, next morning, long before daybreak :

"The two French soldiers below thank the good English monsieur of this house for unexpected and unusual kindness, after a long march, on a bad day. May God bless him and madame, and the little children."

A PEASANT GIRL'S LOVE.

A PEASANT GIRL'S LOVE.

THE county assizes had commenced in my native town, when a new batch of Irish tithe arrangers were brought in prisoners by a strong party of police. They had attacked, only the previous evening, a gentleman's house in our neighborhood, for the purpose of rifling it of arms ; had been repulsed by the police, who, aware of their intentions, lay in ambush for them, and lives were lost on both sides. I was idling on one of the bridges when they passed by to the jail, bound with ropes, and with belts and buckles, to the common cars of the country ; the expression of their haggard cheeks, and hopeless or scowling eyes, was sickening in the sunlight of that beautiful spring day. Some of them were wounded too, and brow, or hand, or clothing, gave painful evidence of the fact.

But, although the general impression made by the whole of the wretched groups was disagreeable, one face among them strongly interested me. It was that of a young man, not more than nineteen or twenty. His features were comely, and, I would have it, full of goodness and gentleness. His clear blue eye, too, was neither sulky, nor savage, nor reckless, but seemed to express only great awe of his situation, unless when, from some sudden mental recurrence—to home, perhaps—it quailed, or filled with tears. I involuntary followed the melancholy procession towards the jail, thinking of that young man. After all the prisoners had been ushered into their new abode, a popular anti-tithe attorney, whom I knew, accosted me. He was always ready to conduct, gratis, the defences of poor wretches similarly situated ; and he told me his intention of going into the jail that moment, to try and collect materials for saving the lives, at least, of some of the new comers. I expressed a wish to assist him in his task; he readily consented, observing that as the unfortunate men would certainly be put on

their trials the next day, no offer of aid in their favor was to be
disregarded. So we entered the jail together.

It fell to my lot to visit the cell, among others, of the lad who
had so much struck me. His assertions, supported or not contradicted by most of his band, seemed to argue that I had not
formed a wrong opinion of his character—nay, better still, that
there was a good chance of snatching him from the gallows, even
though he must leave his native land forever. He had been
forced, he said, to accompany the others upon their fatal sortie
had never been out before ; and had not pulled a trigger or raised
a hand against the police. As I have said, his more guilty associates supported, or else did not contradict, his statement. So,
confident that the police would also bear him out at the really
critical moment, I took notes of his defence for my friend, the
attorney, and passed on to other cells ; but of the results of my
continued investigation I will not now speak.

The sagacious attorney was right. By twelve o'clock the next
day, four of the men, including my favorite client, were placed at
the bar of their country: three others were too ill of their wounds
to be at present produced. All was soon over, and over to my
affliction. Instead of swearing that the young lad had been comparatively forbearing during the battle outside the gentleman's
house, the police, one and all, through some mistake—for surely they
thought they were in the right—distinctly deposed that his was
the hand which slew one of their force, and badly wounded
another. In vain did he protest, with the energy of a young
man pleading for dear, dear life, and all its array of happy promise, against their evidence ; in vain did his fellow-prisoners support him : he and they were found guilty in common. But his
fate was the terrific one—of him the example was to be made.
While the other men were only sentenced to transportation for
life, he was doomed to be hanged by the neck within forty-eight
hours, and his body given for dissection.

As the judge uttered the last words of his sentence, a shriek I
shall never forget,—it rings through my head now, and makes my
nerves quiver and cringe—a woman's shriek, and a young woman's
too,—pierced up to the roof of the silent courthouse, and then I
heard a heavy fall. The young culprit had been trembling and
swaying from side to side during his sentence. At the thrilling
sound he started into upright and perfect energy ; his hands,
which had grasped the bar of the dock, were clapped together with a loud noise; the blood mounted to his very forehead;

his lips parted widely ; and, having almost shouted out, "Moya! it's she! I knew she'd be here!" he suddenly made a spring to clear the back of the dock. Obviously no impulse to escape dictated the action ; he wanted to raise Moya—his betrothed Moya —from the floor of the courthouse, and clasp her in his arms— and that was all. And, doubtless, in his vigorous and thrice-nerved strength, he must have succeeded in his wild attempt, but that the sleeve of one arm, and the hand of the other, became impaled on the sharp iron spikes which surmounted the formidable barrier before him. Thus cruelly impeded, however, he was easily secured, and instantly led down, through a trap-door in the bottom of the dock, to his "condemned cell," continuing, till his voice was lost in the depths beneath us, to call out, "Moya! cuishla-ma-chree! Moya!"

I hastened with many others into the body of the court, and there learned from her father and mother and other friends, the connection between her and the sentenced lad. They were to have been married at Easter. This did not lessen my interest in him. My attorney joined me, and we spoke of all possible efforts to obtain a commutation of his sentence, after Moya's parents had forced her out of the courthouse on the way to their home, rejecting all her entreaties to be led into the jail, and— married.

We thought of hearing what the wounded policeman might say. But he was fourteen miles distant, on the spot where the affray had occurred, and, even though his evidence might be favorable, we knew we must be prepared to forward it to Dublin, as the judge would leave our town for the metropolis that day. We set to work, however, mounted two good horses, and within three hours learned from the lips of the wounded man that the Rockite who had fired at him was an elderly and ill-favored fellow. It was our next business to convey our new evidence into the town ; we did so, in a carriage borrowed from the person whose house had been attacked. He was confronted with all the prisoners ; we cautioned him to say nothing that might give a false hope to the object of our interest ; but, after leaving the cell, he persisted in exculpating him from having either killed his comrade or wounded himself ; and, moreover, pointed out the real culprit among those who had not yet been put upon their trial.

This was a good beginning. An affidavit was soon prepared, which the policeman signed. A few minutes afterwards the attorney, helped in his expenses for the road by some friends, my-

8

self among the number, started for Dublin as fast as four horses
could gallop with him.   Ten hours out of the forty-eight allowed
to the condemned to prepare for death had already elapsed.
Our good attorney must do the best he could within thirty-seven
hours.   It was fearful not to leave an hour to spare—to calculate time when it would just be merging into eternity.   But he
had good hopes.   If horses did not fail on the road, going and
returning, and if the judge, and, after him, the Lord-lieutenant, could be rapidly approached, it was a thing to be done.
That *if*, however!   I scarcely slept a wink through the night.
Next morning early I called on the clergyman whose sad duty it
was to visit the poor lad in his condemned cell ; he and I had
been schoolfellows ; and he was a young man of most amiable
character.   He told me "his poor penitent" was not unfit to die,
nor did he dread the fate before him, notwithstanding his utter
anguish of heart at so sudden and terrible a parting from his
young mistress.   I communicated the hopes we had, and asked
the clergyman's opinion as to the propriety of alleviating the lad's
agony by a slight impartation of them.   My reverend young friend
would not hear of such a thing : his conscience did not permit
him.   It was his duty, he said, his sacred duty, to allow nothing
to detract the mind and heart of his penitent from resignation to
his lot ; and should he give him a hope of life, and then see
that hope dashed, he would have helped to kill a human soul,
not to save one.   I gave up the point, and endeavored to seek
occupations and amusements to turn my thoughts from the one
subject which absorbed and fevered them.   But in vain ; and
when the second night came I had less sleep than on the first.

Early on the second morning, I took a walk into the country,
along the Dublin road, vaguely hoping to meet, even so early,
our zealous attorney, returning to us with a white handkerchief
streaming from the window of his postchaise.   That idea had
got into my head, like a picture, and would recur every moment.
I met him not.   I lingered on the road.   I heard our town-clock
pealing twelve.   The boy had but an hour to live.   I looked
towards the county jail, whither he had been removed for execution—the black flag was waving over its drop-door.   Glancing
once more along the Dublin road, I ran as fast as I could towards the jail.   Arrived at the iron gate of its outer yard, I
was scarce conscious of the multitude who sat on a height confronting it, all hushed and silent, or of the strong guard of soldiers at the gate, till one of them refused me way.   I bribed the

sergeant to convey my name to the governor of the prison, and was admitted—first, into the outer yard, then by the guard-room door, and along a colonnade of pillars, connected with iron work, at either hand, into the inner courts of the jail. The guard-room was under the execution-room, and both formed a building in themselves, separated from the main pile—the collonnade, or which I have spoken, leading from one to the other. What had sent me where I now found myself was an impulse to beseech the sheriff, whom I knew, and was necessarily in the jail, to accompany the condemned to the door of the execution-room, for some short postponement of the fatal moment. He came out to me, in one of the courts at either side of the collonnade ; we spoke in whispers, as the good and kind-hearted governor and I had done, though there was not a creature to overhear us, in the deserted sunny spaces all around. I knew the sheriff must at his peril make any change in the hour ; but I told him our case, and his eyes brightened with zeal and benevolence, while he put his watch back three-quarters of an hour; and asseverated, with my Uncle Toby's oath, I believe, that he would swear it was right, and that all their clocks were wrong, and "let them hang himself for his mistake."

Our point arranged, we sank into silence. It was impossible to go on talking, even in our conscious whisper. One o'clock soon struck ! The governor, pale and agitated, appeared, making a sad signal to the sheriff. We beckoned him over to us, and he was shown the infallible watch, and retired again, without a word. My friend and I continued standing side by side, in resumed silence. All was silence around us too, save some few most melancholy sounds ; one caused by the step of a sentinel under the window of the condemned cell, at an unseen side of the prison ; another, by the audible murmurings of the condemned and his priest, heard through that window—both growing more fervent in prayer since the jail clock had pealed one ; a third, made by some person, also unseen, striking a single stroke with a wooden mallet, about every half minute, upon a large, muffled bell at the top of the prison. Yes, I can recall two other sounds which irritated me greatly, the chirping of sparrows in the sun—and I thought that their usually pert note was now strangely sad— and the tick, tick of the sheriff's watch, which I heard distinctly in his fob. The minutes flew. I felt pained in the throat, burning with thirst, and losing my presence of mind. The governor appeared again. My friend entered the prison with him. I re

mained alone, confused. In a few minutes, the governor came
out, bareheaded, and tears were on his cheeks. The young clergyman and his younger penitent, followed ; the former had passed an arm through one of the manacled ones of the latter, and
the hands of both were clasped, and pointed upwards ; and they
both were praying audibly. My old schoolfellow wept like a
child. My poor client had passed the threshold into the colonnade with a firm step. His knees kept peculiarly stiff as he paced
along ; and his cheeks and forehead were scarlet, while his eye
widened and beamed, and was fixed on the steps going up to the
execution-room, straight on before him. He did not yet see me
gazing at him. As the sheriff appeared behind him, and his
priest, also bareheaded, I rapidly snatched my hat from my head.
The action attracted his attention. Our glances met ; and oh !
how the flush instantly forsook his forehead and his cheeks, and
how his eyes closed, while cold perspiration burst out on his
brow ; and he started, stopped, and faltered ! Did he recognize
me as the person who had spoken kindly to him in his cell, before his trial, and, perhaps, with all my precaution, gave him a
vague hope ? Or was it that the unexpected appearance of a
human creature, staring at him in utter commiseration, in that
lonely courtyard, had touched the chord of human associations,
and called him back to earth, out of his enthusiastic vision of
heaven ? I know not. I cannot even guess—who can ? As
he faltered, the young priest passed his arm round his body, and
gently urged him to his knees, and knelt with him, kissing his
cheeks, his lips, pressing his hands, and, in tender whispers, man-
ning him again, for facing shame, and death, and eternity. The
governor, the sheriff, and I instinctively assumed the attitude of
prayer, at the same moment. But I hate to give a character of
clap-trap to a real, though wonderful occurrence, by continuing
too circumstantially. Moya's "own boy" never even mounted
the steps of the execution-room. We were first startled, while
we all knelt, by, as it afterwards proved, her shrieks at the outer
gates. She had escaped from the restraint of her family, and
had come to the jail, insisting on being married to him " wid the
rope itself round his neck, to live a widow for him forever."
Next, there was a grand shout from the multitude on the rural
heights before the prison ; and my one ceaseless idea of our attorney, with a white handkerchief streaming through the window
of his postchaise, was realized, though every one saw it but I
And Moya, self-transported for life, went out to Van Die

men's Land, some weeks afterwards, a happy and contented wife, her family having yielded to her wishes, at the instance of more advocates than herself, and put some money in her purse also.

THE END OF A PEASANT GIRL'S LOVE

THE HALL OF THE CASTLE.

THE HALL OF THE CASTLE.

NOTWITHSTANDING that the castle of Kilkenny generally held a strong garrison, upon an October evening, in the year 1390, its bastions, towers, and other points of defence, were almost unmanned—its courts almost silent. But a few very old or very young domestics sat in its great hall, with arms in their hands, and with doubt and anxiety impressed on their features. It had sent out its last regular soldier, together with its able-bodied serfs, to support its lord, James, Earl of Ormonde, in a battle against the Desmond, touching the rights and bounds of certain lands. Intelligence of the result of the fray was upon this evening every moment expected at its gates.

The lady of the fortress knelt in her private chapel, at " the altar of the holy stone," in fervent, but not faltering prayer. The pride of name, the pride of feudal animosity, and the pride of her love of her martial husband, equally kept her unconscious of fear. The utmost condescension of her anxiety was to doubt ; but nothing did she, or would she, doubt upon the subject which engrossed her soul, so far as regarded its issue by mortal means. Uncontrolled by a superior power, the Botiller, the Ormonde, the lord of her heart and her life, ever commanded success against a Desmond. She knelt, therefore, only to pray that the will of God might not, on this occasion, fight against her and hers.

Her orisons ended, she slowly arose, and after bending her head and crossing her calm and high forehead before the alter, paced along the solitary chapel, and issued from it through a low arched door. Many flights of narrow stone steps, twining upward from the foundations of the castle, upon a level with which was the chapel-floor, conducted her to the suite of small rooms leading into her sleeping-chamber ; thence she gained a

8*

lobby, which gave entrance to what was called, "The Long
Gallery" of the edifice, where, finding herself alone, the Lady of
Ormonde blew a shrill and loud call upon the little silver whistle
which hung from her neck.

` But no person answered her ; and while her commanding
brow assumed a severe expression, she was again about to put
the whistle to her lips, when the notes of a trumpet, sounding
the signal for defence, reached her from, as she believed, the
embattled wall which faced and fell down to the Nore full forty
feet, although its top was still much lower than the foundation-
stone of the fortress it helped to defend. The point from which
the martial strain seemed to arise was fully commanded by the
spacious end-window of the long gallery ; thither the Lady of
Ormonde now repaired, with a more rapid step than was habitual
to her.

Arrived at the window, she boldly flung open its casements
and gazed directly downwards. Two figures only met her view
—those of the individuals whom she had reckoned upon meeting
in the gallery after her return from the chapel ; namely, Simon
Seix, the half-witted foster-brother of her only son (and only
child, too), and that only son himself mounted on Simon's shoulders, who galloped, or pranced, or curvetted along terre-plein of
the wall.

"The poor born-natural !" she muttered, "again will he dis-
obey my commands not to leave the castle with his young lord ?
And leave it for such antics, too, and to be playing upon that
perilous wall. Doubtless it was he who erewhile mimicked the
sound of trumpet which so challenged us !"

The lady recollected Simon's talent for imitating the tones of
all the instruments of music which he had ever heard played, as
well, indeed, as of the voices of many animals ; and even at the
moment her surmise was confirmed ; for, after he had exceedingly well performed the loud neighing and snorting of an enraged battle-charger, as an accompaniment to a devious and (still
the lady thought) perilous caracole, she saw and heard him blow
a second trumpet blast through the hollow of his hand, which
might well be mistaken for the martial music it faithfully copied.
It was a strain of victory and triumph ; and Simon seemed
enamored of his own execution of it ; for he prolonged the
sounds, as though he would never end them, until, at last, they
suddenly stopped, breaking off in a ludicrous cadence of terror
as the overmastering shrillness of his lady's whistle cut them short,

Turning up his large gray eyes to the open window far above him, he saw the awful figure of his offended mistress half bending from it. Her arm was raised, her hand clenched, and she stamped her foot, and pointed to him to re-enter the castle. The Lord Thomas—so was called the little boy of seven or eight years on his back—looked up also. But while Simon assumed a face of the utmost fright and affliction, he only laughed merrily and graciously, in answer to his mother's signs; and then, resisting his foster-brother's preparations to place him on his own feet, he obliged Simon still to bear him on his shoulders.

In a few moments the little Lord Thomas appeared before his mother in the gallery. Her first look towards him was one of grave reprehension; but when, presuming on her love for him, as well as prompted by his love for her, the boy came bounding forward, the stately lady's brow relaxed, and, thinking of his father, she opened her arms to receive him.

"But where tarries Simon Seix, boy? With him, at the least, the overgrown adviser and contriver of all thine antics, I shall call a strict reckoning," she said, after some previous words between them.

Lord Thomas made a gleeish signal to his mother of a confidential understanding sought at her hands; then composing his features he spoke in a voice of mock solemnity, as he turned towards the door by which he had come in.

"Enter, Simon," he cried, "and face my lady mother."

The ill contrived figure of Simon—short, thick, and bandy-legged—dragged itself through the door-way, and stood still a few paces past the threshold. His arms dropped at his sides, his jaw fell, his crooked eyebrows became proportionately elevated, his heavy-lidded eyes turned sideways upon the floor; altogether he presented a very ludicrous caricature of repentance, fear, and self abasement, of which one-half was, however, only affected; for, with his young lord for an advocate, he really apprehended no bad consequences.

"So, knave," the lady began, "neither your respect for my commands, nor your love and fear of the Lord of Ormonde, exposed at this moment to utmost peril, can keep you within the castle with Lord Thomas, sage and sedate, as the time requires him and you to be?"

Simon, whiningly, yet with a certain sly expression of tone and manner, replied:

"I wot not, gracious lady, wherefore, at this time, aught is required from Lord Thomas, his father's son, or from me, his poor, simple servitor and body-man, save the bearing which bespeaks joyousness and trouble passed."

"And why, sirrah, wot you not ?"

"Because, by this hour of the day, our good battle hath surely been fought and won, and a Botiller's foot again planted on the neck of a Desmond," answered Simon, confidently.

"Say you so," continued the lady, her eyes brightening ; "and whence come your tidings, sir ?"

"From our common thought of whatever must be the fortunes of the Ormonde against his present foe, lady," said the reputed fool.

While he spoke he gave his noble foster-brother an anxious sign to second his interested sycophancy, in consequence of which, as well, indeed, as in assertion of what he really felt, the boy answered :

"True, Simon ! And it would, in sooth, ill become the Ormonde's only son to show, by wearing of a sad face this evening, a doubt of his own gallant father."

"List, excellent lady !" adjured Simon, "his nobleness repeats the very words which drew me from the castle by his side."

"Peace, knave !" said the lady, her face, voice, and manner suddenly changing into great energy as she heard the well-known sounds of lowering the drawbridge before the principal gate in the walls of the castle. "Nay, by my holy saint !" she went on rapidly, while a burst of wailing voices reached her from the hall below ; "here I have been sinfully bandying words with an idiot at the moment that I should have bent my knee to Heaven ! Who comes to greet us ?—who waits below ?" she cried, pacing towards a side door of the gallery.

She was about to issue through it, when the sound of many feet echoed on the lobby without. She paused and grew pale. Old John Seix, the father of Simon, completely clad in mail, and looking jaded and agitated, presented himself before her, the few servants left in the castle crowded at his back. Her eyes met his, and during their short but eloquent glance, she drew in her lips hard, crossed one hand over her bosom, and with the other extended at full length, motioned him to speak.

"The noble Ormonde lives, dear lady," answered the old man, and then he paused.

"But the battle is lost, John Seix ?" she said, apparently with calmness.

Evasively he replied, that his lord, in quick retreat upon Kilkenny, close pressed by the Desmond, had dispatched him to bid his lady summon the citizens of the town to arms, that some of them might help to garrison the castle, and some hasten to join his army at Green's Bridge, half a mile up the river, where he purposed making a last brave stand against his old foe.

"All things shall be tried," answered his lady.

Thereupon she dispatched one domestic to the civil authorities of the town, over whom the house of Ormonde held despotic sway, and another to the steeple which held the great clock, in the courtyard, with orders to ring the alarm.

"John Seix," she resumed, walking up and down the gallery, "however may betide this last struggle at the bridge, I give way to no fears for the dear and precious life of the Ormonde. Supposing him a war-prisoner at the present moment, a Desmond hath never lived who dares to harm a hair of his head."

"Nor ever shall live to but think of it, mother," said the almost infant Lord Thomas, coming to her side and taking her hand—his childish tears, which had flowed at John Seix's first news, being now almost dried up. She raised him in her arms and pressed him to her bosom, but she did not weep. After setting him on the floor again, she continued :

"No, old and faithful servant. I fear not the poor Desmond on my lord's account ; but should he a second time prove fortunate at yonder bridge, and afterwards break his rude way into our castle here, then, John Seix, ungarrisoned and alone as we are, then would I fear him on mine own account."

"And wherefore, mother?" demanded the boy at her side, while old Seix sighed heavily and assentingly.

"It needs not that I inform you of the broad grounds of my fear," she resumed, still addressing her old house-steward. "Before my marriage with my noble lord, you remember his bold pretensions to my favor—they were plain to all the world. Nathless, no living creature, save myself, can now tell you the reason why—woman, wife, lady, and mother, as I am"—her accents trembled ; she stopped her rapid walk, and put her hand on her son's head, while he looked into her face most intently, though not as if he comprehended her present discourse—"the especial reason why my soul begins to shrink before the Desmond."

"Hark to the noise which comes faintly down the river, lady,' said, to her great surprise, Simon Seix, the half-fool, speaking seriously and steadily, as he gracelessly moved from a corner in which he had hitherto been standing unnoticed, though, perhaps, not without noting all he saw and heard, and, edging round by the wall, approached the end window of the gallery.

" Ay, and so it does !" exclaimed the mistress, hurrying to the point of observation before him ; " and, for the nonce, Simon, well have you spoken."

She gained the open window. Quick as a flash, her glance shot at once up the river to the bridge, and there fixed itself. The October evening began to close in, and it was sunless and heavy. Yet the twilight did not so much prevail as to hinder her from distinguishing the general features of things at a good distance.

The faint shouting and uproar still came down the Nore ; but nothing to interest her as yet occurred upon the bridge. In a very short time, however, the wild tumult growing louder, as she saw a large body of armed men pour over it, rapidly and in disarray. Some rallied at the country side of the bridge, some between its battlements, and some at its town side. The Lady of Ormonde knew that these were her husband's men, hotly pursued by the Desmond, and that they now prepared to make the last stand of which old Seix had spoken to her. They were not allowed much time to prepare themselves ; nor did they long resist the fierce attack of their assailants. The particular incidents of the struggle she could not see; but in the furious shouts of the Desmond, at first confident and insulting, and then cruel and triumphant—in the haughty blasts of their trumpets—in the gradual receding from the bridge of her lord's bands as those of his enemy thronged thick upon it—and in the frequent plunge of men and horses into the river, at that point evidently possessed at first by her friends,—in all these occurrences the unhappy lady saw too plainly signs of discomfiture and of woe to her husband, his child, and herself.

Old Seix, watching her from the interior of the gallery, needed nothing but her action and the expression of her countenance to tell him the issue of the fray, and to impart to his own bosom the successive emotions which agitated hers. When she first looked out from the window he knew, by her bending attitude, extended neck, and unwinking eyes, that, as yet, she saw naught which she had expected to see. Suddenly, in answer to the rush of the Ormondes over the bridge, she stood upright, and clenched her hands at her sides : then she bent low again, and her fingers

grasped her knees. Then she started a second time to her full
height, stamped with one foot, waved an arm round her head
with a quick action of impatient command. Finally she threw
up her hands, locked them together, and dropped her head between her arms.

"All is over, Lady of Ormonde?" demanded Seix.

"It is, John," she answered, "our base hinds fly, like poor
deer they are only fit to tend, scattered and wild, over the distant country."

"Do the Desmonds pursue?" again asked the house-steward.

"Gallantly!" replied the lady; "and all in a body—not a
man stays on the bridge."

"Then we have some pause, dear mistress, since none of them
hasten this way."

"Ay, I grant you, if our townsmen enter the castle in time.
But where linger they—false, bourgeois churls! Begone, thou,
John Seix, and essay to rouse their sluggish spirit! But no!
hold an instant! It may—it may be so!" She interrupted
herself by speaking these last words in a joyous, hopeful tone, as
she again looked up the river.

"The Ormondes, lady?" questioned the old man.

"By Heaven! I do believe it is, John Seix! Some five or
seven mounted men have parted from the confused body of pursuers and pursued beyond the bridge, and now regain it—now
spur fiercely over it—and one keeps ahead of the others. Now I
lose him and them as they turn into the town. Quick, quick,
John Seix, and mount the turret over the grand gate; thither
they repair, whoever they be. Quick, old man! I wait you
here."

The house-steward did as he was commanded. In a short time
after he had taken his position in the turret, seven horsemen galloped up the ascent which led from the near end of the town to
the castle; and one of noble bearing led the rest. But as it was
now deep twilight, and as the riders kept their vizors down, he
could not, at a first look, pronounce whether they were friends or
foes. Coming nearer, he fixed his glance upon a banner which they
bore, and his heart beat with joy, for it was the banner of the
Ormonde. He challenged them, as they pulled their reins before
the gate; they, one and all, shouted the gladdening word, and
he hastened from the turret to admit them within the walls of the
castle.

Meantime, his lady impatiently, pantingly awaited his return to the gallery. Leaving the window, she cast herself at first into a seat; then quickly arose, paced the gallery, stopped, listened, took her son's hand, and rapidly walked with him to the door at the remote end.

She had again heard the unbarring of the gate and the lowering of the drawbridge. Now she distinguished hasty steps ascending through the castle to the gallery. A few paces from the end door she stood still; a knight, clad in full armor, entered. In height and figure he resembled her husband; but his vizor was down. Upon that she fixed her eye. An instant passed in silence, neither moving. The knight slowly raised his hand, and put up his vizor—it was the Desmond!

She did not scream not start, nor even step back, for her heart had misgiven her, and spared her a surprise which might have betrayed the heroic lady into some weakness which she would have scorned to show.

"I know you, Desmond," she only said, nodding her head, and endeavoring to look down his deep and fearful stare; "ay, and I knew you before you put your hand to your casque."

"You did, Petronilla?" he asked, in a low voice.

"Call me by my better name, here in mine own castle, Desmond. The Lady of Ormonde is that name; none other have you license to utter. And then tell me what would Piers Gerald of Desmond with the Lady of Ormonde—with her, and with her son, whom she holds by the hand?"

"It pleasures me," he answered, evasively, "that you knew me, as you say."

"And wherefore should it?"

"Because the knowledge so little angered you towards me, when I feared far otherwise of our meeting, lady of this castle."

"Is that all? Then I tell you Desmond, build not upon such a seeming. Learn rather that there be some in the world who deeply feel, though they despise much outward show of *what* they feel, and who leave actions, in the stead of words, to decide between them and those they love or hate, honor or spurn."

"And 'tis well, passing well, that thus calmly we *do* meet," he resumed; "for it hits the fashion of the time, and the change of—"

"Of what?" she interrupted—for a woman, almost sternly "The change of what? What change? Think you, Desmond, that for an hour's mishap—the first he ever knew from *your* hand, at the least—the Lord of Ormonde, or I, his wife, will brook that

word? Think you that spirit bends or snaps so soon? Think
you that the cowards who fled from you on yonder bridge make
a tithe of the Ormonde's truer and loyaler vassals and fighting
men? or, granting that he stood alone to-night in some nook of
his own wide lands, think you no other friends may be near, although come from far, to take his part, and give you back to him,
hand to hand, and foot to foot?"

"What other friends?" asked Desmond.

"Hark in your ear—true English friends! Ay, Desmond!
and with one who loves the Ormonde to bid them on—with England's king to bid them on!" she continued, exultingly.

"Who hides behind this arras, to witness our discourse?" demanded Desmond, striding to the place of which he spoke, his
hand placed on his sword.

"Harm not my poor jester, black Desmond! cried the little
Lord Thomas, springing after him from his mother's side. "None
but he, Simon Seix, the half-witted, is there ; and he has only
crept behind the arras to sleep."

The child pulled aside the arras as he spoke, and discovered,
indeed, Simon Seix sitting behind it—his clumsy, bony knees
crippled up into his mouth, and his whole figure curiously
twisted into the smallest possible size, while he seemed, at least,
to sleep profoundly.

"Bid him awaken, and to the hall with you for pastime, my
brave man," said Desmond, shaking Simon with his mailed hand
till he opened his eyes, uttering a strange cry, and starting to
his feet. "May they not leave the gallery, lady?" resumed
Desmond ; "our speech grows of import."

"But surely of no value to an infant and a simpleton," answered the lady of Ormonde ; "wherefore, Desmond, they may
not leave the gallery for the hall."

"Dicken Utlaw, my proved body-man, will there do service
and ward upon your fair son," continued Desmond.

"And *is* he there? *he?* Dicken Utlaw, your *proved* body-
man?" asked the lady. "I know of him. In my days of unwedded youth I had a reason to know of him—the which you
can tell. And, oh! Heaven forgive you, Desmond, the intents
in furtherance of which you bring the stony-hearted Dicken into
this castle!"

"If the child and the fool are to rest here," rejoined Desmond, "I pray you let it be at the end of the gallery, out of
hearing."

To this she assented, and the young Lord Thomas and Simon Seix accordingly withdrew to the window.

"Now, lady, touching your wild speech of the English king's coming to Ireland—"

"He lands to-day at Waterford, Desmond; 'tis as wild as that—England's Second Richard—at Waterford!"

"Hush!" cried Desmond, as he perceived that Simon had again drawn near them alone, so cautiously that his steps were not heard. "Now, sirrah, do you dare to pry into the discourse of your lady and myself?"

Simon humbly and earnestly denied any such bold and sinful design; and, reproved and chidden, he again withdrew, while Desmond went on with what he had to say.

"Lady, 'tis passing strange I should not have heard of this. But let the king be at Waterford. I shall have loyal friends to wait on him there before midnight. You can have none—"

"The Ormonde may think of having some there before midnight, Desmond."

"Alack the day, lady!" said Desmond, sighing.

"Ha!" she cried, receding from him; "when *you* put on that seeming grief, there must be a black tale for me to hear, in good sooth! Speak, man! You have jumped upon his body, laid prostrate by thousands for you, and then passed your coward knife through his noble heart."

"The Ormonde forced me to the field, lady, in just defence of my bounds of lands; but otherwise I bore him no ill blood. His life I never sought; and had I seen it threatened, would have saved it. But the last melée was fierce upon the bridge, and he fell ere I knew that—"

"Dead! my Ormonde dead?" she cried, clasping her hands, and fixing her eyes on Desmond.

"I bore his banner to your gate—please you to see it in the hall? Could he have drawn living breath when that was done?"

"I think no," she answered. "And you have reached him, then? Now, Desmond, 'tis in your mind that all looks clear for the fulfilling of an old oath." Stern despair was in her tones, as she uttered these words.

"Sweet lady, pass we that worthless matter—an error o. mere youth, and naught besides—unless we add an outbreaking of passionate love, as pure and true as—"

"Insolent fool as well as villain!" again interrupted the lady. "Where are you, boy? Come hither to my side, and hold fast

by my hand—hither, hither! ha!" as she turned round, and
looked towards the end of the spacious and dusky apartment.
"My child hath left the gallery—with his poor fool, too! and
left it, for what company! for what chances! Desmond, I
leave you to go seek him. Aid me in the task; and promise
not to part us, when I find my boy, and I will kneel down to
bless you."

Terrible fears of Desmond's designs began to press on her
mind, and she scarce knew what she said. Her unwelcome visitor earnestly promised to do so as she requested of him; and
they left the gallery by different doors. Desmond hastened to
the hall, where taking Utlaw aside, he said to him in a whisper—

"Dicken, if by some secret outlet the young spawn of the
Ormonde hath evaded us, we nearly lose our present game.
Search well the courts and outbuildings—"

The calls and cries of the afflicted mother, echoing through
the castle, interrupted his speech. She rushed into the hall, still
uttering the name of her child.

"You have murdered him, too!" she exclaimed, wildly, stopping before Desmond. "Ay, you! even while we spoke, above,
some devils in your service spirited him away. Give place!"

She darted past him, and left the hall, to engage in another
search.

Desmond followed close in her steps to receive the child, for
himself, if he should be found. His confidential follower explored
every hiding-place out of doors. None of them succeeded.
Then Dicken and some trusty comrades mounted their horses
to ride to the town, and through all the surrounding country.

Half an hour before the lady of Ormonde missed them, Simon
Seix, stealing on tiptoe to the nearest side-door, had carried the
child out of the gallery in his arms. By private and obscure
passages, which, as he whispered to his young charge, the Desmond's men would not be found to have yet mounted guard upon,
they then gained nearly the same spot, under the window of the
long gallery, where, some hours before, he had enacted, together
the parts of battle-charger and of trumpeter to the little Lord
Thomas. Here he put the boy upon his feet, and stooped down
upon the terre-plein of the wall. "John, the father of Simon,
showed it to me more than once," he said; and, while speaking,
he contrived to loosen a small stone, and extract it from the surrounding ones. A ring appeared; he tugged at it with all his
strength, and a square portion of smooth small flags moved, were

displaced, and discovered narrow steps winding down in darkness through the thickness of the wall.

"Now, noble son of the noble Ormonde, and most noble foster-brother of a born natural, remember all you promised me while we whispered together at the window over our heads," resumed Simon. "Here be the steps which will free us of the castle; and, though it seemeth somewhat dark a little downwards, still trust to my guidance; for the sake of thy dear lady-mother, and of thy—"

"I am not afraid, witless," interrupted the child; "take my hand, and lead me after you."

Without another word, Simon safely conveyed him to the bottom of the turning steps. Here they stood in utter darkness; the misnamed fool groping with his two hands over the rough surface which temporarily opposed their further progress. A joyful exclamation soon told, however, that he found what he sought; and the next moment, a part of the wall, here but of slight thickness, framed in iron, moved inward on hinges, and they saw, through a low, arched opening, only a few feet from them, the river, whose rapid dash and chafe had come on their ears as they descended.

A rugged bank, often interrupted by eddies and little coves of the river, fell from the foundation of the wall into the Nore. Along this, his back turned to John's Bridge and the town, and his young foster-brother once more astride on his shoulders, Simon was soon hurrying. The wall made an abrupt turn, striking off at right angles, inland; he turned with it, and still pursued his course.

"There is the paddock, truly; but where is my lord's favorite horse for the chaise?" he said, after having made considerable way. "Nay, I see him; and now for a hard ride, without saddle, and a *suggaun* bridle in hand."

Some hay was piled in the paddock; from it he adroitly and quickly spun his *suggaun*, fastened it on the head of the fleet courser, placed the child on the animal's back, vaulted up behind him, and a few minutes, over hedge and ditch, brought them to a highway.

"For Waterford, Raymond!" cried Simon, shaking his hay bridle; "and we have need to see the end of the twenty-and-four Irish miles in little more time than it will take to count them over."

"'Tis well to be a fool, ay, and a sleepy fool, too, at times,

Simon, else neither Raymond, nor his riders for him, would know the road so well," said the child.

"There be tricks in all born crafts, your little nobleness," replied Simon, "else how would fools, or even wise men, win bread! In sooth, I deemed I might catch a needful secret behind the arras. Though I wot not of the road till I bethought me of treading lightly back from the window to hear another word."

It was night, but a moonlight one, when the hoofs of their courser beat hollowly along the banks of the Suir. They had avoided the town, and followed the widening of the river a little distance beyond it. Unpractised as were his eyes to such a sight, Simon soon was aware that a great many ships floated on the moonlit water, that boats moved to and from them, and that large bodies of soldiers, destined for taking the field against the formidable young Irish chief, Arthur MacMurchad O'Kavanah, were every moment landing.

While he looked, a sentinel challenged him. He reigned up his foaming horse, and answered, by giving the name of Lord Thomas of Ormonde, and demanding to see the king. The soldier scoffed at his request; and, as Simon insisted, his words grew rough and high. A group of noble-looking men, who, from a near elevation of the bank, had been watching the disembarkation, were attracted to the spot; and one, a knight completely clad in splendid armor, advanced alone from the rest, saying—

"The Lord Thomas of Ormonde to have speech with the king! Where bides this Lord Thomas, master mine?"

"I am the Lord Thomas of Ormonde!" answered Simon's little charge, spiritedly, and as if in dudgeon that he had not been at once recognized.

"Thou, gramercy, fair noble!" continued the knight, good-naturedly, as he touched his helmet. "And on what weighty matter wouldst thou parley with King Richard?"

"An' you lead me to him, like a civil knight and good, Richard himself shall learn," replied the child.

"Excellent well spoken," whispered Simon to his charge "Abide by that fashion of speech."

"By our lady, then, like civil knight and good, will I do my devoir by thee, Lord Thomas of Butler," resumed the knight, "little doubting that the king will give ready ear to thy errand; for passing well he affects one of thy name, the Lord James, Earl of Ormonde."

"Which noble earl is my own father," said the boy.

The knight showed real interest at this intelligence ; and, commanding the horse which bore Simon and the child to be led after him, walked towards the town of Waterford.

Half an hour afterwards, mounted on a fresh steed, and accompanied by their patron and a body of well-armed soldiers, our adventurers galloped back to Kilkenny. The knight had pressed their stay till morning ; but Lord Thomas and Simon convinced him that, for the sake of the Lady of Ormonde, this ought not to be. She required not only to have her son restored to her, but also to be protected against the Desmond, who, ere morning's dawn, might work her irremediable harm. Finding these reasons good, the friendly knight resolved to bear them company.

Upon the road, he arranged with Simon various plans of proceeding ; and, upon a particular point, was wholly governed by the simpleton's advice. Simon said that there was but one vassal of the Desmond in Kilkenny Castle, who, after the tidings they had to communicate, would, at all hazards, attempt to spill blood.

"Then, can ye not make free with his before I enter the castle-hall ?" demanded the knight.

Simon demurred, but proposed an alternative : " We will make him drunk with wines, till he sleeps soundly," said Simon · " and then, upon hearing my signal, a child may enter the hall."

The knight assented ; but added—" Good success still rests upon the chance of the Desmond's army not having yet marched from the field to greet their lord in the Ormonde's fortress. For, though our liege comrades here may well suffice to master the knaves already within its walls, they could not withstand thousands."

Notwithstanding this chance against them, the travellers held on, however, and by midnight gained the secret door, through which Simon had escaped from the castle wall upon the rough and scanty bank of the Nore. Previously, all had dismounted, and, conducted by him, were now ushered, stealthily, into the interior of the castle ; and their hopes grew high when it appeared evident that Desmond's army had not yet come to garrison it.

Few moments then elapsed until Simon entered the hall of the castle, leading his foster-brother by the hand. By the light of a tripod, suspended from the arched roof, he saw his old father stretched on the tiled floor, mournfully supporting his head upon his hand, guarded by a soldier ; at the oak table, immediately under a Scotch broadsword and buckler, won by the Ormonde, some years before, in a battle against the Bruce, when that chieftain made pretensions to the crown of Ireland, sat Dicken Utlaw, the man whom Simon had meant, when he spoke of the single follower of Desmond, whose hand would be prompt to shed the blood even of his liege king in defence of his lord, or in revenge of his discomfiture. A wine cup and a flagon stood at the ruffian's hand, by means of which he had already anticipated, half-way, Simon's designs upon him.

Utlaw's voice was high and angry, as the two truants appeared before him ; and, in fact, he was roundly expressing his wrath against them for the useless chase they had led him over all the neighboring roads, and from which he had only lately returned. So soon as his eyes met theirs he started up, roaring forth commands to the armed man who stood guard over old Seix to secure the door of the hall.

" It does not need," answered the boy ; " we come hither to be your prisoners, good Dicken."

" Ay, thou vagrant imp ! and whence come ye so suddenly, after all our chase, as if ye grew out of the ground, or were blown in upon a wind ?" asked Utlaw.

" Perchance, even as thou sayest, we come," answered Simon ; " for, all this evening, we have footed it merrily with the fays of Brandon Hill. Be patient now, sweet Dicken Utlaw," as the bravo raised his sheathed sword, " and but suffer us to enact for your pleasure one of the good dances they have taught us, and I will bribe my father here, the house-steward, to whisper thee in what corner of the cellar thou mayst chance on a magnum of such renowned wine as has scarce filled to-night the empty flagon at thy hand."

Dicken became somewhat soothed, and, growling an exhortation to the sentinel to guard all his prisoners well, strode off to avail himself of the ready instructions of old Seix. During his short absence, Simon studied the features of the soldier who rested on his tall spear near the door, and drew comfort from their tranquil and even benevolent expression. Utlaw returned to his seat at the oak table, called the wine good, and gulped it down rapidly. It was of great power, and Simon knew the fact well ; but it also seemed capable of making him obliging, for he consented to see the fashion of the dance practised by the hill-elves ; and accordingly, Simon, with a whisper to the child, performed a vagary so grotesque that the drunken savage laughed hoarsely in his cup, and the guard smiled quietly on his post.

Simon continued his frolics till the critical powers of Dicken began rapidly to desert him. Very soon afterwards he slept profoundly—snorting like the swine he was. Simon, now preparing for his most important feat, proposed that Lord Thomas should take a war-horse—namely, an old weapon at hand—and ride it about the hall to the notes of the trumpet. The boy was soon mounted, and Simon taking up a useless scroll of parchment, and rolling it loosely, applied it to his mouth.

Before he would blow his signal blast, however, he glanced into the face of the sentinel, and afterwards to the half-open door of the hall. The man was still smiling good-naturedly at the gleeish gambols of the little Lord Thomas ; and, in the gloom without the hall, Simon caught glimpses of armed men, one of whom presently entered, unseeen by the soldier, and bent watchfully over the snoring Dicken.

"Now to the charge!" cried Simon, addressing his foster-brother ; and, to the astonishment of the sentinel, of the knight, who had just stealthily come in (Simon's friend at Waterford), and of every one in the castle, a perfect trumpet sound ran through the spacious building.

Dicken sprang to his feet, half conscious, and was instantly felled to the ground by a blow of the knight's battle-axe, who had been watching him. Old Seix arose, and seized his sword. Simon armed himself with the weapon upon which the child had been astride, and placed himself spiritedly, though grotesquely, before him. The sentinel quickly brought his spear to his hip, and stood upon the defensive, regarding the stranger knight (who wore his vizor down) with a threatening look ; but a second knight now gaining that person's side, rendered his hostility vain. Almost at the same moment an uproar and a clash was heard through the castle. Presently the Lady of Ormonde ran shrieking into the hall ; and she shrieked wildly again, though not in the same cadence, as she caught up her child to her bosom. She was quickly followed by Desmond, now the prisoner of some of Simon's friends. The bold lord had fought desperately, and bled from his wounds, though the rage which was upon him did not allow him to think of them.

"What treachery is this? and what villains be these?" he exclaimed, as he came in. "Who calls himself chief here?"

The knight, who wore his vizor down, raised his arm, and touched his breast, in answer.

"Then call thyself by such name no longer," continued Desmond; and with that he suddenly freed himself from his guards, snatched the sentinel's long spear, and aimed a thrust at the knight.

"Traitor! stay thy hand!" exclaimed his antagonist, in a voice of high and dignified command. "Thou knowest not what thou doest, nor that, indeed, thy feudel sceptre is here broken in pieces. Look at me now!" He exposed his face.

"Richard, the king!" faltered Desmond, dropping on his knee, as the Lady of Ormonde and all the hall knelt with him.

THE END OF THE HALL OF THE CASTLE.

THE HALF-BROTHERS.

THE HALF-BROTHERS.

LUCY HAWKINS, at sixteen, was the belle, if not the beauty, of her little sea-washed village on the coast of Kent. Other girls might boast a more perfect shape and handsomer features, but her air, her expression, or—if a fashionable French word may, with allowances, be applied to a lowly maiden—her *tournure* eclipsed them all. She was also celebrated for a vivacity of manner and conversation unusual among young women of her class ; nay, in the opinions of a numerous circle of good judges, who constantly enjoyed her company and discourse, Lucy Hawkins deserved to be termed witty.

Her mother kept the post-office of the village, together with a general huckster's shop, and a hotel in one of her outhouses for very humble wanderers or sojourners—beds, three-pence per night. Upon a large deal chest, the good dame's flour-store, which stood under her shop window, opposite to her counter, hard-worked laborers, employed in the neighborhood, would sit and eat their four penny-worth of bread and cheese, and drink their half-pint of small-beer, by way of the morning's or afternoon's meal. And Lucy generally served them, or else stood by while they were served ; and her good-humor materially helped to give zest to their meagre breakfast or dinner. At the upper end of the counter was a rush-bottomed, curiously-legged, old oak-chair, a fixture, put forward for any chatty neighbor or visitor who might like an hour's gossiping. Since its establishment it had, indeed, seldom been left empty, as was indicated, even during its leisure moments, by a little round cavity worn in the tiled floor, just at the spot where its successive occupants necessarily rested their heels. And with the revellers on the chest, and the numerous patrons of this oak-chair, to say nothing of ordinary customers and her own particular friends, Lucy became quite a public character, and, as has been hinted, quite a favorite. The poor people who, towards night, crept through the shop to their straw beds over the hen-house in the yard, also shared her sparkling conversation, and acknowledged its cheery influence.

There were other visitors who also admitted her attractions, though it would have been better for Lucy if we could limit her encomiastic friends to those already mentioned. Over one department of the manifold concern, she had absolute sway. Her mother did not know how to read handwriting, and, considering the frequency of almost illegible superscriptions on the backs of letters, the deputation of authority alluded to became a matter of prudence, if not of necessity. At the inquiry of every claimant for letters "to be left till called for," it was Lucy, therefore, who always unlocked the little rude deal box—about the size, and much in the shape of a salt-box—which, clumsily nailed against the wooden pane with the slit in the shop-window, formed the whole apparatus of the post-office branch of the establishment.

Many officers of the preventive service, although they had abundance of unemployed men to go to Mrs. Hawkins's shop in their stead, would call in every morning to ask for their letters, and at different hours of their idle day return to purchase a quarter of an ounce of Scotch snuff, or something else of which they could have less use—such as a row of pins, a yard of tape, or a reel of thread. In fact, it became evident that three of them were rivals for the smiles of Lucy Hawkins.

Two of the three soon insured to themselves, however, any thing but her smiles. For offences separately received at their hands, she invariably left the shop whenever they entered at it ; and as Lucy's conduct was not a mere show of feminine anger, they absented themselves, and gave up their unmanly pursuit. The third, whose visits were still received, was more seriously in love with Lucy than either of his friends ; but, whether from a nicer sense of honor, or that the fate of the others had taught him a lesson, Lieutenant Stone dip not lightly or hastily tell her so. Much younger than his rivals, perhaps he was more romantic, and, particularly since Lucy's late specimen of self-assertion, would not indulge his admiration with a view to any mean indulgence of it. In fact, when, after sitting in the shop upon the flour-chest or in the old chair, day after day, for more than six months, he at last whispered his sentiments to Lucy, the declara-

tion sounded seriously and respectfully to her ear, and, she concluded, could be made only in one hope—that of obtaining her
hand, with the due consent of father and mother.

The scene must now be very abruptly changed, with a breach
of the three unities of time, place, and action.

Twelve years after Lucy Hawkins accepted the suit of her
chosen lover, we enter a small wooden house, indeed a very poor
shed, in another little seacoast hamlet, many miles distant from
her native one. The walls of its only sitting-room, a kitchen, are
bare, the floor is tiled, and the few articles of indispensable furniture are old, common, and crazy. Yet the poor apartment
looks clean, or, to use an humble but expressive and very English
word, tidy. A woman, as ill clad as her house is ill appointed,
but, like it, tidy too, sits on a stool, teaching a sturdy, sunburnt
boy of seven years to read out of a "Reading Made Easy." She
seems about forty, but may be much younger than she looks, for
her composed features would suggest long acquaintance with misfortune—the often successful anticipator of time's utmost efforts
to destroy. A half-finished female dress, of materials too costly,
and of shape too fashionable, to be destined to the use of the
lowly occupant of the lowly abode, lies, together with the little
implements of woman's industry, upon a table at her side, hinting
the mode of pursuit by which she earns scanty bread for her
young pupil and herself.

The task is over, and Billy is kissed, and called a good boy;
and, while his mother combs his yellow hair in smooth and equal
portions, towards either temple—

"There, my king," she says. "And now, where is brother, to
take you out to play?"

"The naughty great boys were *quarrelling* Charley on the
shingles, mother, when he sent Billy home to his task to be rid of
them."

"And what game did they quarrel over, Billy?"

"No game, mother; but Dick Saunders called Charley a bad
name."

"Tell mother the bad name, my man."

"Billy can't; he doesn't know it now, mother."

Their conversation was interrupted by the quick entrance of
Charley himself. The moment his mother saw him, she uttered
an alarmed cry. His clenched hands were thrust into his
trousers' pockets; he frowned, for the first time in his life his
mother had seen him do so; his lips quivered; tears glazed his

eyes; his face, nay, his forehead and ears, flamed scarlet, and blood trickled down his cheeks. Obviously he had been fighting a hard battle, but, as obviously, was the victor. The boy was about twelve.

"Let Billy go play at the door, and I'll tell you mother," he said, after she had addressed many anxious inquiries to him

She led the little fellow out, and shut the door upon her self and Charley. He dropped in a chair, flung his arms over the table, laid his face upon them, and burst into a furious fit of crying.

"Naughty Dick Saunders has hurt you, Charley, mother's darling!" she cried, approaching him.

"No, not so much as I have hurt *him*, the story-teller! the puppy!" sobbed Charles. "Mother, Dick Saunuders spoke ill of me and of you."

"What did he say, Charley?"

"I can't repeat it after him—I won't. But, mother, I be old enough to ask you what I'm going to ask. Was Master Turner, who died last year, Billy's father?"

"To be sure he was, Charley." She grew uneasy.

"And your husband?"

"Yes."

"And *my* father, too?"

She changed color, and dropped her eyes beneath the deep glance of her child.

"Now, Charley, I know what they said of you and me; and the time is indeed come for me to speak to you of what nearly concerns you."

"Did Dick Saunders tell no story, mother?" interrupted Charley, sitting upright, and again unconsciously scrutinizing her face.

She raised her eyes, met his for an instant, and then sank back in her chair, covering her features with her hands, and weeping dolefully.

"I ask pardon, mother," said the generous, and hitherto gentle boy, as he gained her side, and put his arms round her neck. You always loved me, and I shall always love you, let them say what they will of us. Kiss Charley, mother, won't you?"

Fondly, almost wildly, she embraced him, and resumed—

"No, Charley; Master Turner, my husband, was *not* your father. Stop a moment."

She stepped into her little bedroom; returned with a small,

square red-leather case ; placed it in his hand ; sat down ; averted her head ; began to move the work on her table ; and would vainly hide her continued tears, as she added—

"Open that, and you will know more of your father."

While he obeyed her commands, Charley recollected that he had more than once detected his mother weeping over the little red-leather case. When the miniature met his eye, the boy started.

"My father was a ship's captain !" he cried.

"He was an officer in the king's navy," she answered.

" And a gentleman, mother ?"

" His commission made him one, Charley, but he would have been a true gentleman without it."

"And he married you before Master Turner married you, mother ?"

" Charley, your father and I never were married."

A pause ensued. Charley's features betrayed a bitter and fierce inward combat, as his glance still fixed on the miniature.

" Is he dead ?" he at length asked.

" I hope not, but I am not sure. Sometimes I think one thing, sometimes another. Listen, my king. I was very young when I met your father, and I wondered, and many others wondered, what he could see in me to love. I was his inferior in every way. To be sure, my poor mother had managed to keep me at good schools till I was a great girl, and perhaps this made me something in his eyes. Then, when we began to keep company, with father's and mother's consent, he taught me, like a master, himself, a great many things that improved my mind and my manners, ay, and my heart, too ; but I am not going on with my story. We were to be married at the end of two years. Before the first year came round he was ordered from the blockade service to a ship, at only a few hours' notice. He ran down to our shop, and showing the letter, prayed mother to let us be made man and wife that very evening. She would not hear of it, saying I was too young, and did not know my own mind, and would not know how to behave as his wife. He begged and prayed once again, and cried tears, and went on his knees ; she held firm to her word. But alas Charley, it had been doing better if she had not held so firm to it, or else not have left us alone to take leave of each other that evening. And next day, ay, before it was day, your father left our village, and I have never seen him since."

" But he has sent letters to you, mother ?"

"I got none, if he did : though I believe he did, and that an enemy kept them from my hands. A very short time after he left us, my father died, my mother grew poor, and we were turned out of our comfortable little house, not being able to pay our rent The shop was reopened by a woman and her daughter who bore me no good-will, and on your father's account, too. He had paid some compliments to the daughter before he met me, and they blamed me for taking him from them. God, forgive me if I wrong either mother or daughter! but I do fear that letters from your father to me, and from me to him, were stopped by the new keepers of our post-office. Well, Charley, you were born while my mother and I lived in a very poor way, trying to support ourselves with our needles, and keep out of the workhouse. Your father's silence almost broke my heart. I did not suspect foul play about the letters then—'tis only lately people gave me some hints ; and all I could think was that he had forsaken us both, my king. My mother died too, and you and I were quite left alone, Charley. Years after, when, try as I would or could, we were getting worse and worse off, Master Turner came from his village to ours on business, and knowing my whole story asked me to marry him. He was a man well to do in the world at that time, and a kind man too; and so, after giving up all other hopes, I thought, Charley, that, even for your sake, I ought not to refuse a comfortable home and comfortable living. But it seemed as if every one was to have ill-luck with me. Good Master Turner began to grow poor from that very day till last year, when he died, leaving us as badly off as he found us. And that's the whole story, Charley ; only, here are you and I living alone again, with your little half-brother Billy to keep us company.

"Well ; and I be glad of his company, mother," said Charley. "I always loved little Billy for his own sake, and because he loved me." The mutual affection of the boys was indeed very remarkable. "And now, though as you say, he turns out to be only my half-brother, I'll love him better for his father's sake, who was a friend to you when you wanted a friend. But we must open the door and let him in."

Billy's voice had been heard calling on Charles to run down with him to the beach, and see the grand three-masted ship that was passing but a little way out, and people said, seemed about to send a boat ashore. Ere Charles went to the door, he held out the miniature and asked,

"May I see it often again, mother ?"

"Keep it ; 'tis your own, Charley. Here"—passing a riband through a loop at it's top—"hang it round your neck."

As his mother secured it, he once more felt her tears droppiₙg fast on his head, and looking up into her face, he stole his arms around her.

"Go, now, mother's darlings," as, hand in hand, they left huᵣ humble threshold. "But, Charley, do not stray out far on the sands : it will be a spring-tide, I fear, and the breeze comes fresh from the sea."

Still, hand in hand, they proceeded on their walk—Billy uₙ usually communicative, and Charles unusually silent. Indeed thᵤ younger boy remarked his brother's taciturnity, and taxed him. with it. They met groups of their former playmates in the village street, whom the child wished to join ; but Charles, chucking him closer to his side, passed them by, knitting his brow and holding up his head. On the shingles appeared other groups, and the young misanthrope would not descend to the water's edge until he had proceeded several hundred yards above their position.

It was a beautiful spring day. The breeze lashed the waves into a sportive fury. Sun and cloud, light and shade, alternated their effects over the wide bosom of the sea, streaking it with gold and pea-green, with dark purple or deep blue. Now a distant sail was a white speck on the horizon, now a spot of dark, dotting a clear sky. The three-master, of which little Billy had spoken, lay-to about a mile from shore. Charles knew her to be an East Indiaman. His brother urged him to approach her as close as the sands permitted. Still wrapped up in his own thoughts and feelings, Charles silently stepped down the shingles, looking jealously around to note if they were alone.

Behind him, as he began to move towards the waves, was a low line of cliff, forming, at a particular point, a jutting platform, from the outward edge of which the continuation of the cliff swept like a buttress to the shingles. Before him stretched the strand to nearly the distance of half a mile, where it was met by an irregular circle of black rocks, closely wedged together, and inclosing the last patch of sand visible even at low tide. Charles had not intended to approach this spot, but as he walked in an oblique direction from it, some straggling boys appeared coming against him, and he hastily led his little charge to the convenient screen of the tall rocks.

The tide had for some time been coming in. Often before,

however, Charles had ventured further out when it was more ad
vanced, and returned to shore with only wet feet and a splashing. The rocks could not at any point be easily scaled, so high
and broad was their barrier ; nor did they admit of ingress into
the sandy area they girded, save at a particular spot seaward,
where, some feet from their base, appeared a narrow fissure, still
difficult of access. Charles, therefore, walked round them until
he gained this opening ; then, assisting his little brother to climb
up to it, the two boys soon stood upon a projection inside the
rocky belt, and turned their faces towards the sea.

They could perceive, by a bustle on the deck of the Indiaman,
now so near to them, that a boat would soon be lowered from
her side. They looked out, much interested, until the boat
lightly touched the tossing waves near the vessels prow, and became strongly manned, as if to put off for shore. Still, however,
the men rested on their oars, and seemed waiting for some other
person to descend. And, in a mood that sympathized with the
scene, Charles continued to watch the boat dancing to and fro,
and sometimes almost jumping out of the water, for the breeze
grew stiffer and the waves rougher. Half an hour he stood motionless, disregarding, for the first time in his life, the prattle of
the little boy at his side. At last the individual for whom the
boat waited, clad in blue and white, and gold lace, to Billy's
great delight, jumped in among his men, stood up at their head,
pointed to shore, and was rapidly rowed towards it.

For some time the near roar of waters had been ringing in
Charles's ear, but he made light of the warning, for he confidently argued from experience, whenever his thoughts reverted
to the matter, that there was still sufficient time to return to
the shingles with scarce a wet shoe ; but he did not reckon
that the spot of sand with which he now stood inclosed, was
much higher than the outer sands which stretched to the bases
of the rocks. He did not reckon that the tide, at a certain
period of its flow, after turning a near point of land, usually ran
with almost the rapidity of a mill-stream against the right-hand
sedgment of the barrier, and then, directed by its curve, inundated in a trice the previously open space between it and the
shingles ; above all, he did not remember what his mother hinted at parting, for, indeed her omen proved true, it was a spring
tide.

The ship's boat, still seen at a distance, glanced athwart the
patch of sea revealed through the fissure at which the boys

looked out. More alive, after its disappearance, to the unusual noise of the waters, Charley took his brother's hand to lead him home by the way they had come. To his consternation, a fiercely crested wave leaped into their faces through the narrow opening, drenching both to the skin. He let go Billy's hand, and sprang up to the top of the circular wall of rocks. A foamy sea tossed all around him. His eye caught the gallant boat, about a quarter of a mile distant. He screamed to it; jumped down to his little brother; dragged him up to the spot he had just quitted, and screamed again. There was a little cavity, formed by the irregular junction at their sharp extremities of the rocks, and in this he placed the now bewildered and weeping child, to preserve him from being dashed inward by the quickly increasing sea, and clinging himself to the highest pinnacle he could grasp, once more he wildly hailed the boat.

Most probably he had now caught its notice. It put round and pulled towards him, but soon seemed deterred from venturing too near the dangerous rocks.

"O God! O mother, mother! your Billy! Mother's darling! *he* at least will be drowned, though I may swim till they pick me up—and all *my* fault! But, no, no!" He pulled off his jacket and waistcoat, and tore his shirt into long stripes. No! he shall not! Come, Bill! I will tie you to my back! Never fear, my king—and see if I don't swim like a fish for you!"

The child, having heard and noted all his words and actions, had stopped crying, and, as if struck with Charley's noble conduct and sentiments, and unconsciously sympathizing with them, answered—

"I won't, Charley; I won't. I should sink you, and we should only be drowned together, then; and no one will be left with mother."

All this while breakers had been dashing from without nearly up to the summits of the rocks at the opposite sweep of the circle, and as Charles eagerly, indeed violently, renewed his entreaties, they at last came leaping and plunging up to its very edge, like dark, white-maned war-horses, trying to rear and paw over some high and well-guarded embankment. Once again he hoarsely cried out to the boat. It was nearer to him, but still seemed cautious of actual approach. He turned for the last time to Billy, and seized him in his arms to compel him to do his bidding. The riband which held his father's miniature round his

neck snapped in the exertion ; the miniature itself was rolling
outwardly into the surf ; he snatched at it, and secured it,
but lost his balance, and the next instant was kicking among the
breakers.

The captain of the East Indiaman had, with his pocket-glass,
witnessed the greater part of the scene between the young broth-
rs ; and, as he saw Charles tumble from the rocks, gallantly
ordered his men to dare a good deal, and pull towards the spot
where the boy had sunk. Presently, Charley reappeared, swim-
ming stoutly ; not for the boat, however, but back again to the
now almost invisible rocks. The captain and his men called to
him, but he did not heed them. It has been mentioned that
when the boys walked out to the sands, they directly turned
their backs upon a platform in a low line of cliff. At that moment, not only the platform and its rugged buttress-base, but the
shingles beneath, were perfectly dry. Now the raging surf of a
spring-tide, excited by a stiff breeze, foamed up to the level of
the former ; and almost simultaneously with Charley's reappearance, a woman, screaming loudly, descended the difficult passage
from the brow of the cliff, and gained the slippery shelf. Many
people followed her to the top line of the precipice, but no one
ventured to her side. Her cries reached the young swimmer
through all the roar of the sea, and he redoubled his vain efforts
to reach his little brother. But very soon exertion became useless. At one enraged and re-enforced charge of the breakers, the
area inclosed by the rocky circle, hitherto little intruded on, was
inundated, and no part of the black barrier-line remained visible,
except that formed by the pinnacles amid which the child stood
wedged : a curling chain of foam supplied its place. And now,
his mother from the shore, his brother from the sea, and the
captain and his men from their boat, witnessed the conduct of
the little sufferer. He had been sitting ; he stood up : a break-
er struck him ; he staggered : another came ; he fell, disappeared : was still seen, however, upon a point of rock, raising
his hands, and clapping them over his head, until at the third
blow the little fellow became engulfed in the whirling waters.

The boat was now very near to Charles ; and, at last seemingly attentive to the remonstrance of its crew, he turned, and
languidly swam towards its side.

" What the deuce has the young grampus fished up between
his teeth ?" said the captain, as he assisted in reaching out an oar.
" A boiled crab, I reckon ; though, where they got a fire to

boil it, at the bottom of this surf, is more than I can imagine."

Charles was dragged into the boat, and without a word or a cry, fell stupefied upon its bottom. The miniature dropped from his unclenched teeth ; the captain took it up, opened it, and startled his men by uttering a loud exclamation. Then he stooped to Charley's face, and peered into it ; then glanced to the cliff ; and finally, ordering every oar to pull for the shingles, he knelt on one knee, raised Charley's head to the other ; and his crew were still more surprised to see their bluff captain embrace the almost senseless lad, kiss his cheeks and forehead, and weep over him profusely, though in silence.

The boat had not shot far, when little Billy floated ahead. The captain gently, though hastily put Charles down, and with much energy assisted in picking up the child, who soon lay stretched beside his half-brother, rescued indeed from the sea, but, it seemed evident, quite dead. Still the captain cried, "Pull, men, pull !"

Vigorously and skilfully obeying his orders, they ran the lively boat upon the shingles, a good distance below the point at which the low cliff gradually dipped to their surface. The mother flew down to meet her children and their unknown friends. The anxious crowd followed her. She received Charley from the captain's arms ; a sailor followed, holding Billy, wrapped in the captain's jacket, to his bosom. At her first word the elderly boy opened his eyes. After straining him to her heart, she flew to his brother. No word had effect upon him. The captain called out for a surgeon : the village practitioner and the blockade surgeon were both at hand. They caused the child to be conveyed into a neighboring cottage, and there, in the presence of the mother and the captain, promptly engaged in all the usual measures for restoring animation : but all failed. They repeated their exertions, still without effect ; and at length, pronouncing Billy to be a corpse, left the cottage.

Charles had been stretched across the foot of the bed upon which, wrapped in blankets, lay his little half-brother. At first he did not comprehend his situation, or notice the occurrences around him. Now, however, he seemed to hear the departing words of the surgeons, for, raising himself upon his elbow, he gazed first into his mother's face, as she sat in silent anguish by the bedside, and then he tried to move upwards towards Billy. While making this effort, the captain, gently laying his hand on the mother's shoulder, asked to speak aside with her. She arose, in the languid indifference of grief, and followed him into a corner of the room, out of view of the bed.

"Lucy !" was the captain's only word, soothingly whispered at her ear.

She drew back, looked up into his face, and was in his arms.

A brief explanation proved that her suspicions of her revengeful rival at the village post-office were well founded ; while, from the suppression of the captain's letters to her, Lucy had believed him cruel and faithless, the holding back also of her letters to him had caused her sincere lover to conclude that she was no better than a village coquette, who, the moment he left her presence, forgot him, and insulted his memory and his devotion in the smiles of a new admirer. Hence, after her seeming silence of many years, he had proudly struggled to give up Lucy Hawkins for ever ; and though, since their parting, he could often have returned to her village, he would not so far humiliate himself. Some inquiries, however, he condescended to make by a confidential person sent for the purpose, merely with a view of ascertaining if Lucy were alive or dead,—for death alone, he argued, could explain her supposed conduct. About the very time his emissary arrived in the village, she had become the envied wife of the rich Master Turner ; and this intelligence necessarily confirmed his former angry resolutions.

The captain and Lucy were yet speaking, when Charles's voice sounded shrill and joyfully from the bed :

"Yes, Billy, yes ! 'Tis Charley, Billy !—mother's darling !"

They stepped round to the bedside. He had crept under the blankets, and clasped the child close to his bosom ; and now, indeed, the efforts of the surgeons, although despaired of by themselves, began to yield a good result.

"He would not die, to let you see I killed him, mother," said Charles, laughing through his tears.

"The child lives, by heavens !" cried the captain.

That day Captain Stone was married to the woman of his early choice ; and having dispatched, before evening, the trifling business which first called him to shore, he conveyed his wife to his ship, together with her two sons, and pursued his voyage.

.

THE END OF THE HALF-BROTHERS.

TWICE LOST, BUT SAVED.

TWICE LOST, BUT SAVED.

PERHAPS there is no country so little susceptible, generally speaking, of public sensation as England. Events which agitate the peasant, nay, the peasant's wife, at the other side of the straits of Dover, would scarce reach John Bull in his village chimney-nook ; certainly would not disturb the serenity of his countenance, if they did. And yet there is one species of occurrence which excites and pervades English people, through every grade of society, more than it could, or at least more than it does, any other civilized nation. A murder, a downright murder—broad-featured, well-marked, unequivocal, refined—arouses into unusual vivacity all England, from the banks of the Tweed to the Land's End. Its fame spreads from cities and towns into the recesses of the small mountain hamlet. Men, women, girls, and children talk and think of nothing else. The newspapers teem with nothing else, excepting only and always the unheeded advertisements of new books. Literary talent of really a high order is vented in descriptions, speculations, deductions, and sentimental discussions on the subject. Artists hurry down to the rural scene of the atrocity to make money by making drawings of it, as well as of all the innocent scenery and accompaniments within view. Thousands of people who cannot wait for their second-hand information, hurry after them, or anticipate them, to see with their own eyes, or to hear with their own ears, the whispered anecdotes of the half-petrified carter, who, in the gray dawn of the drizzling morning, found the stained bread-knife or the discharged pocket-pistol (the first dreadful intimators of the deed) in the lonesome bridle-road, or by the side of the stagnant pool. Or they pay round sums to have to say that they sat down in the little back-parlor or scrambled through the brake where the murderer so lately sat or passed. A bit of the chair upon which he reposed while contemplating his crime, as he glanced into his victim's face, or a branch of the briars among which they struggled together, is eagerly purchased, and reverently and tenderly preserved, like a saint's relic or a true-love token. Is all this to be called honest, national abhorrence? What would Rochefoucault call it—particularly after detecting in the cabinet of the collector of curiosities the last possible mementos of the sentenced and executed hero, in shape, perhaps (lavishly bribed from the law's humblest officer) of a inch of twisted hemp, the corner of a flaming red cravat, or a gentle lock of redder hair?

So thoroughly had the tidings of such an event as is alluded to penetrated the nooks and corners of the land at the commencement of this little tale, that naught else was discussed around the fireside of the humblest and most isolated country cottage ; and scarce aught else upon the truant and noisy forms of the lowliest village school. While manhood and old age rehearsed the tale with the profoundest interest, boyhood and childhood commented upon it in whispers which bespoke a little interest deepened by awe and fear. The murder had, indeed, been of a fearful character. But it must be remarked that weeks had now passed over since its occurrence ; that its wretched perpetrator had undergone the earthly expiation of his tremendous crime ; and that, notwithstanding, it had not yet begun to relax its influence upon the general mind of the country. And this part requires to be explained.

Justice had gained her victim with difficulty. Circumstantial evidence was slight and loose against him, and although he had been apprehended upon strong suspicions, it seemed that, after repeated examinations before the magistrates, he must have been discharged from prison. Upon the eve of his contemplated day of enfranchisement, a woman visited him in his cell. A person was so posted as to listen to their conversation. She had been suspected of carrying in spirits to the prisoner, but the irregularity was overlooked by the jailor in hopes of the results it might produce. The miserable beings caroused together, first speaking in cautious whispers, but gradually high enough to be imperfectly overheard by the eavesdropper. It appeared that although married, they had only recently met with each other, previous to which event the female had been a poor outcast, glad to avail herself of any protection. The listener thought he then could recognize allusions to the murder, but that the man stopped them, his husky voice sinking into a low and ominous tone. The topic changed. The woman slightly upbraided her companion with having deceived her. She said it was whispered that he had a wife living. His answer came abruptly and savagely. She repeated her charge in an angry voice ; they quarrelled ; she reeled and shrieked under his blows ; and during her fit of indignation, he who listened caught, though still imperfectly, enough to authorize the jailor in making more objections to her departure than he had done to her admission. In fact, she was speedily removed to a separate cell, and carefully secured under lock, and key, and bolt.

The object now was to induce a disclosure of all she knew. Magistrates, officers of justice, ministers of religion, visited her alternately or together. At first it became surmised that she was an actual accomplice. Her gradual confessions, however, if they could be believed, combatted this opinion ; and finally, as if a heart, once good and never irremediably depraved, had been touched in her bosom by a horror of the insinuated accusation, she fell upon her knees, and, with clasped hands and streaming eyes, called Heaven to witness that, so far from having participated in the hellish crime, she had often, though vainly, interfered to prevent it during the unhappy moments that the murdered man remained alive in her presence.

This was enough, or nearly so, for executing justice upon her wretched associate. The details were elicited at subsequent intervals ; repeated by her before a judge and jury ; the murderer perished, as a deliberate spiller of blood should perish. The doors of her prison-house opened, and she passed out into the world—free.

Free—but it was not freedom to her. Hatred, abhorrence, avoidance, curses, execrations, met her at every step, and left no path open for her to choose among her fellow-creatures. All hearts were shut against her as close, ay, closer than the iron door of her cell had been. Public opinion, particularly in such cases, is rapidly and tyrannically made up. In the interval between her confession and the trial of the greater criminal, the notion first adopted by her visitors in the jail, that she had been a real accomplice in the cruel and abominable murder, seized upon the minds of the community at large. Nay, immediately before the day of trial, every one bandied about the belief that she was the sole homicide, and that she had accused her former companion only in order to save herself. Whether or no these rumors reached that individual in his solitary dungeon cannot be said, but he acted so as to give them a seemingly unquestionable confirmation. After the verdict of the jury had been returned, and again upon the trembling verge of eternity, he declared his own innocence and her guilt. The decent crowd, male and female, graybeards and piping children, fully credited his assertions, and gratified him with three horrid growls upon the name of Martha Hall—for so was the wretched woman called—befor his ears grew dull forever to the sounds of this world. Th only person who, at that moment, seemed to doubt his sincerity was the clergyman who attended him. For the culprit's heart had continued hard and obstinate to the very last, against every exhortation to die in peace with God and with his kind.

But the miserable Martha Hall could gain little from the single doubt of the good priest. It was the crowd, the arbitrary, the inhuman crowd she had to face, and, one and all, they rose up against her. Unnerved and ill after her release from jail, she had sought a squalid lodging in the suburbs of the town in which her nominal husband suffered death. Half an hour subsequent to his mortal exit, the howl of the people came towards her door ; her old landlady thrust her out to them, and she fled through their recoiling masses, stunned with curses, with yells, with hissings and hootings, with blows of offal and of hands. The constables could scarce save her life. Half-clad, faint, weeping, screaming, tottering, they finally succeeded, however, in escorting her beyond the bounds of the town, and then left her panting on the road-side, her back leaning against the fence, and her feet resting in the putrid water at its bottom. Did she find peace here? Did any good Samaritan pass that way? No ; but some who had seen her in the neighboring streets did, and taking the other side of the road, they refrained from heaping more cruelty, more dirt and revilings upon her head, only until they could summon to their aid in the task, the fellow-creatures in whose parish she had now dared to set the sole of her foot. Soon the fresh crowd gathered around her ; and, amid renewed yellings and blows, she was again hunted, like a mad dog, into another parish, the local officers still scarce able to save her from perishing under the hands of an indignant Christian community, most of whom went, each Sabbath-day, to one place of worship or another, and listened to the interpretation of the doctrine of Christian charity.

So, from place to place, wherever she sought a refuge or a breathing-spot, Martha Hall was pursued. Her name and the curse upon her ran like wildfire before her ; so that she was dreaded, and expected, and prepared for, ere she made her appearance in a near town, or village, or hamlet, or parish, and received and welcomed accordingly. Reports of the outrages committed upon her regularly found their way into the newspapers. And thus the more remote haunts of man became acquainted with her "whereabouts ;" and people living a hundred miles from the latest scene of her disgrace were able to trace her wretched wanderings, and calculate the likehood of her shaping her course towards them.

These were the circumstances which kept up in every mind, long after such a public fever generally abates, the interest of the late murder. At each new account of the expulsion of Martha Hall beyond the new bounds within which she vainly hoped to find an asylum, all the circumstances of the event that led to her persecution became discussed over again, with a vivacity which lost little by the repetition. And, as has been said, the commotion and the dread of her was general throughout the kingdom. But it will readily be concluded, that the districts nearest in turn to the fugitive outcast experienced the greatest panic and abhorrence.

We must now visit a remote and thinly inhabited parish, in the west of England, of which almost all the inhabitants, at least of the middle and the lower orders, had passed an anxious and idle morning, under the apprehension that their neighbors would send the vagrant within the pale of their jurisdiction. A better illustration of the state of the people's minds can scarce be given, than to notice the fact that, in expectation of Martha Hall's public entry, mothers, although they flocked towards the public road themselves, left behind them, under lock and key, such of their children as were young enough to be so controlled.

In one only humble house of the parish was the topic of general interest treated as it ought to have been. This was the dwelling of Laurence Hutchins, a man advanced in years, a widower, and, compared with older sojourners or with natives, a stranger. He had come from a distant county, with his wife, a little girl, and an infant son, only some seven or eight years before. Shortly afterwards, his wife died, people said of a broken heart, the seeds of which malady she had brought with her to her new residence ; and if Laurence Hutchins did not follow her to the grave, it was not that he too seemed not to share the hidden grief of his companion, but that his frame proved stronger than hers, or his mind more resisting, or, perhaps, that Providence had given him the nerve to endure life for the sake of his two orphans. The deepest sorrow, indeed, was fixed on his hard-featured, though not displeasing face; and all his actions, and his whole manner, agreed with its expression. He worked laboriously, as a common day-laborer, whenever he could get employment. In his disengaged hours, he dug, or raked, or weeded, or planted, or transplanted, in the little garden attached to his solitary cottage; but he made few acquaintances, and no companions. To those who knew most of him, little as that was, he spoke seldom, and never mirthfully. He had no person, male or female, to assist him in the many cares claimed at his hands by his two helpless children. If a visitor dropped in, although Laurence did not demean himself uncouthly, there was no welcome such as might induce a second call. To sum up the opinion entertained of him by his surrounding friends, his poor cottage was termed, "the sad house," and its master, "sad Laurence."

And yet it was in this "sad house" that the expected arrival of Martha Hall within the parish bounds created no indecent commotion. From the time of the first report of the murder, down to the present morning, little Mima, or Jemima Hutchins, now a growing girl of about twelve, observed that her father never bestowed a word on the subject. He had listened, indeed, to the account of it given to the lonely family, by a gossiping neighbor; but, when the tale was ended, Laurence only took his hat and spade, and strode heavily into his garden. Mima, however, could not remain ignorant of the tidings which reached her secluded district, day after day. If no other person acted as her informant, little brother Dick ran in to her, during her discharge of such household duties as she was now able to undertake, with the free translations of the newspaper, and other anecdotes, supplied to him by urchins like himself, on the roadside, or at "the steps" by the brook—a favorite rendezvous of the junior truants of the parish, as it was also the place where the girls of the adjacent cottages went to fill their pitchers for domestic uses.

Nor could Mima help feeling a portion of the excitement created in all around her, by the exaggerated stories of the innocence of the executed man, the guilt of Martha Hall, and her flight from parish to parish, from town to town. Although the practical virtues and benevolence taught her by her father, always in act and deed, and sometimes in sound doctrine, hindered the child from fully sharing the thirst of persecution towards the fugitive, so ostentatiously encouraged in themselves and others by the good people who surrounded her, still she imbibed a strong aversion for the object of all hate and all loathing, and felt a surpassing terror of coming in contact with her. These sentiments gained strength in her breast, from the necessity of keeping them to herself, and brooding over the chimeras they engendered ; for, though she could not tell precisely why, Mima would not renew the topic with her father, and she had no one else to claim confidence of, except her little brother, of seven years, and he was nobody.

The family of " the sad house" sat down to their frugal breakfast. One after another, idlers dropped to report the news of Martha Hall's approach from the neighboring parish. Still Laurence Hutchins took no notice. Mima, however, listened eagerly and breathlessly. An additional piece of information did not increase her happiness. The last over-zealous friend who came to unburden himself of his babbling at Laurence Hutchins's hearth strongly advised the melancholy man to keep his children within doors, and to stand at his threshold with a bludgeon in his hand, in order to obstruct the probable entry of the vagrant ; inasmuch as the brook which ran by the falling ground at the back of his cottage was the boundary of the parish in that direction, and most likely Martha Hall would be driven in among them all at that point or near it. Then she would make for " the steps," and up them, straight for his house, and so—

Laurence Hutchins again interrupted his obliging orator by putting on his hat and leaving the cottage, his little boy's hand in his, to cut rushes in a neighboring marsh, for the purpose of making salable mats of them.

The gossip sat a moment, much offended, opposite to Mima. Then, starting at some ominous sound which, he said, reached him from a distance, also arose and left her alone.

Mima sat listening in great fear, more than once inclined to bolt the door and secure herself. But hearing nothing to suggest immediate danger, and also recollecting that she ought not to barricade her father's house without his permission or advice, she continued fixed upon her stool. Presently she bethought herself of her forenoon duties ; and, at a recurrence of the thought of the first and most necessary, poor Mima turned pale. It was to go down the bushy declivity at the back of the cottage and fill a pitcher of water from the brook at " the steps" wherewith to

prepare her father's dinner ; the very brook which, in that quarter, ran between her parish and the parish whence the execrated
Martha Hall was to be expected ; the very steps up which, in
the opinion of their anxious visitor, she would most probably
escape into new bounds.

At the first view, the child deemed it to be impossible that she
could run such a risk. But her father must not be left without
is dinner at the usual hour—her good father, who, when she
was a little girl, took care to have hers ready every day. Besides, would he deem her reasons for the omission of her duty
sufficient? From a recollection of his habits of thinking and
and feeling, she believed not. ` Finally, after some time had worn
away, she knelt down, as she had been taught to do from her infancy, and praying to God to be saved from harm, Mima lifted
up her pitcher, and took her way to the brook.

There were two distinct descents to "the steps" from the back
of the house. At the bottom of the first ran a broad pathway,
leading to the marshes whither her father had gone with little
Dick to cut rushes. This pathway she gained, stepping firmly,
if not courageously, and was mounting over the stile which would
usher her upon the first of the rude steps leading down the second descent to the water, when a distant uproar really reached
her. She hesitated and stopped. The sounds grew louder. She
was turning to race home again. Her father and her little
brother appeared coming back from the marsh, having finished
their work sooner than she had expected. As they must pass her,
she waited for them. Laurence Hutchins expressed some surprise to find her loitering at the stile. She wept. He looked
earnestly into her face, and took her trembling hand as he added—

"But I see ; you durst not go down to fill your pitcher, Mima,
for fear of Martha Hall?"

Fresh tears were shed by Mima, and she could give no other
nswer. Her father patted her on the head, and continued :

"Trip down to the brook, my maid, however ; do your duty,
and fear no one. Besides, why should you fear this poor woman?"

"I hate her more than I fear her, father?" replied Mima, the
sudden liveliness of her manner emulating what she had seen
among her Christian neighbors.

"Hate her, Mima, do you?" pursued Laurence. "And who
gave you leave to hate *her*, or any living creature? Not Him
who commands us to love all."

"All, father ! Even the guilty and the bad ?"

"All, Mima. Even the guilty and the bad ! Even them we are to love, though we hate the bad that is in them. But who says that Martha Hall is so bad? A judge and jury have believed her innocent of the great crime, at least, laid by less wise people at her door. Go down, my little maid ; go down the steps and fill your pitcher ; and go with courage. I will not even stay here to give you false heart. You will find me and little Dick in the house."

He fondled and kissed her as he spoke—a rather unusual manifestation of his love, though he was practically a very affectionate parent. This, and the reliance placed on her strength of mind, suddenly encouraged Mima. Dashing the tears from her eyes, she trotted down instantly to the brook's edge ; and, while Laurence Hutchins and his almost infant son turned away from the stile to pursue the easy path to the house, each carrying his bundle of rushes, she seated herself on the steps, laid her pitcher at her side, crossed her hands on her lap, and unconsciously indulged for an instant the pleasing sensations which had so suddenly taken possession of her breast.

The clamor she had heard at the stile above, although unheeded during the conversation of her father, here came loudly on her ear. From the opposite side of the brook the ground swelled, though not so suddenly as at her own side, and ran for about a quarter of a mile, until it met a high road. It was a succession of stubble fields. From the high road, at its far edge, Mima heard the uproar. Her eyes eagerly turned in that direction. She was left but a short time in doubt. A crowd broke over the fence of the road into the most remote field, shouting, yelling, groaning, and hissing, and came in almost a straight line towards her. She started up, but a thought of her father kept her stationary. The rabble rout drew nearer ; some running on before Martha Hall, others at her side, others pressing upon her from behind, and all—men, women, boys, and young girls—all similarly engaged pelting her with clods and mud, spitting in her face, cursing her, and hooting her. The thrice unhappy woman was just protected, and no more, from their utmost fury by two overseers, each of whom held one o. her arms as they hurried her along ; and by a beadle, who ex erted himself to keep off the virtuous viragos, and the manful husbands and fathers at her back. Exhaustion, terror, almost madness stamped her ghastly features, her rolling eyes, and her parched and dust-clotted lips. Blood-stained her forehead ; her long black hair streamed around her ; her clothes were half torn off ; her feet were bare, weather-cracked, and swollen ; her step altogether uncertain. Indeed, but for the support and tugging of the stout overseers, she must have fallen prostrate among the sharp stubbles.

Such was the appearance of Martha Hall in her present plight ; and yet more than half of Mima's dislike, remaining after her father's words, was conquered by that appearance. The child, shaping a phantom to suit her prejudices, had fancied the outcast into a personification of something monstrous, ugly, and horrible ; now she beheld a woman not more than four or five-and-twenty, handsome featured, well formed, and looking no more like a murderess—and a double murderess, and traitoress, too—than any other comely female she had before seen. Mima only felt that she looked scared almost to death, faint, and very wretched. Upon this feeling followed another—that she was barbarously treated.

They brought her to the edge of the brook, a few paces below the steps, on the opposite side. Until now, Mima had thought that she spoke not a word. At this close view, however, it was evident that her lips often moved in an effort to shape words, although her voice was only a hoarse, struggling whisper. Seemingly she craved mercy—humbly, most humbly. A pause took place. The abhorred vagrant was to be forced across the shallow water ; but how? Her bitterest haters did not feel inclined to wet their shoes, even to satisfy their magnanimity.

"In with her ! in with her alone !" arose the cry. "In with her ! and we shall soon pelt her over to our neighbors !"

They gathered close and clutched her. The overseers resisted a little, as in duty bound. The wretch herself, with clasped hands, bloodshot eyes, bending knees, and cringing body, mutely implored. The next instant, shrieking wildly, she was splashing in the water. The next, stimulated as well by a dread of a shocking death as by a shower of clods, sods, and stones, she had, with a desperate effort, scrambled across the brook, crawled up its easy bank, and disappeared among the trees and bushes, which, at that point, thickly clothed the base of the ascent thence arising towards Laurence Hutchins's house. Shortly afterwards, with a parting yell, her persecuters hurried back to the road from which they had come ; the overseers and the beadle slowly followed, and little Mima was left alone on the steps.

Terrified, shocked, and now full of pity rather than of hate, the child dipped her pitcher in the brook, and hastened to her home. Half-way up the steps, groans and hard breathing reached her from a clump of bushes to one side. She leaned, not without awe and some fear still, over the spot. Stretched upon her back, some distance beneath her, she saw Martha Hall. The woman was staring vaguely straight upwards. Her eyes and those of the child met; she started through her whole frame; her glance became more intelligent; she half arose on her knees, grasped her hands together, and now, in the deep silence, Mima could distinctly hear her piercing whisper.

"Mercy! mercy and pity, young girl! Save me from them! Oh, save me this time—only this time! Let me have a day —an hour—to breathe! *Here*—I ask no more than to lie *here*, and of you no more than not to tell them where to find me! Oh, my maid! my maid! take compassion on me! You are young and innocent, and of *you* I beg some pity!"

"If I am innocent," replied Mima, weeping, "are you as bad as they say?"

"No!" answered the supplicant, her vehement whisper forcing itself into a wheezing scream. "No! of blood I am free—I am, I am! and not for what they lay to my charge do I deserve this! Though I *do* deserve it for great wickedness—for early disobeying and shaming a good father and mother—for sending them upon the world, wanderers, till they have gone—I know not where— gone where I cannot find them—where I cannot find them, to lay my head at their blessed feet, and die! But, hush! does not some one come? Oh! will you promise not to betray me?"

"No one comes. Wait a moment," answered Mima.

She hurried home, and told her father every word the woman had said. At the last words he seemed suddenly and greatly aroused, looked hard into Mima's face, and said, in a very low voice—

"Go back to her, child, and ask her, as she hopes for the mercy of God or men, to tell you her real name and her birthplace. My mind misgives me that the name she bears is not her true one."

Mima, though wondering at the nature of her commission, did as she was commanded; and having got the woman's answers, returned to her father and said—

"As she hopes for mercy from God or from men, she sends

you word that her real name is Mary Ware, and her birthplace
a village in Devon."

"Ay, Mima," questioned the old man, shuddering, while his
head drooped, and his eyes fell glaringly on the floor. "Come
here, then, my maid; come here."

The child went over to him; he took her hand, strove to continue speaking, closed his eyes, and fainted.

His child's cries called back his senses. Summoning up, with
a great effort, self-command and presence of mind, his first en
deavors were to calm her. When he saw her assured, Laurence
Hutchins asked—

"Is there not a cup of elder wine and a mouthful of meat since
supper last night, Mima?"

Mima, rapidly answering, "Yes," went to make hot the elder
wine—often the poor English cottager's greatest luxury; and
when she had done, she brought it, with a plate of cold meat and
bread, to her father.

"Not for me, my little maid, not for me," he resumed. "Take
It to—*her*," speaking in a constrained manner, and pointing
through the back door; "and tell her she is safe with us. But
talk no more with her till you have come back to me."

Mima returned from her errand, and found her father seated in
the same spot, weeping. At her appearance, he strove to hide
his tears, beckoning her to him with an extended hand and arm.
A second time she came to his side. He put the arm round her
neck, made her stand between his knees, and continued:

"The time has come, Mima. After believing that the offender
had suffered for crime committed, I had hoped, mostly for your
sake, my maid, that it would never come. But it has; and, because it has, listen to what I have prayed, morning and night, you
should die, without hearing from a living tongue. Listen to our
shame, Mima. Eight years ago she left her precious mother
and myself—left us, after growing up, under our love and care,
and in the love and fear of God, into a beautiful creature—the
light of our eyes, the pride of our hearts, and the boast of our
vain lips. Neither had her mind been neglected; for I was then
in what is called a respectable way of life, and had received some
education myself, and was therefore doubly able to attend to hers.
But she left us, Mima, after being a child to us—and *such* a
child!—for seventeen years. I own that her first temptation was
not small. The man—the robber—was of rank in the world,
young and handsome; he promised her marriage—a secret mar

riage—ay, and flattered even her old love for her father and mother by swearing to enable her to raise them above a chance of want all the days of their life.

"So much I have learned since, though it was not from her I learned it—no, nor any thing else ; for she would hold no intercourse with me after her elopement. I pursued her. The man's servants turned me from the door. I wrote to her ; she did not answer my letters. Then came the news of his abandoning her, and then a terrible rumor of—no matter what. I believed in it for some time, because in no other way could I account for her still avoiding us. Well, my maid, you were four years old then ; and when your mother and I looked at you, we said to each other, 'This child is now our care ; let us save her from the curse of her sister's shame in after life.' So we resolved to leave our native place, ruined in fortune on account of the numb that came over me, and changing our names, we settled here. But your mother, Mima, could not bear up against it. She died, you know ; and I was left alone to meet this day."

"Then, father," said Mima, pale and trembling, "this woman, Martha Hall—that is, Mary Ware, I mean—"

"She is your sister, my maid. You want to ask why I never mentioned her name before—why, in fact, I never told you you had a sister ?"

"No, father, no ; I understand why now. You made me understand it when you began to speak. Are you able to come with me to her yet, father, and help her up to the house ?"

He groaned wretchedly, and then said—

"I will at least hear her denials more at length of what she spoke of to you, my child. But I must go alone ; and before I go—"

He walked into his little sleeping nook, leaving the sentence unfinished. But Mima knew what he meant, and as she went on her knees, was sure that she joined him in prayer. Providence had been preparing some alleviation of misery for both.

The child was disturbed in her innocent devotions by the sound of men's voices at the back of the house. Alarmed for her unfortunate sister, she sprang to her feet ; her father, also startled, came out of his chamber. The fears of both were not allayed by meeting, on the threshold of the back door, the overseers and the beadle of the next parish, preceded by an elderly person in black, who seemed to be a clergyman. Nor did the question of one of the overseers appear to bode good.

" Have you seen the woman, Martha Hall, pass this way?"
Father and child could not conceal their embarrassment.

"Yes, you have seen her, thank God! for the poor creature's
sake," said the clergyman. "Fear nothing, my good people, on
account of your Christian act towards her. She has undergone
much—oh! much, much wrongfully. But her trials are over—
she is proved innocent; and the proof having reached my hands,
it became most peculiarly my duty to hasten after her upon her
wretched pilgrimage, and save her from future persecution. Tell
me, my good man, is she not under your protection? in your
house? and how has she borne her misfortunes? life not in danger? Where is she? Let me see her. Oh, thank God that she
is found?"

"Thank God!" repeated the father, and he staggered backwards
against the wall.

Mima flew out of the cottage—the father knew where.

"You seem greatly overcome by your first fears for her and
yourself, master," continued the clergyman. "But compose
yourself, for I assure you again that there is nothing to apprehend."

"And so she is quite, quite innocent of it, sir!" demanded old
Ware, grasping the hand which the good priest had kindly laid
on his arm.

"You shall hear. You know the whole previous story, of
course. You know that the declaration of the real culprit formed
the chief grounds for the popular fury against the poor, unhappy,
and greatly wronged woman."

"Poor, unhappy, and greatly wronged woman!" echoed Ware;
and then added, "I do know, sir."

The clergyman went on.

"It was I who attended the miserable man in his last moments.
I could not credit his assertions for reasons of my own. A subsequent event proved my judgment correct. The clothes of such a
wretch as he was became, after death, the property of the almost
as depraved being who executes the law's sentence. Weeks after
the nominal husband of Martha Hall had expiated his hideous
crime, a half-written letter, found in a secret pocket of his coat,
was brought to me. It would seem that the murderer had been
interrupted, almost in the act of writing it, by the officers who arrested him, and that afterwards it escaped his recollection : but
we have proved it to be in his hand. It is addressed to a brother
profligate in London, and, although the language is disguised, not

only admits his commission of the crime for which he has suffered, but alludes, petulantly and savagely, to the vain interruptions he had received, during his perpetration of it, from Martha Hall. And now you know all, and will hesitate no longer in introducing me to the poor woman, that I may carry her, if she is able to be moved, to some asylum where she can be comforted, cherished, and saved in body and in soul."

"This is her asylum while she or I live, sir," answered Ware ; "and here, and here alone, she shall be comforted, cherished, and, if we can, saved in body and soul."

"Your intentions do you honor, my good friend ; but let me ask you, do your circumstances allow you to offer her a home?"

Ware started, looked towards the overseers and the beadle, who stood at some distance, put his lips to the clergyman's ear, and replied—

"Let me whisper you, sir. This *is* her home ; and home will be home to her, be it never so homely."

"Walk out with me," resumed the clergyman, much moved. "What am I to understand?" he continued, when they stood alone in the open air. "Is she any thing to you?"

"She is my child, sir !" answered Ware, as he covered his face with his hands.

A short explanation followed, and they went together in search of Mary Ware. Mima met them at the stile leading down to the brook. She was crying heartily, and yet smiling. Her sister had heard all she could tell.

"And she expects you, father," continued Mima : "and oh ! pray make haste ; for it troubles her so that I fear, I fear—"

They quickened their pace, Mima running on before them, and disappearing, at the bottom of the steps, into the thicket. When they gained a sight of Mary Ware, her head drooped over her little sister's shoulders, who knelt beside her, her arms hung helplessly, and her eyes were closed. Her father embraced her before she seemed aware of his presence. At last she opened her eyes, and fixed them on his : then a great change took place in her features, and she could no longer support herself on her knees. Evidently, however, she strove to speak, and after much dreadful struggling, whispered—

"What word, father? what last word from you ?"

"God forgive and bless my poor child as I do," answered Ware.

Again she made a feeble and useless effort to utter a seem· ingly joyous and comfortable ejaculation

10*

"Come here, sir," resumed the father, addressing the clergyman, who stood apart. "She wants both our help, now."

The benevolent man understood him, knelt by his side, and prayed aloud. Ware repeated his words, as so did little Mima, though weeping convulsively.

Mary seemed for many minutes aware of the sounds they uttered, and her voiceless lips moved, too, as if her mind prayed.

The father stopped suddenly, as her head lay heavier on his shoulder, after a long sigh had escaped her.

"She is dead, sir," he said, in an even, solemn tone.

"But saved," replied the clergyman.

"We hope it, sir. And I am not impatient under this ending of all her faults and sufferings. It pleases me better to hold her dead in my arms to-day, than it could have done to have held her alive in them yesterday."

"Let me be your friend," sobbed the clergyman, grasping his hand.

THE END OF TWICE LOST, BUT SAVED.

THE FAITHFUL SERVANT.

THE FAITHFUL SERVANT.

Azineb, the son of Omar, succeeded to his father's crown at an early age. All his subjects, the old and wise men as well as the unlettered and the humble, instead of withholding their confidence from his youth, blessed Alla and the Prophet for the prospect of a good and happy reign. For although nineteen years had scarce rolled over the head of Azineb, he was known to be matured in wisdom and virtue. From his boyhood he had devoted himself to books, and the conversation of the learned and the accomplished; his days and nights of study being relieved only by practising such manly and warlike feats and sports as would at once prepare him for probable future hardships in in battle, and exercise the physical strength and skill with which God had blessed him, and which, therefore, were not to be permitted to remain uncultivated. So that while few or none of his subjects of his own years rivalled Azineb in a knowledge of the grave literature of his country—in science, in poetry, and, above all, in his Koran; and while the wisest, the oldest, and the most religious men of his court wondered at the sedateness and vigor of his discourse—he was also unsurpassed, if not unequalled, in graceful feats of horsemanship, in the use of the scymitar, in courage and adroitness in hunting the lion, the leopard, and the tiger. His own hand had given the deathblow to many of these ferocious animals: indeed, he bore home more of their skins than did any other adventurer of the chase. Yet, so tempered with skill and prudence was his intrepidity, that from tusk or talon he had never received a wound.

The learned fathers of his mind were justly proud of their scholar, and boasted of his acquirements and talents more than they did of their own. It was whispered, however, by some satirist of the court, that they thus took the best way of insuring

royal tributes of admiration and gratitude to themselves. Another
of Azineb's instructors might also be allowed to feel honored in
his pupil—namely, Mustapha, a man high in military command,
and his master ever since childhood (until the princely boy first
equalled, and then eclipsed his own skill) in warlike exercises and
in the hunting-field. But whatever were Mustapha's inward
feelings on this subject, he never boasted of his pupil, as did the
more superior and reverenced men who had aided in forming the
mental and moral excellence of the (so-called) Royal Wonder.
Had any one raised a question of Azineb's manly prowess, he
would have gainsayed the slander at the risk of his life : but he
seemed too sure of the fact to insist upon it, and of its general
acceptance to talk about it. Making it a theme of self-praise,
either in vanity or that his master might hear his speeches and
show a pleased consciousness of them, never entered into his
mind. The sole privilege which Mustapha appeared to think he
had acquired by his successful instructions of Azineb, was that
of loving him the more. And in this love of the subject for the
prince, was essentially included the zeal of serving him faithfully.
Azineb, understanding and feeling the claims of Mustapha, not
only recognized and admitted his love, and afforded opportunities for its indulgence, but returned it also with his heart, and
rewarded it with his bounty.

It was amazing, if not irksome, to the philosophical, the poet
cal, nay, the pious colleagues of Mustapha, that he should succee
so well at court, merely by saying nothing on the topic which, o_
all others, seemed calculated, if well kept alive, to insure him
success. None of them got on better, if so well, by the contrary and, as they argued, more advisable rule of conduct. Their
individual reveries on this point, for they were too wise to communicate at present their sentiments to one another, began to
create a jealousy of Mustapha. And upon the occasion of a
grand banquet given by Azineb in the palace, in honor of all
his former tutors, this jealousy rankled into something akin to
hatred, in consequence of a particular mode of designation
adopted by the prince towards his old riding-master.

During the feast, the young monarch proposed in succession
the healths of his guests. One was his " most reverenced helper
in reading the Koran ;" another, " his honored tutor in astron-
omy ;" a third, his " most useful assistant in languages ;" a
fourth, his " accomplished playfellow in the bowers of poetry !"
but Mustapha he simply called, " My faithful servant." And

one would have thought that, by complimenting in their own polite style each of Mustapha's rivals, Azineb had taken the best means of gratifying their laudable pride, and of leaving them nothing to complain of. Indeed, so he had, until the proposal of his last toast ; but that was too much for logic, rhetoric, rhyme, and piety united. From that hour, Mustapha had active enemies at court, and they at length began to make common cause against him.

The ethical sage of the cabal, sitting down to consider a plan for disgusting Azineb with his faithful servant, soon built up a formidable battery of syllogisms. His first assumption was a simple one, an axiom, in fact, or something else more true, if possible, namely, " Azineb is very young." Then he proceeded to the following effect, though with greater order. " Very young, and blessed with robust health and a vigorous constitution ; consequently, notwithstanding his precocious philosophy, religion, and morality, containing within him all the springs of natural passions. Suppose some of these excited—what then ? Mustapha is an austere man ; a crabbed man ; and somewhat of a rough-spoken man. He deems he loves the prince ; would he relish Azineb's backslidings ? Would he let them pass without reproof ? And then, how would the prince take his constant moralizing, either in its matter or manner ? Let us see."

The professor consulted his colleagues, and they admired his system, and pledged themselves to each other to carry it into effect. The master of belles-lettres began the attempt. He composed beautiful verses in praise of the most lovely and fascinating maiden of the royal city, and sang them, and caused them to be sung repeatedly in the presence of Azineb. From admiring the poetry, the prince unconsciously was led to ask questions about its object, and received answers which heightened his curiosity. In due time, the charming Zobeide supped at the palace ; and after an evening of song, smiles, roses, perfumes, music, wit, and wine, her youthful entertainer proved mortal. So far were verified the inverted ethics which conjectured this event.

Little was now necessary but to continue an application of excitements, sufficient not only to satisfy the cravings of now-born passions, but also to smother the occasional pangs of remorse ; and the conspirators were not idle in their duty. Day by day, step by step, Azineb surrendered himself into the arms of sensual pleasure and licentious enjoyments. To his great comfort—for

during his first hours of repentence he had feared the contrary—
neither the moralists nor the divines of his council troubled him
with their reprehensions. As they had calculated, however,
there was one man who did exercise the duty of affection
towards his royal master.

Not after the first lapse of Azineb, nor yet after his third or
fourth, were the unwelcome hints of Mustapha addressed, notwithstanding, to his ear. The beloved and princely boy had
sinned long, and impulses were on the verge of becoming habit
(hideous change!) before his faithful servant uttered a word o.
expostulation; and then, indirectly, he would say, "The wisest
man, in his youth, is made weak. Who therefore wonders? It
is so." Again. "When the young man is wise and virtuous,
and has fallen into no snares, the old bless him, though they
wonder, and say the snares have not been spread in his path."
Or, at another time, "The stumblings of the good, and the sins
of the hardened in evil, are two things. It is so."

To such gentle admonitions Azineb gave little heed, though he
lent them an ear. The temptations to disregard them were too
strong for their refraining tenderness. By degrees, the sincere
Mustapha grew bolder in the stern task of love. But his idolized
prince had become less sensitive of admonition, and still he produced no effect. He gained his utmost possible point of reproof,
beyond which even his feelings dared not to pass. Now Azineb
heard him impatiently, because he was still more self-devoted to
licentiousness, and therefore still more removed from sympathy
with Mustapha's heart. The sole thing he could or would eventually distinguish was the uncouthness of his monitor's manner.
This he called rude, at first, and then bold, and at last auda-
cious; knowing not, or seeing not, that here he was confounding
manner and motive, and so misrepresenting true friendship.

The learned and accomplished conspirators could not long remain ignorant of such a change in Azineb's sentiments towards
his "faithful servant;" for exactly such a change they had
hoped to produce, and were watchful accordingly. Thereupon
they sharpened other weapons for Mustapha's overthrow. The
poet took an occasion to exhibit, garishly, the old soldier's lack
of accomplishments, by calling upon him for an impromptu, of
which all the world knew he did not even comprehend the
the nature; and Azineb, to whom, at that moment, the power
of saying a witty thing in verse was a great talent (because he
could excel in it himself, and because it hit the vein of the hour),

joined in the scoff against his old friend's simple rejection of the challenge. Upon a less elated occasion he agreed with the astronomer, that any man who was ignorant of at least the rudiments of heavenly science was a disgrace to the cabinet of a civilized court. And it was not long till he listened to an insinuation of Mustapha's orthodoxy, originating with the sage or the Koran, the uncle of the unrivalled beauty who had been introduced to the royal palace.

In fact, Azineb soon admitted, nay, believed, or thought he did, that, for many weighty and virtuous reasons, he ought to dismiss Mustapha from court, and confine him to a provincial military command, hundreds of miles distant. Yet a cowardliness of purpose, the common attendant curse of the sensual, or else a lingering recollection at his heart, hindered him from issuing the necessary order. Meantime, he tried to palter with the embarrassment. His queen of the hour would be amused by assuming a part in a tiger or lion hunt ; and he desired Mustapha to prepare for taking the field upon a certain day, with extraordinary pomp and preparation, supposing that his old tutor might thus be diverted from present thoughts into the bias of former enthusiasm.

Upon the morning of the appointed day, the hunting cavalcade left the palace in as much pomp as Asiatic gorgeousness ever witnessed. The beauty and trappings of the Arabian coursers, the highly ornamented castles of the elephants, the surpassing splendor of the palanquin which contained Azineb's reigning favorite, beside which the youthful prince rode upon a steed of unmatched proportions and fleetness, the bands of music, the ensigns, all formed a magnificent spectacle.

Intelligence had just been gained that a lion had descended the night before upon the herd of a neighboring noble, and, after having been surprised and scared from his prey, had retreated into an adjacent wood. Those skilled in the knowledge required for a good hunt decided that he should be tracked, roused, and challenged in his temporary lair, because they concluded that his balked appetite would render him peculiarly disposed to manifes the true spirit of his nature. Mustapha, the conductor of the sport, agreed to these reasons and arrangements, and the cavalcade accordingly got into motion for the wood pointed out by the guides.

It was approached across an almost barren plain, scorched by the sun, and scantily studded here and there with sharp rocks, which afforded root, among their crevices, to some meagre shrubs and blades of brown grass. A broad and rapid river divided this plain from the leafy retreat of the lion, and was to be crossed only by a rude bridge, a good distance up its stream from the cavalcade's line of advance. The middle of the wood, deemed to be the beast's crouching place, was, however, straight before the hunters, close by the river's opposite bank ; and a flat country, stretching to the right and to the left from its skirts, and a gentle ascent beyond and above it, showed the only ground over which, after having been scared from his lair, he could be pursued. As all stopped on the sterile plain, some distance from the near bank of the turbulent water, Azineb understood, at a glance, that upon this spot he ought to halt his beautiful favorite. From it she could fully see any possible turn of the chase, excepting the start in the wood, without sharing one of its perils. He accordingly gave orders to have her palanquin rested, its bearers halt, and a body of horse form around her, while he turned to cross the bridge, with his attendants, and so approach the wood.

Mustapha had been considering the opposite ground as attentively as his master, and, from his own conclusions, respectfully objected to the proposed arrangement, so far as concerned the safety of the lady. The wood was not thick, he said : it afforded numerous temptations to an angry lion to break through it, regardless of any line of men who might be left to guard its edges ; in reasonable anticipation, the beast they were about to rouse would prefer attempting a return to the prey from which he had been scared the previous night to a retreat into the hungry wilderness he had abandoned upon his late adventure.

Rendered obstinate by his self-opinion, Azineb laughed at this advice. Whispers from some of Mustapha's enemies prompted him to treat it even more despotically. He told Mustapha that he believed it arose rather from a design to betray the lady into danger than to save her from possible harm.

"Then Mustapha will watch by the palanquin to share the dangers of his own treachery."

To this, still prompted by a whisper, Azineb made a cruel and tyrannical retort.

"The old hunter fears for himself," he said.

"If Mustapha has taught the young hunter to fear for himself, it is so," replied Mustapha, with more spirit than the highest subjects were allowed to use towards an Asiatic prince.

He had scarce spoken the words when Azineb struck him on the shoulders with the flat of his sabre, and ordered him to quit the hunting-ground and retire down the bank of the river. A great struggle was seen in Mustapha's features, and his hand involuntarily moved towards his own sabre. But pure love of the royal boy, whom he had often helped to his saddle, and pure love alone, subdued all his majestic wrath. Making a low salutation, he rode slowly in the direction in which he was com manded to go.

He halted about the same distance from the palanquin down the stream as was the bridge from it towards the water's source. Proud, bitter, yet tender tears filled his eyes. At first he felt no wish to notice the proceedings of the pompous and gallant train from whom he had been ignobly banished. Their music and their cries aroused his interest, however, and he glanced to the bridge and then to the wood. The greater number were just entering the latter, after having stationed a weak line round its skirts. Further he could not observe the chances of the hunt. But the continued cries, now of a changed cadence, which broke from the lion's umbrageous lair, told his experienced ear that the animal had been tracked, and that his anger had been roused into an attack upon his assailants ; and the next sound Mustapha heard was the explosive, almost crashing roar of the terrific beast himself, as he sprang out of the wood, overwhelming two or three of his scared enemies on its outposts, and plunging into the river exactly opposite the bank where the palanquin rested.

His fiery eyes were scarce seen glaring in the water by the horseman left to guard the lady ere they fled across the plain, like one of its own hurricane-blasts ; the equally frightened horses not requiring spur or whip to urge them to the utmost speed. Then Mustapha heard piercing shrieks issue from the palanquin, and saw its glittering silk curtains shaken violently in the sun, and white arms tossed in agony through their openings towards the wood. The following instant, Azineb's worshipped one and all her young slaves ran, still screaming, along the river's bank, approaching the point where Mustapha had stationed himself.

"She is very young and beautiful," muttered Mustapha, "and but for *him* would have been innocent. He loves her, too," he continued, as, in answer to her startling calls, the young prince just then issued from the wood, and, casting his eyes abroad over the river, began, after bounding forward a few steps, to return her cry for cry, tear his hair, rend his garments, beat his breast, and exhibit all the actions of utter anguish and despair ; for now the lion gained the confronting bank, and as Azineb and all his attendants had left their horses at the bridge, pursuit was useless

"Loves her," resumed Mustapha, "as the apple of his eye ! loves her, even as he hates me. What then ?"

He took another glance at the terrified girl. From excess oi fear, or lack of strength, she had been left far behind by her slaves ; and the lion, evidently selecting her as an object of vengeance, closed fast upon her.

"What then ?" Mustapha made but a moment's pause, when he added, "it shall be so. He shall see it—" and suddenly taking off a loose part of his dress, he threw it over his courser's eyes, to hinder him from seeing the lion, and galloped amain to meet the poor fugitive.

Shouts, in applause of his heroism, arose from the prince and many of the attendants.

Azineb now ran along his own side of the river towards the bridge, obviously bent upon seconding, if possible, the daring attempt of Mustapha. During his hurry thither, accompanied by his hunters, he lost sight of the appalling scene. When he and they had remounted and crossed the bridge, Mustapha held his prize before him on the saddle. Again all shouted tremendously —now to overawe the lion, and turn him from his unremitted pursuit. The enraged beast paused an instant, looked back upon them, and then, as if ascertaining that the distance between them and him allowed him scope for his present purpose, uttered a roar of defiance, and renewed his bound after Mustapha. That roar gave him fearful odds. Hitherto, Mustapha's steed had not been aware of his proximity, for his eyes were hoodwinked ; now he *heard* the voice of the king of beasts, and it was enough. Swerving aside, he shook the piece of drapery from his eyes, and, with tottering and failing limbs, remained paralyzed. Again and again Azineb and his train uttered wild cries, and urged on their own fear-stricken coursers.

"It is vain !" shrieked the prince. "Behold ! Yet shout ! still shout !"

The lion had sprung against the side of Mustapha's horse, and fastened upon a limb of the rider. Mustapha saw him prepare for his last bound, and with one arm holding her up, and another holding her back, endeavored to place his charge out of immediate danger. It gave him pleasure instead of pain when he felt the beast's fang tearing his own flesh. . . .

"Come on !" he exclaimed to the approaching hunters, "I can hold her till ye vex him away from us !"

They jumped from their saddles and ran forward with spears and scymitars. Mustapha felt his strength failing, and his eyes growing heavy, and frame cringing, in spite of him ; for the lion had now fastened his tusks in his body. But he faintly caught the sound of more feet and louder cries, and was sensible of being released by the lion. The next moment he recognized the prince' voice making quick inquiries, and could just utter, "She is un touched to the hair of her head. Mustapha, whom you love no longer, says it ;" when he fell from his saddle dead.

That day won Azineb back to virtue, but it lost him his faithful servant.

THE END OF THE FAITHFUL SERVANT.

THE ROMAN MERCHANT.

THE ROMAN MERCHANT.

THE Norman and Welch lords of the Pale in Ireland determined, in the first instance, upon building themselves in from the natives of the country in which they colonized—that is, at such seasons as they did not deem convenient for voluntary rencounter in the field, or by wile, with their detested neighbors. The rudely wrought and ungraceful square castles, without adjunct of any kind, which to this day are found in the. Pale districts of Ireland, were the results of their earlier attempts to indulge this love of solitude. Soon after, walled towns sprang up in the land, still to keep out all pure-blooded descendants of Heber and Heremon. But this could not last. The general similarities of human nature began, in the course of time, to attract and approach each other among the two people. Common wants, suggesting common interests, had the usual and inevitable effect of levelling the barriers of exclusiveness on the one hand, and of qualifying hatred on the other. And long before Cromwell's devastating visit to Ireland, neither double-curtained walls, nor lines of circumvallation, nor massive gates, nor yet laws stronger than any of these, were able to keep the Anglo-Normans and the mere Irish from mixing comfortably together.

It may appear, however, that the natives were not all at once received into the bosoms of the towns and cities of the strangers, even when liberality and common sense had begun to legislate in their favor. Most probably they were only permitted at first to settle *extra muros*, and there erect dwellings of their own.

By degrees that part of the wall of the Pale-town running between the two communities was thrown down, or suffered to fall into decay, and the quickly blending races then agreed to let one continued wall inclose and protect both.

In this manner two towns would have become a single town,

11

known to the world by a single name. Such was the case with respect to Dublin, Cork, Limerick, Kilkenny, and other places of considerable and even of much less note in the west, the south, and the middle of Ireland. Either a relic of the old spirit of making distinctions, or else common parlance, continued, however, to designate separately the two clusters of houses thus massing together, by the names of English-town and Irish-town; or else, while that quarter originally English was distinguished by the geographical name equally applying to both, the streets of Milesian architecture retained their mere Irish title.

This "distinction without a difference" (no common-place quotation) exists at the present day; and so we arrive at our story.

The Irish-town of our dear and not uncelebrated native city is now before our eyes as vividly as when we roamed through it in childhood. One side of its main street reposes in the sunshine of a sunny Saturday. (Why has the word occurred? rather, why ask that question? what reader who has been a schoolboy will not comprehend the associations that suggest it? A sunny Saturday! school dismissed at noon; the whole day and evening, ay, and the next day too, lengthening out before our minds in a most luxurious prospect of leisure and enjoyment; and the blessed sun shining! Oh! to this hour a sunny Saturday wears its own peculiar radiance to our eyes, and gladdens our heart like a very act of happiness! But we must describe—not be guilty of sentiment.)

We have said that the main street of our Irish-town appears to us this moment as vividly as when we were children; yet not exactly so. Memory is at best but a camera-obscura, in which, though there be true forms, there are sobered colors and subdued lights; even the sunlight cannot be brought to mind in it as brilliant as in reality it has been. It is promised, however, that our little sketch shall be faithful enough. And so, look once more down the main street. The sunny side shows a straight line of humble houses—some very humble—the most considerable not more than two stories high; they are all old, or oldish, and here and there runs up a gable-front with round stone chimneys, that speaks of absolute antiquity. They are all the abodes of shopkeepers—not a single gentleman's hall-door, with a heavy brass knocker, is to be seen in the row. Some of these honest men ("comfortable" folk, neither affluent nor struggling like certain of their contemporaries "in town," who

figure, or try to figure, on a larger scale), are standing at their
thresholds talking across to their opposite neighbors, or leaning
over their closed half-doors doing the same thing. And they
happen to be almost all of an age, that age some fifty years.
And you may perceive in the fashion of their respectable clothes,
and in their sleek, three-curl wigs, as well, indeed, as in the char
acters of their faces, a sober attachment to the usages and to
the mind of old times, which strikingly distinguishes them from
their brethren only a few streets off. The narrow flag-way before their shops is worn from age rather than from the bustle of
the street at any time. Even upon this day, at noon, there is
little crushing or pushing by their doors. When one of the respectable householders raises his voice, you can hear him talking
from the steps going up to the cathedral, all the way to the little bridge that connects the street, quite at the other end, with
the English-town; the shouts, gabble, laughing, and crying of
the urchins who are at play in the middle of the road, make
the air ring; and when a horse trots over the stones, or a cart
or car rolls over them, you would think the little old houses
were about to tumble down with the noise.

This outline bears date some—no matter how many—years ago.
Enough to say that we were schoolboys when we studied (unconsciously indeed) the original. A grand-uncle, then about sixty,
told us he remembered the Irish-town just the same when *he* was
a boy. It may hence be inferred that the present sketch will stand
good for from seventy to eighty years, past and gone, according
to the reader's good-natured allowance for our objection to be
called middle-aged. And so, seventy or eighty years ago, we are
in the main street, seeing nearly the same houses, shop-windows,
and shop-doors, and nearly the same kind of shopkeepers standing
at them, or leaning cross-armed over them, which have already
been described. It is past noon, too, and the summer sun is un-
·loudly shining.

Amid all the quiet and listlessness of the little street, a remarkable man, leading a small cart, drawn by an ass, entered it by a
cross-street, at the country side of the Irish-town, and attracted
immediate attention. He wore a costume which, to whatever nation or tribe it belonged, proclaimed him a stranger, not only in
that town, but in Ireland. This consisted of a loosely fashioned
greatcoat, of a brown color, reaching nearly to his toes, secured
tightly at his throat, and girt round his middle with a leathern
belt and buckle; of russet boots, falling in folds to his ancles;

and of a headdress of red linen, or some such cloth, wound round and round his forehead. Having turned the corner of the street, he raised his eyes, which had been previously fixed on the ground, as if to note the situation of a little inn, to which he might have been directed. Then the interest of the shopkeepers of Irish-town increased tenfold. Those eyes were very large, deep black, sad, mysterious, and yet tranquil; his nose was long, slightly hooked, and prominent ; his cheeks and whole visage swarthy and thought-worn : but what most attracted notice was his short, thick, coal-black beard, which completely hid his chin, and his mouth almost, and, when again he bent his head to his breast, made a black spot even on the surface of his dark-brown robe. Those who looked at him could not call him old, nor even advanced in years, though they hesitated to call him young. His pace was as heavy as his face was serious. The dust of travel was on his dress, his hair, his whiskers, and slightly on that strange beard. Although he appeared leading the little cart, no one thought of classing him with the vulgar of any country, who perform such humble offices ; nay, whether from natural character, or from former rank, he impressed himself vaguely as a person of superiority. His cart was well loaded with trunks, boxes, and bales packed in sackcloth or in matting.

It seemed, that the one glance he gave after entering the street, assured him of the point to which he walked ; for, as if content with it, he passed along the middle of the way, looking neither to the right nor to the left, nor, indeed, again lifting up his eyes. If he were conscious of the general attention he attracted, he was also indifferent to it. The little inn was the last house but one to the bridge, at the further end of the street. He gained the open gateway which led into its stable-yard ; halted his ass ; turned his face towards the opposite houses ; fixed his regards on one— a very humble one—of which the closed door and shutters told that it was uninhabited and to be let ; and wiped his heated brow with the wide sleeve of his gaberdine. Then, still taking not the least notice of the many curious eyes bent upon him, he again put his hand to his ass's halter, and let it to one of the stables of the inn.

More than one of the shopkeepers of Irish-town, after debating with their neighbors the probable country, rank, profession, and religion of the stranger passed over to the inn to hold consultation on the same points with its shrewd and observant landlady. But they found her as much surprised and as curious as they were themselves. Her new guest, after seeing his little beast well disposed of, had summoned her servants to unload his cart, and caused them to convey its trunks, boxes, and packages into a private room. Then, placing a purse in her hands, he had retired after his property, ordering a frugal dinner. Since that moment, neither she nor any one in her house had seen him. He kept his door locked, and objected to open it till the hour of dinner. His language was English, broadly marked with a foreign accent and idiom ; yet he made himself sufficiently intelligible.

Conjecture continued at a stand for many hours. At last, in the cool of the evening, the good folk of Irish-town saw the same man issue from the inn, dressed like one of themselves, his beard gone, and a decent three-cocked hat on his head, instead of the unchristian-looking pile of red linen. He crossed the little bridge, and passed "into town." Again his landlady was consulted, and her answers, while they gave more information than before, caused more surprise. At dinner he had asked of her the name and residence of the proprietor of the house which was to be let in the street, and noted down both in his tablets. After his meal, he a second time went up to his chamber; there cut and shaved off his beard, and changed his dress. When he had done dressing, he locked his door on the outside, and finally left her house, as her neighbors had observed, without speaking another word.

This unknown, and perhaps infidel and dangerous wanderer, was about to become, then, a citizen of Irish-town ! And what were his means of support, and what were they to be ? Would he live in the house as a private gentleman, or would he open the shop and carry on some business ? If so, what business ? The well-laden cart here occurred to the thoughts of his future neighbors, and good-hearted and straight-minded people as we wish them to be believed, it will not be wondered at, if fears of rivalry, and (considering that the stranger must have travelled much, and seen many markets) of eclipsing rivalry, too, made some of them look grave.

Perhaps the least liberal among them it was who started the comforting thought, that the proprietor of the uninhabited house might "look two ways," before he consented to accept a tenant of such a questionable description. Different opinions were being exchanged on this point, when the stranger reappeared, crossing the little bridge, followed by the clerk of the attorney, who did legal business for the gentleman whom he had gone to seek. Both gained the house in question : at its threshold the clerk handed a key to his companion, and wished him a good evening ; the new comer unlocked the door, and entered the premises, which had now evidently become his.

In a short time he was seen standing at the door, looking up the street. An upholsterer and two of his apprentices came in view, bearing a few of the most necessary articles of household furniture. He beckoned to them : they passed into his house, as if to arrange their goods. He went over to the inn ; returned with all its spare hands carrying the baggage of his cart. Before nightfall he had secured his door, and was alone in his house, the light of a candle shining through the clinks of one of the windows. That was a memorable night in the charitable club-room of Irish-town.

The earliest riser among his neighbors next morning saw his shop open, and an ample stock of various articles handsomely disposed in its little bow-window, and hanging at its door. These consisted of a strange medley : woollen and linen ; cheap showy jewelry; tobacco and snuff; books and pamphlets; knives, scissors, needles, and such matters ; ready-made shoes and boots ; and flaunting colored engravings, mostly of Divine or sacred subjects. All Irish-town were soon up and stirring ; and, one by one, his competitors walked observantly by his door, or entered his new establishment in a more blunt and friendly manner, to wish him good-morrow and a welcome. They found him sitting behind his counter gravely,, and like a man of business, "taking stock," as they believed, in a large book. He received all his visitors politely ; and if he did not return their smiles or good-humored sayings, was not backward in replying to their merely complimentary or friendly expressions. All curious inquiries about strange articles in his shop he answered off-hand and satisfactorily. He was asked if he proposed to stay some time among his new neighbors; and said, "I hope so ; I have taken the house for seven years." Was he not a foreigner? "Yes ; a native of Rome." And his name ? "Bartolini."

When public anxiety had been pretty well allayed, the old householders of Irish-town began to compare opinions upon the stranger ; and, notwithstanding previous prepossessions, and even a present certainty that he must prove a formidable rival to more than one long established shop in the street, no man said or felt that he disliked Bartolini. The sad suavity and unpretending composure of his manners were openly admired ; then, the irresistible conclusion that he was a friendless wanderer, who had suffered much, gained him pity; and a vague sense of mystery completed the simple interest raised in his favor. As to his name, it was judged to be, indeed, foreign enough; so much so, that plain Irish tongues could scarce be expected to get round it. And after various laughing attempts to pronounce it as he had done, his friends, as they said, "left it to himself to go through the trigonometry of it." But as he had informed them that he was a native of Rome, this fact and his present occupation suggested a substitute appellation; in a few days Bartolini went by the name of "The Roman Merchant," and never afterwards was otherwise designated.

The first morning of his residence in Irish-town he went out among his neighbors to purchase provisions for breakfast and dinner, and conveyed them home with his own hands. From this it was concluded that he meant to live quite alone without a servant; and such, indeed, proved to be the case. Neither man nor woman, girl nor boy, resided during his life, under his truly solitary roof. When the night of that morning drew on, he put up the shutters of his shop-window, secured them, locked his door, and walked forth, as if for exercise. Close by the corner of the street by which he had entered Irish-town, it has been passingly said, were steps which led up to the cathedral. These, a long flight, he was observed to ascend. Then he passed into the churchyard of the venerable and beautiful edifice spoken of, by a small door, at that time always left open; through it, and out of it by another door at its opposite side; thence into the suburb, and the open country; returned to his residence in about two hours, and went to rest for the night.

His proceedings on this day are minutely mentioned, because, for years, he scarce ever made any alteration in them from sunrise to sunset, winter or summer. It is to be particularly observed, that a solitary stroll invariably closed his day of serious and unremitting attention to his shop. Add to which, he was often noticed in the cathedral churchyard, for a longer time than seemed necessary to pass through it into the adjacent environs of Irish-town. The only occasions upon which he was not found behind his counter, or met in the street purchasing his breakfast or dinner, or seen upon his evening walk, were when he was absolutely absent, for a while, in Dublin or elsewhere, laying in a new stock of goods. Then the Roman Merchant's house remained shut up, till his return with a fresh pile of bales in his little ass's cart.

Soon after his settlement in Irish-town he was more than once invited to a neighbor's house : he declined the civility with his usual blandness, but so firmly and gravely as to put an end to future solicitations. He asked no one to his house : in fact, from the night it became his until he was no longer master of it, it never was entered by any one, except by the customers, or chance visitors of his shop. Proposals were made to him to become a member of the charitable club of the parish. He readily consented, and sent in treble the amount of the specified subscription, but never went to the club-room. Here it may be mentioned, that to the poor of every description, to the wandering beggar at his door, and to distressed objects in the suburbs, he gave liberally and continually. And thus passed his life for years ; holding no communication with his kind, beyond what a return of mere passing good manners demanded of him ; indeed, never speaking, but when spoken to ; a true hermit, though not of the desert ; a man esteemed and thought well of, though from year to year still as much unknown, and as much a mystery to his neighbors, as he had been the first day of his appearance in the street.

It was more than five years after his coming to Irish-town, that, one morning the Roman Merchant's shop appeared shut at an unusually late hour. People wondered, but supposed he had overslept himself. Hours wore away, and still he was not seen engaged, as usual, in taking down his shutters. They knocked loudly at his door—they thundered at it ; no one stirred within. A little alarmed, they began to surmise that he might have gone to purchase goods before daybreak ; for it was winter-time.

To ascertain this point, some went to the cabin of an old woman who took care of his ass and cart. The ass and cart were under their shed, in her yard ; of course, he had not left the town, as had been supposed, as he never did so without them. Consternation as to his fate took possession of the minds of his neighbors.

Noon came ; night was drawing on. Authorities of the borough caused his house to be forcibly entered. He was not in it ; he had not slept in his bed the previous night, for it was undisturbed after having been made up. In his little back-parlor an humble supper was found laid out, a bottle of water to one hand, his single chair placed to the table, and the ashes of a turfen fire on the hearth. All his property seemed untouched.

Every thing was sealed up, the house again secured, and inquiries set on foot in all directions.

Days elapsed, and he was not heard of. The moment and the circumstances, at and under which he had last been seen, now were carefully established. His street neighbors, the night before his disappearance, had noticed him locking his shop-door, and then going towards "the long steps," upon his accustomed walk. Other individuals had met him in the suburbs afterwards ; and one had seen him at a late hour roaming through the churchyard. No further could he be accounted for.

At about the end of a week, spent in vain searches and con jectures, some youths of the suburbs were amusing themselves, vaulting over the tombstones in the churchyard of the cathedral. It was now dark, and the winter's moon began to rise,* shining ghastily upon a light sheet of snow, which for some days had covered the ground. They recollected what description of place they were so merry in, and half serious, half in jest, began to banter each other's superstitious misgivings. One, stepping back in mock terror upon his companions, pointed to a far corner, among the stems of two rows of trees, and said that "the sperit of the Roman Marchant was watching them !" . All took to flight in laughing confusion, along the narrow pathway, pushing and jostling each other. Two of them slipped on the snow, and fell to one side among the graves. Their kicking and struggling displaced a loose and carelessly heaped mound, and the hand and arm of a man, gloved and clothed, started up between them from the earth. They were the hand and arm of the Roman Merchant. The fact was established when by the light of lanterns and torches, a crowd, whom their cries had summoned, disinterred the body.

It was fully dressed. Even the poor man's hat was found in his ill-made grave. Closer investigation showed that, along with the key of his shop, his purse had been left in his pocket, his old-fashioned but valuable watch in his fob, and a mourning ring, of value, too, upon his finger. They touched some thing hard at his breast. It was the handle of a dagger, which they could not at first pull out. The blade traversed the middle of his heart, and

* Since writing the above, we have returned to the scene of the story, and been informed that we made an important omission, as regards the moon, in this part of it ; for that, upon the night of the discovery of the body of the Roman Merchant, the planet, strange enough to say, was eclipsed.

11*

its point appeared at his back.   The death-blow had been un-
erring and vehement, and must have killed him before he could
have felt it.

Who struck it ?   That was the question of every tongue, but
it remained unanswered.   It remains unanswered to the present
hour; although the motives of the unknown assassins are darkly
imagined and hinted at. whenever this true and unvarnished story
is related—and it is still related—in our Irish-town.

The fact of finding his money, watch, and ring untouched upon
his person, removed the first natural suspicion that the Roman
Merchant had been set upon in a thirst for plunder.   It then became almost evident that hatred or revenge alone could have
done a murder of which the object was life—poor life only.   And
of the primitive community which he had chosen for his last
earthly associates, not a heart or mind was found to attribute to
its neighbor either of these baleful sentiments against the Roman
Merchant.   Although he had not permitted that close and con-
tinual intimacy which produces lively feelings of friendship, all
had respected him for his demeanor, admired and esteemed him
for his charities, and compassionated him, as well for his hermit-
life as for the unexplained misfortunes that must have influenced
and shaped it.   In what direction, then, was the deadly enemy to
be sought ?   The dagger, when unsheathed from his heart, suggested the first vague elucidation of the mystery.   It was at once
seen not to be of Irish, or even of English manufacture.   An old
military gentleman of the city, a native, who, after half a life of
foreign service, had returned to repose himself among his early
friends, unhesitatingly pronounc: ' it to have been made in Spain
by a hand well known to him and to others who wrought with
such tools.   But other evidence much more important, though
still not giving a clue to the identity of the murderer, came to light

The Roman Merchant's little abode was again entered by com-
petent authority.   A more careful and minute search took place
in it after any documents likely to tell who he really was, and
who might have been his early friends and connections in a distant land.   In the drawer of his desk was found a sealed packet,
with a superscription in a foreign language, which none of the
persons then present could translate.   An old friar, half hiding
in the suburbs, from the enactments of the time, was summoned
to their councils ; he had been a Salamanca student ; he declared
the direction on the back of the packet, as well as the writing in
the body of it, to be Spanish ; and he supplied the following

translation—first convincing all that the writing was dated only some days before, from the residence of the murdered man:

To MY RUTHLESS AND TERRIBLE ENEMY :

"You are upon my track again! After more than five years of quiet, gained by successfully eluding you, you are upon my track again! After escaping you seven times, in the four quarters of the globe, you have hunted me into this little nook of earth! I know it—I am sure of it! Your bloodhound has crossed my path—the subtle devil whom you always sent forth to course after me through deserts and cities, over the most silent places, and into the thickest abodes of men, to mark me, and to fix me for your blow. I have once more seen him! This very day, though he does not think it—ay, beneath all his consummated disguises of feature and of person, I knew his eye!—this very day, among a crowd of humble peasants, in my little shop, and at the very moment that he bargained with me for one of the paltry articles by the sale of which to them I gain the only bread you have left me—this very day, he and I stood face to face. And now he has gone to tell you he has found me, and you will surely come for the last time! Yes!—my relentless enemy!—my fate!—my destruction-cloud!—already you have cast forward your thick shadow upon me!

"You will come for the last time, I say—ay, for the last time —because I will not try to baffle you now. Heretofore, I exerted the utmost skill and energy of man to save your soul from future fire (yes—you will die without regretting it!) and my own life from your hand, becaused I had injured you—because you were *her* blood—because she prayed for *you* to her God in heaven, and forgave *me*—and because, penetrated with a Christian's sorrow for the past, it was my duty, as well as my heart's great yearning, to preserve my wretched existence from one who had well forewarned me of his thirst to end it. But now, if, after five years' time for thought, you come—after sending me out, a Cain upon the earth—after taking from me name and rank, fortune, friends, a country, humankind—after using your power and your sway to disgrace and beggar me—after trampling me, treading me with your heel down, down into the dust—if now, once more, you come, let it be for the last time! I cannot save you—it is doomed! Or, perhaps, notwithstanding my uncharitable fear of the stoniness of your fierce heart, perhaps my life alone stands between you and the capability of feeling forgiveness and remorse. Perhaps, when you can see me stretched stiff at your feet—perhaps, then, and then alone, it is decreed that you may relent—that out of the last of my earthly punishment will grow the first of your earthly repentance. Come, then!

"And yet, have I not already been punished enough? Oh, very hard has been my life since I injured you! That you have sent me out to earn my bread in the sweat of my brow—me, nursed on the very knee of luxury and honor—I count as nothing. So much, at least, I can thank you for. Humility, in all things, became my quick and full sense of my sin, and it has been my only solace.

"But, remember!—your hand has, before now, struck sharp steel into my body; and, when you thought I fell to rise no more, whose foot spurned me?

"Yet why remonstrate with you on this paper?—you can never read the words I write, nor hear them read, till you have shed my blood. And I *do* write them, only to hint to the Christian people who shall find my lifeless body some shadowy explanation of the cause of my coming death. Give me no praise for suppressing your name, and all allusions that might lead to a discovery of it. An angel—and your child—your only, only child (alas! alas!—strike home when you strike next!—I merit it!)—she now watches my heart and its workings, and she can feel, if you cannot, why, at more than the hazard of a thousand lives, I refrain from bringing to disgrace a name that I have already tarnished, through my treacherous love of the brightest creature that ever bore *it*, or any other. If they who shall find this paper ever publish it, then you may further reflect that, with a good omen of your coming, I called not on the arm of justice to shield me from you; but still, thank me not, nor on this account alone indulge remorse. Oh, may the expressions of sincere sorrow and misery I now give vent to, move you to a more lively regret!—and that is a cheering hope. You have never before allowed my voice to reach you; you have stopped short my words with execrations, boisterous as a raging sea; you have interrupted them by outrage on my person; you have sent back my letters unopened; you would have struck down any messenger from me. It is probable, then, that, all along, you have believed me a hard-minded villain, untouched by the results of my own fearful crime. If so, let these, my last protestations, undeceive you. I *am* penitent—humbly, crawlingly penitent. Come!—you will not find me raise a hand, an eye, against *your* hand, *your* eye.

"I am certain you will be minutely informed of my usual haunts abroad, in this little place, that so you may surprise me upon a secret spot. Knowing this, it is my resolve to tempt you to a haunt of mine, the most favorable for your purpose. Every night, henceforward, till the last—my last—I will loiter in a lonely corner of the burial-ground of the cathedral, already, or soon to be described to you ; for thither, I am assured, your spy must have watched me repair, during my accustomed evening walk. There, among the graves, and perhaps standing upon my own—there, in the dark, I will expect you. Not a cry, not a loud word, shall expose you to detection. Come ! Could I avoid you still, I would do it—no matter what words may have escaped me ; but is there the slightest hope that I can ? After all that has passed, what corner of the wide earth is able to hide me from *his* glance and *your* arm ? And, by walking out in the night, as is my wont, and in the places I am accustomed to—particularly when you know not that *I* know--how shall I be accessory to my own death ? True, I might await you trebly armed—but against whom ? *Her* father !—unutterable horror is in the thought. Ay, come !—and let the last words I shall hear on earth be even her name ! Hers—growled forth as you will !"

Thus ended the document. Of that anticipated meeting in the silent churchyard, nothing but the result is known. The paper *was* published, and that it produced some of the effects hoped for by the writer is thought by the good and Christian. For, some six months afterwards, a large wooden case came, directed to the mayor of the city, from Dublin, where it had been imported ; and upon opening it was found a marble urn, with a pedestal, inscribed to "The Roman Merchant."

THE END OF THE ROMAN MERCHANT.

ILL GOT, ILL GONE.

ILL GOT, ILL GONE.

"Well—it's my turn, now, sure enough, genteels, to tell my story; and it will be most about how ould Square (Squire) M'Cass come by the great fort'n, that he couldn't keep with as strong a hand as he got it—'ill got, ill gone,' ye know, neighbors." In these words, one of a circle of Irish villagers, assembled round a winter fire, and beguiling the long holiday evening with their favorite amusement of story-telling, began his imposed task. The tale is preserved in his words, or as nearly so as possible.

"Every one that hears me, young and ould, knows who I mean by Square M'Cass, though he's dead and gone from among us many a year. Let any gorsoon or little girl that doesn't know—or, at laste, that has heard tell of him, but not of what a great man he was in his time—just step over the trassel of the door of this good friend's house, and look up the slant of the hill, in the moonlight. There is to be seen the remains of a big barrack of a place he built for himself, more than fifty years ago, though its tall gables and chimblies are now tattbered and torn with the weather, and the bat and the scallcrow have more to say to it than Square M'Cass. And when any one looks at that ould ruin, and is tould, more-be-token, that all the land you can see from the highest window-hole, at every side of it, belonged to him that built it once upon a time, then, certain sure, it will be guessed what a man he was.

"Well, genteels; 'tisn't of Square M'Cass, alone, I have to say, 'Ill got, ill gone;' the word fits them he got his money from as well as it fits himself: but ye shall hear what ye shall hear. I had the story, in bits and scraps, from more than one knowledgable body, and from time to time. From the poor darling mother o' me—rest her soul in glory!—from cousins and cousin's childher

of some of the people I'm to talk about ; and from Jude Murphy,
the misthress of the Fighting Cocks, below in the village, and
own granddaughter of the Widow Murphy that kept the same
house before she was born.   And, sure enough, it's into the kitch
en of the Fighting Cocks we are to step, the first going off.

" A nate, cosy kitchen it was ; kept clane and well swept ; a
full barrel always in the corner, and a fireside almost as snug as
this one we are sitting at—every thing befitting man and horse
that came that way, supposing them the first in the land—and
barring that the horse had his own good lodging in the warm
stable, nigh at hand.   And so, Biddy Murphy was sitting fornent
her man o' the house (they were newly married at that same time)
by the pleasant fire, of a winter's evening, like this, only earlier,
when she hears a sound she was always glad to hear—the noise
of horses' feet, stopping at her dour.   And, when she hurried to
the trassel, two decent, well dressed, mannerly men were stepping
down from their saddles.   She made her curtshee to them, and
called Mickle Murphy to put up their horses ; and soon she had
them settled in the warmest corner, a can of good ould *shibbeen*
(home-brewed ale) a-piece in their hands, and the fresh eggs and
the nice bacon screeching in the pan for their supper.   Certain
sure, she said in her own mind, that she had the luck to have two
responsible (respectable) pleasant bodies in her house that night ;
and, when Mickle came back from the stable, and made one at
the fireside, they all chatted jocosely together, of one thing or
another, though nothing particular till afther.

" Biddy Murphy's hand was on the fryingpan, to turn out the
eggs and bacon on the dish, when she stopped herself, and said,
' Hushth ! merry Christmas to me ! but I hear another man and
horse for the Fighting Cocks this blessed night!' and, sure enough,
she whipped to the door, laying the pan on the hearth, and stepped
back with a new comer.

" He was a sogering man, a throoper, discharged from the wars,
as it turned out to be, afther ould Shamus ran from the Boyle,
but still in his soger's clothes, and carrying his long sword at his
side, that clanked at every step he made across the flure, in his
jackboots and spurs.   His tongue betokened that he came from
the Black North, where they don't spake either English, or Irish,
or Scotch, but a kind of a mixtrum-gatherum of their own, made
up of the three together, that's not like any dacent Christian speech
—much good may it do them.   The way he had with him tould
of the place he had come from, more-be-token ; for he was not

sprightly nor pleasant in his looks or his words to Misthress Murphy, nor any one about him, but as serious as a pig getting a sundial by heart, and stand-offish, and apt to find fault with other people's discoorse, and quite full of himself. The greater the shame for a young man like him, that night, at Biddy Murphy's hearth, and she doing her best to plase him ; for, young enough he was, not above thirty, and a tall broad-shouldered throoper into the bargain.

"When he took his stool at the fire, afther seeing his horse in the stable, the hearty gossip that had been going on there, afore he came to the door, was a'most put a stop to. He would not laugh at any thing that the woman o' the house or the man o' the house said, to cheer up the hearts of their customers, or that the two jocose-looking men, who had come in before him, said in return. So, by degrees, everybody grew as down in the mouth as himself : or, if the discoorse was taken up now and then, it had no laugh in it, but turned on sarious things. Even the good supper that he had his share of, and the *cruiskeen lawn* (full cup or pitcher) left at his hand, couldn't make him put on a merry face, so that the people round him might find heart to be jocose again ; no, nor as much as make him to join in the most in-earnest talk. Only from time to time he said a cross word, blaming the victuals, or the *shibbeen*, or making out that his companions were discoorsing like fools, or not like Christian cratures. By and by, howsomever, he found a little more of his tongue, though it was the bad tongue still.

"'Ye are not of our parts, genteels,' says Misthress Murphy to her other two customers.

"'No, ma'am,' says one of them, making answer, 'this is the first time we ever came into the County Louth.'

"'And ye come a good way up the country, I'll go bail,' says Misthress Murphy again.

"'All the way from Kerry, ma'am,' the man said to her, very civil and hearty.

"'Musha, ay, that's a good step, of a sartainty. And is the place round about here very sthrange to ye, afther laving your own place, so mortial far in the south ?' asked Biddy over again.

"The two men looked hard at each other, before he that had spoken first said, 'We have a quare answer to that question, ma'am ; for, though this *is* our first journey into Louth, as I tould you afore, and though the night fell on us just afther crossing the bounds of the next county, only a stone's throw from your snug house, we think we could describe ɪvery tree and bush of—'

" 'Hushth, Aby !' says the second man, taking the word out of his gossip's mouth.

" 'Never fear, Dick,' Aby made answer, 'I'm not going to make a fool of myself or you—every tree and bush, ma'am,' he went on, turning to the woman o' the house, 'and every thing in the world besides, of a certain spot, not very far from the spot we are talking on this blessed minute. It's a truth, sir,' he repeated, nodding to the throoper, who, at his last words, raised up his eyes from the hearth to look at Aby.

" 'Well, and that's quare, of a sartinty, as you promised ɪt would be, sir,' says Biddy Murphy. 'Ye got your knowledge of the spot ye mane out of a book, I'm thinking ?'

" 'No, indeed, ma'am,' says he.

" 'Then ye saw it dhrawn out and painted in a pictur, and the name printed undher it ?' Biddy a second time demanded of the man.

" 'Nor that either, upon my word and credit, ma'am,' he replied to her.

" 'But some body that knew it well described it to ye, stock and stone, afore ye came—sure that must be it,' says Misthress Murphy for the last time, very curious to find out, as ye may suppose.

" 'No living tongue has ever made mention of it to us, ma'am !' was all that Aby answered, only he spoke in a remarkable way, very slow, and half undher his breath.

" 'Blessed hour !' cries Biddy, opening her mouth and her eyes at her two customers. The throoper also grumbled out something, and kept staring.

" 'Biddy,' says the man of the house, handing her the pipe, 'I'll guess it for you. The two genteels saw the place in a dhrame, whatever place it is.'

" 'Hoot-toot,' grunted the throoper, shifting himself on his stool, and turning sideways to the company, eyes and all, mighty wise and scornful.

" 'The Lord save us !' cries Biddy again, while the two Kerry men only looked more and more serious.

" 'You may hoot us, sir,' the husband went on to the throoper; 'but I'll lay you a small wager I'm in the right ; and, more than that, I'll lay you the same wager that the dhrame was about money being hid in the place, and that the two genteels have dhremt it together, over and over, and that they are come into Louth to-night to see their drame out.'

" 'All nonsense, and turf, and butter-milk,' the throoper made answer, in words like my words, though maybe not the very same, for I don't pretend to spake his north bad English ; 'and all come of the errors and superstitions of ould Papistry.' And he gave himself another swing round, and spoke down in his throat, and turned up his nose like my lady's lapdog at cowld pee-aties. And, upon that, every sowl that heard him snapped at him, because they were all good Christians like ourselves, or had the name of it, at laste. And Biddy Murphy's husband dared him to make the wager ; and her two customers promised to decide it, by making oath of the truth one way or another. And she called him names, and told him he ought to be ashamed of himself. And at last he consented, and wagered his sourd agin two gould guineas that the Kerry men could and would not uphold what Mike Murphy had said. So, the sourd and the money were put on the table together, and he swore the men on a little Bible he took out of his pocket ; and, sure enough, the sourd was lost, for they made oath that every word Mike had spoken was gospel.

" 'Now, what's the rason you don't take it up, man o' the house ?' says the throoper, speaking to Mike, who didn't make the laste motion for the sourd, but only looked at it as a body would look at a live thing that might turn on a body, and bite. He thought he had a rason for keeping his hands to himself— or, maybe, two rasons. Biddy used to say that, first and foremost, he didn't half like to meddle with it, and its gruff-looking owner to the fore, even supposing he had won it quite fair But she used to say, besides, that he cotch the Kerry men winking and smiling at one another, in a knowing way, just when they were going to kiss the little Bible ; and, upon that, Mike wasn't sure of them, out and out ; and, moreover, he thought the throoper saw them doing the same thing, and had a maning in his words and look, when he said, 'What's the rason you don't take it up, man o' the house ?'

" ' Never lay a finger on it, Mike !' cried Biddy, as soon as the speech was out of his mouth. ' Huth, sir,' facing herself about to the throoper, ' put your purty sourd at your own side, where it ought to be, its little use I or my good man have of such things ; and sure it was all out of fun we laid the wager with you, and no more did we want than just to show you that Mr. Murphy can make a sharp guess at a riddle, now and then.' And Mike himself bid the throoper take it, saying the same words that Biddy said ; and so he stretched out his big long arm for it, at last, with a grave kind of smile on his own face, for the first time that evening.

"Very well. You must not think, genteels, that Mike Murphy had any doubt of the guess he made ; no such thing. He believed firmly, and so did Biddy, that the Kerry men, Aby and Dick, as they called each other, had dhremt the dhrame, and came into Louth to dig for the money. And when I said that he did not depend on them, out and out, for winning the wager, it was to give ye to understand that he feared they did not kiss the book right—only their thumbs, maybe—that was all. Very well, again. Mighty unasy he was, to thry if they would tell him whereabouts in the neighborhood they expected to find the threasure ; and so, giving a sign to Biddy—and Biddy wanted little asking—he got her to thry Aby on that head. But Aby was not entirely the fool she took him for ; and all she had for her trouble was, 'Ah, ma'am! and sure that would be telling !'

" It was growing late, and the two men got up from the fire, as if going to shake themselves, and make ready for bed. The saddles of their horses lay in a corner, where they had put them down ; they took them on their arms, and stood a while together whispering. The throoper was nearer to them at that time thau the masther or the misthress of the Fighting Cocks ; and it's said he heard a word or two, for all his not seeming to take notice. In a minute or so, Aby said to the other, spaking loud, 'Come up the loft with me, Dick, till we take care of the saddles, and then we'll settle who is to go out, and have a peep first.'

" ' It's talking of looking at the place, out of doors, they are,' says Biddy to Mike. And then she tould them not to be uneasy about the saddles, for that they would be quite safe in the kitchen—as safe as if they put them undher their heads, for pillows, in the loft where they were to sleep. But they made answer that the saddles did not belong to them, that they had borrowed them of a friend or two in Kerry, that they were new and of value, and that they did not like, for the same rasons, to trust them out of their sight.

" ' Of great value they must be, surely,' said the throoper, getting up, too, from his stool ; ' of great value, to make you so careful of them ; I ought to know a good saddle from a bad one. Let me handle one of them.' With that, he whipped

Dick's saddle off his arm, before any one could hinder him ; and, 'sure enough,' says the throoper, says he, 'this is a serviceable sort of a saddle ; but what makes it so heavy, I wondher !'

"'Huth, that's the virtue of it,' answered Dick, snapping it back again. And then he and Aby went up the laddher to the loft, and stayed there a long while, whispering over agin.

"No one had 'come down, when the throoper said he would walk out a bit, to sthretch his long legs, afther his hard day's ride, before he went to bed. 'He's slipping out to lie in wait for them, Mike,' says Biddy to the husband, 'let you step out too, and who knows but you might have a share of what's going.' And many a time she bid him thry his fortune ; but Mike Murphy was a quiet man, and stayed where he was.

"While they were talking under their breath, Dick ran bould ly down the laddher, and, looking pleasantly at them, and speak ing as if he wanted to make no great secret of any thing except the real spot where the money was, said, ' Now for it !' and darted out of the house. The man and wife sat at the fire, going on with their gosther. Aby soon made one among them agin. In a short half-hour's time Dick came in, rubbing his hands and dancing about, now on one leg, now on another.

"'You have found the place,' asked Aby.

"'The very place, sure enough,' says Dick. 'And honest people, we'll tell you. Lend us a spade, a crow, and a pickaxe, or borrow them for us from the neighbors, and wait here till we go try our luck—'twould be unmannerly for any one to follow us—and, according to what we may find, ye will be the better of your civility.' And no sooner said than done. Mike and Biddy got the things they asked for in a jiffy, and out they went together, stripping off their coats and waistcoats to be ready for their work.

"For the hundredth time, ay, and more, Biddy wanted Mike to stale easy afther them, but she could not get him to stir.

"' Well, then, salvation to me, but I'll have an eye afther them myself,' says she ; and, putting on her cloak, she was as good as her word, sure enough, crossing the trassel, and leaving Mike alone at the fire.

"The place, above all others, nigh at hand, that a body would dhrame of finding money in, was an ould castle, built by the thieves of Danes the time they had all Ireland to themselves, before Brian Boru the Great dhruve them all into the say, at Clontarf, like a flock of half-starved wolves. And Biddy Mur phy was not the woman to forget that same the moment she left her house, but sthraight away she bent her steps to the ould four walls. Round about the narrow window-holes, and the low door-way, she went peeping like a cat, and it was easy for her to see the Kerry men inside on the ground floor. But they were not digging, and did not seem as if they were much in earnest about going to dig—not at all ; but there they sat, side by side, on the big, loose stones that had tumbled in from the top of the castle, and the moon shining strong on them through the door-way ; and Biddy thought they were only listening, as if to hear some footstep they expected might come, laughing low to one another, and looking very 'cute and knowledgable all the time.

"And at last she heard one of them say to the other, with a big curse—asking your pardon, genteels—' The hussy, won't she stale over here to watch us, afther all ? If she doesn't, half our good plan fails.'

" ' She will, man alive,' the other made answer ; ' she's the woman to do it, I tell you. Her husband is a gom (ass), but Biddy has the right curiosity in her.'

" ' Thank ye kindly, gossips,' says Biddy to herself, ' and faix 'tisn't a bad guess ye have, no more than Mike Murphy, and so here goes to give ye a notion that I *am* here, but not that I know that *ye* know any thing about it.' For Biddy had it in her mind in a minute that they wanted her to see them raise the treasure, and be a witness for them that it was honestly dhremt of and come by. And with that she stirred her feet among the weeds and rubbish outside o' the ould place where she stood, so that they might hear her a little, which they did, at the same time, and then, with signs to each other, the two rogues of the world began to clear away the big stones, and to dig at last.

"They were but a short time at work when Aby cried out, as his spade sounded like music against something, ' Here it is, by the piper !' and down they threw their spades, and began to clear around the treasure with their pickaxes, and, one by one, drew out of the earth a great many little tin cannisthers like. ' Goold in them all! goold in every one o' them ! and the whole lot full to the brim!' they said, dancing like wild men, the same that Dick had done in the Fighting Cocks, according as they examined the little cannisthers one afther another. ' Goold enough to make rich men and gentlemen of us forever and a day !' they went on ; ' goold enough to buy a nate bit o' land out of ould Ireland's ground!'

" 'Yes,' said some one else that Biddy did not see at first ; 'yes, but not for ye!' and behold, ye genteels, with that the big throoper came jumping down upon them from a hiding-hole in the ould wall of the room, or whatever we are to call it, and his sword in his hand, and his cross face now looking terrible entirely. Down he jumped and rattled jackboots, spurs and all, among the loose stones, and the first thing he made bould to do was to split poor Aby's skull to the chin, before any one could say, 'Don't, sir, and I'll be obliged to you.'

" Biddy was goin' to screech murder as loud as she could, when something flew, whistling—for all the world as if one of the good people (fairies) did it—by her ear, and stopped her breath ; and to tell the truth, she was more and more frightened at the noise of a gun or pistol going off, entirely at the same time ; for it came into her mind that it was the bullet she heard so close by her ear, and that she had what might be called a great escape, for the same rason. And the second Kerry man fired the shot, sure enough, at the throoper, thinking to have revenge for his gossip's death, only he missed his mark somehow ; and he drew another pistol from his bosom and presented it, when the throoper knocked it out of his hand, and then they closed and had a brave wrastling match.

" Biddy now found her voice, and pillalooed, and clapped her hands, and danced on her heels, at the narrow window-hole, enough to bring down the remains of the ould castle on all their heads, though she had not the thought, nor maybe the strength, to do a better thing by far—that is, run home to Mike Murphy.

" 'Hould your tongue, woman !' cries the throoper to her roaring all the time that he was shaking the Kerry man, like a dog worrying a rat ; 'hould your foolish bastely tongue, and come in here to us ! I am glad you came in time to bear wit ness.'

" 'Musha, and I'm in great request with you, one after an other, for bearing witness,' says Biddy, 'and what good can I do you, misther throoper, by giving a true account of what I have seen ?'

" 'Come in, and you shall learn,' he grumbled, and in speaking these words he got the Kerry man on his face, and was strapping his arms behind him.

" 'Come in ?' asked Biddy ; 'come in to you to be murdered, as you are afther doing te one of my honest, civil customers, and are going to do wid the other ?'

13

"'Fool of a woman!' roars the throoper, madder than ever, 'you do not know what you say ; but I care little, so you listen to me, and heed me. The man I have cut down with my sword was a great highway robber, and so is the man who lies bound at my feet. For many years they have pursued their bad call-ing in the south ; nor are their hands clane of the blood of some of the people they plundered. They had gained a power o₄ ⁻iches by their evil deeds, and thought to leave Ireland with it, nd live like graudees in a foreign counthry. But the govern-ment, and the great gentlemen of the south, hearing of their plan, sent descriptions of them, printed, all over Ireland, and to every port where they could take shipping, in particular ; so that after many attempts, they gave up their notion of going abroad, and laid another plan to enjoy their riches at home. And it was this last plan that sent them into Louth, a good distance from every place where they were well known, and set them upon inventing their story of the dhrame, at your fireside.'

"'Blessed hour, sir!' says Biddy, speaking in through the split in the ould wall ; 'but how did you come to know all this ? and did not they find the threasure nigh to the spot you are standing on, at any rate ?'

"'He that hides can find,' the throoper made answer. 'Be-fore they left your home together, for this place, one of them came here alone, and put the goold into the ground, and haped stones over it. I saw him at the work. Ay, and I suspected his intent before he quitted your roof.'

"'You did, sir, did you ?' asked Biddy again.

"'I did ; and from the moment that I took his saddle in my hand, too, for it was almost as heavy as so much lead, by rason of the goold that was hid in it. Ask me any other question you like'—he went on spaking in a very slow, determined voice—'any other question ; but be quick ; my business must be finished.'

"'Why, then, it's only what I asked you before, sir,' says Biddy.

"'That is,' says he, taking the word from her, 'how have I come to know all the rest I have told you. You shall learn. Afther the man who now lies dead had concealed the goold, he went back for his comrade, and I remained where I was till they came side by side, carrying their spades, and other things. Here they sat down to wait for you ; and from their discoorse together, I larned who and what they were ; and the hopes they had that, upheld by your evidence, the fable of their having found the

money, by virtue of a dhrame, might pass current in your superstitious neighborhood. I also recollected a description of them,
which I had often read in the printed hue and cry raised afther
them, and not a doubt was left on my mind. Then my part
was soon taken. You have seen me go half through with it.
Having to face two bould men, both well armed, of course, I
knew that it behoved me to rid myself of one of them at the
first blow.'

" 'And so you did, sir, to a sartainty. But who does the
threasure come to ?' says Biddy.

" 'To me !—fool, I call you agin for asking !' cries the throoper. 'Do you think a single man will dare what I have dared
for nothing ? Larn that the proclamation made for taking these
men gives all the money found in their hands to the person who
does its bidding on them, dead or alive, ay, and a good reward
besides. And so you may tell whom you like, that you have
seen me gather up my own ;' and saying these words, he stooped
down, sure, enough, and put the little cannisthers into his pockets, one afther another, as many as twenty of them. ' You are
looking at me, too,' he says agin, turning his eyes on the sham
Kerry man, who, to tell the truth, was watching him mighty
close ; ' but " ill got, ill gone," you know, comrade. And come,
now, stand on your legs, and walk with me down to the village,
till we can see about sending you to be well looked afther ; help
me, woman, to lift him.'

" Biddy, none afeard, did as he bid her ; her mind not at all
asy on the head of which of them was the real robber, and which
not. But the throoper's story turned out to be true enough.
The man he had bound was sent to jail, put on his thrial and
hanged, upon the oaths of many who knew him well, and there
was no law to take a single goold piece from the throoper ; but,
as he tould Biddy it would happen, he got more and more riches
and the greatest of praise, and who but he from that day out.
And, now, genteels, ye'll be guessing the throoper's name, afore I
tell it to ye ; and, sure enough, it was M'Cass ; the very M'Cass
that bought all the land in these parts, and was the great Square
M'Cass among us. And 'ill got, ill gone,' was his word to the
bould highwaymen ; but men and women are now living that can
say the same word of himself; for, afther, the first spurt of his
good luck, nothing went right with him ; he soon became a struggling man, canting (selling) and dhriving, early and late, to make
both ends meet for the keeping up of his big house, and his

hounds, and his horses, and his ladies. Ay, and a sorrowful man he was, too ; without wife or child, kith or kin, true friend or kind neighbor ; and so he spent his life, and so he died ; in poverty he was put into the ground, without any Christian show of a funeral, without a tongue to *keenth* (wail) him, or a hand to fix a stone at his head. And people have it, that the night he departed, Squire M'Cass talked as if the man he cut down in th ould castle was sitting by his bedside ; and that the last say ing heard from his lips was his own saying of ould—' Ill got, ill gone' ; ill got, ill gone'—repeated over, and over, till he was stiff."

THE END OF ILL GOT, ILL GONE.

THE CHURCHYARD WATCH.

THE CHURCHYARD WATCH.

THE dead are watched lest the living should prey on them. A strange alliance of the living with DEATH!—that his kingdom and sovereignty may remain untrenched upon. In different parts of England we have seen watch-houses, almost entirely composed of glass, built in lonesome churchyards, of which, generally, the parish sexton, and perhaps his dog, are the appointed nightly tenants ; with liberty, ceded or taken, to leave their dull lamp in the watch-box, and roam here and there, at their pleasure, among the graves until daylight. What stern necessities man forces upon man! There can scarce be a more comfortless lot, or, making allowance for the almost inborn shudderings of the human heart, a more appalling one, than that of the poor grave scooper or bell-puller who is thus doomed to spend his night, summer and winter. Habit, indeed, may eventually blunt the first keenness of his aversion, if not terror : he may serve a due apprenticeship to horrors, and learn his trade. After a thousand secret and unowned struggles to seem brave and indifferent, he may at last grow callously courageous. His flesh may cease to creep as he strides on, in his accustomed round, over the abodes of the silent and mouldering, and hears his own dull footstep echoed through the frequently dreary hollowness beneath. But what has he gained now, beyond the facility of earning his wretched crust for himself and his crying infants! We have seen and spoken with one who seemed to have lost, in the struggle with conquered nature's especial antipathy, most of the other sympathies of his kind. He had a heavy ox-like expression of face ; he would scarce speak to his neighbors when they passed him at his door or in the village street ; his own children feared or disliked him, and did not smile nor whisper in his presence. We have watched him into the churchyard, at his usual hour, after nightfall. When he began to stalk about there, he appeared to be in closer fellowship with the dead he watched than with the fair existence which he scarce more than nominally shared. It was said, indeed, that, upon his initiation, at a tender age and under peculiar circumstances, into his profession of churchyard watchman, temporary delirium had prepared him for its regular and steady pursuit ever since. That, although he showed no symptoms of distinct insanity when we knew him, the early visitation had left a gloom on his mind, and a thick, nerveless insensibility in his heart, which, at forty-five, formed his character. In fact, we learned a good deal about him, for every one talked of him ; and, as has been hinted, much of that good deal from himself, to say nothing of his wife, in his absence. If he did not deliberately invent fables of his past trials, for the purpose of gratifying a little mockery of our undisguised interest, as mad as the maddest bedlamite he must have been upon the occasion alluded to. Nay, to recount with a grave face (as he did) the particulars of the delusions of his time of delirium, did not argue him a very sound-minded man at the moment he gave us his confidence. We are about to tell his story at length, in our own way, however—that is, we shall try to model into our own language what his neighbors, his spouse, and his own slow-moving and heavy lips have, from time to time, supplied us with.

He was the only child of an affectionate and gentle-mannered father, who died when he was little more than a boy, leaving him sickly and pining. His mother wept a month, mourned three months more—and was no longer a widow. Her second husband proved a surly fellow, who married her little fortune rather than herself, as the means of keeping his quart-pot filled, almost from morning to night, at the village tap, where he played good-fellow and politician to the expressed admiration of all his companions. He had long been the parish sexton, and took up his post night after night in the churchyard. Little fear had he of what he might see there. He had outgrown his fears ; or, if he thought or felt of the matter, the lonely debauch which he was known to make in that strange banquet-place, served to drug him into obliviousness. He deemed his duty—or he said and swore he did—only a tiresome and slavish one, and hated it just as he hated daily labor. And—as he declared and harangued at the tap—he had long ago forsworn it, only that it paid him well. But now that his marriage made his circumstances easier, he was determined to drink alone in the churchyard no longer.

He fed an idle, useless lad at home, who, with his dog—as idle as he—roamed and loitered about, here and there, and had never yet done a single thing to earn his bread. But it was full time that both were taught the blessings of industry ; and he would teach them. Why should not Will take his place in the watch-box, and so keep the shillings in the family? His friends praised his views, one and all, and he grew thrice resolved.

Returned the next morning from his nocturnal charge, he reeled to bed in solemn, drunken determination. He arose, towards evening, only half reclaimed by sleep to ordinary sense, and set about his work of reformation. He ate his meal in silence, turned from the table to the fire without a word, looked at the blaze, grimly contemplative.

"Where is that truant now?" he asked suddenly of his wife. "Down by the marshes with his cur, I suppose ; or gone a-nut-ting, or lying stretched in the sun, the two idlers together. What! and must I work and work, and strive and strive! I, I, forever! and will he never lend me a hand? Go where he likes, do what he likes, and laugh and fatten on my labor?"

"Master Hunks," said the wife, "Will is sickly, and won't fatten on either your labor or mine, not to talk of his own. You know he's a puny lad, and wants some favor yet awhile. With God's help and ours he may be stronger soon."

Will and his dog here came in. From what followed this evening it will be seen that the ill-fated lad promised, in early youth, to be of an open, kindly, intelligent character, very different indeed from that in which we found him husked up at five-and-forty.

He saluted his step-father, and sat down quietly near the fire.

His poor dumb companion—friend of his boyhood, and his father's gift—coiled himself up before the blaze, and prepared to surrender his senses to happy sleep, interspersed with dreams of all the sports he had enjoyed with his master that day. Hunks, his eye glancing from one object of dislike to the other, kicked the harmless brute, who jumped up, yelping in pain and bitter lamentation, and ran for shelter under Will's chair. Will's pale cheek broke out into color, his weak eye sparkled.

"Why is my poor dog beaten?" he cried shrilly.

"The lazy cur!" said Hunks ; "he was in my way, and only got paid for idleness."

"'Twas ill done," resumed Will ; "he was my father's dog,

12*

and my father gave him to me. If my father were alive and
well, he would not hurt him nor see him hurt !" Tears interrupted his sudden fit of spirit.

"Cur, as much as he is !" retorted Hunks ; "do you put upon
me here at my own fireside ? *You* are the idler, you, and he
only learns of you ; and I hadn't ought to have served him out
and you so near me."

"It has been God's will," said the boy, "to keep my strength
from me."

"Be silent and hear me!" roared Hunks ; "this is your life, I
say, playing truant forever. And what is mine and your own
good mother's here ?"

"Master Hunks," pleaded the wife, "God knows I don't
grudge nothing I can do for my poor Will's sake."

"And you—not a word from you either, missis !" grunted
Hunks ; "I am put upon by one and t'other of you ; ye sleep
in comfort every night, and leave me to go a-watching out o'
doors there in all weathers. But stop a bit, my man, it sha'n't
be this way much longer. I'll have my natural rest in my bed
some time or other, and soon ; and you must earn it for me."

"How, father ? how can I earn it ?" asked Will. "I would if
I could, but how ? I haven't learnt no trade, and you know as
well as any one knows it, I am not able to work in the fields or
on the roads, or get my living any one way."

"Then you can sit still and watch, that's light work," muttered Hunks.

"Watch !" cried mother and son together ; "watch what ?
and where ? or whom ?"

"The dead folk in the churchyard."

"Heaven defend me from it !" cried poor Will, clasping his
hands and falling back in his chair.

"Ay, and this very night," continued the despot. "This very
night you shall mount guard in my place, and I shall have my
lawful sleep, what the whole parish cries shame on me for not
having months ago."

"Master Hunks, 'twill kill the boy !" cried the mother in
agony.

"Missis, don't you go for to cross me so often !" remonstrated
her husband, with a fixed look, which, short as they had been
one flesh, she had reason to understand and shrink at. "Come,
my man, stir yourself ; 'tis time you were at the gate ; the church
clock has struck ; *they will expect us.*" He interrupted him-

self in a great rage, and with a great oath. " But here I keep
talking, and the cur never minds a word I say ! Come along !"
" Don't lay hands on him !" screamed the mother as he strode
towards the boy. " What I have often told you has come to
pass, Master Hunks, you have killed him !"

Hunks scoffed at the notion, although, indeed, Will's hands
had fallen helplessly at his side, and his chin rested on his breast,
while his eyes were closed and his lips apart. But he had only
become insensible from terror acting on a weak frame. Sighs
and groans soon gave notice of returning animation. His mother
earnestly besought their tyrant to go on his night's duty, and,
at least till the following night, leave her son to her care. Half
in fear of having to answer for a murder, incredulously as he
affected to speak, Hunks turned out of the house, growling and
threatening.

" Is he gone ?" asked Will, when he regained his senses ;
"gone, not to come back ?" Having heard his mother's gentle
assurances, he let his head fall on her shoulder, weeping, while he
continued—

" Mother, mother, I could not bear it for an hour! The dread
I am in of it was born with me! When I was a child of four
years, I had dreams of it, and I remember them to this day ;
they used to come in such crowds round my cradle ! As I grew
up, you saw and you know my weakness. I could never sit still
in the dark, nor even in the daylight, out of doors in lonesome
places. Now in my youth—a lad, almost a man—I am ashamed
to speak of my inward troubles. Mother, you do not know me
—I do not know myself ! I walk out sometimes, down by the
river, and, listening to the noise of the water over the rocks,
where it is shallow, and to the rustling of the trees, as they nod in
the twilight, voices and shrieks come around me. Sometimes
they break in my ears—and I have turned to see what thing it
was that spoke, and thought some gray tree at my side had only
just changed, and become motionless, and seemed as if, a moment
before, it had been something else, and had a tongue, and said
the words that frightened me ! Oh ! it was but yesterday evening, I ran home from the banks of the river, and felt no heart
within me till I had come in here to the fireside, and seen you
moving near me !

" You know the lone house, all in ruins, upon the hill—I fear
it, mother, more than my tongue can tell you ! I have been
taken through it, in my dreams, in terrible company ; and here I

could describe to you its bleak apartments, one by one—in vaults pitch dark, and half filled with stones and rubbish, and choked up with weeds, its winding, creeping staircases, and its flapping windows—I know them all, though my feet never yet crossed its threshold ! Never, mother—though I have gone near it, to enter it, and see if what I had dreamt of it was true ; and I went in the first light of the morning. But when close by the old door-way, the rustle of the shrubs and weeds startled me, and I thought—but sure *that* was fancy—that some one called me in by name. Then I turned, and raced down the hill, never looking back till I came to the meadow-ground, where cows and sheep are always grazing, and heard the dogs barking in the town, and voices of the children at play !"

"Will, my king," said his mother, soothingly, "this is all mere childishness, at your years. God is above us, and around us ; and, even if evil and strange things are allowed to be on earth, He will shield us from all harm. Arouse up like a man ! for, indeed, your time of boyhood is passing—nay, it has passed with other lads not much older. Only you have been poorly and weakly from your cradle, Will. Come, go to sleep ; and, before you lie down, pray for better health and strength to-morrow."

"To-morrow !" he repeated, "and did my step-father say any thing of to-morrow ?"

His mother answered him evasively, and he resumed—"Oh, how I fear to-morrow ! Oh, mother, you have loved me, and you do love me, for my weakness, my ill-health, and my dutiful-ness ! and you loved my father ! Oh! for his sake, as well as mine, mother, keep me from what I am threatened with. Keep me from it, if you would keep me alive another day !"

After spending a miserable night, he stole out of the house next morning, and wandered about the private walks adjacent to the town, until he thought his father might have arisen and taken his usual walk to the tap. But as the lad was about to re-enter the house, Hunks met him at the threshold. Will shrank back. To his surprise and comfort, however, his fears now seemed ill-founded. The man bade him good-morrow, in as cheerful and kind a tone as he could command, shook his hand, tapped him on the head, and left the house. Delighted, though still agitated, Will sought his mother, within doors, told her his good omens, and spent a happy day. At dinner, too, notwithstanding Hunks' presence, the mother and son enjoyed themselves, so amiable had the despot become, at least in appearance.

When their meal was over, Hunks, as if to attain the utmost civility, invited Will to go out with him for a walk by the river —" and let's have Barker (Will's dog) for company," continued Hunks. " He may show us sport with a rat, or such like Will."

Accordingly, the three strolled out together, Will leading the way, by many a well-known sedge or tuft of bushes, or undermined bank, the resort of the water-rat, and sometimes of the outlaw otter ; and Barker upheld his character, by starting, hunting down, and killing one of the first-mentioned animals. As twilight came on, they turned their faces towards the little town. They entered it. Its hum of life was now hushed ; its streets silent, and almost deserted ; its doors and windows barred and bolted, and the sounds of the rushing river, and the thumping mill, were the only ones which filled the air. The clock pealed ten, as they continued their way. Hunks had grown suddenly silent and reserved. They passed the old gothic church, and now were passing the gate which led into its burial-ground. Hunks stopped short. His gray, cruel eye fell on the lad— " Will," he said, " I be thinking, we've walked enough for this time."

" Enough, indeed ; thank you for your company ; and goodnight, father," answered Will, trying to smile, though he began to tremble.

" Good-night, then, my man ; and here be your watch-light ;" and Hunks drew a dark lantern from his huge pocket.

" Nay, I want no light home," said Will ; " I know the way so well. 'Tis not very dark ; and you know you can't do without it on your post."

" My post !" Hunks laughed villainously ; " your post you mean, Will. Take it ; I be thinking I shall sleep sound to-night without a dead-light—as if I were corpse to need it. Come along."

" You cannot have the heart to ask me !" cried Will, stepping back.

" Pho, my man." Hunks clutched him by the shoulder with one hand ; with the other unlocked the gate and flung it open. " In with you ! You'll like it so in a few nights, you'll wish no better post. The dead chaps be civil enough ; only treat them well, and let them walk awhile, and they make very good company." He dragged Will closer to the gate.

" Have mercy !" shrieked the wretched lad, trying to kneel ; " or kill me first, father, to make me company for them, if that will please you."

"Get in!" roared the savage, "get in! Ay, hollo out, and twist about, so, and I'll pitch your shivering carcass half-way cross the churchyard!" He forced him in from the gate. "Stop a bit, now; there be your lantern." He set it down on a tombstone. "Good-night; yonder's your box. Just another word: don't you be caught strolling too near the murderer's corner, over there, or you may trip and fall among the things that turn and twine on the ground, like roots of trees, to guard him."

With a new and piercing shriek, Will clung close to his tormentor. Hunks, partially carrying into effect a threat he had uttered, tore the lad's hands away, tossed him to some distance, strode out at the gate, locked it, and Will was alone with horror.

At first an anguish of fear kept him stupefied and stationary. He had fallen on a freshly piled grave, to which mechanically his fingers clung and his face joined, in avoidance of the scene around. But he soon recollected what clay it was he clung to, and at the thought, he started up, and glanced shrinkingly about him. High walls quite surrounded the churchyard, as if to part him from the habitable world. His lamp was burning upon the tombstone where Hunks had placed it—one dim red spot amid the thick darkness. The church clock tolled eleven. It ceased; his ears ached in the resumed silence; he listened and stared about him for what he feared. Whispers seemed to rise near him; he ran for his lamp, snatched it up, and instinctively hurried to the watch-box. How he wished it made of solid rock; for it was chiefly framed of glass, useless as the common air to his terrors. He shut his eyes, and pressed his palms upon them—vain subterfuge! The fevered spirit within brought before his mind's vision worse things than the churchyard could yawn up, were all that superstition has fancied of it true. He looked out from his watch-box in refuge from himself.

That evening a half-moon had risen early, and, at this moment, was sinking in gathering clouds behind distant hills. As he vaguely noticed the circumstance, he felt more and more desolate. Simultaneously with the disappearance of the planet, the near clock began again to strike—he knew not what hour! Each stroke smote his ear as if it would crack the nerve; at the last sound he shrieked out, delirious. He had a pause from agony, then a struggle for departing reason, and then he was at rest

At daybreak his step-father found him asleep. He led him home. Will sat down to breakfast, smiling, but did not speak a word. Often, during the day, his feverish eye turned to the west; why, his mother could not tell, until, as the evening made up her couch of clouds there, drawing around her the twilight for drapery, he left the house with an unusually vigorous step, and stood at the gate of the churchyard. Again he took up his post ; again the hour of twelve pealed from the old church, but now he did not fear it. When it had fully sounded, he clapped his hands, laughed, and shouted.

The whispers he had heard the previous night—small, cautious whispers—came round him again ; first from a distance, then nearer and nearer. At last he shaped them into words. "Let us walk," they said ; "though he watches us, he fears us." *He!* 'twas strange to hear the dim dead speak to a living man, of himself ! The boy laughed at the fancy, and replied to them :

"Ay, come! appear! I give leave for it. Ye are about in crowds, I know, not yet daring to take up your old bodies till *I* please. But up with them! Graves, split on, and yield me my subjects ! Am I not king of the churchyard? Obey me, ay, now your mouths gape—and what a yawning! Are ye musical, too ?—a jubilee of groans ! Out with it, in the name of Death! Blast it about like giants carousing !

"Well blown! Now a thousand heads pop up at once—their eyes fixed on mine, as if to ask my further leave for a resurrection. They know I am good-humored now, and grow upwards, accordingly, like a grove of bare trees that have no sap in them. And now they move—passing along in rows, like trees that glide by one on a bank while one sails merrily down the river. Yet all is still. See others stand bolt upright against their own headstones to contemplate. I wonder what they think of ! Move! move! young, old, boys, men, pale girls, and palsied grandmothers—my churchyard can never hold 'em! Yet, how they pass each other from corner to corner! I think they make way through one another's bodies, as they do in the grave. They'll dance anon—minuets, at least. Why, they begin already! And what partners! That tall, handsome young officer takes our village witch-of-the-wield—she that died at Christmas. Our last rector smirks to a girl of fifteen—ha! ha! Yon tattered little fellow is a radical, making a leg to the old duchess! Music! music! Go, some of you that look on there, and toll the dead-bell! Well done! they tie the murderer to the bell-rope by the neck (though he was hanged before), and the bell swings out merrily! But what face is here ?"

It was the vision of a child's face which he caught staring at him through the glass of his watch-box—the face of an only brother who had died young. The wretch's laughter changed into tears and low wailings. By the time that his mother came to seek him, just at daybreak, he was, however, again laughing ; but in such a state as to frighten mirth from her heart and lips till the day she died. As has been said, symptoms of positive insanity did not long continue to appear in his words or actions ; yet, when he recovered, there was still a change in him—a dark and disagreeable change, under the inveterate confirmation of which, the curious student of human nature may, at this moment, observe him in his native village.

THE END OF THE CHURCHYARD WATCH.

THE LAST OF THE STORM.

THE LAST OF THE STORM.

AT a very early hour of a July morning, an admirer of the picturesque stood alone upon the top of a hill, on a spot best calculated to give him a bird's-eye view of the town in which he was a temporary resident, together with its adjacent scenery. The prospect he commanded was indeed most pleasing, notwithstanding that some blotches occasionally offended the eye, and produced disagreeable associations in the mind.

The extensive "haunt of men," containing twenty thousand souls, peeped out, here and there, about a mile distant, through groves, gardens, and orchards, mixed up with its outskirts, and through more rural foliage between him and them. The river that ran under its bridges from a remote hill-source, widened as it approached the stranger; uplands sloped from behind it; all around to a great distance the country was spotted with villas and mansions, and relieved with masses of trees, rich and abundant for an Irish landscape, though somewhat meagre if compared with a parallel scene in woody England. Beyond them, from twenty to forty miles off, towered blue mountains—shapeless, excepting in the general outline; blank, pale; the mere spectres of what, in reality, they were. Upon their peaks alone the rising sun had begun to shine, while all the rest of the picture remained untouched by his beams, though visible in their promise—not vague in twilight, but distinct and fresh, however cool. A white mist curled up at different points of the widespread slopes, the river gray and dim, showing only black wrinkles where at noontide it used to sport its dimples, and interweave its maze of little lines of light.

The dark spots of this fair view remain now to be noticed. Part of the suburbs of the town consisted of dingy ruins: cabins, and small farm-houses beyond them appeared half burned. No

cattle grazed or sauntered, or reclined in their trampled pastur-
ages—few, indeed, could be seen over the whole landscape. In
other fields, hay had rotted, and wheat and barley were going to
decay for want of the sickle. Many mills upon the brink of the
river, or of its tributary streamlet, showed signs of recent and
present idleness ; before one of them, which the stranger knew
had lately been converted into a temporary barrack, a sentinel was
pacing. These and other things indicated that civil war, not yet
quite subdued, had recently visited, in its bitter wrath, one of the
fairest districts of his country. In fact, it was the end of July,
1798.

"But the storm is about to pass away," said he, "never again,
I hope, to gather on our hills and desolate our plains. A few
weeks more, and in this town and county, at least, we shall be
amendable to our own civil magistrates, and not to the arbitrary
administrators of martial law. A few days more, and our sisters,
wives, and daughters, need not tremble through the livelong night,
cowering together like woodpigeons from the hawk. A few
days more, and you, my Bessie, now dreaming of me, I h
 in
yonder garrisoned town, may be permitted to accept of y protection."

Indulging the last feeling, he employed himself, lover-like, in
trying to make out, among the different groups of houses that
broke through the foliage in and beyond the town, the identical
roof under which he imagined his fair dreamer to slumber, when
he heard shrill cries from a by-road that skirted the hill upon
which he stood, although its convex sweep was so abrupt as to hide
that road from his view. Suddenly the cries were hushed—then came
a clashing of weapons from the same quarter. Indifferent to the
danger of interfering, in such times, in an unknown quarrel, he
hastened to the road, not, indeed, by plunging directly downwards
from the spot on which he had been standing, which was impracti-
cable, but by running along the hill's ridges towards the town until he gained a path which, winding obliquely over its bosom,
would tardily usher him upon the road, at a point considerably
above the spot he was so anxious to gain.

Before he had got half-way down, the clashing ceased, as the
cries had previously done. He stopped to listen in the *boreen*,
horsemen approached him, yet hidden by a turn of the road.
Prudence now qualified his first chivalrous ardor, and he secreted
himself behind a fence. Presently, two Hessians, belonging to a
regiment quartered in the town, came slowly up to his hiding-place.

They were conversing in their own language, with which he was acquainted ; and their first words strongly interest.d him. They came close—he held his breath to catch every syllable they uttered, and just as they passed, he ventured, for a reason drawn from their discourse, to glance observantly, though cautiously, at them. He became satisfied, so far ;—the face of one bled profusedly ; the right arm of the other was bound up, and hung disabled at his side. Soon after clearing his ambush, the Hessians trotted briskly towards the town. He jumped over the fence, and, greatly excited, ran along the road in the direction they had come. He arrived at a stile, leading into a pasture-field, which belonged, as he was aware, to a farm-house, distant some fields more from it, and skirting a little retired hamlet—almost the only one in the immediate district still free from the visitations of civil war. The mark of horses' hoofs on the dust near the fence, recently impressed, made him pause at this spot. He vaulted over the stile, and remarked, even during his quick transit, that it was bloody. At the end of a path running from it, he saw two cows standing together holding down their heads ; a pail, overturned, was near them ; and beyond them were some men and women, with eyes bent upon the ground. A few bounds brought him into the midst of the group, and he now saw what he had expected—the poor owner of the pail lying senseless, if not dead, on the grass ; her head bruised, and a severe wound in her neck.

He called on the bystanders for an explanation ; one and all, they professed complete ignorance of the accident. They had only heard screams at some distance ; and when, after waiting for each other to advance in a body, they arrived on the spot, they saw no one—nothing, in short, but the poor girl lying there, her pail upset, her milk spilled, and the two cows standing over her ; and "she could not yet spake for herself, if it was the Lord's will that she was ever to spake agin at all ;" but one of the women surmised that "Brown Beck, the young cow wi' the sharp horns, that now an' then was a giddy, cross-grained cow, might have done the mischief, for as sorry as she now looked on the head of it."

The catechist did not regret the ignorance of the peasants, and, with praiseworthy caution, resolved not to make them wiser on the subject. He only assisted in conveying the wounded milk-maid to the farm-house, having first dispatched a messenger for a surgeon. The girl moaned when they stirred her, but gave no sign of consciousness. Her new friend saw her laid on a bed ;

and, taking the dame of the house aside, soon convinced the good woman's understanding that, till the arrival of a surgeon, she alone ought to sit by the sufferer's couch, and hear her explanation ; if, indeed, she should be able to give one by that time. The next instant he was on the road to the town.

In the suburbs he met the surgeon proceeding to visit his patient. It was most advisable to make a confident of this gentleman, also ; accordingly, our young acquaintance stopped him, repeated much of what he had said to the farmer's wife, obtained the assurances he wished, and walked quietly forward.

It did not surprise him to observe, at the entrance of the town, groups of people looking around, as they conversed in a low tone, and turned their heads and eyes in the direction which the two bleeding Hessians must so very recently have taken. But he was startled—though expecting something of the kind, too—when, as he gained the main street, drums beat to arms, trumpets sounded to the field, and soldiers of every description, regulars, militia, and the local yeomen, hurried, obeying the summons, to a well-known place of rendezvous.

He was received at the friend's house in which, for many months, he had been a visitor, with a welcome that suggested that his family had expected his return, in some alarm. His host, and his host's son, stood at the back of the servant who opened the door, and shook his hand warmly. A voice yet gentler than theirs whispered his name through a half-open door in the hall, and he disappeared into the apartment to answer the summons as became him. He did not lead Bessie Gordon to the breakfast parlor until he had made her the exclusive confidante of his morning's adventure, detailing every circumstance very minutely, for her satisfaction and assurance.

Breakfast was nearly over, when he asked, "And now, my good friends, what is the meaning of the excitement in which I find you all ?"

"No one has told you as you came along, Harry," said Mr. Gordon.

"No !"

"Then you have yet to hear disagreeable news. Two of the Hessians of our garrison, on their way to General Sir A. D—— with dispatches, this morning, have been attacked by a body of rebels, who, unfortunately for me, seem to be composed of my tenantry about Killane."

"Ay !" cried Harry, drily.

"Ay, indeed ; and the two poor fellows are badly hurt ; and Sir A. D—— is going to march out almost the whole garrison, to burn every cabin of the hamlet, if he cannot meet with the treacherous rascals."

"Ay!" repeated Harry, his brow knitting and his cheek reddening, to the surprise of his host ; and have *the poor fellows* described the appearance of the rebels, sir ? Were there any *women* among them ?"

"Why, yes, as is almost always the case ; one of whom, the men think, they have wounded."

"Ay!" again cried Harry, rising sternly. Here a party of horse trotted up to the hall-door, and a loud knocking resounded through the house.

"The general," resumed Mr. Gordon, "following up his intimation to me, even sooner than I expected."

"What intimation, sir ?"

"That, before he proceeded to Killane, he would require my opinion as to those of my tenantry there, most likely, from symptoms of previous disaffection, to have headed the insurrection this morning.*v*

"Mr. Gordon," resumed Henry, while they heard the general and his party ushered into an adjoining room, "there is now no time to inform you why I am very anxious to stand by your side during this interview, but I particularly request you to afford me that privilege."

"Henry Lane," answered his host, "your expression when you came home just now ; the preference I know you have for that morning walk towards Killane ; your manner at breakfast ; your present request—all convince me you can say something about the matter in question. Is it so ?"

"It is, Mr. Gordon."

"And you *do not fear* to stand by my side ?"

His young guest scouted the notion

"Although your old enemy, Kirk, is at the general's elbow ?"

"Although the devil, instead of a dear friend of his, were there, Mr. Gordon."

They entered the general's presence together. He was a sharp-featured man ; having a military air certainly—but one of an inferior kind. A scar through his lips, and down his chin, argued, indeed, effective service ; but it also added to the ungentle expression of his countenance, and did not combat the presumption that fitness of natural character, rather than high achievement in the field, had recommended him to his late and present situation of despotic chief, judge, and all but hangman, at a terrible and merciless crisis.

At his right hand stood Mr. Sheriff Kirk—also Captain Kirk ; the second title having been conferred by a command in one of the yeomaury corps of the town: He wore, of course, his military uniform, and did not lack the air of a soldier. Nor were his cool, gray eyes, his yellow checks, and his steady mouth, evidences of a merely civil energy of official character. A few words more, glancing at his previous history, are required, for the knowledge we need to have of this individual.

Ten years before he had kept a very humble shop in the town. A large reward was offered for the apprehension of a notorious robber. Mr. Kirk courageously issued into the country; returned with the highwayman ; got the reward ; and never afterwards knew a poor day. Under the patronage of the noble person who dispensed corporate honors, he rose rapidly in the world. At the breaking out of the rebellion, no man could be more active in discovering hidden traitors, and dragging them to justice ; some said, indeed, that on the principle of " sure hide, sure find," he might be supposed to be peculiarly adapted for the service. In the field, as a yeomanry officer, his zeal was equally conspicuous. For instance, after a skirmish with a band of United Irish, in a village some miles distant, two of the retreating peasants ran for shelter into a thatched chapel on the road-side, and Mr. Kirk pursued them, sword in hand, and dispatched the superstitious rebels on the steps of their little altar.

Henry Lane, when his host presented him to Sir A. D——, wondered at the coldness of the general's bow. The undisguised sneer of Mr. Kirk did not surprise him. Upon his arrival, as the visitor of his father's oldest friend, Bessie Gordon was from home, and, amid the mixed society of the town, a daughter of the captain-sheriff received at his hands more passing gallantry than perhaps fell to the lot of the young ladies around her. But Bessie came—looked—and conquered ; and, in consequence, Mr. Kirk and his " darling child" chose to consider themselves ill-used people. But we dare say the gentleman felt even more keenly a second injury. Henry Lane had snatched from his gripe an innocent man, from whose condemnation as a rebel Mr. Kirk had expected to reap peculiar advantages.

Mr. Gordon preferred his own and his young friend's request that Harry might be permitted to remain during the interview about to commence. The general and Mr. Kirk exchanged very expressive glances ; and while to Henry's increased amazement, the former said, "Certainly ; though we could not suppose the young gentleman would be so anxious about it." The latter, almost to his consternation, smiled.

"In fact, sir," resumed Sir A. D——, "our principal business here is—making as little noise as possible—to desire you to consider yourself a prisoner."

"On what account?" asked Henry.

"Why, sir, we hope you may be able to tell us something of the insurrection of this morning. You were observed on the road to Killane, hiding behind a fence, when, as is presumed, you found yourself likely to be overtaken by the retreating Hessians."

Henry Lane now asked another, and a very impolitic question —one that seemed almost to imply guilt—instead of at once communicating the information it was his duty to submit. But his curiosity to ascertain who had observed him, when he felt convinced the Hessians had not, threw him off his guard.

"Observed! by whom?" he demanded.

"I regret to say, by me, Mr. Lane," continued Captain Kirk ; "I happened to be in the fields, at your back."

"Then you dogged me like the spy and informer you are, sir," said the accused, giving way to youthful passion. He was severely checked by the general, and advised to speak more to the point. Much grieved and alarmed, his old host whispered him to be cool and collected. This, as is sometimes the case with persons in his situation, only made him less tractable. He vociferated ; he gesticulated ; he unbuttoned his coat violently; and there was an exclamation from the general and his prime minister, as both pointed to a large blood stain on his waistcoat. Henry had received it while assisting the unfortunate young woman to the farm-house ; had buttoned his coat over it, as he returned to the town ; had almost forgotten it since ; and had now unconsciously disclosed it. Feeling aware how much it must tell against him, he became silent and confused ; and, to the scrutinizing eyes which observed him, appeared really guilty.

"Pray, Mr. Lane," continued Sir A. D——, "inform us, at least, if you please, why you concealed yourself from the Hessians, and in what manner your waistcoat became soiled."

Courageously rallying, Henry said frankly what he had to say.

13

The general and Mr. Kirk again glanced at each other ; and the former, shaking his head, expressed his regret that, in the very improbable story submitted—and so tardily submitted—he saw little that ought to keep the matter from the ordinary test of a court-martial.

"Very well, sir," said Henry, "only send for the poor girl, and if she is able to attend "—and his blood grew chill at the thought that she might be dead, without having uttered a word !—"I can laugh with scorn at the result."

The general believed that, whether she could attend or not, Mr. Lane would hardly be benefited. It was already in evidence from the two Hessians, that they had wounded one, and only one, of the motley rabble ; that one a woman, and necessarily the witness appealed to ; and any convenient story she might tell was scarcely worth the trouble of sending for ; particularly, as a dispatch to Killane must put the rebels on their guard against the intended attack. "And," continued Sir. A. D——, "as we only await the closing of the present case to march for their position."

Well aware of the prompt manner in which the general had hitherto deemed himself compelled to "close" such "cases" as "the present," Henry again began to exclaim against his mode of proceeding. "What ! is an innocent man to be destroyed by the very villains he seeks to bring to justice ?"

Mr. Gordon, quite terrified, raised his voice in entreaties for time and cool investigation. A whisper from the captain-sheriff disposed of his appeal; and that gentleman then stepped out, and returned with two dragoons, who placed themselves at either side of the prisoner.

"In the name of common sense !" still conjured Henry, "how can I be supposed capable of the absurdity laid to my charge ? My father's loyalty as well known as are his rank and high character ; my friends here—the first in your town—free from all taint ; how can suspicion fall on me ? *I* a rebel ! *I* join with rebels in the fields !"

"Mr. Lane may recollect that his late zeal on behalf of a known and marked rebel might not have left *motives* quite unsuspected,' said Mr. Kirk.

"Silence, paltry fellow !" cried the accused. "Sir A. D——, I have but one remaining appeal to make from your court-martial —from even your order for a court-martial—from even yourself personally It is to the distinguished man who has been publicly

appointed to succeed you in your command over us all. Understand, therefore, distinctly, that I protest, in his name, against
your authority, and demand to be left, a prisoner if necessary, for
his disposal."

"You will understand, in return, sir, that although the gallant
individual to whom you allude has, indeed, been nominated to relieve me of my painful responsibilities, I retain, even with his assent, the full powers they confer, until he personally requires a
transfer of them at my hands," answered Sir A. D——.

"But accountable to him, surely, for the use of what can
be but delegated power, since his appointment," urged Mr.
Gordon.

"You mistake, sir," said the general.

"He is expected this very day," resumed Henry.

"He *was*; but he is not, Mr. Lane. Two men of our garrison—of whom you know something—brought me a dispatch
from him a few hours ago, stating that, from a great anxiety to
cultivate anew an old friendship, he will stop and sleep at Lord
N——'s, on the road to us. And so I have answered all your
demands at length, and, out of respect to your host, perhaps
without considering the situation in which I am placed. Now,
please to attend us to the courthouse."

"Come, then!" cried the prisoner. "How could I have
hoped better from a man, whose cruelty, and not whose honorable services, procured him his ˉpresent butchering commission;
and who dare not stand an appeal to the dignified commander, at
length selected to rescue us from his despotism of blood?"

"My old friend's son!" exclaimed Mr. Gordon, extending his
arms, as Henry was led out after the general and Mr. Kirk. A
shriek reached them; and ere he could embrace the father, the
daughter was clinging to his neck.

"Fear nothing, Bessie; I am innocent."

"I know you are," answered the poor girl; "but is that a
reason why I should fear nothing? Is that a reason why I
should forget the sights we have unwillingly seen. Oh! Harry,
remember the horrible day, when, in less than an hour after he
was dragged from our table, we beheld poor young S—— led to
their rooted gibbet, opposite their courthouse! But *you* must
be saved! how—how—what is to be done?"

"I will go to General K——," stammered Mr. Gordon, who,
since Bessie's appearance, had stood with his back against the
wall. Even while he spoke, he fell. His daughter, screaming

again, flung herself down by his side. The dragoons gained the hall with their prisoner ; she flew to him ; they forced her back A second time she was at her father's side, now as insensible as he ; and Henry, accompanied by her brother, proceeded to the courthouse.

Lord N——'s mansion, at which General K—— was spending the day, was about twelve miles distant from the town. An hour and a half after the occurrences related, he stood with his old friends before the steps of their hall-door, his hands behind his back, his gray head bent towards his breast. The urbanity of a gentleman, and the light of a good heart, cast a dignity over his massive hard-marked features. A lady, followed by a servant, galloped up the avenue, seated on a spirited little steed, as was evident from the animal's fiery though graceful motions. She wore a riding-habit, but her head was bare—her hat had fallen from her unheeded on the road ; and when she swept nearer, her golden hair appeared flowing down her shoulders and around her face, young and fair as the morning ; but like morning when its hues are washed out by tears. She must have caught a view of the persons she wished to see, at some distance, for she waved her light whip before they could hear her voice. When the words she had long been uttering grew at last distinct, she pronounced the general's name. He stepped forward.

"For life and death, General K——! for life and death!" she continued ; "and not a moment—and not a word to spare. Order your horses, sir! you are deputed to act for Heaven, this day—you alone! Come, sir, come!"

Amazed, admiring, sympathizing, and much excited, he prayed an explanation.

"Not if you mean *to act!* not if you *will* discharge your duty! not if you shrink from murder done in your name! Your horses, sir!" the girl cried wildly.

Overpowered by her contagious vehemence, he gave the order required.

"The carriage!" said Lady N——, whose pale cheeks and streaming eyes bespoke the excitement in which she also observed and listened. The carriage was in waiting, to take the party through the grounds.

"Thanks," said the general ; "and it is better, if this young lady must."

"Must and will go back with you!" interrupted Bessie Gordon, jumping from her saddle. Though almost stumbling, she was at the carriage-door before he could offer his arm. The next moment they were whirled off, attended by the aids-de-camp, who had been ready mounted to accompany him on a very different excursion.

In broken sentences, Bessie now gave an explanation of her hasty summons. Henry's confidential communication to her, before breakfast, enabled her to detail the whole of his case. Her companion listened most attentively. He inquired her lover's name. Bessie at last burst into tears as she gave it.

"Why, I know him," said General K——; "at least, I know his father; and may have seen him, when a child, at his father's table. He must be saved, even if he were guilty; but we shall see."

"The time, sir! the time!" sobbed Bessie; "and we go so slow!" The horses were proceeding at full gallop.

The general spoke out of the window to an aid-de-camp, desiring him to push forward at the utmost speed of his charger, and announce his approach to the court-martial. The young man, stimulated by his interest for the beautiful and wretched Bessie Gordon, as well as by zeal in the service of his beloved commander, soon seemed to substantiate Bessie's charge against the very best gallop the carriage-horses could assume. They lost sight of him in a few minutes.

"Is it over?" was her question, addressed to the first stranger she saw, as, an hour afterwards, the carriage rattled into the town; and twenty times she repeated it, although, either that it was not understood or heard, or that the people feared to answer her, no one replied. Approaching the courthouse, she leaned out of the window to look at the hideous gibbet; its rope wavered in the breeze—no more.

"Look! sir," she said, catching the general's arm, as she sank into her seat; "what do you think—are we too late?"

The carriage stopped; the door was instantly opened, and an officer of the garrison appeared at it, saluting the general.

"My aid-de-camp, sir?" asked the new commander, getting down.

"I have the honor to await you here with a verbal dispatch from him," replied the officer.

"Where is he, sir?" asked Bessie, jumping to her old protector's side who repeated her question.

"He is gone forward to Killane, sir, fresh mounted."

"Then the court-martial has decided," continued Bessie.

"It has, madam."

"And Mr. Lane?"

"Has been marched out with the troops, to undergo his sentence, upon the spot where"—

The officer ceased speaking, as Bessie dropped at his feet He and the general raised her, and she was placed in her brother's arms, who came running down the street.

"Fresh horses for us also, sir," said General K——, addressing the officer, as he pointed to his remaining aids-de-camp. While his commands were being obeyed, he walked up and down an open space before the courthouse, his hands joined at his back, and his head bent, as was customary with him. Other officers of the residue of the garrison left in town, and several of the persons who, before the proclamation of martial law, had wielded civil authority, approached to pay their respects. Suddenly he stopped, and glancing up at the gallows, said to the group generally: "Take that down; its day is over." Then he resumed his short walk, and again stopping, and scowling at the triangle which appeared in a corner of the space, added: "And down with that, too; *its* day had passed even before it was put up."

His horses were led out, and he and his aids-de-camp proceeded towards Killane, by the narrow hill-road upon which Henry Lane had seen the Hessians in the morning, the officer of the garrison riding in advance to show them the way. Approaching the hamlet, they met the second officer, who had gone forward before them, standing over the sorry steed with which he had been supplied at the town; the animal had fallen under him. After a few words they passed him.

"Shall we come up with them?" asked General K—— of the officer.

"I should hope so, sir, unless they have marched at almost double-quick time. Yet see there, sir! and hear that!" A wreath of smoke burst up into the sunshine beyond a quick turn in the road, and a cheer simultaneously reached the party. "That must be the first firing of the enemy's cabins; the exe-ution of Mr. Lane's sentence must have preceded it."

General K—— spurred forward, passing his guide, so as to be the first at the turn of the road; here he said: "You are wrong, the troops are still in motion towards their point"

It was so. Sir A. D——, with his force, had not yet gained the thatched hamlet of Killane, and the smoke that had been observed, arose only from a solitary cabin on the road-side, which, having been found deserted by the terrified inmates, was fired by Mr. Kirk's zealous yeomen. Now, within hearing of the rear-guard of the column, General K—— cried: "Halt! halt!" and desired his aid-de-camp to advance, who, obeying his command, repeated the magical word, "Halt!" and added, in still louder tone, his commander's name. A halt quickly ensued, and the general galloped forward. Gaining the head of the line, he saw a young man sitting on a horse led by a dragoon, his arms pinioned. Their eyes met; the general touched his old-fashioned cocked hat, and smiled. Henry Lane, who, till that moment, had worn a firm brow and a flushed cheek, turned sickly pale, and would have fallen from his saddle but for the assistance of his guards.

The veteran joined Sir A. D—— and his staff, still more in front. The two generals exchanged bows, and stood uncovered, as also did their attendant, while the whole line presented arms, and the trumpets and kettle-drums of the horse and the bands of the infantry played a salute. Now the little hamlet appeared in view, and from it came a wild and alarmed cry, in answer to the startling though cheery burst of martial music. Presently, groups of men, women, and children of every age, were seen run-ning before the cabins in great terror and disorder.

"The enemy, I suppose," said General K——, smiling "not in arms, though, and, therefore, scarce worth our attention. Let us send out to reconnoitre, however, in hopes that they deem us entitled to a better reception. Meantime, Sir A. D——, I go towards the cabins."

Attended only by an aid-de-camp, he arrived at the farm-house to which the wounded milkmaid had been carried. The surgeon, still in attendance, pronounced her out of danger, and at last able to speak. General K—— heard, at her bedside, th communications she had already made to her mistress and to th surgeon. Of the latter, he inquired whether she could safely be removed to the town, travelling in an open litter, only as fast as the troops should march. The surgeon said she could; then, giving the necessary orders, he left the farm-house.

In a contiguous field he summoned back the reconnoitring parties, and learned from their report that no enemy of any kind appeared in view. After this he rode to the nearest group of peasants, who, with much entreaty, awaited his approach; told the terrified people to go home and keep quiet. Lastly, he returned to the troops on the road, and ordered them to march back the way they had come.

At the entrance to the town he whispered to his aid-de-camp, who trotted briskly forward. Arrived at the public parade, he halted the soldiers and dismissed them to their barracks. He then desired Sir A. D——, the officers who generally formed his court-martial, and the prisoner, Henry Lane, to attend to him to the courthouse. As they proceeded up the steps of the building, Mr. Kirk, and many of his friends, exchanged eloquent glances at the disappearance of the gallows and the triangle.

The aid-de-camp, who had gone forward, met his general in the court, and pointed out the two wounded Hessians, one in the dock the other at a side bar.

" Have you kept them separate, sir ?" he asked.

" Strictly so, sir," answered the aid-de-camp.

" Gentlemen," he resumed, " we require some additional information touching the rebel movement of this morning ; and without yet sitting as a court-martial, I wish to examine, in succession, these wounded men. Let one of them be led quite out of hearing ; let the other come on the table."

He was quickly obeyed. The Hessian selected as a first witness again affirmed that he and his comrade had been surprised by a band of rebels at Killane that morning ; and after wounding one only of the assailants—a woman—barely escaped with their lives. General K—— put questions, requiring minute accounts of the details of the affair, and received certain answers which he desired should be carefully written down. He then seemed casually to inquire what conversation had passed between the witness and his comrade upon the route home after their escape. The man hesitated. He raised his voice, knit his brow, and desired instantly a report of their whole conversation along the hill-road, whatever it was. The Hessian now gave answers, which were also committed to writing.

" Let him withdraw, and bring up the other—still keeping them apart," resumed General K——.

The second Hessian appeared in the evidence chair. His general statement of the attack corroborated that of the first ; but his account of the specific details, already described by his comrade, was a new story altogether. And when asked to recollect and repeat their discourse on the road homewards, he made it consist of topics, which did not remotely resemble, even in matter, those sworn to by his friend.

"Let them come face to face," was the general's next command. Accordingly, they confronted each other ; heard read the extraordinary clashings of their separate testimony, and were called on to reconcile them if they could. The men were silent.

"Has the prisoner, Mr. Lane, any questions to propose to the witnesses ?" asked General K——.

Henry said he would prefer to have them ask questions of one another, at his dictation. This was agreed to ; and he proceeded fluently in their own tongue :

"The man whose sword-arm is disabled shall say to his comrade, ' Hans, bad work you have done for me, and I for you, all about a silly girl.' "

The Hessians started at these words ; exchanged glances ; looked consciously around ; and then bent their eyes on the table.

"If he does not speak, shall I give him the answer Hans gave *him ?*" continued Henry.

"Do so, prisoner."

"Listen then, Hans. ' Ay, Quinton ; but blame your own greediness of the girl's smiles, by the side of an old friend.' "

Again the Hessians showed agitation.

"I continue, sir, speaking for Hans and Quinton, alternately."

Still the general assented.

" ' Well, Hans, here we ride back to headquarters, without a smile of hers to boast of between us.'

" ' Ay, and in a plight we must account for, too, Quinton.'

" ' Oh ! the rebels have surprised us !'

" ' Der deyvil ! good ! But the girl may prate, unless her mouth is stopped.'

" ' And I think I've stopped it, Hans. Or, no matter. She was one of the ambuscade—half-wild Irishmen, half-wild Irishwomen. So, let her tell her story : who will believe it ?'

"Such is the conversation," resumed Henry Lane, speaking for himself, "which I overheard between these two men, upon the hill-road from Killane, early this morning."

In answer to questions from General K——, he ended by describing his proceedings, after the Hessions passed him, down to the moment at which he had left the farm-house.

"Place them at the bar," said the general ; "and now we form our court-martial."

The Hessians were formally arraigned, and the contradictions of their own testimony, coupled with Henry Lane's story, were taken as evidence against them.

13*

"I have yet another witness," resumed General K——, glancing at his aid-de-camp.

The young officer withdrew, and speedily returned, ushering to the table a litter, borne by soldiers, on which lay the wounded milkmaid. Her cruel assaulters stared in stupid terror upon her reclining form. The surgeon stood beside her, as in feeble and hoarse accents, she deposed to the following facts:

"While employed in milking her cows, two troopers, 'with beard on their lips,' stopped at the side of the pasture-field, looking towards her. It was 'just the gray of the morning.' Presently they dismounted, and separately crossed the stile; one walking fast before the other, and both speaking loudly and angrily in 'a fur'n speech.' She screamed, attempted to run, and fell from terror. Nearly at the same moment they broke into open quarrel, drew their swords, and cut at each other. She fainted. On regaining her senses, she saw them standing, exhausted and bleeding. In a frenzy, she called out the names of her friends, and spoke as if many people were speeding to help her; the troopers looked around; again exchanged words, in a more friendly tone; came close to her, and desired her to cease screaming; finally, beat her about the head and stabbed her in the neck. Further she could tell nothing."

"The prisoner Lane has had an opportunity to arrange this improbable story with the cunning girl," said Mr. Kirk.

"Impossible," answered the surgeon. "When I reached the poor creature, she was unable to utter a word; and she must have been still more unable to do so before my arrival."

"She does not identify the men," resumed the sheriff.

"The men confess their guilt," said the aid-de-camp, who stood near them.

"Let them die before the sun sets, notwithstanding," said General K——, "and release Mr. Lane."

"Come home, Hal," cried young Gordon, grasping Henry Lane's hand.

"How is Bessie?" asked the liberated prisoner, on their way through the streets.

"In good hopes, since your return with old K——; and her father still able to congratulate you upon your escape from THE LAST OF THE STORM."

THE END OF THE LAST OF THE STORM.

THE RIVAL DREAMERS.

THE RIVAL DREAMERS.

Mr. Washington Irving has already given to the public a version of an American legend, which, in a principal feature, bears some likeness to the following transcript of a popular Irish one. It may, however, be interesting to show this very coincidence between the descendants of a Dutch transatlantic colony and the native peasantry of Ireland, in the superstitious annals of both. Our tale, moreover, will be found original in all its circumstances, that alluded to only excepted.

Shamus Dempsey returned a silent, plodding, sorrowful man, though a young one, to his poor home, after seeing laid in the grave his aged decrepit father. The last rays of the setting sun were glorious, shooting through the folds of their pavilion of scarlet clouds ; the last song of the thrush, chanted from the bough nearest to his nest, was gladdening ; the abundant though but half-matured crops around breathed of hope for the future. But Shamus's bosom was covered with the darkness that inward sunshine alone can illumine. The chord that should respond to song and melody had snapped in it ; for him the softly undulating fields of light-green wheat, or the silken surfaced patches of barley, made a promise in vain. He was poor, penniless, friendless, and yet groaning under responsibilities ; worn out by past and present suffering, and without a consoling prospect. His father's corpse had been just buried by a subscription among his neighbors, collected in an old glove, a penny or a half-penny from each, by the most active of the humble community to whom his sad state was a subject of pity. In the wretched shed which he called "home," a young wife lay on a truss of straw, listening to the hungry cries of two little children, and awaiting her hour to become the weeping mother of a third. And the recollection that but for an act of domestic treachery experienced by his father and himself, both would have been comfortable and respectable in the world, aggravated the bitterness of the feeling in which Shamus contemplated this lot. He could himself faintly call to mind a time of early childhood, when he lived with his parents in a roomy house, eating and sleeping and dressing well, and surrounded by servants and workmen; he further remembered that a day of great affliction came, upon which strange and rude persons forced their way into the house; and, for some cause his infant observation did not reach, father, servants, and workmen (his mother had just died), were all turned out upon the road, and doomed to seek the shelter of a mean roof. But his father's discourse, since he gained the years of manhood, supplied Shamus with an explanation of all these circumstances, as follows :

Old Dempsey had been the youngest son of a large farmer, who divided his lands between two elder children, and destined Shamus's father to the Church, sending him abroad for education, and, during its course, supplying him with liberal allowances. Upon the eve of ordination, the young student returned home to visit his friends ; was much noticed by neighboring small gentry of each religion ; at the house of one of the opposite persuasion from his, met a sister of the proprietor, who had a fortune in her own right ; abandoned his clerical views for her smiles ; eloped with her ; married her privately ; incurred thereby the irremovable hostility of his own family ; but, after a short time, was received, along with his wife, by his generous brother-in-law, under whose guidance both became reputably settled in the house to which Shamus's early recollections pointed, and where, till he was about six years old, he passed indeed a happy childhood.

But, a little previous to this time, his mother's good brother died unmarried, and was succeeded by another of her brothers, who had unsuccessfully spent half his life as a lawyer in Dublin, and who, inheriting little of his predecessor's amiable character, soon showed himself a foe to her and her husband, professedly on account of her marriage with a Roman Catholic. He did not appear to their visit, shortly after his arrival in their neighborhood, and he never condescended to return it. The affliction experienced by his sensitive sister, from his conduct, entailed upon her a premature accouchement, in which, giving birth to a lifeless babe, she unexpectedly died. The event was matter of triumph rather than of sorrow to her unnatural brother. For, in the first place, totally unguarded against the sudden result, she had died intestate ; in the next place, he discovered that her private marriage had been celebrated by a Roman Catholic priest, consequently could not, according to law, hold good ; and again, could not give to her nominal husband any right to her property, upon which both had hitherto lived, and which was now the sole means of existence to Shamus's father.

The lawyer speedily set to work upon these points, and with little difficulty succeeded in supplying for Shamus's recollections a day of trouble, already noticed. In fact, his father and he, now without a shilling, took refuge in a distant cabin, where, by the sweat of his parent's brow, as a laborer in the fields, the ill-fated hero of this story was scantily fed and clothed, until maturer years enabled him to relieve the old man's hand of the spade and sickle, and in turn labor for their common wants.

Shamus, becoming a little prosperous in the world, rented a few acres adjacent to his cabin and—married. The increase of his fields did not quite keep pace with the increase of his cares, in the persons of new comers, for whose well being he was bound to provide. His ray of success in life soon became overclouded, by the calls of the landlord and the tithe-proctor. In truth, three years after his marriage, he received a notice which it were vain to oppose, to quit both his farm and his cabin, and leave his few articles of furniture behind.

At this juncture his father was bedridden, and his wife advanced in her third pregnancy. He put on his hat, walked to the door, fixed his eyes upon the ruins of an old abbey which stood on the slope of an opposite hill, and formed his plan for present measures. By the next evening he had constructed a wattled shed, covered with rushes and leaves, against a gable in the interior of the ruin. Clearing away the nettles and other rank weeds inclosed by his new house, he discovered a long slab on which was carved a cross and letters illegible to his eye ; this he made his hearth stone. To furnish the abode, he fetched two large stones, as seats for his wife and himself, shook straw in either corner, and laid in a bundle of twigs. Then he went to the cabin that was no longer his, sent on his wife and two children to the abbey, followed with his father on his back, and laid him upon one of the straw couches. Two days afterwards the old man was a corpse. From his pauper funeral we now see Shamus returning, and to such a home does he bend his heavy steps.

If to know that the enemy of his father and mother did not

thrive on the spoils of his oppression could have yielded Shamus
any consolation in his lot, he had long ago become aware of circumstances calculated to give this negative comfort. His
maternal uncle enjoyed, indeed, his newly acquired property only
a few years after it came into his possession. Partly on account
of his cruelty to his relations, partly from a meanness and vul-
garity of character, which soon displayed itself in his novel
situation, and which, it was believed, had previously kept him in
the lowest walks of his profession as a Dublin attorney, he found
himself neglected and shunned by the gentry of his neighborhood.
To grow richer than any one who thus insulted him, to blazon
abroad reports of his wealth, and to watch opportunities of
using it to their injury, became the means of revenge adopted by
the *parvenu*. His legitimate income not promising a rapid ac-
complishment of this plan, he ventured, using precautions that
seemingly set suspicion at defiance, to engage in smuggling adventures on a large scale, for which his proximity to the coast afforded a local opportunity. Notwithstanding all his pettifog-
ging cleverness, the ex-attorney was detected, however, in his
illegal traffic, and fined to an amount which swept away half his
real property. Driven to desperation by the publicity of his failure, as well as by the failure itself, he tried another grand effort
to retrieve his fortune ; was again surprised by the revenue officers ; in a personal struggle with them, at the head of his
band, killed one of their body ; immediately absconded from
Ireland ; for the last twenty years had not been authentically
heard of ; but, it was believed, lived under an assumed name in
London, deriving an obscure existence from some mean pursuit,
of which the very nature enabled him to gratify propensities to
drunkenness and other vices, learned during his first career in life.

All this Shamus knew, though only from report, inasmuch as
his uncle had exiled himself while he was yet a child, and without previously having become known to the eyes of the nephew
he had so much injured. But if Shamus occasionally drew a
bitter and almost savage gratification from the downfall of his
inhuman persecutor, no recurrence to the past could alleviate
the misery of his present situation. He passed under one of the
capacious open arches of the old abbey, and then entered his
squalid shed reared against its wall, his heart as shattered and
as trodden down as the ruins around him. No words of greeting ensued between him and his equally hopeless wife, as she sat
on the straw of her bed, rocking to sleep, with feeble and mourn-

ful cries, her youngest infant. He silently lighted a fire of withered twigs on his ready-furnished hearth-stone ; put to roast among their embers a few potatoes which he had begged during the day ; divided them between her and her crying children ; and as the moon, rising high in the heavens, warned him that night asserted her full empire over the departed day, Shamus sunk down upon the couch from which his father's mortal remains had lately been borne, supperless himself, and dinnerless, too, but not hungry ; at least not conscious or recollecting that he was.

His wife and little ones soon slept soundly, but Shamus lay for hours inaccessible to nature's claims for sleep as well as for food. From where he lay he could see, through the open front of his shed, out into the ruins abroad. After much abstraction in his own thoughts, the silence, the extent, and the peculiar desolation of the scene, almost spiritualized by the magic effect of alternate moonshine and darkness, of objects and of their parts, at last diverted his mind, though not to relieve it He remembered distinctly, for the first time, where he was—an intruder among the dwellings of the dead ; he called to mind, too, that the present was their hour for revealing themselves among the remote loneliness and obscurity of their crumbling and intricate abode. As his eye fixed upon a distant stream of cold light or of blank shadow, either the wavering of some feathery herbage from the walls, or the flitting of some night bird over the roofless aisle, made motion which went and came during the instant of his alarmed start, or else some disembodied sleeper around had challenged and evaded his vision, so rapidly as to baffle even the accompaniment of thought. Shamus would, however, recur, during these entrancing aberrations, to his more real causes for terror ; and he knew not, and to this day cannot distinctly tell whether he waked or slept, when a new circumstance absorbed his attention. The moon struck fully, under his propped roof, upon the carved slab he had appropriated as a hearthstone, and turning his eye to the spot, he saw the semblance of a man advanced in years, though not very old, standing motionless, and very steadfastly regarding him ; the still face of the figure shone like marble in the nightbeam, without giving any idea of the solidity of that material ; the long and deep shadows thrown by the forehead over the eyes, left those unusually expressive features vague and uncertain. Upon the head was a close-fitting black cap, the dress was a loose-sleeved, plaited garment of

white, descending to the ground, and faced and otherwise check-
ered with black, and girded round the loins ; exactly the costume which Shamus had often studied in a little framed and
glazed print, hung up in the sacristy of the humble chapel
recently built in the neighborhood of the ruin, by a few descendants of the great religious fraternity to whom, in its day of
pride, the abbey had belonged. As he returned very inquisi-
tively, though, as he avers, not now in alarm, the fixed gaze of his
midnight·visitor, a voice reached him, and he heard these strange
words :

"Shamus Dempsey, go to London Bridge, and you will be a
rich man." ·

"How will that come about, your reverence ?" cried Shamus,
jumping up from the straw.

But the figure was gone ; and he stumbling among the black
embers on the remarkable place where it had stood, he fell prostrate, experiencing a change of sensation and of observance of
objects around, which might be explained by supposing a transi-
tion from a sleeping to a waking state of mind.

The rest of the night he slept little, thinking of the advice he
had received, and of the mysterious personage who gave it. But
he resolved to say nothing about his vision, particularly to his
wife, lest, in her present state of health, the frightful story might
distress her ; and, as to his own conduct respecting it, he determined to be guided by the future—in fact, he would wait to see
if his counsellor came again. He did come again, appearing in
the same spot at the same hour of the night, and wearing the
same dress, though not the same expression of feature ; for the
shadowy brows now slightly frowned, and a little severity mingled
with the former steadfastness of look.

"Shamus Dempsy, why have you not gone to London Bridge,
and your wife so near the time when she will want what you are
to get by going there ?   Remember this is my second warning."

"Musha, your reverence, an' what am I to do on Lunnon
Bridge ?"

Again he rose to approach the figure ; again it eluded him.
Again a change occurred in the quality of the interest with
which he regarded the admonition of his visitor.   Again he
passed a day of doubt as to the propriety of undertaking what
seemed to him little less than a journey to the world's end,
without a penny in his pocket, and upon the eve of his wife's
accouchement, merely in obedience to a recommendation which,

according to his creed, was not yet sufficiently strongly given, even were it under any circumstances to be adopted. For Shamus had often heard, and firmly believed, that a dream or a vision, instructing one how to procure riches, ought to be experienced three times before it became entitled to attention.

He lay down, however, half hoping that his vision might thus recommend itself to his notice. It did so.

"Shamus Dempsy," said the figure, looking more angry than ever, "you have not yet gone to London Bridge, although I hear your wife crying out to bid you go. And, remember, this is my third warning."

"Why, then, tundher-an-ouns, your reverence, just stop and tell me"—

Ere he could utter another word the holy visitant disappeared, in a real passion at Shamus's qualified curse ; and at the same moment, his confused senses recognized the voice of his wife, sending up from her straw pallet the cries that betoken a mother's distant travail. Exchanging a few words with her, he hurried away, professedly to call up, at her cabin window, an old crone who sometimes attended the very poorest women in Nance Dempsy's situation.

"Hurry to her, Noreen, acuishla, and do the best it's the will of God to let you do. And tell her from me, Noreen,"—he stopped, drawing in his lip, and clutching his cudgel hard.

"Shamus, what ails you, avich?" asked old Noreen ; "what ails you, to make the tears run down in the gray o' the morning ?"

"Tell her from me," continued Shamus, "that it's from the bottom o' the heart I'll pray, morning and evening, and fresh and fasting, maybe, to give her a good time of it ; and to show her a face on the poor child that's coming, likelier than the two that God sent afore it. And that I'll be thinking o' picturing it to my own mind, though I'll never see it far away."

"Musha, Shamus, what are you speaking of ?"

"No matter, Noreen, only God be wid you, and wid her, and wid the weenocks ; and tell her what I bid you. More-be-token, tell her that poor Shamus quits her in her throuble, with more love from the heart out than he had for her the first day we came together ; and I'll come back to her, at any rate, sooner or later, richer or poorer, or as bare as I went ; and maybe not so bare either. But God only knows. The top o' the morning to you, Noreen, and don't let her want the mouthful o' praties while I'm

on my thravels. For this"—added Shamus, as he bounded off to
the consternation of old Noreen—"this is the very morning and
the very minute that, if I mind the dhrame at all at all, I ought
to mind it ; ay, without ever turning back to get a look from
her, that 'nd kill the heart in my body entirely."

Without much previous knowledge of the road he was to
take, Shamus walked and begged his way along the coast to the
town where he might hope to embark for England. Here, the
captain of a merchantman agreed to let him work his passage to
Bristol, whence he again walked and begged into London.

Without taking rest or food, Shamus proceeded to London
Bridge, often put out of his course by wrong directions, and as
often by forgetting and misconceiving true ones. It was with
old London Bridge that Shamus had to do (not the old one
last pulled down, but its more reverend predecessor), which, at
that time, was lined at either side by quaintly fashioned houses,
mostly occupied by shopkeepers, so that the space between presented, perhaps, the greatest thoroughfare then known . the
Queen of Cities. And at about two o'clock in the afternoon,
barefooted, ragged, fevered, and agitated, Shamus mingled with
the turbid human stream, that roared and chafed over the, as
restless and as evanescent, stream which buffeted the arches of
old London Bridge. In a situation so novel to him, so much
more extraordinary in the reality than his anticipation could have
fancied, the poor and friendless stranger felt overwhelmed. A
sense of forlornness, of insignificance, and of terror, seized upon
his faculties. From the stare, or the sneers, or the jostle of the
iron-nerved crowd, he shrank with glances of wild timidity, and
with a heart as wildly timid as were his looks. For some time
he stood or staggered about, unable to collect his thoughts, or
to bring to mind what was his business there. But when Shamus became able to refer to the, motive of his pauper journey,
from his native solitudes into the thick of such a scene, it was no
wonder that the zeal of superstition totally subsided amid the
astounding truths he witnessed. In fact, the bewildered simpleton now regarded his dream as the merest chimera. Hastily escaping from the thoroughfare, he sought out some wretched place
of repose suited to his wretched condition, and there moaned
himself asleep, in self-accusations at the thought of poor Nance
at home, and in utter despair of all his future prospects.

At daybreak the next morning he awoke, a little less agitated,
but still with no hope. He was able, however, to resolve upon

the best course of conduct now left open to him ; and he arranged immediately to retrace his steps to Ireland, as soon as
he should have begged sufficient alms to speed him a mile on the
road. With this intent he hastily issued forth, preferring to
challenge the notice of chance passengers, even at the early hour
of dawn, than to venture again in the middle of the day, among
the dreaded crowds of the vast city. Very few, indeed, were
the passers-by whom Shamus met during his straggling and
stealthy walk through the streets, and those of a description
little able or willing to afford a half-penny to his humbled, whining suit, and to his spasmed lip and watery eye. In what direction he went Shamus did not know ; but at last he found himself entering upon the scene of his yesterday's terror. Now,
however, it presented nothing to renew its former impression.
The shops at the sides of the bridge were closed, and the occasional stragglers of either sex who came along inspired Shamus,
little as he knew of a great city, with aversion rather than with
dread. In the quietness and security of his present position,
Shamus was both courageous and weak enough again to summon up his dream.

"Come," he said, "since I *am* on Lunnon Bridge, I'll walk
over every stone of it, and see what good that will do."

He valiantly gained the far end. Here one house, of all that
stood upon the bridge, began to be opened ; it was a public house,
and, by a sidelong glance as he passed, Shamus thought that, in
the person of a red-cheeked, red-nosed, sunk-eyed, elderly man,
who took down the window-shutters, he recognized the proprietor.
This person looked at Shamus, in return, with peculiar scrutiny.
The wanderer liked neither his regards nor the expression of his
countenance, and quickened his steps onward until he cleared the
bridge.

"But I'll walk it over at the other side, now," he bethought,
after allowing the publican time to finish opening his house, and
retire out of view.

But, repassing the house, the man still appeared, leaning
against his door-jamb, and as if waiting for Shamus's return,
whom, upon this second occasion, he eyed more attentively than
before.

"Sorrow's in him," thought Shamus, "have I two heads on
me, that I'm such a sight to him? But who cares about his pair
of ferret-eyes? I'll thrudge down the middle stone of it, at any
rate?"

Accordingly he again walked towards the public house, keeping the middle of the bridge.

"Good-morrow, friend," said the publican, as Shamus a third time passed his door.

"Sarvant kindly, sir," answered Shamus, respectfully pulling down the brim of his hat, and increasing his pace.

"An early hour you choose for a morning walk," continued his new acquaintance.

"Brave and early, faix, sir," said Shamus, still hurrying off.

"Stop a bit," resumed the publican. Shamus stood still. "I see you're a countryman of mine—an Irishman ; I'd know one of you at a look, though I'm a long time out of the country. And you're not very well off on London Bridge this morning, either."

"No, indeed, sir," replied Shamus, beginning to doubt his skill in physiognomy, at the stranger's kind address ; "but as badly off as a body 'ud wish to be."

"Come over to look for the work ?"

"Nien, sir ; but come out this morning to beg a ha'penny, to send me a bit of the road home."

"Well, here's a silver sixpence without asking. And you'd better sit on the bench by the door here, and eat a crust and a cut of cheese, and drink a drop of good ale, to break your fast."

With profuse thanks, Shamus accepted this kind invitation ; blaming himself at heart for having allowed his opinion of the charitable publican to be guided by the expression of the man's features. "Handsome is that handsome does," was Shamus's self-correcting reflection.

While eating his bread and cheese, and drinking his strong ale, they conversed freely together, and Shamus's heart opened more and more to his benefactor. The publican repeatedly asked him what had brought him to London ; and though half out of prudence, and half out of shame, the dreamer at first evaded the question, he felt it at last impossible to refuse a candid answer to his generous friend.

"Why, then, sir, only I am such a big fool for telling it to you, it's what brought me to Lunnon Bridge was a quare dhrame I had at home in Ireland, that tould me just to come here, and I'd find a pot of goold ;" for such was the interpretation given by Shamus to the vague admonition of his visionary counsellor.

His companion burst into a loud laugh, saying after it—

"Pho, pho, man, don't be so silly as to put faith in nonsensical dreams of that kind. Many a one like it I have had, if I would bother my head with them. Why, within the last ten days, while you were dreaming of finding a pot of gold on London Bridge, I was dreaming of finding a pot of gold in Ireland."

"Ullaloo, and were you, sir?" asked Shamus, laying down his empty pint.

"Ay, indeed; night after night, an old friar with a pale face, and dressed all in white and black, and a black scullcap on his head, came to me in a dream, and bid me go to Ireland, to a certain spot in a certain county that I know very well, and under the slab of his tomb, that has a cross and some old Romish letters on it, in an old abbey I often saw before now, I'd find a treasure that would make me a rich man all the days of my life."

"Musha, sir," asked Shamus, scarce able prudently to control his agitation, "and did he tell you that the treasure lay buried there ever so long under the open sky and the ould walls?"

"No; but he told me I was to find the slab covered in by a shed, that a poor man had lately built inside the abbey for himself and his family."

"Whoo, by the powers!" shouted Shamus, at last thrown off his guard by the surpassing joy derived from this intelligence, as well as by the effects of the ale; and, at the same time, he jumped up, cutting a caper with his legs, and flourishing his shillelagh.

"Why, what's the matter with you?" asked his friend, glancing at him a frowning and misgiving look.

"We ax pardon, sir." Shamus rallied his prudence. "An' sure sorrow a thing is the matter wid me, only the dhrop, I believe, made me do it, as it ever and always does, good luck to it for the same. An' isn't what we were spaking about the biggest *raumaush** undher the sun, sir? Only it's the laste bit in the world quare to me, how you'd have the dhrame about your own country, that you didn't see for so many years, sir,—for twenty long years, I think you said, sir? Shamus had now a new object in putting his sly question."

"If I said so, I forgot," answered the publican his suspicions of Shamus at an end. "But it is about twenty years, indeed, since I left Ireland."

"And by your speech, sir, and your dacency, I'll engage you were in a good way in the poor place, afore you left it?"

"You guess correctly, friend." (The publican gave way to vanity.) "Before misfortunes came over me, I possessed, along

* Nonsense.

with a good hundred acres besides, the very ground that the old ruin I saw in the foolish dream I told you stands upon."

"An' so did my curse-o'-God's nucle," thought Shamus, his heart's blood beginning to boil, though, with a great effort, he kept himself seemingly cool. "And this is the man fornent me, if he answers another word I'll ax him. Faix, sir, and sure that makes your dhrame quarer than ever ; and the ground the ould abbey is on, sir, and the good acres round it, did you say they lay some where in the poor county myself came from ?"

"What county is that, friend ?" demanded the publican again with a studious frown.

"The ould County Monaghan, sure, sir," replied Shamus, very deliberately.

"No, but the county of Clare," answered his companion.

"Was it ?" screamed Shamus, again springing up. The cherished hatred of twenty years imprudently bursting out, his uncle lay stretched at his feet, after a renewed flourish of his cudgel. "And do you know who you are telling it to this morning ? Did you ever hear that the sisther you kilt, left a bit of a *gorsoon* behind her, that one day or other might overhear you ? Ay," he continued, keeping down the struggling man, "*it is* poor Shamus Dempsey that's kneeling by you ; ay, and that has more to tell you. The shed built over the old friar's tombstone was built by the hands you feel on your throttle, and that tombstone is his hearth-stone ; and"—continued Shamus, beginning to bind the prostrate man with a rope, snatched from a bench near them —"while you lie here awhile, an' no one to help you, in the cool of the morning, I'll just take a start of you on the road home, to lift the flag and get the threasure ; and follow me if you dare ! You know there's good money bid for your head in Ireland—so here goes. Yes, faith and wid this—*this* to help me on the way !" He snatched up a heavy purse which had fallen from his uncle's pocket in the struggle. "And sure, there's neither hurt nor harm in getting back a little of a body's own from you. A bright good-morning, uncle dear !"

Shamus dragged his manacled relative into the shop, quickly shut to and locked the door, flung the key over the house into the Thames, and the next instant was running at headlong speed.

He was not so deficient in the calculations of common sorse as to think himself yet out of his uncle's power. It appeared, indeed, pretty certain, that neither for the violence done to his person, nor for the purse appropriated by his nephew, the outlawed murderer would raise a hue and cry after one who, aware of his identity, could deliver him up to the laws of his country. But Shamus felt certain that it would be a race between him and his uncle for the treasure that lay under the friar's tombstone. His simple nature supplied no stronger motive for a pursuit on the part of a man whose life now lay in the breath of his mouth. Full of his conviction, however, Shamus saw he had not a moment to lose until the roof of his shed in the old abbey again sheltered him. So, freely making use of his uncle's guineas, he purchased a strong horse in the outskirts of London, and to the surprise, if not under heavy suspicions of the vendor, set off at a gallop upon the road by which he had the day before gained the great metropolis.

A ship was ready to sail at Bristol for Ireland ; but, to Shamus's discomforture, she waited for a wind. He got aboard, however, and in the darksome and squalid hold often knelt down and, with clasped hands and panting breast, petitioned Heaven for a favorable breeze. But from morning until evening the wind remained as he had found it, and Shamus despaired. His uncle, meantime, might have reached some other port, and embarked for their country. In the depth of his anguish he heard a brisk bustle upon deck, clambered up to investigate its cause, and found the ship's sails already half unfurled to a wind that promised to bear him to his native shores by the next morning. The last light of day yet lingered in the heavens : he glanced, now under way, to the quay of Bristol. A group who had been watching the departure of the vessel, turned round to note the approach to them of a man who ran furiously towards the place where they stood, pointing after her, and evidently speaking with vehemence, although no words reached Shamus's ear. Neither was his eye sure of this person's features, but his heart read them distinctly. A boat shot from the quay ; the man stood up in it, and its rowers made a signal.

Shamus stepped to the gangway, as if preparing to hurl his pursuer into the sea. The captain took a speaking-trumpet, and informing the boat that he could not stop an instant, advised her to wait for another merchantman, which would sail in an hour. And during and after his speech his vessel ploughed cheerily on, making as much way as she was adapted to accomplish.

Shamus's bosom felt lightened of its immediate terror, but not freed of apprehension for the future. The ship that was to sail

14

in an hour haunted his thoughts : he did not leave the deck, and, although the night proved very dark, his anxious eyes were never turned from the English coast. Unusual fatigue and want of sleep now and then overpowered him, and his senses swam in a wild and snatching slumber ; but from this he would start, crying out and clinging to the cordage, as the feverish dream of an instant presented him with the swelling canvas of a fast sailing ship, which came suddenly bursting through the gloom of midnight, alongside of his own. Morning dawned, really to unveil to him the object of his fears following almost in the wake of her rival. He glanced in the opposite direction, and beheld the shores of Ireland ; in another hour he jumped upon them ; but his enemy's face watched him from the deck of the companion vessel, now not more than a few ropes' lengths distant.

Shamus mounted a second good horse, and spurred towards home. Often did he look back, but without seeing any cause for increased alarm. As yet, however, the road had been level and winding, and therefore could not allow him to span much of it at a glance. After noon, it ascended a high and lengthened hill, surrounded by wastes of bog. As he gained the summit of this hill, and again looked back, a horseman appeared, sweeping to its foot. Shamus galloped at full speed down the now quickly falling road ; then along its level continuation for about a mile ; and then up another eminence, more lengthened, though not so steep as the former ; and from it still he looked back, and caught the figure of the horseman breaking over the line of the hill he had passed. For hours such was the character of the chase ; until the road narrowed and began to wind amid an uncultivated and uninhabited mountain wilderness. Here Shamus's horse tripped and fell ; the rider, little injured, assisted him to his legs, and, with lash and spur, reurged him to pursue his course. The animal went forward in a last effort, and, for still another span of time, well befriended his rider. A rocky valley, through which both had been galloping, now opened at its further end, presenting to Shamus's eye, in the distance, the sloping ground, and the ruin which, with its mouldering walls, encircled his poor home ; and the setting sun streamed golden rays through the windows and rents of the old abbey.

The fugitive gave a weak cry of joy, and lashed his beast again. The cry seemed to be answered by a shout ; and a second time, after a wild plunge, the horse fell, now throwing Shamus off with a force that left him stunned. And yet he heard the hoofs of another horse come thundering down the rocky way ; and, while he made a faint effort to rise on his hands and look at his pursuer, the horse and horseman were very near, and the voice of his uncle cried, " Stand !" at the same time that the speaker fired a pistol, of which the ball struck a stone at Shamus's foot. The next moment his uncle, having left his saddle, stood over him, presenting a second pistol, and he spoke in a low but distinct voice.

" Spawn of a beggar ! This is not merely for the chance of riches given by our dreams, though it seems, in the teeth of all I ever thought, that the devil tells truth at last. No, nor it is not quite for the blow ; but it is to close the lips that, with a single word, can kill me. You die, to let me live !"

" Help !" aspirated Shamus's heart, turning itself to Heaven ; "help me but now, not for the sake of the goold either, but for the sake of them that will be left on the wild world without me ; for them help me, great God !"

Hitherto his weakness and confusion had left him passive. Before his uncle spoke the last words, his silent prayer was offered, and Shamus had jumped upon his assailant. They struggled, and dragged each other down. Shamus felt the muzzle of the pistol at his breast ; heard it snap—but only snap ; he seized and mastered it, and once more the uncle was at the mercy of his nephew. Shamus's hand was raised to deal a good blow ; but he checked himself, and addressed the almost senseless ears of his captive.

" No ; you're my mother's blood, and a son of hers will never draw it from your heart ; but I can make sure of you again— stop a bit."

He ran to his own prostrate horse, took off its bridle and its saddle-girth, and with both secured his uncle's limbs, beyond all possibility of the struggler being able to escape from their control.

" There," resumed Shamus, " lie there till we have time to send an ould friend to see you, that, I'll go bail, will take good care of your four bones. And do you know where I'm going now ? You tould me, on Lunnon Bridge, that you knew *that*, at least" —pointing to the abbey—" ay, and the quare ould hearth-stone that's to be found in it. And so, look at this, uncle, honey"— he vaulted upon his relation's horse—" I'm just goin' to lift it off o' the barrel-pot full of good ould goold, and you have only to cry halves, and you'll get it, as sure as that the big divvle is in the town you came from."

Nance Dempsey was nursing her new-born babe, sitting up in her straw, and doing very well after her late illness, when old Noreen tottered in from the front of the ruin, to tell her that "the body they were just speaking about was driving up the hill mad, like as if 'twas his own sperit in great throuble." And the listener had not recovered from her surprise, when Shamus ran into the shed, flung himself kneeling by her side, caught her in his arms, then seized her infant, covered it with kisses, and then, roughly throwing it in her lap, turned to the fireplace, raised one of the rocky seats lying near it, poised the ponderous mass over the hearth-stone, and shivered into pieces, with one crash, that solid barrier between him and his visionary world of wealth.

"It's cracked he is, out an' out, of a certainty," said Nance, looking terrified at her husband.

"Nothing else am I," shouted Shamus, after groping under the broken slab; "an', for a token, get along with yourself out of this, owld gran !"

He started up and seized her by the shoulder. Noreen remonstrated. He stooped for a stone ; she ran ; he pursued her to the arches of the ruin. She stopped half-way down the descent. He pelted her with clods to the bottom, and along a good piece of her road homewards ; and then danced back into his wife's presence.

"Now, Nance," he cried, "now that we're by ourselves, what noise is this like !"

"And he took out han'fuls after han'fuls of the ould goold, afore her face, my dear," added the original narrator of this story.

"An' after the gaugers and their crony, Ould Nick, ran off wid the uncle of him, Nance and he, and the childer, lived together in their father's and mother's house ; and if they didn't live and die happy, I wish that you and I may."

NOTE TO THE RIVAL DREAMERS.

LESS than a century ago, as we learn from tradition, deposits of treasure were frequently exhumed from interment in Ireland, by lucky dreamers; the spot where such lay concealed being invariably revealed in a dream—that is, a dream three times dreamt. Those deposits being made, it was supposed, during the almost continuous change of inhabitants, when civil wars, and transplantations, and confiscations, were the order of the day.

Now-a-days, however, such good fortune is scarcely heard of. People grow rich, to be sure; and often unaccountably fill their granaries—that is, unaccountable to the gleaners in the stubble fields. But "crocks of goold" are neither dreamt of nor dug up, that I can hear of.

An occurrence took place, somewhat beyond seventy years ago, which, even now, it would be heterodoxy to disbelieve, and which I give, on the authority of the principal actor concerned in the adventure.

Phelim Bryan, a broguemaker, residing in Kilkenny, dreamed three dreams, that in a corner of the mouldering priory of Kells, within seven miles of him, a "power of gold" lay concealed. Phelim Bryan placed implicit faith in his three dreams. But the place was so distant from his residence, so lonely, and so thickly tenanted by the dead, that, being of a timid nature, he shrank from the idea of going alone to disinter the treasure. If the exhumation were to be made while there was daylight, he might have ventured, and without intrusting his secret to any one. But his good sense told him, that if the "crock of goold" were brought to the surface, under the eye of day, he could expect nothing less than a general scramble for it by the inhabitants of the entire neighborhood; and he was of opinion that he might be the "Paddy-last" in the scuffle; and so his three dreams and all his labor go for nothing.

Phelim Bryan could not screw up his courage to the resolution of wending by himself, at night, to the priory of Kells; particularly, as the whole world knew that hidden gold was always watched over by a supernatural guardian, whether such watcher might be the troubled spirit of the hider, or a dangerous fiend, had not been satisfactorily ascertained.

In his embarrassment, Phelim Bryan took to his confidence two brethren of his craft—three is admittedly a lucky number. The three held council together, and they agreed to go in company. They set out from Kilkenny, well provided with tools, and with a lantern; and, at the hour when labor, the veritable Morpheus, bestows the blessings of profound slumber on his disciples, the three expectant broguemakers stole quietly into the gloomy ruin at Kells, a fitful moon throwing mysterious gleams of white, ghastly light occasionally through the roofless building.

Phelim Bryan, during a more than usual moon-glinting, pointed out without hesitation, the precise spot thrice indicated to him in his dream; and lighting the candle in his lantern, by means of his tinder-box and matches, he and Andrew Treahy fell to work to delve among the graves; while the third broguemaker, Paddy Dullard, kept watch for them. This duty was assigned to Paddy Dullard, inasmuch as he was known to be a stout-hearted fellow, not easily daunted, either by flesh or blood, or by less tangible interference.

Phelim Bryan and his co-laborer had shovelled away, might and main, for more than an hour; and, during the progress of their task, had pitched up more than one skull, with other human relics, to be glanced at by the moon, during her capricious inspection of what was going on.

"By the life, we are ou it," whispered Andrew Treahy to Phelim Bryan; "there's something hard under the spade."

"Good-fellow, good-fellow," Phelim Bryan whispered, in return.

While Phelim Bryan was whispering his approval of Andrew Treahy's welcome intelligence, both the whisperers withdrew spade and shovel hastily from their work, and endeavored to read each other's faces, which the moon, shining brightly for an instant, enabled them to do.

Phelim Bryan saw that Andrew Treahy was frightened. And Andrew Treahy ascertained, during the hasty view he was enabled to take of Phelim Bryan, that Phelim Bryan's eyes were starting from their sockets, as their glances met. And no wonder that the resurrectionists should be terrified. Immediately following the interchange of whispers between them, a deep, melancholy groan, or, more properly, a sound, partly groan, partly angry bellow, partly discordant wail—such an indescribable minglement of pain, grief, and fury, as could not possibly emanate from living, human breast—travelled round and round through the mouldering archways and crevices of the ruin.

The two coldly perspiring broguemakers ceased their work and leaned on their shovels, listening to the unnaturally prolonged lamentation, when Paddy Dullard, the watchman, stumbled over the graves and other impediments until he reached them. The cool nonchalance of Paddy Dullard on the occasion was afterwards honorably mentioned as a proof of the unflinching bravery of his nature. There was no sign of trepidation or apprehension in the tone of his voice as he addressed his colleagues; on the contrary, he spoke in the accents of a triumphant adventurer; he spoke as an Australian miner would speak when turning up nuggets: "Work away, my hearties," he said cheerily; "work away, body and soul, my hearties. By the piper that played before Moses, you'll be on the crock o' goold in no time; didn't you hear that wicked shout? And look, look, standing by the tall headstone near yon, the thieving spirit of the fellow that hid the goold is watching you! Work, work, my men, and to the devil with broguemaking, while grass grows and water runs."

The moon, that had been playing fast and loose all the night, favored the explorers, so far as to enable the diggers to discern a tall, unearthly figure, standing on a headstone not more than three feet from them; and the same terrible lamentation they had heard before was repeated.

Phelim Bryan snatched up his lantern; but he did not pause to secure his spade and shovel. He scrambled away, as fast as the inequalities of the graves would permit; and Andrew Treahy ran, or stumbled close at the heels of Phelim Bryan. As for Paddy Dullard, when he found himself left alone with the "spirit" of the fellow who had hidden the "crock o' goold," he slowly and unwillingly withdrew, shaking his head at the fruitlessness of the night's adventure.

Next market-day, when all the broguemakers of Kilkenny had assembled in the portion of the street where their bog-defying foot-gear was exposed for sale, in their large baskets (brogues and broguemakers were then forty to one more numerous than they are now), a certain Luke Shortall inquired, in a jeering kind of way, of his neighbor, Phelim Bryan, as to the value of the "crock of goold" that he, Phelim, had dug up in the ruins of Kells. Phelim Bryan was somewhat taken aback, by having this inquiry made. How could Luke Shortall have got his knowledge? He had not told his secret to any one, barring Andrew Treahy and Paddy Dullard.

THE END OF THE RIVAL DREAMERS.

THE SUBSTITUTE.

THE SUBSTITUTE.

NAPOLEON wanted a fresh supply of "food for powder," and
so urgently that the time usually allowed, even during the
war, between the choice of a conscript and his departure for
actual service became limited upon this occasion to a few days.

In many a village through France, the winter's morning
which ushered in the day upon which the peasant lads were to
"*tirer leur sort*," in the different adjacent towns, presented
scenes of trembling bustle. We are upon the high-road outside
one little hamlet. Two young fellows pass us arm in arm, talking earnestly, though in a low tone. They are brothers, the only
support of an aged and feeble mother. The elder being *chef de
famille*, since his father's death, is not called upon to attend the
mayor and sub-prefect, in the town towards which they walk ;
he only conveys the younger lad a little way on the road, to bid
God bless him, and deliver him from a "*mauvais numero.*"
You may guess, indeed, from the patched, working dress of the
one, that it is not his intention to accompany his (unwillingly)
holiday-clad brother far out of the village ; and you may infer
that the necessity of not missing a single day of agricultural
labor sends him back to the farmer's team or barn ; he must
retrace his steps already. The brothers stop at the bottom of
the first little hill, speak a moment to each other, doff their caps,
kiss cheeks, and part. The *cadet* bounds up the road bravely,
at once to disguise his feelings and make a little show of response to the call of "glory and country." As the *ainé* repasses
you, his step is heavy, his head drooped, his hands clenched, as
they swing at his side, and his eyes—but he will not let you see
them.

Another pair approach—a lad and a girl. He is laughing, or
doing his best to laugh ; she is shedding tears, though sometimes

14*

she smiles, too. Are they brother and sister? Hardly. Their
arms happen to be interlaced at one another's backs, and observe how expressively he, or she, or both, kiss. Let them go
their ways in peace, and without arousing excessive sympathy.
He is the youngest of five stout sons, whose father and mother
are living and thriving, and may pretty well be spared as a con-
tribution from his native village to national honor and glory.
And though 'tis interesting and pleasing to witness the romantic distress of the young couple—lovers according to the rules—
that is, with the consent of both their families—yet they are *too*
young to get married yet awhile ; and Arriette will be constant
—if she can ; and he may come home an officer, or a corporal
at least ; or if he never come home, why then Arriette will be
very, very much afflicted. They disappear from us over the hill
together, and it seems she has got leave to accompany him to
the town, that she may the sooner learn whether he is to
"*tomber*" or not.

A middle-aged man and his wife, leaning at either side upon
their son, now attract our notice. "Still, one should always
live in good hopes, my child," says the mother, while passing by
us ; but even her voice does not support the recommendation of
her words. In fact, her hopes of Clovis drawing a good number are very slight, and a kind of superstition augments her apprehensions for his lot. Among the peasantry of France it goes
as a rule that if one of a family of many sons is cast as a conscript, the others, from time to time, are sure to share his fate ;
and she has some reason for putting vague faith in the influence
of the supposed fatality. About seven years before, her eldest
boy, after drawing a "bad number," joined the army, and fell in
his first battle-field. Another conscription was ordered, and her
second fared as his brother had done ; another, and her third
left her, and soon returned, badly wounded, and now creeps
about her cottage, drooping, pale, and unable to work. The
fourth is on his way to try his fortune, and he is her last, too—
that is, the last able to help her and his father, for little Pierre
is only ten. God speed them, the old couple this day, and may
they march home, Clovis betweed them to supper, a happy pair.

Standing by the road-side to witness the departure of these
and many other villagers, for the town, our position was at one
of the piers of an avenue of elm-trees, which lead up to a
chateau of some respectability. Presently voices sounded coming down the avenue, and many humble groups on the high-road

stopped to take off their caps and bow, or else to simper
courtesy, and give their "*bon jour*" to the speakers, who soon
joined them.

"Good-day, Mademoiselle Hortense—good-day, Monsieur
François," said many kind and respectful voices, accompanied
by the smiles, and looks, and action which peasants out of
France know nothing of.

Mademoiselle Hortense was a young lady of about twenty,
her height good, her figure straight as a poplar, her carriage
free, noble—all but haughty—and yet it was simple, too. No
one called her beautiful; but every one spoke of the spirit and
expression of her face—and, indeed, it could not be seen once,
and soon forgotten. Its complexion was almost Moorish ; perhaps her ancestors had not escaped, in times gone, some contact
with Oriental blood, when the south of France was partially inhabited by swarthy children of the sun—and from the south, we
have heard, her family first came into the almost extreme northern
province which is now country to her. Hortense's eye, too—her
round, powerful, fascinating black eye, shaded by her intensely
black hair, had a fitfully firm glance, such, it is said (though
softened in her), as struck with astonishment, if with nothing
else, the good citizens of Paris, when the bold and brave Marseil-
lais suddenly appeared in their streets, chaunting their tremendous
hymn, and glaring upon the new objects around them, with an
expression traced to their mixed descent from infidel and Christian. But let not an illustration unfeminize, in the slightest degree, our Hortense. If nature gave her a feature which truly
revealed spirit and power, another was conferred abounding with
softness and goodness ; her mouth—beautiful mouth ! narrow,
full, richly colored, out-breathing, and constantly putting in play
two dimples. Nay, a particular individual has averred that Hortense's eyes, when they met his, were, of all features of her face,
the gentlest, softest, tenderest, kindest, best.

However, this is a little too much of Hortense, devotedly as
we love her. Her companion, whom the peasants have called
Monsieur François, is to be introduced. He was a young man of
two-and-twenty, it was said—nay, insisted on—else he would not
have appeared in the avenue this morning. Yet, from his slight
figure, a little stooped and not strongly knit, and from his boyish, pale, unbearded, and unwhiskered face, he did not appear to
be as old as the girl who leaned on his arm.

"And is no one to be spared, in these times, Mademoiselle

Hortense," continued an old man, after he had saluted her, "not even the best among us ? And must Monsieur François take his chance with the poorest ?"

" My brother," answered Hortense, " is proud to take his chance for serving his country and his emperor, at the side of the other brave youths, no matter how poor, of our district."

" The call to war, Oudard," added François, smiling at his old neighbor, " has never yet been neglected by one of my family."

The old man with his parting compliment, bowed, put on his battered old hat, and left them. The brother and sister stood still at the bottom of the avenue, both looking in the same direction.

" 'Tis time Eugène were here, if he *is* to accompany me to the town," resumed François.

" Yes, indeed," replied Hortense, " and he is not generally so unpunctual. But, my brother, you must feel the morning air very cold, for you tremble a little ?"

" Do I ? 'tis nothing, Hortense ; ten minutes' brisk walking towards the town will cure it, if our friend would only come as he promised."

" Here he is, then," said Hortense, as the young man they expected jumped over a stile at the other side of the road, nearly opposite to them.

Eugène was twenty-five ; well-formed, well-featured, manly looking, but rustic. He wanted something of the elevated character which stamped the appearance of Hortense and François, though in such different ways. Hortense, however, did not seem to think contemptuously of his agricultural mannerism, as he walked across the road, bowing and smiling to her. She blushed, to be sure—that is, her deep brunette cheeks became, of a sudden, of a rich, red color. But we are certain it was not because she was ashamed of him that Hortense blushed.

After greetings, a few words served to make François and Eugène ready to start for the town.

" God bless you, my brother !" said Hortense, offering her cheek, while her noble eyes were now moist and half closed ; " God bless you ; and though, as you have yourself just said, no man of our ancient family ever yet turned an indifferent ear to the call of country and of honor, still, my brother"—her voice failed her, and the tears would not keep bounds—" still, I will pray, all this day, that for the present, you may be spared to those who love you. Eugène, good-morning!" She turned quickly up the avenue, drawing round her her little brown cloak, and pulling forward her coarse straw bonnet.

"For glory and country!" cried François, taking his friend's arm to lead him off.

"Stop one moment; I've forgotten just to ask Hortense one word," said Eugène; and he ran after his mistress.

"Folly!" cried François; "soft nonsense at the moment we have hard blows to think of! you may overtake me if you can, Eugène!" He spoke in a brave, shouting tone, and disappeared from the avenue.

"I will catch you in two jumps," shouted Eugène in return. "Hortense," he continued, joining her, "there will be no one at home with you in the house to-day, except your poor sick mother and the servants."

"Well, Eugène, and what of that? I thank you for your anxiety about me; but can I not take care of the house and servants, and of my dear mother, too, for a few hours? Besides, Antoine" (her elder brother, and *chef de famille*) "may be home from his long journey before evening. You know he has been many days expected."

"Well, Hortense, good-by—you know you have not bid me good-by yet"— a moment's break here in the dialogue—"and Hortense"—

"What, Eugène?" as he paused.

"This day, of all days, would not be the day to"—

He stopped short again, but Hortense knew what he meant, and went on for him.

"To receive a visit from your rich rival, Eugène? he"—she continued, contemptuously—"who has the chateau hard by, with a window for every day in the year in it? you are right, my friend. If ever his company was disagreeable to me, it must be till I see you again—you and François, together, I mean. Eugène"—she paused, in her turn, looked most wistfully into her lover's face, laid her hand on his arm, and beginning with the word "François," was about to make an important request; but she suddenly checked herself, and saying—"but no; time enough for that—for even a breath of it—*when* I shall see you both again"—she again turned from Eugène, and he bounded down the avenue to overtake his friend.

Hortense gained the open space before the inclosed *cour* of the chateau. It had originally been covered with soft grass, but the constant irruptions of the poultry, pigs, horses, and cows, from the farm, which bounded it on one side at right angles with the chateau, left it at present little appearance of verdure, or even of uniformity or cleanliness. We have, indeed, often been outraged in taste and patience, in France, by observing how frequently the immediate vicinity of a respectable and comfortable house is thus littered by fixing the abode of the small farmer, with its almost endless appendages of stables, cow-sheds, sheep-sheds, pigstyes, etc., close within view and contact. But that is scarcely to our present purpose.

As Hortense, treading her way cautiously between beasts, brutes, and fowls of many kinds (to speak of nothing else), approached the farmer's thatched house, she saw his stalwart, though comely daughter, holding out a flat basket of breakfast-mess for the poultry, while she screamed an invitation to them, on their predatory wanderings far and near, in a succession of shrill and nearly diabolical cadences.

" Good-day, mademoiselle," said the maiden, interrupting her summons to the cocks and hens, and turkeys, the ducks, and their offspring of low degree ; yet she bawled to her young mistress almost as loud as she had to them. " Good-day, mademoiselle ; and may God make this day end happily for you."

" The eggs, Madeline, for breakfast," said Hortense, distantly, for she did not like the prayer put up by Madeline, for certain reasons ; " since I am abroad so early, I may as well take them home myself."

" Ay, ay, abroad so early indeed," resumed Madeline ; " and too early, for any good is to come of it, I am sure. Mademoiselle, if Monsieur François should *fall* to-day, what is to be done ?"

" Done? What do you mean, my child?" asked Hortense, in real or feigned surprise.

" Oh, I have heard my father and my mother talk it over, mademoiselle ; and they say it will be quite impossible to get a substitute, this time, the drain of men is so great everywhere, and the price so very high."

" And who told *thee*, Madeline, or *thy* father and mother, either, that we—my brother and his family—are so poor as not to be able to purchase a substitute—high as the price may be ?" asked Hortense, now putting Madeline at her distance, as she used the *tu-toi*. " Or suppose Monsieur François *does* draw a bad number, who told thee he may not prefer to serve his country personally, rather than by a substitute ?"

"Hélas, poor Monsieur François!" sighed Madeline, with a snowing shake of the head.

"Girl!" cried Hortense, "what dare you say of my brother?"

"Nothing, mademoiselle—nothing, upon my honor—it is not I that say it—"

"Say what?"

"Nothing, indeed; nothing, mademoiselle,—only that he has often been sickly and weakly, and might not have health or strength enough for a soldier."

"Bah! the eggs, girl—and the freshest." Hortense soon had them in the little basket, and crossed over to the chateau, seemingly unconcerned and unmoved by Madeline's chatter, but really and deeply agitated by it.

She did not, however, allow any one in the house to notice her feelings by her manner. To prepare for the old and feeble mother's descent to breakfast, she closely watched, as was her wont, the labors of the rustic servant, whose business it was to pile up the logs on the hearth, in the *salle à manger;* to wheel round the immense, old-fashioned, half-decayed arm-chair to their blaze; and sweep, and dust, and arrange; and, in a word, do the best to make the spacious appartment not have the air of being badly and poorly furnished. When, with the assistance of the same attendant, Hortense had placed her mother in her usual seat, the earnest, fond, coaxing devotion with which she induced the half-doting invalid to take her morning's meal, showed nothing of a reserved care preying upon her very heart. They spoke little together of François, or of the interests of the day connected with him; for, in fact, the old woman's mind was so decayed, nothing distinctly affected her.

After breakfast, Hortense left her mother to the care of a young girl, and ascended to her brother Antoine's chamber, with the professed purpose of seeing that it was in order for his expected return to his family. "I must keep myself employed, except when I kneel down to pray," was Hortense's mental resolve. "O God, grant that Antoine may come back with the money he has gone to borrow of our rich uncle—God, grant it!" she continued, entering his chamber. A look around, informed her that little was wanted in the arrangement of the apartment. Before she turned out of it, she could not help remarking how like her elder brother's mind and character were many of the appendages of the place, added to it by himself: the fowling-pieces, the pistols; an antique sword, once wielded by a distinguished war-

like ancester ; a wolf-spear; roots of flowers, preserved on rough
shelves from the frosts of winter ; paper bags of seeds hung
against the wall ; ponderous, country-made shoes, calling to mind
the manful, almost rude, tread and stride of their owner, in all
weathers, here and there, over the few acres which misfortune
had 1.ft to the descendants of a once wealthy and powerful fam
ily.   And for the private library of Antoine, his sister smiled
to think how easily its volumes could be numbered ; they were,
in fact, but two—one an odd tome of an old, fabulous history or
France ; the other, a great folio, quite as old, entitled *La Maison
Rustique*—containing loquacious and quaint instructions how to
make, and keep in order, gardens of various kinds, shrubberies,
vineyards, pleasure-grounds ; how to make all descriptions of
wines ; and how to brew, and how to bake, within doors.

But Hortense did not smile when, by association, her mind,
and with it her steps, turned to her younger brother's study,
contrived next his sleeping apartment.   Here, as she paused at
its door, none of the indications of a rough masculine mind, like
Antoine's were visible ; no weapons, nor implements of country
sport ; no spear for the wolf, who was occasionally, though not
often, to be met with in the adjacent forests ; no relic of family
heroism ; no arms of defence ; even no symptoms of attention to
the garden or the farm.   Of books, indeed, there were enough;
but all, whether poetical or prosaic, of a soft, or dreamy, or gentle cast ; and a guitar lay on a chair beside the student's table;
and landscape sketches, mostly unfinished, were pinned to the
walls.

"Amiable and beloved François !" sighed Hortense, as she
sat to the table; "my brother, my friend, my tutor ; you to
whom I owe almost a mind, and whose goodness and gentleness
have improved my heart—woman's as it is ! O my brother ! my
brother ! a merciful Providence grant I may be deceived in my
fears for you !" She fell on her knees, and the prayers of Hortense were long and fervid.

The wind, entering through a half-opened window, wafted to
her side a piece of torn paper, written upon, but blotted, and
scratched over here and there. Its rustle disturbed her devotions;
her eye fixed upon it; she knew her young brother's hand ; and
the first words of it, unconsciously perused by Hortense, made her
hurry, in spite of herself, through the whole. It was but a frag
ment of, seemingly, an aspiration to Heaven, torn in pieces by its
writer ; and, doubtless, he had never meant it for any eye but

his own. "But even this is like him, thought Hortense;" the want of presence of mind, which, in the nervous bustle of leaving the house this morning, could make him overlook an evidence so tremendous."

Hortense could decipher only a few sentences of the paper; but she had read enough to make her start to her feet, from her knees, in consternation, anger, and horror; enough to make her mutter, and—so soon after her prayers—almost imprecate; enough to make her tear the scrawl into a thousand little bits, and stamp them under her feet, as if she would annihilate them, and with them the sense of the written words within the breast of her brother. And then she rushed out of the room, her uttermost feeling being that of detestation of it, and almost of him.

But love and pity soon reasserted themselves over her; and after them came, upon confirmation of her worst fears long indulged, intense, agonizing solicitude, and dread of her own and her family's honor, as much as for her brother's. She flung herself on her knees again, in her own room, and her only prayer now was, either that François might not draw a bad number that day, or else that Antoine might come back with money to purchase a substitute for him.

The step of a horse in the paved courtyard drew her to a window. It was Antoine come back; but, after flying to embrace him, Hortense soon knew that half of her prayer was denied. Their rich relative would not lend him a sous, although the necessities of the family, accumulating for years, now seemed to threaten them with literal ruin.

After this, Hortense rested but upon one slight and tremulous hope; to prove which vain or true, she must still wait many hours. For the rest of the day, she scarce opened her lips; and, mostly sitting alone in her chamber, the anguish of suspense was fearful to her. Eugène's rich rival came a-wooing, as he often did: she would not descend to him. He loitered in the house and in the gardens: she was inexorable.

At length the winter evening fell—the hour for the return of her brother and her lover. Hortense stole out of the house unobserved, down the avenue, and so posted herself within the fences of the road near its termination that she could observe every one who came by. One after the other, the groups who had passed the avenue in the morning, or the greater part of them, appeared returning to the little village, some silent, or only speaking in sad tones, others talking loud and laughing; and now and then was heard the smothered sob or the repressed lament of a woman or a girl. The poor *chef de famille* strode by with his only brother (the first group we have noticed in the morning), whom, after his day's labor, he had gone to meet on his way home; his herculean arm encircled the lad's neck, but his head was bent to his chest, and he moaned to himself. Arriette appeared by her lover's side, weeping so determinedly that his false spirits, the good things he said, and the better things he did, could not make her give over. But Clovis was marched home to supper between his father and mother, a delivered youth; and it seemed, from the occasional difficulty he found in keeping the old man steady by his side, and hindering him from singing in a very loud and very cracked voice, that some good beer or *eau-de-vie* had celebrated in the town or on the road, the triumph of the family.

Hortense looked close as each group passed by: her brother came not. But she heard him named, now and then, in whispers, and caught disjointed words and tones which entered into her brain like adders' fangs. She could comprehend that something had already happened, disgraceful—and destroying because so—to him, to her, to their family, to their ancient honor and name—the idols of her worship since childhood, and now the only good left to them all. A daring determination already began to dawn in her mind. The sound of carriage-wheels diverted her, and broke it up. She came upon the moonlit road. The heads of François and Eugène appeared alternately from the window of the vehicle, as if looking to note if their return was watched for. It was singular to see them come home in a carriage. No matter: now, at least, she could learn what the whispers of the passing villagers had not yet told her, though they alluded to other things—namely, was François, or was he not, a conscript?

She hurried to meet the carriage. The driver knew her, and pulled up.

"Ah, my sister!" shouted François, from the window, "I have fallen—I am a soldier!"

Along with the shrinking of her feelings from this announcement, her reason and understanding recoiled upon their own "foregone conclusions." Could François greet her in so laughing and brave a tone, if she had done him justice in her former thoughts of him?

Scarcely noticing Eugène, she tenderly and weepingly embraced her brother in the carriage, which now conveyed all up the avenue. François supposed she must be surprised that they had returned not a-foot ; but, in fact, as Eugène could tell her, what with getting up so unusually early that morning, and taking a long walk fasting, and then the crowd of the place where they had assembled to draw their lots, he had been put out of sorts, and could scarce muster strength enough to get home without a carriage.

"Were you ill before or after you drew?" asked Hortense.

"Before—no, after, I think. Was it, Eugène?—I forget," answered the conscript.

"After," said Eugène, solemnly and sadly.

Hortense spoke not another word, although her brother continued to talk, in a bantering and hearty voice, of the suddenness with which he must enter upon his new trade, and the full practice which the new conscripts were promised just as suddenly ; and how glad he would be to acquire, by the habits of a soldier's life, sufficient hardiness of frame to keep off such absurd fits of faintness as that morning had shown him subject to.

Arrived at the chateau, Hortense, instead of asking Eugène in, bade him good-night in so abstracted a manner that the lover thought her indifferent; and remarked that if his friend Antoine were at home he might not be treated so inhospitably.

"He is at home, Eugène," replied Hortense (and she felt François start at her side) ; "but, even for that reason, you will not ask to sit down among us to-night."

"And why not, Hortense? Has the chevalier been visiting here to-day!"

"I do not know ; good-night. *Mon frère*, I wait to have you hand me down." In fact, Hortense scarcely knew or cared what she said.

"Good-night, then," said Eugène quickly, as he jumped from the carriage before François moved ; then he hastened home.

"Stop one moment, dear Hortense," resumed François yet in the carriage, now speaking in a low and constrained voice ; "Antoine returned, you say? and with the money?"

"With not as much as would purchase a substitute for you, my brother, were substitutes to be had at a franc a-piece."

Her brother sat a moment silently ; but she could hear the hissings of his breath between his teeth. At last, at her repeated urging, he descended from the vehicle, and offered her his arm.

"The evening cold affects you as keenly as that of the morning did," she observed, while she leaned on him into the house.

But, to her surprise, François appeared in high spirits before her brother and her at supper. She watched him close, however, and now and then noted within his eye, or upon his suddenly changing cheek, or upon his moist forehead, or in his fitful, smothering sigh, that which she shuddered to interpret. She noted, too, the expression of his earnest embrace of his brother and herself at parting for the night; and her heart sank within her.

"I will watch him still," resolved Hortense. And she did so, as closely as circumstances permitted, for hours after he retired to his chamber. François bolted himself in; but she heard his uneven steps about the apartment, his groans, his wretched weeping, his mutterings, after intervals of silence, when she imagined he had cast himself in a chair or across his bed. It must have been towards the dawn of the winter's morning that, after a long pause of inaction, during which no sounds escaped his lips, she caught these sudden words, as once more he started from his chair:

"Ay! that will end it, and for that cowardice itself at last gives me courage." Then he walked to the door at which she was listening.

Hortense had scarce time to escape out of his view, and yet keep her eye upon him, when she saw him steal, with a faltering foot and a haggard face, towards his brother Antoine's chamber. She followed him. The fatigued traveller had left his door open, and now slept profoundly. François, continuing his stealthy pace, approached the table where his brother had put down, freshly charged, the pistols he had carried with him on his journey. Hortense waited to see no more, but noiselessly flew to act upon a strange though powerful thought which some moments before had possessed her mind. Her paralyzed mother never slept in her bed, but passed the nights in an arm-chair, well wrapped up from the cold. With a suddenly acquired strength the girl caught up the old woman, ran with her out of the chamber, placed her in her chair inside the threshold of that of François, before he had time to re-enter it, and, standing at her back, waited for him.

The faint screams of the vaguely terrified invalid sounded on his ear, as he staggered, almost blind from agitation, along the corridor, with the pistol in one hand and his night-lamp in the other. Had his mother been dead, and had her ghost confronted him, François could not have felt more consternation than at her sight he did.

"What! what's this, Hortense?" he stammered, his distended eyes wandering to his sister.

"Your mother and I have come to ask you, François, what are you going to do with that pistol?" answered Hortense; it was still in his hand. "Give it me, my brother!" she continued, advancing to him; "give it!" she repeated in a loud tone, as he receded, and, unconscious of the act, hid it behind his back.

"Give it!" echoed his mother, her attention roused by the force of the circumstances; "give it, son François, or I will kneel down and curse you!" Her shrill and scarcely human voice rang through the chateau.

He mechanically extended his hand to Hortense; she put the pistol in her bosom.

"Now help me to bear our mother to her own room, and then I will speak with you," resumed Hortense. He again obeyed her.

An attendant remained with the old woman, and the brother and sister walked back to his apartment.

"I know it all, my brother," said Hortense.

"All what?" demanded François.

"O François, François, do not ask me to give it a name! and you know I speak not of what has just happened, but rather what it is that put the evil thought into your mind! My brother, my brother, I *do* know it all! François, I could have preferred, much as I love you, to have seen you in your early grave, and to have taken my place at your side. Oh, mercies! mercies! I could have perished with you, and with all—mother, brother, and every one of our own name and blood—in utter ruin of worldly prospects, in poverty, in insulted and trampled down poverty, ay, and in the depths of a common prison. François, all that, and more—any thing lips can name, or fancy shadow out, I could have smiled at, my brother. But this—this! O François! François!" She wept bitterly, and wrung her hands.

With scarcely power to pronounce the poor equivocation, he continued to ask what she meant.

"Oh, never!" she resumed, not attending to him; "never, from generation to generation, has a woman of our house been called a wanton—and, O merciful Heaven! never, never *before*, from generation to generation, has a man of our house been called—"

"A what? he interrupted, in false vivacity.

"I was wrong,' she answered, changing her tone; "I was wrong to approach so nearly giving it a name, when I said I would not. I do not want to hurt you, François."

"Tush!" he cried, assuming a higher tone, though still a false one; "I will not bear such vague insult even from you, my sister. Tell me, or retire this moment! tell me what it is that no man of my family has ever *before* been called, but which you would now dare to call *me?*"

"No, no, no, I will not," muttered Hortense.

"Hortense, *I* will call *you* rude and insolent, and false, too, *if* you do not."

Her tears ceased; her brow grew stern; she rose from her seat, fixed her eyes on him, and advancing slowly, while he stepped back, said—

"Listen, then—A COWARD!"

He started and shivered as if she had discharged at his head the pistol she bore in her bosom.

"Yes, wretched brother! you *fear*, you *fear!* Your heart chills in your body. Your brain burns like fire, at the thought of the lot you have drawn this day! You would shriek like a whipped infant to face the noble dangers of a battle-field! A score of strong men, did they bind you with thongs, and urge you with base lashes, could not drag you, drag you upright, standing on your limbs, to face it! Deny not my words—try not to talk me down! So mighty is the fear at your heart, that, but a moment ago, you would have done self-murder to escape its tortures! And what else would the act have proclaimed? Proclaimed to the world, and to men and women yet unborn, of you and of your name— your ancient, your glorious name! What would have been the comment of mankind upon you, miserable brother?—upon *you*, found a corpse this morning, because chance made you a soldier yesterday!"

He had been swaying from side to side, his head hanging down; now he fell without a word. His sister, all her momentary passion gone, flew to him, knelt at his side, and put her arms around him. He had swooned. She started up for water, put it to his lips, and chafed his temples with it. As he recovered, he heard her plaintive and soft murmurs at his ear, asking his forgiveness, and he felt her caresses.

"No, no, my brother, my beloved brother!" she continued; "'tis no fault of yours—however great, however terrible a misfortune—no fault of yours! 'tis the will of God, with, perhaps, my own act. Oh, how often have I thought so, and wept to think it was my own act to provoke so dark a judgment! Yes, dear François, until the day when running up to you, of a sudden, I fired Antoine's pistol, only charged with powder, so close to you—until that day you were a brave and reckless boy—infant almost—and then, I fear, some manful nerve or other gave way! But if 'tis even so, a change may again come over you; and till that happens, let us guard jealously the secret of our honor."

With groans and tears, sitting on the floor, he turned his face from her, covering it with his hands.

"For the present occasion," resumed Hortense, "something must be done."

The action of his figure and attitude showed him more attentive.

"We must find you a substitute."

"How?" he asked, not yet uncovering his face, though he turned anxiously towards her.

"Leave it to me to think of, my brother. True, there is no money in the house, even for our immediate and great wants, much less for the purchase of a substitute; and the only friends we have, Eugène and his family, are almost as poor as we are, and with more claims on them. Yet leave it to me; by to-morrow morning—indeed, this morning at breakfast—you shall know more. Return to your bed; I will go to my own chamber. Farewell, my brother. Only promise that you will wait patiently till breakfast, and all may yet be well."

He gave the promise required. She left him with renewed embraces; recollecting, however, the betraying expression of his own farewell to her and Antoine the previous night, she allowed nothing particular to mark her adieus.

Our story may be ended in not many more words. Noble and strange things are true of women in France, calm English reader, particularly since the old revolution.

Left alone, François did not obey his sister's exhortation to seek repose in bed. Her engagement to procure a substitute took absorbing possession of his soul. What did she mean to do? How, in fact, could she raise the purchase-money! Vague fears of inconvenience, perhaps of humiliation and suffering to her, crowded upon his mind; and, wrought upon by his great love for his sister, François paced the room, his kindling resolves almost verifying Hortense's half prophecy, that "a change might again come over him."

He watched the progress of the winter morning through his windows. He descended to the breakfast-room. A note from his sister awaited him upon the table :

" I am quite sure of obtaining a substitute, only I must be absent some days from home. When you read this I shall be already miles distant from you. As you wish me to succeed, make no inquiries about me till we meet. Adieu, dear brother.
" HORTENSE."

Agitated with he knew not what terrors, François soon disobeyed the injunction of the last lines. He hastened to question the servants about Hortense's departure from the house. No one had seen her leave it. He spoke with his brother Antoine, who rode off to make inquiries in the neighborhood.

François himself walked to Eugène's house. The young man had just gone, galloping hard, and in no amiable humor, towards a distant point, on pretended business, and would not return for three days. François walked home again, and in the course of the day saw Antoine come back without obtaining the slightest information of their sister.

Inquiries and searches were continued for the better part of three days, in the adjacent town as well as in the country, but without effect. Eugène appeared at the chateau, agitated with the news of Hortense's elopement. At first even he could make nothing of it ; but, after a moody pause, he smote his thigh, and asked François to accompany him to the house of his rich rival.

They accordingly went thither together. Eugène prophesied either that Hortense would be found under the chevalier's roof, after obtaining money from him to purchase a substitute ; or, that the chevalier would be reported absent, no one knew where. Although François indignantly flouted his vile suspicions, yet the jealous lover desired him to call to mind how coldly Hortense had treated her old friend the very last evening they had all been together ; and he added that, although upon that occasion she had told him (Eugène) that she knew nothing of the chevalier's visit in the course of the day, yet he had since had good reason to think that they had spent many hours together in the garden.

Neither of Eugène's prognostics proved true. They saw the chevalier, and his assurances of total ignorance of the present fate of Hortense could not be doubted.

It was the day, and near the hour, when, according to notice received, François was to repair to the town to learn the exact time fixed for his march, as a conscript, towards the frontier. Eugène accompanied his friend. In the town, having presented themselves before the proper authorities, they were told that François was now a free man, a substitute having taken his place three days before. It was added, that the young person, from some pressing motive not explained, had urgently required, and eventually obtained, written permission to hasten, as soon as he wished, to the head town of the department, where all the conscripts were to assemble by a certain day.

A dreadful, though true, misgiving seized upon François. He asked to have the features of the substitute described to him. Eugène and he glared, thunderstruck, at each other, while his request was complied with. François, after a moment's pause, requested to know how the substitute had been dressed. In the details given he recognized a suit of his own clothes. The name was the last request, and then the friends mounted two good horses. The next day they gained the chief town of the department. A substitute of the name given had set out the day before, with many others freshly come in, and classed together at random, to join a corps actually in the field, only a a few miles beyond the near frontier. Then François and Eugène put their stout horses to their best.

It was the next morning, just after daybreak, that the noise of musketry and cannon reached them on their rapid journey. A short time after, they gained from a height a view of a smart skirmish. French soldiers were in quick retreat over the plain below them. It would be superfluous to go through all the little events which, in rapid succession, brought the brother and sister together. Enough to say that François outstripped even Hortense's lover when he saw her in immediate danger—brought down with a pistol-shot the whiskered and moustached Prussian whose sabre was descending on her head ; and, after delivering her into Eugène's arms, stood his ground in her place, doing his work like a man and a soldier. The change *did* come over him from that moment. He served many campaigns with honor, and returned to his family, holding some rank as an officer.

For Hortense, we repeat, kind English reader, that she yet lives in the brave country in which we now write ; and more, that she wears (whenever she likes) a military decoration, presented to her soon after the facts of her lofty, and yet tender, heroism had become known to her imperial sovereign.

THE WHITE BRISTOL.

THE WHITE BRISTOL.

THE Defiance, a Bristol stage, or, as its numerous officials along the road called it, "The White Bristol," rolled up to the town, at the rate of nine miles an hour, having four "insides," and fourteen "outsides," including a livery servant, rather smuggled, we apprehend, upon the flat of the roof, where he lay at his length, comfortably bedded on a couch of cloaks, great coats, and empty sacks.

It is known to all travellers on the tops of stages—now a large and diversified portion of the English community, embracing every class, from the nobleman to the old-clothes man—that, be the load of "outsides" full or deficient, or overcharged, it invariably divides itself into three companies, each of which can hold little or no intercourse with the other, although the individuals of each may, if they like—and they seldom do—become good friends among themselves. The coachman, and the knowing young gentleman who, before any one else thought of the advantage, "engaged the box-seat," may be regarded as the first of these sets. Detached from their fellow-travellers, they beguile the time with confidential discussions on "the whip," the turf, the ring, the dog that, at any odds, kills two hundred rats in a minute ; or the great cricket-match of "Kent against all England." And, whether from their foremost place upon one of the high-roads of this world, or from a sense of exclusiveness worthy of Willis's dancing-rooms, or that they dislike the considerable trouble of half turning their heads to answer an occasional question from some one behind them, most commonly they gain their journey's end without doing much more than making one another's acquaintance. The close-packed row, occupying the front edge of the roof, from whom, now and then, arise those questions which, good-naturedly, or satisfactorily at least, are seldom resolved, form the second company. But the most numerous party is to be found at the rear of the coach, where a second row of four slip on and off, and off and on, the roof, confronting yet three more human beings, who are half-caged up in semicircular iron bars, which, the morning after a journey, leave a yellow and green mark, and not a comfortable sensation towards the termination of the lumbar vertebræ.

Elevated above the common sublunary level, our little tale begins then, upon the top of the White Bristol, and among a full circle of its back outsides. With its first two sets, cut off from us by the length of the roof, or with the isolated lounger stretched along the flat of that roof, we have nothing to do. But our chosen company—some of them, at least—shall be severally presented to the reader.

In the right of the iron-railed basket-seat, which jutted beyond all other appurtenances of the manifold machine, sat a smart-dressed, smart-faced young man, who, from the certain kind of leering smile that constantly played in his large gray eyes, and round his gaping mouth, seemed to think himself much better than his circle, yet willing to be inwardly amused at their expense. He had a town air, and might be an emissary from some "London house" to a Bristol correspondent, now returning to his desk, after transacting his employer's business.

Next to him, was a young woman of about twenty, holding on her lap a lively infant, just beginning to gabble, in its own occult—though for that reason not vague—language, and to kiss its little hand, and to nod its little head, and to point to novel objects, in admiration or inquiry ; in fact, to go through its first charming intercourse with its kind ; and its first observance of the mute creation which it had been sent here to comprehend, to use, and to enjoy.

At the left of the young woman and her fairy charge, sat a man, perhaps upwards of thirty ; but the rich, embrowned hue of his countenance, betokening long exposure to foreign suns and weather, would probably induce an over-calculation of his age. There was a buoyancy of expression in his rather handsome features, which, according to the world, belonged certainly to early youth ; if, indeed, one did not account for its attendance upon maturer years, by supposing—what his complexion hinted—that he had passed much of his previous life in the camp or on the wave, cut off from worldly mannerism, and preserving, almost untainted, one of the most bountiful gifts of a good Providence—a cheery and hearty disposition. His observers, upon the present occasion, could not decide, however, in which of the capacities alluded to he might have served his country ; for he was as free of military or of naval as he was of social technicality. His plain, peaceful dress also left curiosity at fault. Indeed, considering that the Peninsular contest still went on, and that few who had a right to exhibit warlike costume usually travelled without it, it was highly probable, after all, that he had acquired his foreign complexion without facing peril either of flood or of field. And the rank which, previous to his assent to the basket of the White Bristol, he might have held in general society, further appeared doubtful. Awkward or vulgar he could not be called, in any thing he said or did ; yet, in his way of saying or doing any thing, polished he as surely was not. He *was* polite ; but it was not the politeness of a coterie, nor of a particular country, it was his own, or else, he had picked it up, here and there, in many countries.

Such were the three passengers who, tightly wedged together, filled the basket of the stage. The first of the four who clung to the confronting roof seemed a very young gentleman. He held his head averted from his opposite companions of the road, looking out upon the fields or the sky : he almost turned his back upon his own row ; he dangled one leg over the iron of his perch. His colorless, thin, rigid face, kept itself as imperturbed as if he had been dead, and his lips as compressed as if they had been settled after death. He was obviously an eminent being. And inasmuch as, during the whole journey, he continued to evince his own sense of this superiority in the manner described, he shall henceforward be passed by, just as if, indeed, he had not that day sat on the White Bristol at all, but was really one of the dead-and-one world he seemed so studious of counterfeiting amid the summer sunshine of our living one.

By his side appeared a man almost as young as he ; like him, pointedly averting his eyes from his *vis-à-vis* friends in the basket, and, particularly from the young woman who held the infant ; like him, serious and silent as the grave. He was a decent-clad, respectable-looking young person ; and deep-seated sorrow, or suppressed agitation, instead of stolid assumption, or well-managed superciliousness, characterized *his* taciturnity.

We need say but little of the personage who sat at his left hand. She was a middle-aged, and very fat woman. She held a wicker reticule, of proportions corresponding to herself, in her hand, from under the lid of which peeped the neck of a small green bottle, often applied, with a care-fraught sigh, to her lips. After it had been so applied she always slumbered, or only started into waking existence, shrieking faintly, and clinging to her neighbors, as her dreams vividly pictured the coach in the act of breaking down under her. And of the last passenger of our set, whom she crushed against the barred irons of the roofs, we can say but little. Owing to the point of sight from which we observed the group, we can only avow that a spare-limbed little man was there, who now and then ventured an expostulating look close into the face of the unconscious heap of fat, flesh, and clothes —the noontide incubus—the daymare that oppressed him; or timidly dared to address his opposite neighbor, the supposed "traveller to a house ;" and, in both cases, had nothing for his trouble.

The first individual of our company who, long before the coach started that morning, had mounted behind, was the young woman with the infant. She came quite alone into the inn-yard at Bristol ; and after standing at the wheels some time, and looking timidly and anxiously around her, was at last assisted up by an hostler. The fat woman soon followed, attended by a crowd of friends ; she and they looked bitterly disappointed when the middle seat in the basket appeared already occupied ; but a place on the roof, far away from the irons at either hand, was, after much qualification with a great many soft things, deemed a tolerably good substitute. Up sprang, next, the tropical-faced young man, and flung himself into the first vacancy which caught his eye—namely, that at the young woman's left hand. The moment he was seated he began to chirp and talk to her charge, and to praise its beauty and its liveliness, and to ask its age ; and, when he had been answered, to wonder that there could be so fine and so intelligent a creature of only thirteen months. Shortly, he had it in his arms, and he and it were very good friends, as also, indeed, were he and its young nurse or nursery-maid, although few words or even looks of hers assured him of the fact. While the helpers put the horses to, the dapper youth, mentioned as sitting at the young woman's right hand, clambered up : the little sufferer under the stout lady then crept into his infelicitous nook—he might have chosen better, but he seemed too nervous for the effort ; and the White Bristol rattled out of the inn-yard, yet wanting, among its rear-outsides, two of the party already enumerated.

At the corner of an outlet street, standing alone, with a bundle in his hand, soon appeared the grave or afflicted young man, who afterwards sat between the stout lady and the stupid, affected young man; and now there was a succession of little incidents.

As the coach stopped to pick him up, the young woman glanced down, and immediately started, trembled, and grew pale; then she quickly turned her head, drew a shawl, like an awning, over the baby, and let down a thick green veil over her own face. An instant after, she half rose up and looked around her, as if impulsively anxious to descend and abandon the stage. But a doleful sigh seemed to intimate that, on second thoughts, she must of necessity resign herself to her situation, however disagreeable it might be. As her sole resource, she held her head steadily turned away from the side of the coach at which she had seen the young man standing, and up which she, no doubt, concluded he would climb to the top.

Evidently, the cause of her uneasiness had not yet caught a sight of her. But this was soon to happen, notwithstanding her precautions. Instead of ascending the vehicle at the side which it was natural to think he would prefer, he must have gone round to the other, for some sufficient reason; for she had scarce averted her face to that other side, when *his* closely confronted it, emerging in the space left open for gaining the roof. No one except himself could now see her look, on account of the depth and closeness of her bonnet; but excessive surprise first worked in his features: immediately came a fiery blush, and a dropping of his eye, not so intelligible; then, in his turn, he grew very pale, then wavered in his insecure position, and the White Bristol again rolling off, after Mr. Coachee's mere warning of "hold fast," he must have dropped under its wheels, but that his future companions grappled him by the arms and the collar, and dragged him into his seat. Even the youthful nurse, with a loud catching of breath, stretched out one of her hands, unconsciously it would seem, when she witnessed his emotion, and foresaw his danger. The moment he was in safety, her repelling manner returned; and after many useless glances, he too assumed the grave estrangement of the eye which has before been noticed. This difference there was, however, between their avoidance of one another; hers seemed prompted by dislike, or at least by anger; his, self-imposed by necessity, whatever that necessity might be.

In a short time their unknown feelings towards each other were again called into play.

The coach had proceeded some miles beyond Bristol, when the automaton young gentleman, doomed to fill the now sole vacant place on the roof, hailed it from the avenue gate of an elegant mansion, a short distance off the road. While the White Bristol pulled up for him, and while he mounted it, our sunburnt friend, the early admirer of the engaging infant, suddenly asked the protectress of his favorite, " Is the dear little soul asleep ?"

This question revealed the baby's father at once. We have yet no name for him ; but, at the sound of the words, he jerked round on his seat and fixed his eyes upon the shawl awning, which completely hid even the shape of the child, and which, it became obvious, he had not—from his first agitation, and his averted glances afterwards—suspected, until this moment, of covering the little creature whose intimated presence now so much absorbed him.

The young woman answered, " Yes," to her companion at her left, in a low voice, and without moving. The father had been about to speak ; his lips were shaping the words, his hands were stirring at his sides ; but when he caught her monosyllable, his straining and glowing eyes grew dim and watery, and his person and features became stilled—all except his under lip, and that he drew in to check its spasm. The child's nurse would not yet look in the direction where he sat. In some time he also resumed, with a low, long sigh, the part he, perhaps, thought himself compelled to adopt from the mute dictation of her conduct.

About two hours elapsed, and all our party were silent, and indeed motionless. Except that the young exclusive swung his ramrod leg over the iron of the roof, and that the young woman's sun-tanned neighbor felt her shrink, once or twice, as if to relieve herself of some bodily inconvenience. He looked back to ascertain whether or no the iron of the basket chafed her ; but she sat forward from it and he only detected the left arm of the "commercial traveller" (may we be forgiven if we pertinaciously assign to this young gentleman an unworthy rank and calling?) quickly snatched home from his observation. The White Bristol stopped to change horses, and with a little cry the infant awoke. A second time the father's eyes flashed upon the shawl. The nurse partially uncovered her baby, and evidently would have kept it quiet on her knee. But up it popped its face, now more rosy than ever after a refreshing sleep, and, swinging round, and catching the eye of its late playfellow, crowed in glee, held out its arms, and writhed, nay kicked, to come to him. He put his hands round it, and petitioned to have it ; the young woman

let it go, silently and passively, and the next instant it was clasped
on his father's breast. " For the first time !" mentally remarked
our pleasant-faced friend, who, indeed, had willingly allowed his
new pet to be snatched from him. Then, humming a tune, he
glanced at the mother—for such he at length would have
her be. Still she had not turned her head ; but it was bent on
her hands. Though her bonnet screened her emotion, he felt
from his unavoidable proximity to her, a convulsive shaking of
her frame, which intimated that she wept profuse, though suppressed, tears.

The infant did not like its new acquaintance : his sobs, his
ardent kisses and embraces, had not the charm of the chirping,
the smiles, and the playful fondlings of its first patron ; and it
struggled, and at last cried, to get free. Obviously chagrined,
he tried in vain to conciliate it, calling it twenty pretty names,
and often looking towards its mother as if he hoped she would
at last ask it of him. But even yet she avoided his eye. The
father, with another heavy sigh, passed it to the arm of his opposite fellow-traveller, and quietness once more reigned among our
circle.

The White Bristol had left the city (which has immortalized
itself by rejecting, after having chosen, Edmund Burke as its
parliamentary representative) at ten o'clock. At two, a fierce
July sun played fully upon our travellers. The young woman
grew faint from the heat, and, taking off her shawl, exhibited a
charming figure, and a fair, delicate, taper neck. To protect the
latter from being assimilated with his own complexion, her left
hand neighbor put up an umbrella over her. In this situation
he again felt her shrink and even start, and, glancing across her
shoulders, saw the arm he had before noticed stealing round her
waist.

" You wish the gentleman to keep his arm where it ought to
be ?" he asked, loud enough to be heard by the whole party.

" What arm ? what gentleman ?" seconded the infant's father,
fiercely.

" Nothing incommodes me now, sir, thank you," she said, replying only to the first speaker. The impertinent arm had been
withdrawn.

" And you would rather not be incommoded in future ?"

" Certainly, sir."

" Then I am sure the gentleman will remember"—speaking
over to him.

"He had better, or I will make him remember!" added his ally, bending a hostile glance on (still we hope he is) the commercial scout. At last, the young woman quickly looked up into the speaker's face, plainly, though mutely, remonstrating against any quarrel on her account; and, had he as promptly responded, they would probably have been better friends for the rest of their journey. Though he must have been aware of this decision in his favor, he chose, however, to keep his eyes frowningly fixed on the object of his wrath, perhaps somewhat ostentatious of his zeal in her cause, and inclined to make the most of it while she so closely observed him. But the chidden youth, after one of his leering stares, began to study the beauties of the landscape; and all this being rapidly comprehended by the young woman, she bent her head towards her chest, and allowed her too chivalrous champion to seek her eye, without finding it, at his own convenience.

After daybreak, at about half-past two, next morning, the White Bristol, now within some fourteen miles of the metropolis, approached a spot where our brown-faced friend had told the coachman to set him down. The party shaking off the slumber or the stupor of the short night, engaged themselves in restoring their neglected dress to some degree of good order, suited to the inquisitiveness of "the garish eye of day." The stage stopped at the bottom of a hill, in order that the drag might be taken off its wheel.

"Coachman," said the person we would seem inclined to be most friendly with, "over the next hill, about a mile on, you will see a stile among some trees—put me down there; I have to walk across the fields to the village yonder."

The young woman turned fully round, and gazed into his face.

"Yes, my little queen," he continued, catching up the infant from her knee and kissing it; "good-by—nearest and dearest must part—so, good-by. God bless you, your life-long, ay, with every blessing! (his eyes glistened.) Look, look at yon pretty, taper, little spire, coming up over the green trees—that's my landmark; and 'tis many a long year since I saw it last. Look! is it *not* a pretty thing?"

The infant crowed, and jumped on his lap, and looked and pointed as he looked and pointed, just as if it understood him, or even could discern an object at such a distance.

"Ay, is it. Do you know, fairy, I have seen none half as

pretty ever since I parted with it, though I have seen a good many?"

The child looked down upon the road, and directed his attention to another object. This was a man who sat on a stone by the road-side, his knees widely parted, his elbows resting on them, and his head drooping forward so as to hide his features. A small bundle, having a stick thrust through its knot, lay beside him. Had he appeared standing, his stature must have aproached the gigantic, although his limbs were gaunt and spare. He wore a low-crowned, narrow-brimmed glazed hat, much battered and bruised; coarse linen trousers, tarred, rent, and patched; a bluish shirt-frock, also of some linen or cotton quality, and also soiled, and torn, and here and there clumsily patched. The collar of his check shirt was open; and his bare, brown, bony ankles appeared above very old shoes. He seemed excessively weary, perhaps after walking all night, for the dust of the road covered him from head to foot; or, if he had slept since the sun went down, it might have been in some field by the road, as was intimated by the blades of new hay which adhered to different parts of his person.

"So tired, brother?" asked the infant's friend. The wayworn, or else dogged man, made no answer. At that instant the White Bristol, freed of its drag, resumed its speed, cutting short further efforts to draw him into conversation. But the querist noted that, as the coach whisked by, he arose from the stone, took up his stick and bundle, and seemed to turn his face in the direction opposite to its course.

Shortly after, the infant's mother a third time started more vehemently than she had done before. The two champions, looking at her former persecutor, seemed strongly disposed to be angry, but she interrupted them, saying, in great alarm, "No, no, here behind!" Looking over the back of her seat, she almost screamed at the vision of a great bony hand—from which tar, and other stains, had been but half washed off—perhaps worn off—that appeared grasping the iron rail of the basket, close at her elbow. A louder scream escaped her, when, in reply to her first, a man's face—wasted, though youthful, pale, or rather dingy yellow, though weather-beaten, clouded in coal-black hair, that hung, like ropes, down the cheeks, and surmounted by the old glazed hat just seen upon the road-side—turned upwards, and at only the distance of two or three feet glared its large black eyes into hers. It was, indeed, the tired pedestrian, who, stand-

ing upon a trunk that had been swung in chains at the back of
the coach, underneath, supported himself by holding the basket-
rail with one hand, and some lower stay with the other ; thus
hoping, unnoticed by coachman or passengers, to get himself conveyed a mile or two on his journey.

The infant echoed its mother's scream ; and our party were
thrown into some confusion.

" You had better get down, friend," said the sunburnt traveller.
His former seconder more violently interfered. The owner of the
rawboned, gigantic hand took no notice.

" It seems captious to insist with you," resumed the first
peacemaker ; " and only that you frighten the young woman and
the child, we would not do so ; but come, you really must leave
us more to ourselves."

Still the pertinacious hand showed no sign of relaxing its
gristly gripe, and still no answer was vouchsafed.

"Strike him to the road ?" cried the infant's father.

" Hush, Tom, hush !" said the young woman, in a low voice,
half kind, half commanding.

" Stop," resumed her less boisterous champion, as Tom
(thanks for his name, at last) started up as if to carry into effect
his own advice ; " stop, coachman ! rid us of a fellow who has
got up behind here."

" Take off his castor, sir, and show it the road ; we finds that
always afits them rum uns best," answered coachee, lashing his
horses.

" And a very good way I believe it is, so I'll try it."

Stooping over the seat, he accordingly took off the intruder's
hat, and let it fall on the road. What followed was not to have
been expected. The man's face had been turned downwards ;
now he again turned it up, and darted at our friend a very extraordinary look—or rather, a succession of looks. The first was
hasty, blighting rage ; the next—while his giant fist worked on
the iron—was wild revenge ; then he snatched away his hand—
it was the right—and, clinging to the coach only by the other,
allowed his body to swing back, and it and its arm to knit into
full strength for a destroying blow. A second after, either recollecting that his foe was beyond his reach, or that his own pre-
carious position did not admit of success in his attempt, his
features and attitude changed into a baleful expression of resolved
future vengeance ; his eyes flared less, but it burned deeper ; his
highboned sunken cheeks grew horribly colorless ; his blue lips

parted, showing his set teeth ; his shoulders fell, and his back drawn arm and hand dropped at his side. Some of the spectators laughed, doubtless at the absurdity of such extravagant and impotent anger from such a mean person, and for a provocation so slight, and indeed merited ; but the spectator most concerned did not laugh. He thrilled, as their eyes communed together, if not with alarm, certainly with astonishment ; nay, with interest, too; finally, with admiration. He had often seen the human countenance worked with human passion ; but the intense animal ferocity of that youthful, wasted, and yet finely featured face ; its distinctness ; the deadly frown of those shaggy eyebrows over those beautiful, distorted, devouring eyes ; the mental character that heightened, ennobled the whole—he called it, in his own mind, wonderful and magnificent.

And the tone in which the man at last got out words to syllable his enormous passion well suited the previous eloquence of his countenance; it mastered the noise of the clattering, grinding coach, and the tramping horses ; and yet it was not shrill.

" Rascal !" he said ; " coward ! dog ! I have marked you, till we meet again ! You could not know that, in insulting me, you outraged a man above his present appearance ; but you *saw* me —you saw me ragged, jaded, hungry, and yet a man. And when I would only give my blistered feet a little rest—taking me at a cowardly disadvantage—in every way cowardly—you—you—but no matter : I shall know you another time ! I have looked well at you—ay, marked you, I say, for that other time ! Think of me till it comes !" He recklessly let go his hold of the coach, and was flung by its motion prostrate upon the road.

" Strange, very strange !" mused our friend, his feelings divided between the ludicrousness of the scene—so swelling a result from such a silly cause—and sympathy with the hidden character, the perhaps trampled heart, if not shattered mind, he had roused into morbid fury. Then he recollected that the language addressed to him could not have come from a vulgar man ; and here his own heart smote him, and he anxiously looked back, grieving for the poor fellow's fall. But the coach had gained, and was descending, at the opposite side, the second hill pointed out by himself to the coachman, and the wayfarer could not be seen. " Poor wretch ! perhaps I have, indeed, treated with indignity a spirit not created for its present situation."

His reverie was interrupted by the coach stopping " at the stile among the trees." He snatched a parting kiss from the

baby, wished its mother many blessings, bowed to his other
fellow-travellers, got down, and vaulted over the stile. It had
been arranged that his luggage should go on to the next
town.

In a few moments he only saw the broad, well-beaten path he
had trod so often in childhood, sweeping before him, through
meadows of new hay, down to the umbrageous hollow, in which
rose his beloved spire. "'Tis still the same," he said; "the very
smell of the new-mown hay, and all; see—the stepping-stones
over this little bourne—one, two, three—the identical ones, only
a little worn—and very little, either—not half as much as I am—
ay! the mute, inert things remain the same, while our generations
pass away."

On he bounded; the stile which he had just crossed having
now sunk below the steep, though pleasant, declivity he was descending. The spire, too, seemed to subside gradually into its
rich trees, as he first gained a level with it, and then walked over
ground lower than that upon which it was based. But its top,
still seen, grew more distinct, with its old, well-known features,
its weather slating, its ventilation appertures, its very minute
differences of color : and houses of the little clustering village it
commanded also began to peep out, here and there, through
their embowering foliage.

Tears started to his eyes. He quickened his already quick
pace, and hummed an old song of boyhood to divert them back
again. A wild shout reached -him. He turned ; and along a
narrow path, meeting his at an angle, raced the wayfarer.

Our friend now felt some real alarm, but only such as a brave
man experiences at the prospect of unnatural contest with a
maniac, for such he deemed this frantic person to be. It was a
very early hour, scarce passed three o'clock in the morning. The
place was lonely, too ; and the humble inhabitants of the village
were beyond hail, even if any of them had yet left their beds.
He was unarmed, and though muscular and active, as well as
thoroughly brave, doubted the result of a struggle with the excited strength of the gaunt giant who sought to cope with him.
Not altering his pace, he again looked behind. His enemy was
twice as far from him as he was from the village. He would
walk quicker, and perhaps gain the neighborhood of human beings before they could come in contact. It had occurred to his
mind to imitate his pursuer, and run ; but, whatever might be
the consequences, his spirit disdainfully rejected the idea.

"Stop!" he heard ejaculated at a distance behind him; "stop and face me! Coward!" (when he paid no attention to this command) "you fear to stop! You have insulted me, and you fear me!" At these words he did stop, however, and turned round; and then walked coolly to meet his challenger.

The furious man ran forward at great speed; but he often staggered, as if his strength was failing him; and his broken delivery—for still he spoke—also denoted exhaustion.

"You thought the time I warned you of was not so near at hand—thought, perhaps, that I used idle threats, and that it would never come; but you mistook! And though now—now—it *does* come sooner than I myself hoped, be sure I would have tracked you, mile by mile, day by day—ay, till I fell dead on the road between us, or it *should* have come! Satisfaction for your insult!" he continued, now ending his wild race a few yards from his foe. "Many outrages I have been obliged to bear, but this I will not! You ought to have pistols about you, or else near you. Give me one and take another!"

"I have no such things about me or near me—you are mad to talk such nonsense," he was answered.

"Liar! I should be—I wish I was—mad. But I am not! and you scoff me, because in these rags I demand satisfaction for your ignominious insult? Come, you have something like *this*, at least: hold it in your hand, then!" He drew forth a large pocket-knife.

"Stand off, fellow! I carry no such weapons; nor will I enter into conflict with a maniac. Stand off, I say, at your peril. You vile murderer—you assassin! would you thus attack an unarmed traveller with a butcherly knife!"

"No!" replied the assailant; "I am no cowardly assassin—there goes my weapon"—flinging it far over the hedge. "And now I meet you on equal terms—it is to grapple for life, villain!"

With these words he rushed furiously upon him. But, avoiding his perilous grasp, our friend sprang aside. Clenching his fist, and coolly summoning his strength, he felled him on the grass—where he lay, overcome by exhaustion, as much as stunned by the blow, although it was, indeed, a home one.

The victor, pity and interest still his predominant feelings, resolved to send some friendly aid to the vanquished, and pursued his way to the village. Entering its narrow and straggling street he found greater changes in objects framed by man's hands than he had seen in the features of nature along the meadow path. In one place appeared a new house, where he had expected the familiar face of an old one ; in another arose a human dwelling, where, sixteen years ago, the period of his absence from home, bushes had been growing ; and on many of the little sign-boards above the humble village shops new names were substituted for those to which his boyish eye had been familiar.

His heart fell, as, glancing around, now musing, he walked slowly forward. The echoing of his solitary footsteps through the slumbering village, heightened the sadness of his mood into a feeling of desolation. " I have thought of it by day, and dreamt of it by night, and it is not *old home* to me after all," he said.

Yielding to a heavy foreboding, he now almost feared to place himself before the one well-remembered house, which he had travelled far to enter. He leaned on the swinging stile of the churchyard, that stood between him and it (and how emphatically between him and it he thrilled to think), and gazed up at the old church-steeple. A sudden fancy took him, which he evasively expressed to his own mind—" I will turn in here, and read the headstones to see how many old friends are gone." And on the headstones he found, indeed, most of the names he had missed from the sign-boards. But, at a very humble one he stopped and trembled. It was not higher than his knee, and only bore the inscription—" M. H., 1809, aged 56." They were, however, the initials of his mother's name, and such might be her age, too, four years previously—that is, in 1809. He ran out of the churchyard towards the once decent cottage in which that good mother had (until he last kissed her, and left her to brave the world for their common advantage) been the tutoress of his heart and mind. It was a roofless ruin. He leaned his arm and head against its doorjamb and he wept.

A noise in the street aroused him, and, looking up, he saw a little lame old man wheeling a wheelbarrow, in which were a shovel and a broom. At a glance he recognized "old Master Martin," who, as long as he could remember, used to rise every morning, hours before any one else in the village, to scrape the streets, that he might sell the produce, and live ; and he alone— this decrepit, age-stricken, solitary being, the despised of his own humble community—he, alone, seemed, to the eye of our friend, unchanged in feature, nay, in garb, after the wear and tear of sixteen years. He resolved to speak with Martin ; for still he cherished a doubt of the headstone.

The old man had rested his wheelbarrow, and stood leaning on his broom-handle, attentively eyeing the stranger. They exchanged salutations, and entered into conversation. Recollecting the names he had seen in the churchyard, the traveller—thus introducing his real topic—severally inquired after the persons whom they had once designated, and got an account of their several deaths, and the manner of their deaths. "There was a widow of the name of Martha Hall, too?" continued the querist.

"And so there *was*," replied old Martin, dropping his chin on his breast ; our friend's doubt subsided. "*Her* removal happened just four years ago, come harvest ; and it come about by reason of the first letter she had from from her son Dick, as went after her eldest son to the Hindees, while her daughter Jane was in sarvice in Lon'on, and old Martha herself in the work'se."

"The workhouse? and her little girl in service? how could that be? I have reason to know that her son George regularly sent her remittances, proportioned to his pay, from the time he enlisted as a private soldier till he rose to be adjutant to his regiment. And his very last remittance was considerable, though the former ones were slight."

"*We* know that, too," said Master Martin. "But we know, moreover, that the last money didn't come to hand as soon as it ought to have come ; nor till after Dick Hall went to seek his fortune (a bad one it turned up for him); nor till after little Jane went to Lon'on, and her mother on the parish, and then to the churchyard, just because it didn't."

"And Richard Hall followed his brother to India, more than four years ago, as it appears? And how was his fortune so bad?"

"Why, instead of letting him work his passage out to the Hindees after brother George (that he loved dearly, though he couldn't be said to know him, as why Dick was only in his fourth when George had left us, and the girl only in her second), they pressed him for a man-o'-war's man down on the coast; and took him round the world to fight the French, just wherever they liked ; ay, and gave him the rope's end, I believe, when he wouldn't take to the tar, at the first setting off."

"Good God! bad fortune, indeed, for a lad who had, and has a friend willing and able to help him to a better! His brother often wrote to have his education attended to ; and at twenty he must have been a clever boy."

"The cleverest among us; and the chap had the spirit of a lord; maybe his fault lay on that side. And there came another letter from him t'other day, for his mother, like the first; but as she, poor old soul, was removed, his Uncle Luckhurst opened it, and he said he had just got his discharge at last, and that he would start after it, not waiting for a shilling to help him on the road, to see her and Jane."

"Is Jane Hall still in London?"

"No; poor wench! she has had her own troubles: married a London husband two years ago—a good tradesman, but a wild un. He broke, and ran away from her; and she came down to us, to have her baby; and then she took it with her to Bristol, where she'd got a new place. But we are soon to see her again; her uncle says to-morrow, or next day, if not to-day."

George Hall had reverted, with certain misgivings, to more than one of his late acquaintances of the road, during the narrative of the old chronicler. Now his heart swelled with emotion, as he saw, coming down the street, three of these acquaintances. They were the young woman and her child, and the serious young man to whom, during the journey, she would not speak. At present, however, she leaned on his arm, and he carried her infant. They must have descended from the White Bristol immediately after George Hall, although his bounding speed did not at first allow him to take notice, and the falling ground he traversed soon after caused him to lose sight of "the stile among the trees." Perhaps, too (indeed, it afterwards appeared to be the case), they had tarried some time, just inside the stile, to go through the explanations which, notwithstanding the young woman's determined coldness on the road, ultimately produced the good understanding that seemed re-established between them.

The young woman's eyes met those of George Hall the moment she appeared in the street; and the interest with which they continued to regard each other was probably of a similar kind. She passed him, and proceeded to the door of a house well known to him as his Uncle Luckhurst's. This was the presumptive proof he wanted; and, before she could knock, her brother had made himself known to her.

After their first embrace, and his renewed caresses of his infant favorite, and his salutation of her husband (whom Jane whispered was very contrite and quite a changed man, and had been lately an industrious one, and now brought home proofs of the fact to his wife and child), George Hall led his sister over the crumbling threshold of their former home, seated her on the ruins of a partition wall, which had once bounded their little parlor, and there heard her repetition of old Master Martin's stories. Jane touched lightly on her own sorrows, but wept much while she recounted those of her mother, and even more while she reverted to their brother Richard, whom she endowed with mental and bodily merits, even beyond old Martin's eulogy. At twenty, when he left the village, Richard was the handsomest, tallest, best-hearted, best-learned lad in the whole parish; somewhat too high in his notions, perhaps, but not so, after all, considering the high expectations his brother George had allowed him to form, and the gentleman's education he had sent means to afford him, and for which Richard loved George more than for any other proof of affection. "But God knows how hard usage and great cruelty—too much even for the meanest to bear—may have changed his nature," continued Jane; "and, indeed, in the last letter he sent home, and that Uncle Luckhurst sent to me, there is a bitterness and a sad, sad carelessness of mind, that makes me fear for him."

Their melancholy conversation continued; and George, holding his sister's hand, caused her to rest her head upon his shoulder, while she wept. In this situation they suddenly heard some one jump in through a window-hole at their backs, and come crashing among the rubbish. Before George Hall could stand on his guard, he was overpowered and dragged to the ground, and the revengeful wayfarer held his distorted face to our friend's, keeping him down by the throat, and bending over him, while, amid Jane's shrieks, he cried out, "Soh! here I find you, miscreant,—*here!* and by this woman's side! Jane!" he continued, almost shrieking, as he turned to her, "I knew you this morning at one glance, though, at one glance, you could not know me; but I would not ask you to recollect me, because my rags must have shamed you; and perhaps for another reason—perhaps to watch your conduct with this bully of yours—this scoffing, sneering braggart, who, for *your* smiles—for *your* ruin!"—he bent lower over our prostrate friend, and griped him closer—"for your ruin, for my eternal shame, and for his own destruction, dared to insult your brother!"

Jane redoubled her screams, and clapped her hands, crying, "Richard! Richard!—stop! stop!" Her frenzy did not allow her to say more; but George Hall shook off the young man's gripe with a great effort, and jumped to his feet, as he said, "Yes, Richard, stop! for I, too, am Jane's brother."

Some months following, on the spot where this happened, the two brothers, their sister, her child, and her husband, made a happy family party, at a "housewarming dinner," given by George Hall, after he had built a commodious and handsome house upon the site of the old cottage ; his youngest acquaintance of "The White Bristol" on his knee.

THE STOLEN SHEEP.

THE STOLEN SHEEP.

THE faults of the lower orders of the Irish are sufficiently well known : perhaps their virtues have not been proportionately observed, or recorded for observation. At all events, it is but justice to them, and it cannot conflict with any established policy, or do any one harm, to exhibit them in a more favorable light to their British fellow-subjects, as often as strict truth will permit. In this view the following story is written—the following facts, indeed ; for we have a newspaper report before us, which shall be very slightly departed from, while we make our copy from it.

The Irish plague, called typhus fever, raged in its terrors. In almost every third cabin there was a corpse daily. In every one, without an exception, there was what had made the corpse— hunger. It need not be added that there was poverty, too. The poor could not bury their dead. From mixed motives of self-protection, terror, and benevolence, those in easier circumstances exerted themselves to administer relief in different ways. Money was subscribed (then came England's munificent donation—God prosper her for it!) ; wholesome food, or food as wholesome as a bad season permitted, was provided ; and men of respectability, bracing their minds to avert the danger that threatened themselves, by boldly facing it, entered the infected house, where death reigned almost alone, and took measures to cleanse and purify the close cribbed air, and the rough, bare walls. Before proceeding to our story, let us be permitted to mention some general marks of Irish virtue, which, under those circumstances, we personally noticed. In poverty, in abject misery, and at a short and fearful notice, the poor man died like a Christian. He gave vent to none of the poor man's complaints or invectives against the rich man who had neglected him, or who, he might have supposed, had

16

done so, till it was too late. Except for a glance—and, doubt-less, a little inward pang while he glanced—at the starving and perhaps infected wife, or child, or old parent, as helpless as the child, he blessed God, and died. The appearance of a comforter at his wretched bedside, even when he knew comfort to be use-less, made his heart grateful, and his spasmed lips eloquent in thanks. In cases of indescribable misery—some members of his family lying lifeless before his eyes, or else some dying—stretched upon damp and unclean straw, on an earthen floor, without cor-dial for his lips, or potatoes to point out to a crying infant—of-ten we have heard him whisper to himself (and to Another who heard him), "The Lord giveth, and the Lord taketh away; blessed be the name of the Lord." Such men need not always make bad neighbors.

In the early progress of the fever, before the more affluent roused themselves to avert its career, we cross the threshold of an individual peasant. His young wife lies dead; his second child is dying at her side; he has just sunk into a corner himself, under the first stun of disease, long resisted. The only persons of his family who have escaped contagion, and are likely to es-cape it, are his old father, who sits weeping feebly upon the hob, and his first born, a boy of three or four years, who, standing between the old man's knees, cries also for food.

We visit the young peasant's abode some time after. He has not sunk under "the sickness." He is fast regaining his strength, even without proper nourishment; he can creep out of doors, and sit in the sun. But, in the expression of his sallow and ema-ciated face, there is no joy for his escape from the grave, as he sits there alone, silent and brooding. His father, and his sur-viving child, are still hungry—more hungry, indeed, and more helpless than ever; for the neighbors who had relieved the family with a potato and a mug of sour milk, are now stricken down themselves, and want assistance to a much greater extent than they can give it.

"I wish Mr. Evans' was in the place," cogitated Michaul Car-roll; "a body could spake for'neut him, and not spake for nothin', for all that he's an Englishman; and I don't like the thoughts o' goin' up to the house to the steward's face—it wouldn't turn kind to a body. Maybe he'd soon come home to us, the masther himself."

Another fortnight elapsed. Michaul's hope proved vain. Mr Evans was still in London; though a regular resident on his small Irish estate, since it had come into his possession, business unfortunately—and he would have said so himself—now kept him an unusually long time absent. Thus disappointed, Michaul overcame his repugnance to appear before the "hard" steward. He only asked for work, however. There was none to be had. He turned his slow and still feeble foot into the adjacent town. It was market-day, and he took up his place among the crowd of other claimants for agricultural employment, shouldering a spade, as did each of his comrades. Many farmers came to the well-known "stannin'," and hired men at his right and at his left, but no one addressed Michaul. Once or twice, indeed, touched perhaps by his sidelong looks of beseeching misery, a farmer stopped a moment before him, and glanced over his figure ; but his worn and almost shaking limbs giving little promise of present vigor in the working field, worldly prudence soon conquered the humane feeling which started up towards him in the man's heart, and, with a choking in his throat, poor Michaul saw the arbiter of his fate pass on.

He walked homewards, without having broken his fast that day. "Bud, *musha,* what's the harm o' that," he said to himself; "only here's the ould father, an' *her* pet boy, the weenoch, without a pyntee either. Well, *asthore,* if they can't have the pyatees, they must have betther food—that's all. Ay," he muttered, clenching his hands at his sides, and imprecating fearfully in Irish, "an' so they must."

He left his house again, and walked a good way to beg a few potatoes. He did not come home quite empty-handed. His father and his child had a meal. He ate but a few himself ; and when he was about to lie down in his corner for the night, he said to the old man, across the room, "Don't be a-crying to-night, father—you and the child, there—but sleep well, an' ye'll have the good break'ast afore ye, in the mornin'."

"The good break'ast, *ma-bouchal ?** a-thin, an' where 'ill id come from ?"

"A body promised it to me, father."

"*Avich ?* Michaul, an' sure it's fun you're making of us, now at any rate. Bud, the good-night, *a-chorra,*† an' my blessin' on your head, Michaul. If we keep trust in the good God, an ax his blessin', too, mornin' an' evenin', gettin' up an' lyin' down, He'll be a friend to us, at last. That was always an' ever my word to you, poor boy, since you was the years o' your own

* My boy.   † Term of endearment.

weenoch now fast asleep at my side; an' it's my word to you now, *ma-bouchal;* an' you won't forget id. An' there's one sayin' the same to you, out o' heaven, this night—herself an' her little angel-in-glory, by the hand, Michaul *a-vourneen.*"

Having thus spoken in the fervent and rather exaggerated, though every-day, words of pious allusion of the Irish poor man, old Carroll soon dropped asleep, with his arms round his little grandson, both overcome by an unusually abundant meal. In the middle of the night, he was awakened by a stealthy noise. Without moving, he cast his eyes round the cabin. A small window, through which the moon broke brilliantly, was open. He called to his son, but received no answer. He called again, and again. All remained silent. He arose, and crept to the corner where Michaul had lain down. It was empty. He looked out through the window into the moonlight. The figure of a man appeared at a distance, just about to enter a pasture field belonging to Mr. Evans.

The old man leaned his back against the wall of the cabin, trembling with sudden and terrible misgivings. With him, the language of virtue, which we have heard him utter, was not cant. In early prosperity, in subsequent misfortunes, and in his late and present excess of wretchedness, he had never swerved in practice from the spirit of his own exhortations to honesty before men, and love for, and dependence upon, God, which, as he has truly said, he had constantly addressed to his son, since his earliest childhood. And, hitherto, that son had, indeed, walked by his precepts, further assisted by a regular observance of the duties of his religion. Was he now about to turn into another path? to bring shame on his father, in his old age? to put a stain on their family and their name—"the name that a rogue or a bould woman never bore," continued old Carroll, indulging in some of the pride and egotism for which an Irish peasant is, under his circumstances, remarkable. And then came the thought of the personal peril incurred by Michaul; and his agitation, incurred by the feebleness of age, nearly overpowered him.

He was sitting on the floor, shivering like one in an ague-fit, when he heard steps outside the house. He listened; and they ceased. But the familiar noise of an old barn-door creaking on its crazy hinges came on his ear. It was now day-dawn. He dressed himself; stole out cautiously; peeped into the barn, through a chink of the door; and all he feared met full ccufir mation. There, indeed, sat Michaul, busily and earnestly engaged, with a frowning brow and a haggard face, in quartering the animal he had stolen from Mr. Evans's field.

The sight sickened the father—the blood on his son's hands, and all. He was barely able to keep himself from falling. A fear, if not a dislike, of the unhappy culprit also came upon him. His unconscious impulse was to re-enter their cabin unperceived, without speaking a word. He succeeded in doing so ; and then he fastened the door again, and undressed, and resumed his place beside his innocent little grandson.

About an hour after, Michaul came in cautiously through the still open window, and also undressed and reclined on his straw, after glancing towards his father's bed, who pretended to be asleep.

At the usual time for arising, old Carroll saw him suddenly jump up, and prepare to go abroad. He spoke to him, leaning on his elbow.

" An' what *bollg** is on you, *ma-bouchal ?"*

" Going for the good break'ast I promised you, father dear."

" An' who's the good Christian 'ill give id to us, Michaul."

" Oh, you'll know that soon, father ; now, a good-by ;" he hurried to the door.

" A good-by, then, Michaul ; bud, tell me, what's that on your hand ?"

" No—nothin'," stammered Michaul, changing color, as he hastily examined the hand himself. " Nothin' is on id ; what could there be ?" Nor was there, for he had very carefully removed all evidence of gilt from his person ; and the father's question was asked upon grounds distinct from any thing he then saw.

" Well, *avich,* an sure I didn't say any thing was on it wrong; or any thing to make you look so quare, an' spake so sthrange to your father, this mornin'. Only I'll ax you, Michaul, over agin, who has tuk such a sudd'n likin' to us, to send us the good break'ast ? an' answer me sthraight, Michaul. What is it to be, that you call it so *good ?"*

" The good mate, father." He was again passing the threshold.

" Stop !" cried his father ; " stop, and turn forn'ent me. Mate ? —the good mate ? What 'ud bring mate into our poor house,

* What are you about ?

Michaul ?   Tell me, I bid you again, an' again, who is to give
id to you ?"

"Why, as I said afore, father, a body that—"

"A body that thieved it, Michaul Carroll !" added the old
man—as his son hesitated—walking close up to the culprit ; "a
body that thieved id, an' no other body.   Don't think to blind
me, Michaul.   I am ould, to be sure ; but sense enough is left
in me to look round among the neighbors, in my own mind, and
know that none of 'em, that has the will, has the power to send
us the mate for our break'ast, in an honest way.   An' I don't
say, outright, that you had the same thought wid me, when you
consented to take it from a thief.   I don't mean to say that
you'd go to turn a thief's receiver, at this hour o' your life,
an' afther growin' up from a boy to a man widout bringin' a spot
o' shame on yourself, or on your weenock, or on one of us.   No;
I won't say that.   Your heart was scalded, Michaul, and your
mind was darkened, for a start ; an' the thought o' getting comfort for the ould father, an' for the little son, made you consent
in a hurry, widout lookin' well afore you, or widout lookin up to
your good God."

"Father, father, let me alone !   don't spake them words to
me," interrupted Michaul, sitting on a stool, and spreading his
large and hard hands over his face.

"Well, thin, an' I won't, *avich*, I won't ; nothin' to throuble
you sure ; I didn't mean id.   Only this, *a-vourneen*, don't bring
a mouthful o' the bad, unlucky victuals into this cabin.   The
pyatees, the wild berries o' the bush, the wild roots o' the earth,
will be sweeter to us, Michaul ; the hunger itself will be
sweeter ; an' when we give God thanks, afther our poor meal,
or afther no meal at all, our hearts will be lighter, and our
hopes for to-morrow sthronger, *avich-ma-chree*, than if we faist
ed on the fat o' the land, but couldn't ax a blessin' on our faist."

"Well, thin, *I* won't either, father ;   I won't ;   an' sure you
have your way now.   I'll only go out, a little while from you,
to beg ; or else, as you say, to root down in the ground, with
my nails, like a baste-brute, for our break'ast."

"My vourneen you are, Michaul, an' my blessin' on your head;
yes, to be sure, *avich*, beg, an' I'll beg wid you.   Sorrow a
shame is in that ; no but a good deed, Michaul, when it is done
to keep us honest.   So come, we'll go among the Christians, together.   Only, before we go, Michaul, my dear son, tell me—.
tell me one thing."

"What, father?" Michaul began to suspect.

"Never be afraid to tell me, Michaul Carroll, *ma-bouchal!* I won't—I can't be angry wid you now. You are sorry, an' your Father in heaven forgives you, and so do I. But you know, *avich*, there would be danger in quitting the place without hiding well every scrap of any thing that could tell on us."

"Tell on us! What can tell on us?" demanded Michaul; "what's in the place to tell on us?"

"Nothin' in the cabin, I know, Michaul; but—"

"But, what, father?"

"Have you left nothin' in the way, out there?" whispered the old man, pointing towards the barn.

"Out there? Where? What? What do you mean at all, now, father? Sure you know it's your own sef has kept me from as much as layin' a hand on it."

"Ay, to-day-mornin'; but you laid a hand on it last night, *avich*, an' so—"

"*Curp-an dhoul!*" imprecated Michaul; "this is too bad, at any rate ; no, I didn't—last night, or any other night. Let me alone, I bid you, father."

"Come back again, Michaul," commanded old Carroll, as the son once more hurried to the door ; and his words were instantly obeyed. Michaul, after a glance abroad, and a start, which the old man did not notice, paced to the middle of the floor, hanging his head, and saying, in a low voice, "Hushth now, father—it's time."

"No, Michaul, I will not hushth ; an' it's not time. Come out with me to the barn."

"Hushth !" repeated Michaul, whispering sharply. He had glanced sideways to the square patch of strong, moving sunlight on the ground of the cabin, defined there by the shape o' the open door, and saw it intruded upon by the shadow of man's bust, leaning forward in an earnest posture.

'Is id in your mind to go back into your sin, Michaul, an' tell me you were not in the barn, at daybreak, the mornin?" asked his father, still unconscious of a reason for silence.

"Arrah, hushth, ould man !" Michaul made a hasty sign towards the door, but was disregarded.

"I saw you in id," pursued old Carroll, sternly ; "ay, an' at your work in id, too."

"What's that you're sayin', ould Peery Carroll?" demanded a well-known voice.

"Enough to hang his son," whispered Michaul to his father, as Mr. Evans's land-steward, followed by his herdsman and two policemen, entered the cabin. In a few minutes afterwards the policemen had in charge the dismembered carcass of the sheep, dug up out of the floor of the barn, and were escorting Michaul, handcuffed, to the county jail, in the vicinity of the next town. They could find no trace of the animal's skin, though they sought attentively for it; and this seemed to disappoint them and the steward a good deal.

From the moment that they entered the cabin till their departure, old Carroll did not speak a word. Without knowing it, as it seemed, he sat down on his straw bed, and remained staring stupidly around him, or at one or other of its visitors. When Michaul was about to leave the wretched abode, he paced quickly towards his father, and holding out his ironed hands, and turning his cheek for a kiss, said, smiling miserably, "God be wid you, father dear." Still the old man was silent, and the prisoner and all his attendants passed out on the road. But it was then the agony of old Carroll assumed a distinctness. Uttering a fearful cry, he snatched up his still sleeping little grandson, ran, with the boy in his arms, till he overtook Michaul; and, kneeling down before him in the dust, said, "I ax pardon o' you, *avich*; wont you tell me I have id, afore you go? an' here, I've brought little Peery for you to kiss; you forgot *him, a-vourneen.*"

"No, father, I didn't," answered Michaul, as he stooped to kiss the child; "an' get up, father, get up; my hands are not my own, or I wouldn't let you do that, afore your son. Get up, there's nothin' for you to throuble yourself about—that is, I mean, I have nothin' to forgive you; no, but every thing to be thank-ful for, and to love you for; you were always an' ever the good father to me; an'"—the many strong and bitter feelings which till now he had almost perfectly kept in, found full vent, and poor Michaul could not go on. The parting from his father, however, so different from what it had promised to be, comforted him. The old man held him in his arms, and wept on his neck. They were separated with difficulty.

Peery Carroll, sitting on the road-side, after he lost sight of the prisoner, and holding his screaming grandson on his knees, thought the cup of his trials was full. By his imprudence, he had fixed the proof of guilt on his own child; that reflection was enough for him; and he could indulge it only generally. But he was yet to conceive exactly in what a dilemma he had involved himself, as well as Michaul. The policemen came back to compel his appearance before the magistrate ; and when the little child had been disposed of in a neighboring cabin, he understood, to his consternation and horror, that he was to be the chief witness against the sheep-stealer. Mr. Evans's steward knew well the meaning of the words he had heard him say in the cabin, and that, if compelled to swear all he was aware of, no doubt would exist of the criminality of Michaul in the eyes of a jury. "'Tis a sthrange thing to ax a father to do," muttered Peery, more than once, as he proceeded to the magistrate's ; "it's a very sthrange thing."

The magistrate proved to be a humane man. Notwithstanding the zeal of the steward and the policemen, he committed Michaul for trial, without continuing to press the hesitating and bewildered old Peery into any detailed evidence ; his nature seemed to rise against the task, and he said to the steward, " I have enough of facts for making out a committal ; if you think the father will be necessary on the trial, subpoena him."

The steward objected that Peery would abscond, and demanded to have him bound over to prosecute, on two sureties, solvent and respectable. The magistrate assented ; Peery could name no bail ; and consequently he also was marched to prison, though prohibited from holding the least intercourse with Michaul.

The assizes soon came on. Michaul was arraigned ; and, during his plea of "not guilty," his father appeared, unseen by him, in the jailor's custody, at the back of the dock, or rather in an inner dock. The trial excited a keen and painful interest in the court, the bar, the jury-box, and the crowds of spectators. It was universally known that a son had stolen a sheep, partly to feed a starving father ; and that, out of the mouth of the father, it was now sought to condemn him. "What will the old man do ?" was the general question which ran through the assembly. And while few of the lower orders could contemplate the possibility of his swearing to the truth, many of their betters scarce hesitated to make out for him a case of natural necessity to swear falsely.

The trial began. The first witness, the herdsman, proved the loss of the sheep, and the finding the dismembered carcass in the old barn. The policemen and the steward followed to the same effect, and the latter added the allusions which he had heard the father make to the son, upon the morning of the arrest of the latter. The steward went down from the table. There was a pause, and complete silence, which the attorney for the prosecution broke by saying to the crier, deliberately, " Call Peery Carroll."

" Here, sir," immediately answered Peery, as the jailor led him by a side-door out of the back dock to the table. The prisoner started round ; but the new witness against him had passed for an instant into the crowd.

The next instant, old Peery was seen ascending the table, as-sisted by the jailor, and by many other commiserating hands near him. Every glance fixed on his face. The barristers look-ed wistfully up from their seats round the table ; the judge put a glass to his eye and seemed to study his features atten-tively. Among the audience there ran a low but expressive murmur of pity and interest.

Though much emaciated by confinement, anguish, and sus-pense, Peery's cheeks had a flush, and his weak, blue eyes glit-tered. The half-gaping expression of his parched and haggard lips was miserable to see. Yet he did not tremble much, nor appear so confounded as upon the day of his visit to the magis-trate.

The moment he stood upright on the table, he turned himself fully to the judge, without a glance towards the dock.

" Sit down, sit down, poor man," said the judge.

" Thanks to you, my lord, I will," answered Peery, " only, first, I'd ax you to let me kneel, for a little start." He accord-ingly did kneel, and after bowing his head, and forming the sign of the cross on his forehead, he looked up, and said, " My Judge in heaven above, 'tis you I pray to keep me in my duty, afore my earthly judge, this day. Amen!" Then repeating the sign of the cross, he seated himself.

The examination of the witness commenced, and humanely proceeded as follows (the counsel for the prosecution taking no notice of the superfluity of Peery's answers) :

" Do you know Michaul or Michael Carroll, the prisoner at the bar ?"

" Afore that night, sir, I believed I knew him well ; every thought of his mind, every bit of the heart in his body. Afore that night, no living crature could throw a word at Michaul Carroll, or say he ever forgot his father's rearin', or his love of his good God. Sure the people are afther tellin' you by this time, how it came about that night ; an' you, my lord, an' ye, gintlemen, an' all good Christians that hear me—here I am, to help to hang him—my own boy, and my only one. But for all that, gintlemen, ye ought to think of it. 'Twas for the weenoch and the ould father that he done it. Indeed an'deed, we hadn't a pyatee in the place ; an' the sickness was among us, a start afore ; it took the wife from him an' another baby ; an' id had himself down, a week or so beforehand ; an' all that day he was looking for work, but couldn't get a hand's turn to do. An' that's the way it was. Not a mouthful for me an' little Peery. More betoken, he grew sorry for id in the mornin', an' promised me not to touch a scrap of what was in the barn—ay, long afore the steward an' the peelers came on us—but was willin' to go among the neighbors an' beg our breakfast, along wid myself, from door to door, sooner than touch it."

"It is my painful duty," resumed the barrister, when Peery would at length cease, "to ask you for closer information. You saw Michael Carroll in the barn that night ?"

"*Musha*—the Lord pity him an' me !—I did, sir."

"Doing what ?"

"The sheep between his hands," answered Peery, dropping his head, and speaking almost inaudibly.

"I must still give you pain, I fear. Stand up ; take the crier's rod, and if you see Michael Carroll in court, lay it on his head."

"*Och, musha, musha*, sir, don't ax me to do that !" pleaded Peery, rising, wringing his hands, and, for the first time, weeping. "Och, don't, my lord, don't, and may your own judgment be favorable the last day !"

"I am sorry to command you to do it, witness ; but you must take the rod," answered the judge, bending his head close to his notes, to hide his own tears. At the same time, many a veteran barrister rested his forehead on the edge of the table. In the body of the court were heard sobs.

"Michaul, *avich !* Michaul, *a corra-ma-chree !*" exclaimed Peery, when at length he took the rod, and faced round to his son. "Is id your father they make to do it, *ma-bouchal ?*"

"My father does what is right," answered Michaul, in Irish. The judge immediately asked to have his words translated ; and when he learned their import, regarded the prisoner with satisfaction.

"We rest here, my lord," said the counsel, with the air of a man freed from a painful task.

The judge instantly turned to the jury-box.

"GENTLEMEN OF THE JURY—That the prisoner at the bar
stole the sheep in question, there can be no shade of moral doubt.
But you have a very peculiar case to consider. A son steals a
sheep that his own famishing father and his own famishing son
may have food. His aged parent is compelled to give evidence
against him here for the act. The old man virtuously tells the
whole truth, before you and me. He sacrifices his natural feelings—and we have seen that they are lively—to his honesty, and
to his religious sense of the sacred obligations of an oath. Gentlemen, I will pause to observe that the old man's conduct is strikingly
exemplary, and even noble. It teaches all of us a lesson. Gentlemen, it is not within the province of a judge to censure the
rigor of the proceedings which have sent him before us. But I
venture to anticipate your pleasure that, notwithstanding all the
evidence given, you will be enabled to acquit the old man's son,
the prisoner at the bar. I have said there cannot be the shade
of a moral doubt that he has stolen the sheep, and I repeat the
words. But, gentlemen, there is a legal doubt, to the full benefit of which he is entitled. The sheep has not been identified.
The herdsman could not venture to identify it (and it would have
been strange if he could) from the dismembered limbs found in
the barn. To his mark on its skin, indeed, he might have posi-
tively spoken ; but no skin has been discovered. Therefore, according to the evidence, and you have sworn to decide by that
alone, the prisoner is entitled to your acquittal. Possibly, now
that the prosecutor sees the case in its full bearing, he may be
pleased with this result."

While the jury, in evident satisfaction, prepared to return their
verdict, Mr. Evans, who had but a moment before returned home,
entered the court, and becoming aware of the concluding words of
the judge, expressed his sorrow aloud, that the prosecution had
ever been undertaken ; that circumstances had kept him unin-
formed of it, though it had gone on in his name. And he begged
leave to assure his lordship that it would be his future effort to
keep Michaul Carroll in his former path of honesty, by finding him
honest and ample employment, and, as far as in him lay, to reward the virtue of the old father.

While Peery Carroll was laughing and crying in a breath, in
the arms of his delivered son, a subscription commenced by the bar,
was mounting into a considerable sum for his advantage.

THE END OF THE STOLEN SHEEP

THE PUBLICAN'S DREAM.

THE PUBLICAN'S DREAM.

THE fair-day had passed over in a little straggling town in the southeast of Ireland, and was succeeded by a languor proportioned to the wild excitement it never failed to create. But of all in the village, its publicans suffered most under the reaction of great bustle. Few of their houses appeared open at broad noon ; and some—the envy of their competitors—continued closed even after that late hour. Of these latter, many were of the very humblest kind ; little cabins, in fact, skirting the outlets of the village, or standing alone on the road-side, a good distance beyond it.

About two o'clock upon the day in question, a house of "Entertainment for Man and Horse," the very last of the description noticed, to be found between the village and the wild tract of mountain country adjacent to it, was opened by the proprietress, who had that moment arisen from bed.

The cabin consisted of only two apartments, and scarce more than nominally even of two ; for the half-plastered wicker and straw partition, which professed to cut off a sleeping nook from the whole area inclosed by the clay walls, was a little higher than a tall man ; and, moreover, chinky and porous in many places. Let the assumed distinction be here allowed to stand, however, while the reader casts his eyes around what was sometimes called the kitchen, sometimes the tap-room, sometimes the "dancing-flure." Forms, which had run by the walls, and planks, by way of tables, which had been propp'd before them, were turned topsy-turvy, and, in some instances, broken. Pewter-pots and pints, battered and bruised, or squeezed together and flattened, and fragments of twisted glass tumblers lay beside them. The clay floor was scraped with brogue-nails, and indented with the heel of that primitive foot-gear, in token of the energetic dancing which had lately been performed upon it. In a corner still ap-

peared (capsized, however) an empty eight-gallon beer barrel, recently the piper's throne, whence his bag had blown forth the
inspiring storm of jigs and reels, which prompted to more antics
than ever did a bag of the laughing-gas. Among the yellow turf-
ashes of the hearth lay, on its side, an old blackened tin kettle,
without a spout—a principal utensil in brewing scalding water
'or the manufacture of whiskey punch; its soft and yet warm bed
vas shared by a red cat, who had stolen in from his own orgies,
hrough some cranny, since daybreak. The single four-paned
window of the apartment remained veiled by its rough shutter,
that turned on leather hinges; but down the wide yawning
chimney came sufficient light to reveal the objects here described.

The proprietress opened her back-door. She was a woman of
about forty; of a robust, large-boned figure, with broad, rosy
visage, dark, handsome eyes, and well-cut nose. After a look
abroad, to inhale the fresh air, and then a remonstrance (ending
in a kick) with the hungry pig, who ran, squeaking and grunting,
to demand his long-deferred breakfast, she settled her cap, rubbed
down her *prauskeen* (coarse apron), tucked and pinned up her
skirts behind, and saying, in a loud, commanding voice, as she
spoke into the sleeping-chamber, "Get up now, at once, Jer, I
bid you"—vigorously, if not tidily, set about putting her tavern
to rights.

During her bustle, the dame would stop an instant, and bend
her ear to listen for a stir inside the partition; but at last losing
patience, she resumed—

"Why, then, my heavy hatred on you, Jer Mulcahy; is it gone
into a *surouun* (pleasant drowsiness) you are, over again? Or
maybe you stole out of bed, an' put your hand on one o' them
ould good-for-nothing books, that makes you the laziest man
that a poor woman ever had under one roof wid her? Ay, an'
that sent you out of our dacent shop an' house in the heart of
the town below, an' banished us here, Jer Mulcahy, to sell drams
o' whiskey and pots o' beer to all the riffraff o' the counthry-side,
instead o' the nate boots an' shoes you served your honest time
to?" She entered his, or her chamber, rather, hoping that she
might detect him luxuriantly perusing in bed one of the mutilated
books, a love of which (or, more truly, a love of indolence, thus
manifesting itself) had indeed chiefly caused his downfall in the
world. Her husband, however, really tired after his unusual
bodily efforts of the previous day, only slumbered, as Mrs.

Mulcahy had at first anticipated ; and when she had shaken and aroused him, for the twentieth time that morning, and scolded him until the spirit-broken blockhead whimpered, nay, wept, or pretended to weep, the dame returned to her household duties.

She did not neglect, however, to keep calling to him every half-minute, until at last, Mr.Jeremiah Mulcahy strode into the kitchen, a tall, ill-contrived figure, that had once been well-fitted out, but that now wore its old skin, like its old clothes, very loosely; and those old clothes were a discolored, threadbare, half-polished ker-seymere pair of trowsers, and an aged superfine black coat, the last relics of his former Sunday finery ; to which had recently and incongruously been added a calf-skin vest, a pair of of coarse sky-blue peasant's stockings, and a pair of brogues. His hanging cheeks and lips told his present bad living and domestic subjection ; and an eye that had been blinded by the small-pox, wore neither patch nor band ; although, in better days, it used to be genteelly hidden from remark—an assumption of consequence now deemed incompatible with his altered condition in society.

"Oh, Cauth ! oh, I had such a dhrame," he said, as he made his appearance.

"An' I'll go bail you had," answered Cauth ; "an' when do you ever go asleep without having one dhrame or another, that pesters me off my legs, the livelong day, till the night falls again to let you have another? Musha, stop, Jer, don't be ever an' always such a fool. Never mind the dhrame now, but lend a hand to help me in the work o' the house. See the pewther there. Have it up, man alive, and take it out into the garden, an' sit on the big stone, in the sun, an' make it look as well as you can, afther the ill usage it got last night. Come, hurry, Jer—go and do what I bid you."

He retired in silence to "the garden," a little patch of ground luxuriant in potatoes and a few cabbages. Mrs. Mulcahy pur-sued her work till her own sensations warned her that it was time to prepare her husband's morning or rather day meal ; for by the height of the sun, it should now be many hours past noon. So she put down her pot of potatoes; and when they were boiled, took out a wooden trencher full of them, and a mug of sour milk, to Jer, determined not to summon him from his useful occupa-tion of restoring the pints and quarts to something of their former shape.

Stepping through the back-door, and getting him in view, she stopped short, in silent anger. His back was turned to her, that it might enjoy the warmth of the sunshine ; and while the vessels, huddled about in confusion, seemed little the better of his latent skill and industry, there he sat on his favorite round stone, studiously perusing, half-aloud to himself, some idle volume which, doubtless, he had smuggled out into the garden in his pocket. Laying down her trencher and her mug, Mrs. Mulcahy stole forward on tiptoe, gained his shoulder without being heard, snatched the imperfect bundle of soiled pages out of his hand, and hurled it into a neighbor's cabbage bed.

Jeremiah complained, in his usual half-crying tone, declaring that "she never could let him alone, so she couldn't ; and he would rather list for a soger, than lade such a life, from year's end to year's end—so he would."

"Well, an' do then ; an' whistle that idle cur off wid you," pointing to a nondescript puppy, which had lain happily coiled up at his master's feet until Mrs. Mulcahy's appearance, but that now watched her closely, his ears half-cocked, and his eyes wide open, though his position remained unaltered. "Go along to the divil, you lazy whelp, you !" She took up a pint, in which a few drops of beer remained since the previous night, and drained it on the puppy's head, who instantly ran off, jumping sideways, and yelping as loud as if some bodily injury had really visited him :

"Yes ; an' now you begin to yowl, like your masther, for nothing at all, only because a body axes you to stir your idle legs. Hould your tongue, you foolish baste !"—she stooped for a stone—"one would think I scalded you."

"You know you did once, Cauth, to the backbone ; an' small blame for Shuffle to be afeard of you ever since," said Jer.

This vindication of his own occasional remonstrances, as well as Shuffle's, was founded in truth. When very young, just to keep him from running against her legs, while she was busy over the fire, Mrs. Mulcahy had certainly emptied a ladleful of boiling potato water upon the poor puppy's back; and from that moment it was only necessary to spill a drop of the coldest possible water, or of any cold liquid, on any part of his body, and he believed he was again dreadfully scalded, and ran out of the house, screaming in all the fancied throes of torture.

"Will you ate your good dinner now, Jer Mulcahy, an' promise to do something to help me afther it ? Mother o' Saints !"— thus she interrupted herself, turning to the place where she had deposited the eulogized food—"see that, you unlucky · bird !

May I never do an ill turn, but there's the pig afther spilling the sweet milk, an' now shovelling the beautiful white-eyes* down her throat, at a mouthful!"

Jer, really afflicted at this scene, promised to work hard, the moment he got his dinner, and his spouse, first procuring a pitchfork to beat the pig into her sty, prepared a fresh meal for him, and retired to eat her own in the house, and then to continue her labor.

In about an hour, she bethought of paying Jer another visit or inspection, when his voice reached her ear, calling out in disturbed accents, "Cauth! Cauth! a-vourneen! For the love o' Heaven, Cauth! where are you?"

Running to him, she found her husband sitting upright, though not upon his round stone, amongst the still untouched heap of pots and pints, his pock-marked face very pale, his single eye staring, his hands clasped and shaking, and moisture on his forehead.

"What!" she cried, "the pewther just as I left it, over again!"

"Oh, Cauth! Cauth! don't mind that now; but spake to me kind, Cauth, an' comfort me."

"Why, what ails you, Jer, a-vourneen?" affectionately taking his hand, when she saw how really agitated he was.

"Oh, Cauth, oh, I had such a dhrame, now, in earnest, at any rate!"

"A dhrame!" she repeated, letting go his hand, "a dhrame, Jer Mulcahy! So, afther your good dinner, you go for to fall asleep, Jer Mulcahy, just to be ready wid a new dhrame for me, instead of the work you came out here to do, five blessed hours ago!"

"Don't scould me now, Cauth; don't, a-pet; only listen to me, an' then say what you like. You know the lonesome little glen, between the hills, on the short cut, for man or horse, to Kilbroggan? Well, Cauth, there I found myself in the dhrame; and I saw two sailors, tired afther a day's hard walking, sitting before one of the big rocks that stand upright in the wild place. An' they were ating or dhrinking, I couldn't make out which; an' one was a tall, sthrong, broad-showldered man, an' the other was sthrong, too, but short an' burly. While they were talking very civilly to each other, lo an' behould you, Cauth, I seen the tall

* Pieces of potato.

man whip his knife into the little man. An' then they both sthruggled, and wrastled, an' schreeched together till the rocks rung again. But at last the little man was a corpse ; an' may I never see sight o' glory, Cauth, but all this was afore me as plain as you are in this garden! an' since the hour I was born, Cauth, I never got such a fright; an'—oh, Cauth, what's that now?"

" What is it, you poor fool, you, but a customer, come at last into the kitchen—an' time for us to see the face o' one this blessed day. Get up out o' that, wid your dhrames ; don't you hear 'em knocking? I'll stay here to put one vessel at laste to rights, for I see I must."

Jeremiah arose, groaning, and entered the cabin through the back-door. In a few seconds he hastened to his wife, more terror-stricken than he had left her, and settling his loins against the low garden-wall, stared at her.

" Why, then, dhoul's in you, Jer Mulcahy (saints forgive me for cursing !) and what's the matter with you, at-all-at-all?"

" They're in the kitchen," he whispered.

" Well, an' what will they take ?"

" I spoke never a word to them, Cauth, nor they to me ; I couldn't, an' I won't for a duke's ransom ; I only saw them stannin' together, in the dark that's coming on, behind the dour, and I knew them at the first look—the tall one, and the little one."

With a flout at his dreams, and his cowardice, and his good-for-nothingness, the dame hurried to serve her customers. Jeremiah heard her loud voice addressing them, and their hoarse tones answering. She came out again for two pints to draw some beer, and commanded him to follow her, and " discoorse the customers." He remained motionless. She returned in a short time, and fairly drove him before her into the house.

He took a seat remote from his guests, with difficulty pronouncing the ordinary words of " God save ye, genteels," which they bluffly and heartily answered. His glances towards them were also few ; yet enough to inform him that they conversed together like friends, pledging healths and shaking hands. The tall sailor abruptly asked him how far it was, by the short cut, to a village where they proposed to pass the night—Kilbroggan. Jeremiah started on his seat, and his wife, after a glance and a grumble at him, was obliged to speak for her husband. They finished their beer ; paid for it ; put up half a loaf, and a cut of bad, watery cheese, saying that they might feel more hungry a few miles on than they now did; and then they arose to leave the cabin. Jeremiah glanced in great trouble around. His wife had fortunately disappeared; he snatched up his old hat, and, with more energy than he could himself remember, ran forward, to be a short way on the road before them. They soon approached him; and then, obeying a conscientious impulse, Jeremiah saluted the smaller of the two, and requested to speak with him apart. The sailor, in evident surprise, assented. Jer vaguely cautioned him against going any further that night, as it would be quite dark by the time he should get to the mountain pass, on the by-road to Kilbroggan. His warning was made light of. He grew more earnest, asserting, what was not the fact, that it was "a bad road," meaning one infested by robbers. Still the bluff tar paid no attention, and was turning away. "Oh, sir; oh, stop, sir," resumed Jeremiah, taking great courage, "I have a thing to tell you;" and he rehearsed his dream, averring that, in it, he had distinctly seen the present object of his solicitude set upon and slain by his colossal companion. The listener paused a moment, first looking at Jer, and then at the ground, very gravely; but the next moment he burst into a loud, and, Jeremiah thought, frightful laugh, and walked rapidly to overtake his shipmate. Jeremiah, much oppressed, returned home.

Towards dawn, next morning, the publican awoke in an ominous panic, and aroused his wife to listen to a loud knocking, and a clamor of voices at their door. She insisted there was no such thing, and scolded him for disturbing her sleep. A renewal of the noise, however, convinced even her incredulity, and showed that Jeremiah was right for the first time in his life at least. Both arose, and hastened to answer the summons.

When they unbarred the front-door, a gentleman, surrounded by a crowd of people of the village, stood before it. He had discovered on the by-road through the hills from Kilbroggan, a dead body, weltering in its gore, and wearing sailor's clothes; had ridden on, in alarm; had raised the village; and some of its population, recollecting to have seen Mrs. Mulcahy's visitors of the previous evening, now brought him to her house to hear what she could say on the subject.

Before she could say any thing, her husband fell senseless at her side, groaning dolefully. While the bystanders raised him, she clapped her hands, and exalted her voice in ejaculations, as Irishwomen, when grieved, or astonished, or vexed, usually do.

Now as proud of Jeremiah's dreaming capabilities, as she had before been impatient of them, she rehearsed his vision of the murder, and authenticated the visit of the two sailors to her house, almost while he was in the act of making her the confidant of his prophetic ravings. The auditors stepped back in consternation, crossing themselves, smiting their breasts, and crying out, "The Lord save us! The Lord have mercy upon us!"

Jeremiah slowly awoke from his swoon. The gentleman who had discovered the body commanded his attendance back to the lonesome glen, where it lay. Poor Jeremiah fell on his knees, and, with tears streaming down his cheeks, prayed to be saved from such a trial. His neighbors almost forced him along.

All soon gained the spot, a narrow pass between slanting piles of displaced rocks; the hills from which they had tumbled rising brown and barren, and to a great height above and beyond them. And there, indeed, upon the strip of verdure which formed the winding road through the defile, lay the corpse of one of the sailors who had visited the publican's house the evening before.

Again Jeremiah dropped on his knees, at some distance from the body, exclaiming, "Lord save us! Yes! oh, yes, neighbors, this is the very place. Only—the saints be good to us, again! 'Twas the tall sailor I seen killing the little sailor, and here's the tall sailor murthered by the little sailor!"

"Dhrames go by conthraries, some way or another," observed one of his neighbors; and Jeremiah's puzzle was resolved.

Two steps were now indispensable to be taken: the county coroner should be summoned, and the murderer sought after. The crowd parted to engage in both matters simultaneously. Evening drew on when they again met in the pass; and the first, who had gone for the coroner, returned with him, a distance of near twenty miles; but the second party did not prove so successful. In fact, they had discovered no clue to the present retreat of the supposed assassin.

The coroner impannelled his jury, and held his inquest under a large, upright rock, bedded in the middle of the pass, such as Jeremiah had seen in his dream. A verdict of wilful murder against the absent sailor was quickly agreed upon; but, ere it could be recorded, all hesitated, not knowing how to individualize a man of whose name they were ignorant.

The summer night had fallen upon their deliberations, and the moon arose in splendor, shining over the top of one of the high hills that inclosed the pass, so as fully to illumine the bosom of the other. During their pause, a man appeared standing upon the line of the hill thus favored by the moonlight, and every eye turned in that direction. He ran down the abrupt declivity beneath him; he gained the continued sweep of jumbled rocks which immediately walled in the little valley, springing from one to another of them with such agility and certainty, that it seemed almost magical; and a general whisper of fear now attested the fact of his being dressed in a straw hat, a short jacket, and loose white trowsers. As he jumped from the last rock upon the sward of the pass, the spectators drew back; but he, not seeming to notice them, walked up to the corpse, which had not yet been touched; took its hand; turned up its face into the moonlight, and attentively regarded the features; let the hand go; pushed his hat upon his forehead; glanced around him; recognized the person in authority; approached, and stood still before him, and said, "Here I am, Tom Mills, that killed long Harry Holmes, and there he lies."

The coroner cried out to secure him, now fearing that the man's sturdiness meant further harm. "No need," resumed the self-accused; "here's my bread-and-cheese knife, the only weapon about me." He threw it on the ground. "I come back just to ax you, commodore, to order me a cruize afther poor Harry, bless his precious eyes, wherever he is bound."

"You have been pursued hither?"

"No, bless your heart; but I wouldn't pass such another watch as the last twenty-four hours for all the prize-money won at Trafalgar. 'Tisn't in regard of not tasting food or wetting my lips ever since I fell foul of Harry, or of hiding my head like a cursed animal o' the yearth, and starting if a bird only hopped nigh me; but I cannot go on living on this tack no longer—that's it; and the least I can say to you, Harry, my hearty."

"What caused your quarrel with your comrade?"

"There was no jar or jabber betwixt us, d'ye see me?"

"Not at the time, I understand you to mean; but surely you must have long owed him a grudge?"

"No, but long loved him; and he, me."

"Then, in Heaven's name, what put the dreadful thought in your head?"

"The devil, commodore (the horned lubber!), and another lubber to help him," pointing at Jeremiah, who shrank to the skirts of the crowd. "I'll tell you every word of it, commodore, as true as a log-book. For twenty long and merry years, Harry and I sailed together, and worked together, through a hard gale, sometimes, and through hot sun another time; and never a squally word came between us till last night; and then it all came of that there lubberly swipes-seller, I say again. I thought as how it was a real awful thing that a strange landsman, before ever he laid eyes on either of us, should come to have this here dream about us. After falling in with Harry, when the lubber and I parted company, my old mate saw I was cast down, and he told me as much, in his own gruff, well-meaning way; upon which I gave him the story, laughing at it. *He* didn't laugh in return, but grew glum—glummer than I ever seed him ; and I wondered, and fell to boxing about my thoughts, more and more—deep sea ink, that cursed thinking and thinking, say I! it sends many an honest fellow out of his course—and 'it's hard to know the best man's mind,' I thought to myself. Well ; we came on the tack into these rocky parts, and Harry says to me all on a sudden, ' Tom, try the soundings here, ahead, by yourself ; or let me, by myself.' I axed him, ' Why ?' ' No matter,' says Harry, again ; ' but after what you chawed about, I don't like your company any further, till we fall in again at the next village.' ' What, Harry,' I cries, laughing heartier than ever, ' are you afeard of your own mind with Tom Mills ?' ' Pho,' he made answer, walking on before me ; and I followed him.

"' Yes,' I kept saying to myself, ' he *is* afeard of his own mind with his old shipmate.' 'Twas a darker night than this ; and when I looked ahead, the devil (for I now know 'twas *he* that boarded me!) made me take notice what a good spot it was for Harry to fall foul of me. And then I watched him making way before me in the dark, and couldn't help thinking he was the better man of the two—a head and shoulders over me, and a match for any two of my inches. And then, again, I brought to mind that Harry would be a heavy purse the better of sending me to Davy's locker, seeing we had both been just paid off, and got a lot of prize-money, to boot ; and at last (the real red devil having fairly got me helm a-larboard) I argufied with myself that Tom Mills would be as well alive, with Harry Holmes's luck in his pocket, as he could be dead, and *his* in Harry Holmes's ; not to say nothing of taking one's own part, just to keep one's self afloat, if so be Harry let his mind run as mine was running.

" All this time Harry never gave me no hail, but kept tacking through these cursed rocks; and that, and his last words, made me doubt him more and more. At last he stopped nigh where he now lies, and, sitting with his back to that high stone, he calls for my blade to cut the bread and cheese he had got at the village ; and, while he spoke, I believed he looked glummer and glummer, and that he wanted the blade, the only one between us, for a some'at else than to cut bread and cheese, though now I don't believe no such thing howsumdever, but then I did ; and so, d'ye see me, commodore, I lost ballast all of a sudden, and when he stretched out for the blade (hell's fire blazing up in my lubberly heart !) 'Here it is, Harry,' says I ; and I gives it to him in the right side ! once, twice, in the right place !"—the sailor's voice, hitherto calm, though broken and rugged, now rose into a high wild cadence—"and then how we did grapple ! and sing out one to another ! ahoy ! yeho ! ay, till I thought the whole crew of devils answered our hail from the hill-tops ! But I hit you again and again, Harry, before you could master me," continued the sailor, returning to the corpse, and once more taking its hand, "until at last you struck, my old messmate. And now, nothing remains for Tom Mills but to man the yard-arm !"

The narrator stood his trial at the ensuing assizes, and was executed for this avowed murder of his shipmate—Jeremiah appearing as a principal witness. Our story may seem drawn either from imagination, or from mere village gossip ; its chief fact rests, however, upon the authority of members of the Irish bar, since risen to high professional eminence ; and they can even vouch that, at least, Jeremiah asserted the truth of "The Publican's Dream."

THE END OF THE PUBLICAN'S DREAM.

17

THE ACE OF CLUBS.

THE ACE OF CLUBS.

At English fairs, business and merriment are kept rather distinct. The buying and selling of sheep, oxen, and horses, commonly occur before the gingerbread-booths, the toy-booths, and the dancing-booths (such as the dancing in the latter is found to be) are visited, and take place upon some spot detached from the crowded encampments of pleasure and finery. At Irish fairs, however, important sales, half-penny adventures in gambling, love-making, dancing ("the right sort at a fair"), and perhaps some harmless fighting, used, in our time, to go hand in hand from the opening of the blessed day. Hence, our Irish fair was a less orderly, but a more rousing scene than one in this inveterately decorous island. While the mind of a serious spectator is filled with the important circumstance of groups of "strong farmers" bargaining about the transfer of fifty or a hundred great horned beasts, his livelier or lighter sensibilities might be appealed to by the oratory of the proprietress of a show of fragile nick-nacks, alarmed lest some of those animals should overthrow and shatter at a touch her whole stock in trade; or a rich-cheeked country-girl, laughing loudly, and struggling, "just for dacency," half-caused by her half-proffered lips, the uncouth smack which startles our observer, and which is the payment for her swain's "treat" to a grass-green ribbon, or a pair of scarlet garters; or the rub-a-dub of a set of "jiggers," with their cries of ecstasy, strikes upon his ear from some adjacent public house; or perhaps two "factions," who have been at war, as they would themselves say, "ever since their grandfather's time," emit fiercer shouts, as, huddled among cattle of all descriptions, and striking the animals as often as their own heads, they fight their twentieth pitched battle for some cause of dispute which neither can explain.

About forty years ago, when the writer had most to do with

such an assemblage, an accompanying feature, now almost worn out by the progress of gentility, was observable. While elderly farmers plodded to the important rendezvous, strictly in the spirit of men of business, their sons, or perhaps some youthful landholders of four or five hundred acres, pushed in from the country on nearly whole-blooded horses, arrayed in the Sunday suit, which, at each weekly Mass, made them the stars of their district chapels, purely, or chiefly, to ride up and down through throngs of men, women, and beasts, vouching their attractions in the face of half the assembled county, and also in the faces of rural "darkers" of the other sex, who, perched on pillions behind their fathers, and flaming in all colors, came pretty nearly in the same policy to the great general mart for the day.

A group of such gallant amateurs, standing still because they have been blocked up by surrounding droves of cattle, is presented to the reader, at the fair, holden about forty years ago, to which we direct our attention. The young men were all known to each other; and they talked or laughed cheerily, and seemed fully enjoying their day's adventures.

"But stop, boys," said one, "here comes Martin Brophy; and if he sees us so merry he'll swear we're laughing at himself."

" And then put a quarrel on us all," said another.

" Then ye won't spake to him, boys?" asked a third.

" What's the use, Jack. Ever since things went so conthrary against him, you can't look but he thinks it a slight; so that there's no managing with Martin. I, for one, will just let him go quietly by on his poor, broken-down half-blood."

" Besides, Tom, though an ould head can't be put on young shoulders (a truth we all stand up for), Martin *done the vengeance** entirely, in regard of his behavior to little Catty Morissy."

" Yes; and the priest *calling him*† for it, at last Mass, Sunday se'nnit (week)," added a pious person of the party; " but here he is! See, boys!" speaking loudly, and pointing his whip to a drove of cows and oxen, while the eyes of his companions followed his, " them browns is the clanest cattle in the fair, to my mind."

Martin Brophy passed them with eyes studiously averted in the opposite direction, as if he had determined to anticipate

---

* Went too far. † Rebuking him.

·their slight. Yet his erect carriage, his knitted brow, and his protruded lips, destroyed the ease which should have given to the act its best expression, and suggested, instead, a bitter and haughty consciousness of the presence of his former companions in the carouse and in the sporting-field.

They continued their observations by turns.

"There he goes, the proudest and the poorest grandee in Leinster."

"Look at the hat !—the poor hair will be growing through it with the next crop."

"But the ould green !"—Martin's coat—"*it* ought to bring him new ones by that time, for it's long ago it ran to seed between his shoulders."

"And what brings him to the fair, boys ?"

"To sell ould Nora" (Martin's skeleton steed).

"Yes—to the tanners."

"Or to cut a dash on her backbone."

"Ay, before Dora Marum; only she's not here : I stopped at the house to-day morning, to know if she'd be at the fair with ould cranky Dan, the father of her ; but no, purty Dora couldn't come."

"Then Martin won't take the light out of her eyes entirely this blessed day."

"Hoot, tut, man alive ; in jest or arnest, that's all gone by ; Dan gave him the cowld shouldher long ago."

They separated to resume the exhibition of their handsome steeds and admirable persons through the fair. We follow the individual of whom they have been speaking.

He was a man as young as any of them ; better featured than any, notwithstanding that premature sufferings and the conflict of strong passions had thinned and swarthed his cheek ; nay, his air, and the character of those features, gave him nearer claims than any to a gentlemanlike appearance, although, as they had truly remarked, his attire was shabby.

He had not overheard a word of the jeers spoken at his expense, but his sensitive mind imagined such a dialogue between his former friends, and imagined it to an extent even beyond the reality ; and the petty ferment consequently called up in his bosom, worked his features and temper more violently than greater misfortunes had that day done.

They scoffingly wondered why he appeared at the fair. Martin Brophy could not himself have satisfied their idle and cruel curi

osity. He could only have stated, were he so inclined, that upon
the approach of bailiffs to his house early in the morning, to seize
his furniture—the last of his earthly goods—he had run to the
stable, saddled old Nora, jumped on her back, and while his
mother's low wailings filled his ears, pushed the feeble beast out
of sight and hearing of a scene which maddened his heart, but
which he could not help ; and that then, waywardly yielding to
an unaccountable impulse, he had hurried into the thick of
another scene, the most unlikely of any he might select, to as-
suage his angry feelings.

" And this," he muttered, " this is the end of slashing Mick
Brophy's divil-may-care days ; of his hunting days, and his dancing days, and his cock-fighting days ; ay, and of his good-fellow
nights, with their songs, and their brave cursing and swearing,
and screeling, and tattering. Oh, father! you left us too soon
for Mick's good. Look out of your grave and see him now.
Not worth a lady half-penny, stock, lock, and barrel ; not a dacent tack to his back ; the ould mother crying at home to the
bare walls in the empty house ; Dora Marum lost ; and these
very *kouts,** that you left me a head-and-shoulders over—and
that I made my equals only to let them make me what I am at
last come to—these very scheming, cringing, *palavering*† hounds.
Oh !"—yielding to the bitterness of his immediate position—" by
the light o' the world ! I'd a'most stop thinking of every thing
else that once pleasured me, only for as much good fortune as
would again put me where I was—above them ; and then, with
my foot on their neck, instead of the hand to their hands, as it
used to be !"

His reverie was interrupted by the quick approach of two
bodies of screaming rioters. As they capered past him, he
drew, even from their noise and outrage, a renewed cause for
embittered regret. " Ay! Dullard's faction and Campion's faction !" repeating their war-cries ; and now soliloquizing rather
aloud, " But who shouts Brophy's faction to-day? though I remember the day when if any tenant or follower of his shouted
that name, a hundred good *alpeens* would jump at the sound."

" An' there's one, at laste, to shout it yet, Masther Martin,"
said a low, thick-necked, red-headed lad at his side. " Whoo !"
—jumping among a pacific crowd—" whoo for Masther Brophy!
who'll look crooked at him ? will you ? or you ?"

---

* Paltry fellow.   † Sycophantic.

Martin was much surprised at this unrecognized friend so Quixotically challenging the whole world on his account; but as the hero, after prancing here and there, and peering up hostilely into many faces, only earned for his stunted, burly, unwarlike figure, and for the cause it abetted, contemptuous sneers or loud laughter, on the part of the athletic fellows around him, poor Brophy's wonder changed into increased mortification.

A little old man, dressed in the common peasant garb of the district—namely, coat, vest, breeches, and hose, all gray—with a two-buckled flaxen wig, and a foxy felt hat, staggered up the street, holding a stick, and every now and then stopping and trying to balance himself, in order to make a solemn drunken soliloquy; and upon these occasions he feebly flourished his stick, and seemed to come to the conclusion that he was aggrieved and valiant.

"Or you!" continued Martin's knight, as the old fellow met his eye. "Mind this, Masther Martin"—speaking under his breath, while he passed Brophy—"a friendlier blow was never struck for your good;" and darting on, down tumbled the man of soliloquies; and with a dozen pursuers at his heels, Martin one of them, away scampered the aggressor. For, notwithstanding the lad's whisper, Martin could not think that the little old man had any thing to do with him, nor with his assaulter. There was in the blow a matter-of-fact kind of character; its very sound on the other's skull, might suggest an act without a motive, an effect without a cause.

None of the indignant pursuers succeeded in apprehending the red-haired champion; and Martin returned to condole with the inconsiderable victim, sacrificed, so much against his will, to his feudal importance.

The sire had arisen and gone on. Partly by inquiries, partly by a gory and devious track, Martin traced him out of the fair, and then out of the town. Spurring his sorry nag, he overtook him upon the road towards his own sad home. The sufferer still staggered, but now more from weakness than from inebriety.

"Tell me that young rascal's name, daddy."

"Troth, an' I don't know the poor boy's name."

"Come back into the town, then; he will surely be caught, and you must be ready to take the law of him."

"Why then," in a very kind and simple tone, "I believe we can't do that either, *avich*" (my son); "I owe the poor boy

17*

no ill-will, an' sure I won't go for to put him in raal throuble iest for a little matther of a *clipe*" (blow) " of a stick, that I am sure, afore my Maker, there was no harum in ; an' I'll engage he's a good, honest, poor slob, for all that."

" Then let me help you a bit of the road, daddy." Martin alighted, and throwing Nora's bridle over one arm, caused his tottering companion to lean on the other.

After walking along slowly for some time—" The blessin's be in your path forever, avich ; sure, here's my poor cabin," said the old man, stopping at the closed door of a very inferior habitation even of the kind he named.

" This ?" questioned Martin Brophy ; " why, this, I remember, used to be Musha Merry's—and stop"—looking now attentively into his face—" yes—now I remember you, too : you *are* ould Musha Merry, our great fairy-man."

" Hushth, hushth—a pet—manners to *them*—mainin' you no offence, but the best o' good, conthrary-wise. Poor Musha Merry I am—*their* friend, an' the friend o' the good Christhians, whenever *they* let me."

" Oho !" ejaculated Martin, assuming a sneer ; but from the effects of his early education, not fully feeling it, however ; " and didn't you send a body to me, the other day, to tell me not to let the heart be cast down entirely, for all that's come and gone, yet ?"

" Of a thruth, an' so I did, avich ; just out o' the pity is on my soul for your only throubles, and the kind-of-a-sort of a knowledge I have that there's loock in store for you, let the priest scowld you an' curse you, off o' the althar, as often as he likes, plaise his reverence."

" With help from the fairies ?" laughed Martin.

" Oh, hushth, now again, *avich*, an' call them no names, but lave them to themsefs, my honey, Masther Martin ; an' no, in troth, no ; but wid help from them : sure they haven't the power to give the riches, like others, much as they can do in every thing else."

" Then with help from the Barrymount gang ?"

" Avoch, nien, nien, entirely ; duv you think, Masther Martin Brophy, my pet, I'd go for to give you the advice to take part wid them rapparees o' the arth ? Nien, nien ; and yet," speaking more expressively, " there's a way, so there is—but hushth, again !" The door of his cabin opened, and a group of men and women appeared at it, scraping their feet or dropping courtesies to him. "See, here's some o' the poor neighbors waitin' for me to give 'em the good o' the trifle o' knowledge that's come to me, somehow or someway—a good day to ye, neighbors, honies. Come in, Masther Martin, avich, an' just tie your bridle to the hasp, and rest yourself on the chair a bit, and when I do my endayvors for the poor Christhians, sure, then, you an' I can go on wid our own little *shanachus*" (gossiping).

Doing as he was exhorted, Martin Brophy followed Musha Merry into his cabin. More people than had appeared at the door were tarrying for him under its roof, the greater number women, who sat on the mud floor, with their backs to the mud wall. Martin was aware that, as patients crowd the waiting-rooms of a popular town or city physician, these persons had come to get charms from Musha Merry, for evils inflicted upon themselves, or upon their families, or upon their cows, horses, or crops.

Occupying "the chair," so described, because it was the only one in the house, Martin looked on attentively, and with more deference towards the wise man's gifts, than his language might have expressed at the door ; for unconsciously he agreed in the general homage now paid, in his presence, to the wizard-doctor, if, indeed, he had ever really felt disposed to withhold his share of it.

Musha Merry first retired behind a wicker partition, or screen, which ran half-way across the waste apartment, at its upper end, expressing modestly an intention to charm away his own broken head, before he engaged in the service of any other afflicted person ; and after having been invisible for a short time, he re-appeared, every previous mark of violence effaced from his cheek and temple, or hidden under a more ample wig, while his crabbed old features simpered all over with their usual insinuating good-nature, and his glassy gray eyes were almost shut up in the pucker of wrinkles, which the bland expression induced round them.

A pale, melancholy, overwatched woman, arose, courtesying, and calling him "sir," and stated the first case that claimed his professional attention. "The good people" had sent a great "faver" (fever) to her only son, and the doctor gave the boy up, and the priest gave him up ; what was she to do ? Musha Merry made very light of the matter, and of the skill of his learned brethren, the doctor and the priest, and speaking smooth words of comfort and assurance, gave her a phial filled with

some colored liquid, murmured at her ear directions for administering it, received his fee, and the sorrowful woman slipped
lightly over the threshold.

A half-starved cottier next represented, in a whining, miserable
voice, how his one cow had been "overlooked." The fairy-man
handed him a little bag to tie under her left ham, and smilingly
pocketed sixpence more.

A second woful mother, holding an emaciated, silent, starving
infant upon her arms, rose from her squatting position at the
wall, and her words were, "Avich, Misther Musha Merry, sir,
sure this poor crature of a baby isn't wid me at all, but gone off
wid *them*"—meaning, and plainly understood to mean, notwithstanding the seeming puzzle of two identities, that the child
which, a few months before, she had brought into the world,
had been kidnapped by the fairies; and the certainly preter-
natural looking babe she held out for inspection, left in its
stead.

Another poor peasant applied to have the "fairy-worum pult
out of his tooth, because it wouldn't let him sleep night or day,
wid the atin' it war given him;" and Musha Merry procured a
cow's horn, burnt a reed in it, put the pointed end into the patient's gaping mouth, whispered at the other end, then shook it
over the palm of his hand till a little red worm fell out; and the
man departed with a happy grin on his features, declaring that
his toothache was perfectly cured.

Many more curious complaints received fit attention from the
fairy-doctor. At length Martin Brophy and he were left alone.
Then old Musha Merry bolted the crazy door of his desolate
cabin, and rubbing his hands softly, and simpering in his most
affectionate style, approached the young man, and seated himself upon a large stone at his feet.

"And so this is *not* the way I'm to win the good luck that is
in store for me," said Martin.

The wizard, slightly glancing towards the upper end of the
cabin, softly said, "It is not."

"And yet there *is* a way, you tell me," resumed Martin Brophy,
after a break in the conversation, during which his companion
kept his eyes fixed on the floor, now very serious.

"There *is*," slowly answered Musha Merry; and he did not
offer to go on, nor yet raise his head. Deep silence ensued, except that Martin could distinctly hear every wheezing respiration
of the old man at his feet. The pause and his situation began

to grow disagreeable to Martin Brophy ; he could not tell why. As his eye glanced round, a washy gleam of December sunshine which, entering through a small aperture in the broken thatch of the roof, crept over the rough floor, as unaccountably made him almost start. In fact, the young farmer *was* superstitious ; and the dreary and peculiar lonesomeness and silence of the fairyman's abode, together with the mysterious hint as to " the way" in which he was to retrieve his fortune, and the suspended explanation of that hint, fully called up this weak sentiment.

Still Musha Merry did not go on ; and Martin resumed in a low voice, " Well ; and what *is* that way ?"

His counsellor now looked up into his face, every feature at rest, and his shadowy gray eyes widely opened. The change of expression was, indeed, so remarkable, that Martin Brophy returned, in a kind of fascination, the glassy and vague glare with which he found himself regarded.

"You're afeard o' the priest, so you are, though he done his best on you already, or I'd tell you," said Musha Merry.

" Curse the priest !" cried Martin Brophy, in a mixed feeling of impatience at the wizard's hesitation, and anger at, as he believed, the unmerited disgrace which his clergyman had stamped on him.

"That'll do for a beginnin'," muttered the old man; "an' now I'll *show* you the way, afore I tell it to you"—he arose from the stone—" you haven't much o' the goold or the silver in your pockets, Masther Martin, avich ?"

" Not a cross to keep the devil out o' them ; and my mother is at home without her dinner."

" Ochone! an' sure that's a hard case ; but a friend is near at hand, Masther Martin; never mind me, for a start now ; only observe this."

He drew a dingy card from his bosom, and, holding it out for his companion's inspection, Martin saw it was the "Ace of Clubs ;" and then Musha Merry hobbled to the upper end of the waste apartment, and hid himself behind the wicker partition.

"I'm kneelin' down, *avich-ma-chree*" (son of my heart), he said from his concealment. Martin's bosom beat quick. In a short time the old man's voice sounded again.

" An' now it's time for you to put your hand in your hat that's close by your side."

Martin did so, and his moving fingers caused to jingle in the hat some pieces of coin. He snatched it up, looked into it, and saw three guineas. His bosom's quick throbbing was arrested by a spasm, and as Musha Merry again advanced, smiling in a congratulating and affectionate manner, he saw that his young friend was deadly pale.

"You knelt down, you say, to send me these?" questioned Martin Brophy.

"Throth, ay, on the two poor knees, avich."

"Did you pray?"

"Och, an' sure I did, from the bottom o' my heart."

"Tell me"—Martin slowly stood up, and glanced stealthily round the cabin as he whispered—"tell me, did you pray to God?"

Musha Merry bent his head close to Martin Brophy's face, and also answered in a whisper, "No."

Martin sprang to the door, and began hastily to unbolt it, having put up, however, almost unconsciously, the three guineas.

"An' you won't wait to larn *the way*, yourself?" asked the old man, as he crossed the unhallowed threshold.

Martin muttered an incoherent dissent.

"Well, avich, when it's most pleasin' to you to get the hapes o' goold, instead o' them three beggarly guineas, sure you know who to come to, to larn you; or, if you like, I'll be in the little glin o' Coile at the first light, to-morrow mornin'; it's a good place for talkin' of id."

Without uttering a word, Martin mounted old Nora, and rode off.

"Come out here to me, now, Maurice, you poor creature," continued Musha Merry, again carefully bolting his cabin door.

A man about forty strode from behind the wicker screen. Before he appeared, there had been a rustling, as if of straw; and from his rubbing his eyes, and also from the fact of bits of straws being stuck through his tangled black hair, and to different parts of his attire, it would seem that this concealed inmate of the cabin was asleep, or dozing, previous to Musha Merry's call. His person and limbs were athletic and coarse, his brow scowling; and he held a large pistol in his hand.

"By dad, Maurice, my poor boy, I b'lieve we are nigh hand to our snug little revenge on the Brophys at last, though it cost the simple ould father o' you a'most thirty long years to bring it about," resumed Musha Merry, rubbing his hands, and smiling on his son.

" Will he 'list wid us, father ?" growled Maurice.

" I didn't ax him, and I won't ax him a while yet, avich ; becase, for all his throubles an' ru'nation, the good bringin-up he
got from his mother does be comin' into his head, an' the priest-
talk, an' the Masses, an' them things ; an' if we bid him be
a bould Barrymount-boy, at once, 'twould frighten him, may
be, an' he'd dhraw back from us entirely, not to talk o' the
chance o' tellin' the neighbors some of our sacrets."

" Then, I don't know what you spake of."

" Wait, avich. Sure, I made him believe that the Ace o'
Clubs, wid help from the card's masther, sent him three guineas
out o' the brave booty that came to your share last night ; an'
I'm a big fool in my ould days, Maurice, if he rests night or day
till he spakes to the card himsel' ; an' as soon as he does, tho'
he'll be as far from the hapes o' goold as ever he was, little o'
that *rhaumaush* (nonsense) about the priests, an' the prayers, an'
the Mass-songs, 'ill stay wid Martin Brophy ; an' then we'll have
our own time to 'list him, Maurice, avich, jist by promisin' the
riches in another way."

" The priest was lookin' for him to-day mornin', father ; an'
if he comes across him now, he'll take Martin out o' your
hands."

" We'll do our endayvor to keep the' both broken friends,
Maurice ; Nance Dempsey must throw hersef in the poor boy's
way to-night ; an' afore daylight, the priest 'ill be tould where
to find them together ; Nance is a duck-o'-the-world in regard of
a decoy-duck."

Meantime, Martin Brophy rode homeward. The winter evening fell rapidly. He came in sight of the front of his house ; no
usual lights glimmered through its windows. He turned into
the back-yard, put up Nora, groomed her carefully, gave her a
bunch of musty hay, crossed to the kitchen door, raised the
latch, and heard the low lament of his mother before he saw
her, seated on a low stool at the hearth, and confronted by a
very old woman, her nurse ; the embers of some twigs, gathered
by the latter from the neighboring hedges, flickering between
them.

With a shrill scream, his only living parent sprang up to
throw herself round his neck ; she had entertained fearful thoughts
as to the cause of his absence.

" Come into the little parlor, Martin, my son," she said ; then
changing her voice, " Avich, an' sure I forgot. I left it myself

to sit down here, on this stool, borrowed at a neighbor's cabin, because it broke my heart to look at the four bare walls, that often saw us and ours comfortable and happy between 'em. An' I'm afeard you're dhry and hungry, Martin, my son."

"Cush," said Martin, throwing a guinea to the old woman, "hurry down to the village, and get us something to ate and to dhrink."

The feeble creature, with cries of wonder and joy, tottered off on her errand. His mother, also surprised, inquired how he had procured the guinea. He hesitated. She looked alarmed, and hoped he had not—and she stopped, and with streaming eyes, gazed on him.

"Mother, mother," he said hastily, "don't be afeard; I neither killed nor robbed for it."

Cush returned with food and spirits. She had also providently thought of the fire, and a pile of turf now blazed on the hearth. Martin and his mother ate their meal off their knees: the bailiffs had not left them a table. It was scarce over when horsemen rode up to the front of the house, hallooing heartily. The old nurse went to the hall-door to " discoorse them ;" Martin stepped after her to listen. He soon ascertained that the visitors were two of the "squireens" who had insulted him that day at the fair; and who now, elated with liquor, turned off the main road to taunt him further, by asking a bed at his desolate house ; when, in consequence of Cush's representations, that there was "no one in id," they galloped off, still hallooing. "I'll match ye yet," said Martin, grinding his teeth, "if I burned for it."

"Mother," he resumed abruptly, in some time after, while he liberally helped himself to the whiskey, "tell me some o' your choice old stories about ghosts, an' fairies, an' Ould Nick."

"Christ save us, Martin Brophy," crossing herself.

"Yes, mother ; you know you had plenty of 'em for me when I didn't ask for 'em; an' never mind the night it is ; the blacker to us, the more we want something to put it out of our heads." He drank another deep draught.

"Come, mother, I remember a capital story of yours that I'd thank you to tell me once again—about old Squire Jarvis and a friend of his."

After many demurs, the mother began her tale. It was an old one; or rather a local version of one, common to every country in Christendom. Squire Jarvis was a very bad man, and led a very wicked life, and became very poor in his old age. Everybody forsook him, and he lived in a lone house, a great way off the road, where he did nothing from morning to night but eat, and drink, and sleep, and commit sin, and scold the few servants who remained to share his fortune. One Sunday evening, after dinner, and after a good deal of wine, too, he got into such a passion with his own man, and so abused and swore at him, that the domestic declared he would quit his service as soon as he paid him his wages. Now Squire Jarvis could pay no wages at all, and this made him downright furious; he turned the man out of the room, and fell asleep in his armchair by the fire, still cursing and swearing; and just as he said, "I'd sell myself, body and soul, for one barrel-bag full of goold."

About twelve o'clock he awoke, when every thing was still in the house; and looking across the fire, there was a dark-complexioned gentlemen, decently dressed in black, sitting in the chair opposite to his, and attentively watching him. But the tale need not be continued; Squire Jarvis got the "barrel-bag full of goold" on the usual terms.

"An' sure you're not such a fool, mother, as to b'lieve such a thing can happen?" demanded Martin Brophy.

His mother, mingling pious and frightened ejaculations with her answer, had no doubt but it could. Nor had Martin himself much doubt when he asked the question. He only wanted confirmation from his mother's anticipated assurances; for he misconceived the mode by which Musha Merry proposed to endow him with wealth.

The distressed parent, wearied with grief and watching, began to nod. Martin arose to make up some kind of a couch for her. Cash, again provident, had provided straw; upon part of it, in the corner of the kitchen, next to the fire, he left his mother and her old nurse to stretch themselves; the rest he took into his own chamber. And here he flung it from him, locked himself in, and holding his rushlight in his hand, stared wildly and fiercely around.

"Would he, without Musha Merry's knowledge, make *the call?*" At the thought, his forehead grew moist and cold, his scalp froze, his limbs shook. A glance at his desperate position, aided by the effects of the spirits, controlled his horror. "He would!"—and as the preface to his call, he furiously, though unconsciously, stamped upon the floor. The whole house vibrated to the shock, and something slightly clattered against the wall of the chamber. He looked up. It was an old wooden crucifix hanging by a thread from a nail—the only article which the bailiffs had hesitated to drag away. He riveted his eye upon the symbol of his redemption and his hope ; he trembled again, but it was with new fears ; he dashed down his rushlight, trod on it, plunged on his knees into his straw ; and amid choking sobs, Martin Brophy muttered a prayer ; but it was a prayer to God.

In about an hour, a wailing, soft voice sounded from under his window. He arose, looked out, and saw a girl sitting on the ground, and rocking to and fro, and clapping her hands. He opened the window and spoke to her. She said she had missed her father and her brothers at the fair ; had strayed so far in quest of them ; and now did not know what to do for the night; but the public houses were open in the village, only she had no money. Martin went out to her through the window, and accompanied her to the village. The least respectable of the public houses gave them entertainment and lodging for payment beforehand. Martin, but too well acquainted, from former experience, with the ways of the house, spent his second guinea before he fell asleep, and ere he awoke in the morning, Nance Dempsey had gone off with the other.

With remorse for recent sin, added to his frenzy of the previous night, he hurried out of the house. It was yet scarce daybreak, though not an early hour. As he issued from the door, a horseman, standing still, confronted him, as if watching the egress of some person. At a glance, he knew his rigid parish priest.

"I find you coming out from this house after all, Martin Brophy!" he said. "You have been warned from the altar ; take heed you do not expose yourself to be cursed from the altar."

"Curse away!" answered Martin, bounding across the road into the fields, the worst species of desperation now blackening in his bosom—namely, that of lost character and conscious guilt.

Without thinking of an interview with Musha Merry, he gained the little glen of Coile, where, in happier and better days, Dora Marum and he had often sat together In summer it was a beautiful close scene ; a fairy dell; blocked up at one end by a face of shrubbed rock, adown which trickled a silver line of water, and almost embowered at either side by beech and ashtrees, that dropped their foliage to the very surface of the mossy sod under foot. Now, upon a howling winter's morning, and while twilight yet brooded over it, the place bore, on the contrary, a drear and fierce character. The thread of shining water had become a red and foamy torrent, which tore through the middle of the little valley; the naked trees groaned and clattered their tangled branches in the gust, chorusing its sullen roar ; and the piping of the wind among them sometimes filled Martin's ear like human or superhuman voices. Immediately under the fall of water, there was a deep and boiling basin, and self-destruction, by a plunge into this, was now Martin's impulse. Despairing, and even depraved as his heart had become, he rejected, since his change of feeling the previous night, prolonged and successful life by virtue of a cold-blooded covenant with the enemy of man. He glanced around, to note if he was alone. A figure was just disappearing out of the dell—he thought his champion at the fair ; and now he identified his red-haired friend with Keeraun Dernphy, Dora's foster-brother. Another figure, that of a female, stood watching him. He ran towards her ; it was Dora Marum ; he fell with a cry at her feet.

Dora called on him to "stand up like a man !"

"You do not care for me now, Dora ; and for that reason, little do I care for myself."

" Stand up, Martin Brophy !"—the tall, finely formed. brown-complexioned girl spoke with energy, and her brown cheek reddened, and her black eye grew expressive. " I do care for you, yet ; though, indeed, you care so little for yourself ; and though you have given me no cause to tell you so." He arose. "Stand up, in arnest, Martin ; mend your life ; and your fortune must mend with it ; and then my father will no longer hinder me from showing *how much* I care for you."

"And not till then, Dora? not till I grow rich?" cried Martin, in total despair of his chance of succeeding according to this advice.

"No, Martin Brophy, not till then," answered old Daniel Marum, gaining his daughter's side. "Come home, Dora. It's plain language I spake to you, Martin, my boy : grow as rich as will make you Dora's match ; and then take her with my blessin'." He and Dora went away.

"Grow rich ! haw !" shouted Martin, furiously. Old Musha Merry tottered before him, and repeated his offer to " larn him the way—haw !" Martin angrily desired him to begone, adding,

that "the horned dhoul might have him, body and soul—
and should, soon—but not at a price." His counsellor, smiling,
assured him that he greatly mistook; that no such hard terms
were expected as the bribe for hastening superabundance of
riches. Martin eagerly pressed him to explain. He did so; and
although there certainly was a material difference in the bargain
proposed, from that entered into by old Squire Jarvis, still Martin Brophy listened in unfeigned horror.

"An' see, here it's for you," added Musha Merry, handing his
begrimed card; "the ould one that stood your friend afore; so
you'll have loock wid it, avich." Martin took the card, and
slowly and silently walked out of the little dell.

"There, now," muttered Musha Merry to himself, as he laboriously crawled up the side of the retreat, in a different direction. "An' only use it as I bid you, Martin Brophy, my boy,
an' if we don't list you in the bould Barrymount throop, nan-
bocklish (never mind); an' in a little while after that, plaise God,
you'll be snug in the stone-jug (jail) in their fine town beyant,
an' in a fair way to go under the skibbeah's (Jack Ketch's) hands,
in regard of bein' found out, somehow, for one o' them terrible
robbers that frightens the whole counthry. Ay, just the way it
happened to poor Mechaul, the one brother o' me, about thirty
years agone, by manes of a father you had, rest his sowl, the first
time our brave boys took head together, and opened the fun wid
a call at Dick Brophy's house, after sunset; and maybe it's not
a nate fit for *that* to help your father's son to just the same loock
your father helped poor Mechaul to; ah, an' jest on the same
ould account. Ha, bad stop, isn't that Keeraun Dernphy's red
head watchin' me agin?"

It was Sunday morning. Half an hour after Martin Brophy
left the glen, he was seen hovering about the door of the little
country chapel by the crowds who went in to early Mass. They
wondered that they did not see him at the entrance to the gal-
leries, whither, consistently with his former rank, it had been his
habit to repair. Indeed, they almost wondered at his appearance near the house of prayer, under any circumstances, for
lately he had been absent from all religious observances. But
they concluded that he came to humble himself to the "call" of
his priest, issued the previous Sunday. Arrived in "the body of
the chapel," where the crowds knelt or stood without seats of
any kind, many looked around for Martin, but none saw him.

He was in the chapel, notwithstanding. Avoiding and baf-

fling observation, he had stolen through the throng to a spot
under the rude pulpit, where, inside the sweep of its stairs, was a
small pace, left comparatively unthronged, and where, without
his knowledge of the fact, women who proposed to communicate
after the ceremony of the morning, were in the habit of kneeling,
with their faces enveloped in the hoods of their dark-blue cloaks,
and turned to the wall, so that they might compose themselves
to approach the railings of the sanctuary. And here also, turning his face to the wall, Martin *knelt* to prepare his mind, and
wait his time for his devotional act.

At a certain period of the Mass, the priest elevates the conse
crated bread and wine, which Roman Catholics believe to be the
Real Presence; and Martin Brophy, acting upon Musha Merry's
instructions, intended, when this usual ceremonial should occur,
to turn his back on the altar, hold up before his eyes, in the hollow of his hand, the Ace of Clubs which his tutor had given him,
and bow to it thrice, and worship it thrice, "in the devil's name"
—the only concession, he was assured, required by the great
father of riches, to give him power over mountains of gold.

In a paroxysm of desperation he had so far taken his measures. But after he had knelt down, and that Mass had begun,
the sullen lethargy of Martin's heart became fearfully broken up.
The act of apostasy he resolved to commit was, in its form, of
no ordinary character; and further, Martin Brophy believed in
the Redeemer, of whose atonement for the sins of the world the
sacrament was a memento ; nay, still, according to his creed, a
perpetuation. And this Redeemer, and this sacrament, he came
to forswear on his knees, for the worship of the king of hell ;—
the thought swelled his bosom with tremendous horror.

The pious women and girls around him murmured their aspi-
rations of repentance for their sins, and of joy at the prospect of
partaking of that very sacrament. His heart chilled and col-
lapsed over its own hidden intent. Still he dragged the intent
closer to him, and did not waver. Mass went on—every stage
of its progress familiar to his ear—every response of the sur-
pliced boys who served at the steps of the altar—he had often
served there himself—and a vivid picture started before his mind,
of his mother folding up his newly-washed surplice, and giving it
him to button under his boyish jacket, that he might hasten off
to attend his favorite priest at early prayers. The time drew
near when the bread and wine were to be consecrated. Martin,
shuffling on his knees, fully turned his back upon the altar, and,

shaking in every limb, and teeming with cold moisture, adjusted
the card in the palm of his hand. The little bell, rung by one of
the boys, which gave notice of the approach of " the Elevation,"
tingled in his ears, and pierced into his brain. The hosannah
hymn burst from the village choir, and echoed over him and around
him, first loudly and shrilly, and then louder and confused, then
wildly and faintly, until, as almost madness mastered him, it
swell seemed to break out into scream and laughter. Again
however, he was darkly aware of the second notice of the little
bell, and then, with staring eyes and ghastly features, he raised
the card close to his face. His arm was dragged down. He
uttered a loud cry, and gazed under the head of the woman's
cloak who had thus interfered between him and his terrible apostasy. The eyes of Dora Marum met his. She had learned of
his dread purpose from Keeraun Dernphy, who contrived to listen to Martin's conversation with Musha Merry in the glen, and
who, indeed, had been long aware of the old robber's thirst for
revenge against her unfortunate lover.

After his scream, Martin fell senseless, though in strong con-
vulsions. For weeks afterwards he was a raving madman.
When his senses returned to him, he found himself in the priest's
house, watched by his mother and Dora Marum; they were
softly whispering over his bed. Martin Brophy did not leave
that house till, in an humbled, contrite, and chastened spirit, he
had worthily propitiated Heaven's forgiveness, through the me-
dium of the sacrament he had so recently proposed, along with
that Heaven, to forswear. Restored to health in mind, in
heart, and in body, he seriously set himself to follow the advice
given to him by Dora in the Glen of Coile ; and from very small
beginnings, with perhaps some compassionate allowances for his
griefs and sufferings, became, in a few years, " a match," in old
Dan Marum's eye, for his only daughter, just about the time
that Musha Merry left this world, to seek his unavenged brother
in a better or a worse, and by the same mode of exit vouchsafed
to that worthy brother.